Chicago Public Library

C
P L

Form 178 rev. 1-94

D1595886

Preparing for *Weltpolitik*

PREPARING FOR

Weltpolitik

German Sea Power before the Tirpitz Era

• • •

Lawrence Sondhaus

Naval Institute Press

ANNAPOLIS, MARYLAND

LIBRARY OF CONGRESS CATALOGING-IN-PUBLICATION DATA
Sondhaus, Lawrence, 1958–
    Preparing for Weltpolitik : German sea power before the
Tirpitz era / Lawrence Sondhaus.
        p.   cm.
    Includes bibliographical references and index.
    ISBN 1-55750-745-7 (cloth : alk. paper)
    1. Sea-power—Germany—History—19th century.   I. Title.
VA513.S66   1997   96-52043
359´.00943´09034—dc21

Printed in the United States of America on acid-free paper ∞
04 03 02 01 00 99 98 97   9 8 7 6 5 4 3 2
First printing

CONTENTS

ILLUSTRATIONS

PREFACE

early all accounts of the history of the Imperial German Navy written since World War I have emphasized the era of *Weltpolitik,* the Second Reich's drive for world power in the years 1898–1918. Scholars focusing on the efforts of Admiral Tirpitz in the reign of William II traditionally have offered little comment about the development of the navy, its personnel, policies, and related industries before the 1890s. Ironically, even historians critical of Tirpitz's record as head of the Imperial Navy Office (*Reichsmarineamt*) after 1897 have tended to accept the admiral's own contention that little of importance happened before he came to power.[1] Accounts addressing the period before the great Navy Laws rarely go back as far as the Frankfurt Parliament of 1848–49, where the abortive attempt to create a German navy marked an early convergence of German nationalism with sentiment for a strong fleet.[2] As a comprehensive history of German sea power before the Tirpitz era, when the foundations of *Weltpolitik* were established, the present work represents an attempt to fill a significant gap in the literature.

I conducted my archival research at the Bundesarchiv-Militärarchiv in Freiburg im Breisgau, the Österreichisches Staatsarchiv in Vienna, and the National Archives in Washington, D.C. I am especially grateful to Dr. Fleischer and his staff in Freiburg, *Oberrat* Dr. Gaisbauer in Vienna, and Robert Wolfe in Washington. In my secondary research I used the resources of a number of libraries in Germany and the United States: the Staats- und Universitätsbibliothek Hamburg, the Stadtbibliothek Freiburg im Breisgau, the Library of Congress in Washington, D.C., Olin Library at Washington University in St. Louis, Krannert Memorial Library at the University of Indianapolis, IUPUI University Library in Indianapolis, and the public libraries of St. Louis and Indianapolis. A grant from the German Academic Exchange Service (DAAD) helped fund my research in Germany. I am thankful to *Overarkivar* Dr. Hans Christian Bjerg in Copenhagen for information on the Danish navy. Dr. Patrick Kelly of Adelphi University offered valuable advice on the career of Tirpitz. Dr. Gary Weir of the Naval Historical Center in Washington shared his insights on German armor production and the internal politics of the German navy in the 1890s; he also assisted my search for photographs. I secured other illustrations with the help of Ms. Nicki Marshall of Conway Maritime Press, London. *Kapitänleutnant* Kraus of the German Federal Navy supplied several photographs from the collection of the Marineschule Mürwik. I am grateful to Christine Guyonneau and the interlibrary loan staff of Krannert Memorial Library at the University of Indianapolis for processing my many dozens of requests. I would like to acknowledge the wise counsel of my friend Paul Halpern, especially regarding choice of publisher. I dedicate this book to the memory of my father, Edwin Sondhaus, who encouraged me to persevere in its completion.

Preparing for *Weltpolitik*

1

ORIGINS

he outbreak of the revolutions of 1848–49 and the concurrent German-Danish war over Schleswig-Holstein found German sea power in an embarrassing condition. Among the northern German states only Prussia had a navy; unfortunately, the Royal Prussian navy, formally in existence since the end of the Napoleonic Wars, had an officer corps of just three lieutenants and no full-time manpower. Its only seagoing vessel, a training corvette armed with a dozen light guns, served the needs of a Danzig navigation school that functioned as Prussia's merchant marine academy. The corvette's Dutch captain and cadre crew of two dozen sailors likewise were civilian state employees, whose services would revert to the navy only in case of war. This state of affairs almost defies explanation. Most Prussian monarchs, from the Great Elector to Frederick William IV, at least dabbled in maritime projects. Especially in recent years, many leading generals and cabinet ministers had favored the creation of some sort of navy. Furthermore, the Prussian-led Zollverein had united much of northern Germany in a single customs union, and merchant ships flying the flags of the north German states traded throughout the world. Nevertheless, in 1848–49 tiny Denmark would be able to blockade Germany's busiest ports, strangle their trade, and force a stalemate in the Schleswig-Holstein war. Germans paid a dear price at sea for their lack of political unity on land.

The maritime heritage of Germany, like all of German history before the era of unification, included several threads of development but lacked a central focus. When Brandenburg-Prussia, ultimately the catalyst for

German unity, expanded dramatically in the early modern period, it failed to acquire a seaport of more than secondary significance. The Prussians remained inconsistent in their interest in the sea and rarely enjoyed good relations with the largest port cities. German maritime interests also suffered from a cultural barrier dividing the coast from the interior. Ever since the Middle Ages and the heyday of the Hanseatic League, the Plattdeutsch dialect had been the language of Germans involved with the sea; even merchants used the Lübeck variety of Low German ("*Lübsch*") as one of their written languages of commerce. A Plattdeutsch sprinkled with foreign nautical jargon was baffling to inlanders, and the men of the coast were equally inept at understanding other Germans. In the 1830s future Imperial German admiral Reinhold Werner found this to be the case when he entered the Hamburg merchant marine. Though he was from Prussian Saxony, only 150 miles from the sea, his north German shipmates nicknamed him *Schweizer,* assuming that anyone with his accent must be from the high Alps.[1] In many ways, the cultural barrier to the development of a German navy was as formidable as any political obstacle. It weakened only when the revolutionary enthusiasm of 1848–49 inspired young men from all over Germany to volunteer for naval service.

Some writers trace German naval history back to skirmishes between Roman legions and German tribes along the Rhine and Danube.[2] Especially during the Nazi era, it became fashionable to claim Viking exploits as part of the Germanic experience at sea.[3] The Hanseatic League, established in the late Middle Ages, united the merchant fleets of most German Baltic and North Sea ports. Between the thirteenth and sixteenth centuries, the Hanseatic cities armed fleets for warfare against their rivals, but the league enjoyed only a brief golden age before losing routes and markets to competitors. By 1600 the Dutch controlled 70 percent of the traffic between the North Sea and the Baltic.[4]

The Peace of Westphalia (1648) left much of the north German coast in the hands of Denmark and Sweden. Hamburg, Bremen, and Lübeck continued to coordinate trade policy, but unlike their nation-state rivals, they declined to build permanent navies distinct from their merchant fleets. The initiative soon passed to Brandenburg-Prussia. Frederick William, the Great Elector, established a short-lived East India Company and, in 1675, a small navy, using hired Dutch personnel. Famous Dutchmen in Prussian service included Admiral Cornelius Tromp, whose victories in 1678 gave Prussia temporary possession of the island of Rügen. In 1682 the Prussians founded an African Company, established a fort on the Guinea coast, and secured rights to Emden, their first North Sea port and naval base. The death of the Great Elector, in 1688, dealt a blow to these projects. In 1711 King Frederick William I finally dissolved the African Company, the navy, and the merchant marine. Prussia ceded its Guinea holdings to the Netherlands.[5]

In 1750 Frederick the Great chartered a short-lived Asiatic Company based in Emden. Its ships were the first to fly the royal Prussian flag: a black eagle on a white field, instead of the red eagle of Brandenburg. By then, Britain had emerged as the leading sea power of northern Europe, dominating trade in Hamburg, Germany's largest port.[6] During at least some of Frederick's wars, friendship with Britain left Prussia with little need for a navy. In the Seven Years' War (1756–63) Prussia assembled a dozen small warships to guard the mouth of the Oder River, but the Swedes promptly attacked this flotilla and destroyed it.[7] In his "Political Testament" of 1752, Frederick observed that a navy would be feasible only if Prussia annexed Danzig and West Prussia.[8] When Prussia made these acquisitions in the first partition of Poland (1772), the king declined to build a fleet. Instead, he established the Seehandlung, a trading company charged with encouraging overseas commerce "under our flag, from our harbors." During the War for American Independence (1775–83) most European sea powers either declared war on Britain or joined the anti-British League of Armed Neutrality; the Seehandlung took advantage of the situation and profited by providing a truly neutral flag for its customers. Once these artificial conditions evaporated, the agency sold its ships. It survived the Frederician era by becoming a lending institution for general economic development.[9]

Between 1795 and 1806, Prussia remained neutral in the wars against revolutionary and Napoleonic France. Prussian and Hanseatic shippers prospered, thanks to the French occupation of both Hanover (which limited Britain's access to German trade) and the Netherlands (which crippled the Dutch merchant marine).[10] But in 1806 France ceded Hanover to Prussia, and in return Prussia joined the anti-British Continental System. The British promptly retaliated against the helpless Prussian merchant marine. Later that year, Prussia reversed course and joined the anti-French coalition, only to suffer disastrous defeat at the hands of Napoleon at Jena. During the ensuing years of recovery and reform, the army naturally received the most attention.[11] In 1813, during the War of Liberation, Prussia armed three merchantmen and five customs cutters abandoned by the French along the Baltic coast. The ships were disarmed and sold after the campaign ended.[12]

At the postwar Congress of Vienna, Prussia received the island of Rügen and the last remnant of Swedish Pomerania. Hanover's gains included Emden, which Prussia had lost early in the Napoleonic Wars. Thus Prussia came away without a foothold on the North Sea but with more Baltic coastline than it had ever owned before. The peace settlement also provided for a new German Confederation. The German Federal Act of 1815 included general provisions for a common defense of Prussia, Austria, and the smaller German states.[13] But the confederation would not have an army, much less a navy. From the outset, Prussia and Austria were both partners and rivals in the new Germany. Because Austria held the permanent presidency of the Federal Diet (an assembly of envoys from the state governments), Prussia would often pursue its interests outside the confederation, after 1818 through its customs union, the Zollverein. In the naval realm, Austria maintained its own fleet on the Adriatic, and dynastic ties gave three other federal states foreign naval protection: Hanover with Britain, Luxembourg with Holland, and Holstein with Denmark. The Federal Military Constitution of 1821 ignored the question of a navy or coastal defense, leaving Prussia and other vulnerable states to fend for themselves.

With the acquisition of the former Swedish Pomerania, Prussia inherited two lieutenants, a company of sailors, and six small gunboats (*Kanonierschaluppen*). Each of the 65-ton boats mounted two cannon and required a crew of twelve seamen. Lieutenant Diederick Johan Longé, commander of the force, was a native of Finland with experience in the Swedish army and navy, the British navy, and the British merchant marine. He became head of the Swedish gunboat division at Stralsund in July 1815, just one month before receiving permission to transfer to Prussian service. Longé had spent most of his naval career aboard coastal gunboats; even with the British, he never served on a ship larger than a brig.[14] For Longé and other advocates of a navy, the first peacetime year set the stage for the confusion and indecision that followed. In April 1816 Frederick William III confirmed his commission and that of fellow officer Heinrich Murck, promoted Longé to captain, and personally designed a uniform for them to wear. Two months later, war minister Hermann von Boyen acted as if the navy were dead and tried to find civilian posts for Longé and Murck. But when officials in Pomerania proposed the construction of several schooners, the king authorized one 250-ton, two-masted prototype, designed by Longé and built by J. Meyer of Stralsund. The Pomeranian command also planned to arm a postal yacht, renamed *König Friedrich Wilhelm*, which the Swedes had left behind at Stralsund along with the six gunboats. At the end of the year, however, the yacht and gunboats remained inactive, manned by skeleton crews.[15]

In 1817 a series of positive developments raised the hopes of the navy's proponents. After J. Meyer completed the schooner *Stralsund,* Longé armed it with ten light guns and took it on a cruise from Stralsund to Memel. Chancellor Hardenberg determined that the *Stralsund* and *König Friedrich Wilhelm* would fly a newly designed naval flag, the black eagle on a white field with a black iron cross in the upper left-hand corner.[16] Meanwhile, the king established a navigation school in Danzig to serve the future needs of both the navy and the merchant marine. But the momentum quickly fizzled, and none of the Danzig school's initial graduates received naval commissions. In 1819 Boyen pleaded the navy's case to Hardenberg, arguing that "several trial voyages with the new warship, the schooner *Stralsund,*" had shown that "such armed ships" would be useful to Prussia.[17] Hardenberg acknowledged the need for "the construction of armed ships for the Prussian Baltic harbors" but canceled plans to build more vessels, citing financial considerations. In 1820 the government sold the six former Swedish gunboats. The *Stralsund* served as training ship for the Danzig navigation school in 1818 and 1819, then remained in port until 1823. The *König Friedrich Wilhelm* never left Stralsund.[18]

Far from being discouraged, Longé continued to plan for the Prussian navy of the future. In 1820 he proposed a force of four 18-gun corvettes, four 16-gun brigs, and twenty-four 10-gun schooners on the model of the *Stralsund,* along with four dozen gunboats for coastal and river duty.[19] General Albrecht von Hake, Boyen's successor as war minister, refused to act on the plan, but influential voices continued to support the navy. In 1823 Crown Prince Frederick William (the future Frederick William IV) called for a flotilla of gunboats to be manned by a *Seewehr,* in which conscripts from coastal regions would perform their military service. He also proposed exempting all merchant mariners from army duty.[20] That autumn a commission chaired by General Gustav von Rauch studied the matter. A proponent of naval power since the Napoleonic era, Rauch worked with Longé and the chief of the general staff, Karl von Müffling, to draft guidelines for a twelve-hundred-man *Seewehr* and a force of two schooners and twenty-four gunboats. Despite their modest scope, these proposals met the same fate as Longé's ambitious plan of 1820.[21]

Meanwhile, under the direction of Christian Rother, the Seehandlung emerged as the most dynamic promoter of Prussian maritime interests. In 1822 the agency revived its long-dormant overseas shipping business. Unlike their predecessors a half-century earlier, Rother's vessels operated as armed merchantmen, showing the flag abroad as a sort of "surrogate navy." By 1848 Rother had employed a total of twelve ships, nine of which were owned outright by the Seehandlung. Four were usually in service at any given time.[22] The vessels spent little time in port between missions, enabling the small fleet to complete a phenomenal 133 voyages in barely more than a quarter-century.[23] Nevertheless, the operation failed to turn a profit, and the revolution of 1848 would provide a convenient excuse for the Seehandlung to liquidate the fleet. Its legacy to the future development of Prussian-German sea power amounted to one ship, the *Mercur,* sold to the navy in 1850.[24] Rother's operation did nothing to stimulate Prussian ports. Owing to the location of Danzig and the inadequacies of Stettin, his ships used Hamburg as their entrepôt.

Longé had no connection with the Seehandlung's efforts or the navigation school. In 1823, for the first time in four years, the Danzig cadets used the *Stralsund* for a summer Baltic cruise, but for the most part the school rented merchantmen to train its students.[25] Prussia offered no naval commissions after those to Longé and Murck, making the Danzig school a de facto merchant marine academy with no use for a warship as a training vessel. Like Longé, the school's directors were foreigners: Dr. L. J. Tobiessen (1817–20), a Danish academic, followed by Michael Bille (1820–38), a veteran sea captain from a prominent Danish naval-political family.[26] Because they had different masters—the war ministry for Longé, the finance ministry for the navigation directors—they had very little contact with each other. Of the three disjointed maritime-related initiatives, Longé's efforts ranked far behind those of the Seehandlung and the navigation school in scope and significance. Leading ministers in Berlin considered the navy a small, specialized department of the Prussian army. As the only navy captain, Longé served as technical advisor on everything from coastal mapping projects to lighthouse construction. In 1822 the war ministry transferred him to Danzig, along with Murck. They took the *Stralsund* with them, leaving behind the Stralsund Marine Depot and the yacht *König Friedrich Wilhelm,* which the government soon sold.[27] After the move Longé supervised the construction of three small river gunboats, subsequently manned by a Guard Pioneer (Sapper) Detachment known as the "Garde-Mariniers." During the revolution of 1830–31 in neighboring Russian Poland, two of the boats deployed on the Vistula at Thorn, but in the 1840s all three were sold and scrapped. Longé also designed the 70-ton

Danzig, built in 1825 by J. Meyer of Stralsund. Though designated as a coastal gunboat, it served briefly on the open Baltic as a training vessel for the navigation school.[28]

In 1827 Longé and Murck returned to Stralsund along with the *Danzig* and *Stralsund.* Neither officer, and neither vessel, ever put to sea again. After the sale of the *Stralsund* in 1829, the small cadre of personnel at the Stralsund Marine Depot had little to do other than watch the idle *Danzig* rot from disuse. By 1837 the entire annual navy budget totaled just 2,725 thalers, of which some 1,600 covered salaries for Longé and Murck. The only other personnel were a boatswain and a dozen *Mariniers* from the Guard Pioneer Detachment. The budget shrank even more after the *Danzig* was sold in 1838.[29] For all practical purposes the navy would have died with the sale of the *Stralsund* if not for the personal intervention of the king. In June 1829 Frederick William III authorized the construction of another ship to serve as training vessel for the Danzig navigation school in peacetime and as a coastal "watch ship" in wartime.[30] Although the ship remained on the drawing board, in 1831 an optimistic Longé tried to capitalize on the king's interest with a new plan including seven 26-gun corvettes, three 18-gun "light frigates," and four 16-gun cutters or brigs. The following year, when the king asked for a progress report on his order of 1829, war minister Hake suppressed Longé's plan and revived the Rauch commission's less expensive proposal of 1823, for two schooners and twenty-four gunboats.[31]

In March 1835 General Job von Witzleben, Hake's successor, formed another naval commission. When a frustrated General Rauch refused to chair it, General August von Reiche, director of the army's artillery and engineering school, took his place. Longé, Danzig shipbuilder J. J. Klawitter, and junior artillery officers served under him. This time technological change affected the debate. By the early 1830s merchant paddle steamers under foreign flags were calling in Prussian and German harbors, and even the minor European navies had introduced their first steamships. Meeting from June 1835 to May 1836, the Reiche commission drafted a long-term plan including six steamships and a sail-powered fleet of one 20-gun corvette, one 16-gun schooner, and sixty small gunboats. The corvette and schooner, one steamship, and four gunboats were to be constructed immediately. But any steamships would have to be built abroad, at a cost that alarmed Witzleben. Like Hake, he promoted the Rauch plan of 1823 as a cheaper alternative.[32] After the Reiche commission disbanded, a disappointed Longé returned to Stralsund, never again to be included in naval planning. Though idle, he remained technically on active duty. In 1837 he received a promotion to lieutenant colonel, and in 1842 to colonel.[33]

In 1837 Gustav von Rauch replaced Witzleben as war minister. In a letter to Frederick William III that summer, the staunch advocate of the Prussian naval cause reflected upon the past years of inaction, then made specific recommendations: hiring a foreign officer as navy commander; using the Danzig navigation school to train naval officers; placing other Prussian cadets with foreign navies for training; and finally, purchasing one gunboat in Sweden and constructing four to eight more gunboats in Prussia.[34] The king favored the idea of hiring a foreign commander, but when Bille retired as navigation director the following year, he declined to replace him with an officer holding a naval commission. Like Bille, the new director, the Swede Carl Siegmard Lous, was classified as a civil servant, took orders from the finance ministry, and had no connection with the war ministry. But Frederick William III remained interested in the navy project. Just before his death in March 1840 he finally sanctioned the Reiche plan of 1836, authorizing construction of the corvette and the first two gunboats (*Kanonenjollen*).[35]

The army's Danzig artillery depot launched both of the 21-ton gunboats: *Kanonenjolle Nr.1*, built on a Danish design, in June 1840, and *Kanonenjolle Nr.2*, a Swedish model, in June 1841. Army pioneer lieutenants supervised construction and served as the first officers; the crews came from the *Mariniers* of the Guard Pioneer Detachment, transferred from the abandoned Vistula River gunboats.[36] Between 1841 and 1843, Frederick William IV designated 77,000 thalers to complete the 350-ton training corvette. Because the vessel, in peacetime, would be under the jurisdiction of the navigation school, the finance ministry supervised the project. The contract went to the Carmesin Werft of Grabow, near Stettin, which unfortunately lacked the materials and skilled workers even to get started. The ship, eventually named the *Amazone*, was laid down in May 1842, only after the designer, Carl Alexander Elbertzhagen, imported shipwrights, tools, and hardware from England. By then, thirteen years had passed since Frederick William III first ordered its construction.[37]

Finance minister Ernst von Bodelschwingh persuaded Frederick William IV that the *Amazone* should fly the Prussian naval flag in peacetime and wartime. He reasoned that it would be fully armed at all times, and that Lous's successor as navigation director—a former Danish naval captain, Baron Edwin von Dirckinck-Holmfeld—would operate it on training cruises as a man-of-war, not a merchantman. Hermann von Boyen, who returned as war minister after Rauch's death in 1841, supported Bodel-schwingh's goal of "creating in our merchant marine the cadre of a navy." Boyen considered giving Dirckinck-Holmfeld an officer's rank and commission, but that would have required a definition of his status vis-à-vis the "naval officers already on hand," the idle Longé and Murck. After Dirckinck-Holmfeld arrived to take over the Danzig school in 1842, he did not receive a commission. The navigation director remained a civilian employee of the finance ministry.[38]

From the start, however, Dirckinck-Holmfeld considered his primary duty to be the training of Prussian naval officers. In the spring of 1843 he suggested that four to six boys should be groomed as a cadre; among the older students already enrolled at the school, he saw great promise in "the young [Eduard] Jachmann," a twenty-one-year-old from Danzig and future Prussian admiral. On the school's earlier training cruises aboard rented merchant ships, the director had served as captain and his faculty as officers, but for the *Amazone,* a genuine warship, Dirckinck-Holmfeld saw a need for true naval officers and noncommissioned petty officers (NCOs). Frederick William IV agreed. In the autumn of 1843 the king approved the hiring of a Danish lieutenant and two Danish NCOs to assist the director in training young men "for naval officers' service (*für den Marine-Offizier-dienst*)."[39] Civilian faculty from the navigation school would fill the remaining positions of responsibility, as before. The Carmesin Werft launched the *Amazone* in June 1843 and completed it the following spring. After being fitted out with a dozen Swedish cannon imported from the firm of Baron Gustaf von Ridderstolpe, the corvette left on its first cruise in May 1844. Its mission included showing the flag in the Eastern Mediterranean, where Prussia had growing commercial interests. The ship called at Constantinople, Piraeus, and other Levantine ports before returning home in October.[40]

The construction of the *Amazone* overshadowed Prussia's other "naval" initiative of the early 1840s, involving the army pioneers and their pair of tiny coastal gunboats. The pioneer officers and their *Mariniers* conducted artillery exercises off Danzig in the summer of 1840 with *Kanonenjolle Nr.1,* the following autumn with both gunboats, and in the autumn of 1842 with *Kanonenjolle Nr.2.* After remaining idle in 1843, both gunboats were armed in the summers of 1844 and 1845; on these occasions the "shortage of royal *Mariniers*" compelled the pioneer officers to man the boats with "volunteer seamen." In each exercise, gunboat crews rowed or sailed their vessels into

Corvette *Amazone* (laid down 1842; launched June 1843)   *Historische Sammlung der Marineschule Mürwik*

position, then bombarded stationary targets on the shore.[41] But Boyen and Bodelschwingh clearly favored a seagoing defense. They opposed the construction of more gunboats and further gunnery exercises for the two already built. In 1842, at Bodelschwingh's request, Elbertzhagen (the designer of the *Amazone*) drafted a damning appraisal of the gunboats and the strategic concept behind them. He traced the popularity of the *Kanonenjollen* back to 1807, when the Danes had deployed them successfully against a British blockade. He noted, however, that 1807 was before the age of steam. He concluded that in the future, steamships would provide "the best coastal defense."[42]

Late in 1844 Elbertzhagen, Dirckinck-Holmfeld, and Major General Eduard von Peucker, former head of the war ministry's artillery department, revised the Reiche plan of 1836. Their program still called for a corvette (the *Amazone*, already built) and a schooner, but eliminated the sixty small gunboats, raised the number of steamships from six to sixteen, and added another five steamers for river service. It echoed the views Elbertzhagen had articulated two years earlier, but while he and Dirckinck-Holmfeld favored a focus on warships capable of action at sea, Peucker continued to advocate gunboats such as the *Kanonenjollen*.[43] Indeed, besides Boyen, most military men interested in the navy wanted it to have a narrowly defined coastal defense mission. They perpetuated views promoted earlier by Longé, whose experience at sea had been limited to gunboats and other small craft. Thus the involvement of artillery officers and the pioneer officers of the engineer corps was a mixed blessing, and for the development of a seagoing navy, a detriment.

While Elbertzhagen and Dirckinck-Holmfeld shared a similar vision of Prussia's naval future, they became bitter enemies after the captain questioned the soundness of the *Amazone*'s construction. Dirckinck-Holmfeld resolved to return home to Denmark but agreed to stay on long enough to command the cruise of 1845, which lasted from June to October. An Atlantic and Western Mediterranean itinerary took the ship to Liverpool, Genoa, Algiers, Madeira, and Portsmouth. Eduard Jachmann and another navigation school graduate held two of the officers' positions, albeit without official rank.[44] This fact bothered Boyen, since the two men were Prussian subjects, not foreign hirelings who could be considered an exception to rules. When the remaining Danes followed Dirckinck-Holmfeld home after the end of the 1845 cruise, the Prussians were left with a clean slate and an opportunity to redefine the status of the *Amazone*'s officers, NCOs, and crew. In January 1846 finance minister Eduard von Flottwell proposed to Boyen the hiring of three lieutenants to serve under the navigation director, along with a permanent cadre crew (*Kernmannschaft*) of four NCOs and twenty seamen. This would end the practice of hiring a new crew for each voyage (i.e., for the manpower not provided by the Danzig students), which had failed miserably.[45] That same month Prussia opened negotiations with a Dutch navy officer, Captain-Lieutenant Jan Schröder, to replace Dirckinck-Holmfeld.[46]

In March 1846 Longé retired at the age of sixty-five. In a contemporary evaluation of him, Major General Friedrich von Wrangel remarked that he could "give no verdict on his usefulness as a sea officer," because Longé had not been to sea since 1827. His colleague Murck died in 1845, still a lieutenant after thirty years in Prussian service.[47] Thus, little stood in the way of the war ministry's offering Schröder a commission as an officer or using the *Amazone* to train navy officers along with merchant mariners. At the end of May 1846, Boyen and Flottwell formally proposed Schröder to the king as Dirckinck-Holmfeld's successor. In peacetime he would be a finance ministry civil servant with "the rank of a councillor, fourth class (*Rath*

Jan Schröder *Historische Sammlung der Marineschule Mürwik*

4.Klasse)," while in wartime he would serve under the war ministry with the rank of captain. On 19 June Frederick William IV approved the terms and empowered the new navigation director to hire two lieutenants.[48]

The *Amazone* finally left on its third Mediterranean cruise in July 1846 and returned in November. A modified itinerary enabled Schröder to bring home the body of Prince Henry of Prussia, an uncle of Frederick William IV who had died while on a visit to Rome. The late prince's personal adjutant, the future field marshal Helmuth von Moltke, boarded the *Amazone* along with the corpse. Although seasickness forced him to ship out at Gibraltar and return to Prussia overland, Moltke later praised Schröder for the strict discipline and order of the crew. He recalled that the deck of the *Amazone* had been "cleaner than an Italian dinner table." Apart from the Dutch commander, the voyage was an all-Prussian operation. Schröder employed Jachmann and Arthur Schirmacher of Danzig as his second and third in command; Prussians trained by the departed Danes served as the four NCOs.[49]

In December 1846 Schröder proposed criteria for the selection of navy officer candidates from among the Danzig students: they should be full-paying students rather than scholarship recipients, to ensure proper social background; have good knowledge of German and either English or French; have good military bearing (*Haltung*) and physical fitness; and of course complete the nautical curriculum of the school with satisfactory marks. That same month, General Peucker represented Boyen at negotiations with Schröder that resolved the more pressing questions of the military standing of the *Amazone*'s lieutenants and crew. On 27 May 1847 Frederick William IV formally appointed Jachmann, Schirmacher, and Robert Herrmann of Danzig to the rank of naval second lieutenant. Their status would equal that of first lieutenant in the army. As officers, they would be subject to military law at all times. The same would be true for the crew of the *Amazone* only if the ship were transferred to the jurisdiction of the war ministry.[50] Four days later, the *Amazone* left Danzig with forty-seven navigation school students for its fourth training cruise, a transatlantic voyage to New York. En route the ship survived a collision off Newfoundland with the Hanoverian merchantman *König von Hannover*. During a five-week stay in New York, a local shipyard repaired the damages. The desertion of eight of the ship's thirty-one sailors on the first shore leave distressed Schröder far more than the accident; afterward he limited leave to officers, NCOs, and navigation school students. The *Amazone* arrived home in October after a stormy passage. Schröder assigned Jachmann, Schirmacher, and the *Kernmannschaft* to winter quarters in Danzig, and furloughed everyone else.[51]

Thus, on the eve of the revolution of 1848, Prussia had no warship more powerful than a lightly armed training corvette. This ship, like its commander, Schröder, remained under the jurisdiction of the finance ministry as long as peace prevailed. Naval personnel included three lieutenants, of whom one was on furlough, and a cadre crew of two dozen men. The only other warships were the tiny *Kanonenjollen,* idle at Danzig since 1845 and still under the control of the army pioneers. Indeed, little had been accomplished in the more than three decades since the Napoleonic Wars. But the most significant steps were those just taken, and as a potential leader, Schröder held far more promise than his predecessors. In any event, given the hostilities between Prussia and Denmark that were to erupt in the wake of the March 1848 revolution, the Prussians were fortunate to have only one foreign navy man in a position of responsibility—a Dutchman, rather than a Dane.

In the years before 1848, the military men and government ministers involved with the nascent Royal Prussian navy were far from alone in their promotion of German interests at sea. The cause had a staunch proponent within the ruling Hohenzollern family: Prince Adalbert of Prussia, a nephew of Frederick William III.[52] Adalbert's first experiences at sea came in his early years as an officer in a guards regiment, on trips to Britain in 1832 and Russia in 1834. After the Reiche commission completed its work in 1836, Adalbert entered the naval debate by sending the king a proposal written by a British friend, Captain William Mingaye, suggesting that Prussia order three heavily armed 1,000-ton paddle steamers, at £45,000 per ship, as the core of a future navy. The size and cost of the vessels, much greater than the steamers proposed by Reiche, doomed the plan from the start.[53] Adalbert's next sea voyage followed a second trip to Russia in 1837; his return home included a cruise from Sebastopol to Venice aboard the Austrian navy paddle steamer *Marianna,* in the company of Archduke John. Adalbert and John became good friends, corresponding throughout the following decade. Their paths would cross again in 1848 at the Frankfurt Parliament.[54]

Adalbert's fascination with warships and coastal defense reflected his strong interest in artillery. In 1839 he became commander of the Guard Artillery brigade, a post he retained until Frederick William IV sent him on a state visit to Emperor Dom Pedro II of Brazil in 1842–43. Adalbert made the voyage aboard the Sardinian navy frigate *San Michele* (the *Amazone* was still under construction at the time, and apparently no one considered sending the prince aboard a Seehandlung ship). Upon his return to Berlin, Adalbert became General Inspector of Artillery. His new responsibilities preoccupied him until 1848, but he indulged his naval interests whenever possible. In May 1844, for example, he inspected the two *Kanonenjollen* at Danzig, then witnessed the departure of the *Amazone* on its maiden voyage. In 1847, during one of his inspection tours, Adalbert met a young major, Albrecht von Stosch, who soon became his adjutant. Like Adalbert, Stosch had an artillery background and interest in coastal defense questions. A quarter-century later he would become the first chief of the Imperial German Admiralty.[55]

A memoir of Adalbert's trip to Brazil appeared in 1847 and in English translation shortly afterward.[56] Introduced by Alexander von Humboldt, the work earned praise from Leopold von Ranke. Along with his trav-

Prince Adalbert *Historische Sammlung der Marineschule Mürwik*

elogue, however, the prince included insights into the technological changes then revolutionizing sea power. "A new era in navigation and naval warfare seems to be opening," he observed, as "steamships introduce an entirely new element." Adalbert commented on the latest efforts by the leading navies to equip ships of the line with engines and screw propellers.[57] After the Frankfurt Parliament resolved to create a German navy in 1848, Adalbert naturally became the leading Prussian on the planning committee. Later, when Prussia took the first decisive steps to assemble a navy of its own, the prince would be indispensable.

While Adalbert became the leading voice of pro-navy sentiments in the Hohenzollern inner circle, the arguments of economist Friedrich List filled the void for the broader cause. The ideological "father of the Zollverein" to some extent was also the father of German navalism, or at least the author of its most persuasive economic justifications. List's pro-navy writings coincided with the Near Eastern crisis of 1840 and the ensuing war scare along the Rhine, which raised German nationalism to levels not seen since the War of Liberation in 1813–14. Thereafter, the navy question often went hand in hand with the question of national unity.

As a young professor at the University of Tübingen in his native Würt-temberg, List emerged as the leading proponent of a "national" German economic policy. In the wake of the oppressive Carlsbad Decrees of 1819, List's reputation as an agitator cost him his academic post. He fled to the United States, where he remained from 1825 until 1832. While in exile he be-gan to moderate his economic liberalism with increasingly heavy doses of nationalism. Eventually he concluded that protectionism would be best for Germany, at least while it industrialized. Upon his return from exile, List settled in Leipzig, where a diplomatic appointment as head of the local American consulate shielded him from arrest. He cast his theories in the language of German economic nationalism, ultimately in his definitive work, *The National System of Political Economy* (1841). Not satisfied by the steady growth of the Prussian-led Zollverein, he appealed for a broader German economic unity, a *Mitteleuropa* including all of the German Con-federation as well as the non-German lands of the Habsburg Empire. As for specific proposals, he is best remembered for his agitation for a German railway network; nevertheless, during the 1830s and early 1840s List also promoted a united German front at sea, calling for a national flag to be flown by all German vessels. Opponents argued that a German flag would be an empty symbol, no remedy for the traditional particularism of the states, but List cited the example of the antebellum United States: at home Americans showed an intense state pride, but abroad their merchant sea-men and navy men reflected an American national pride. List believed a flag shown on the high seas could be a catalyst for German national feeling.[58]

List observed that every nation with a coastline "maintains several war-ships, in order at least to defend its dignity as a nation and defend itself against piracy; only the north German coastal states have been an excep-tion." He called for the creation of a navy under the direction of "a federal commission for German sea power" in Frankfurt.[59] Writing in 1841, List noted that "Austria already has its small fleet, and Prussia this year has made its beginning with the construction of a corvette," the *Amazone*. "And as small as the vessel is, . . . so great will Germany's joy be, to christen the little thing and see it take to the sea. This little forefather of a greater progeny will become the darling of the nation, and its remains will be pre-served as a relic, like the boat of Peter the Great" in Russia.[60]

From the Frankfurt Parliament of 1848–49 to the German Reichstag of 1871 and beyond, future advocates of a German fleet would cite List's arguments on the importance of naval power. The colonial lobby in the Second Reich echoed his appeal for colonies as havens for German emigrants. List's promotion of the principle of national interest within a world economy led to his deification during the Third Reich as an early advocate of autarky, the preferred economic theory of Nazism. His own love-hate relationship with Britain, which he saw as Germany's role model, rival, and potential ally, foreshadowed the German view of Britain that would prevail during the Wilhelmine era. But List experienced overwhelming frustration during his lifetime, even after he emerged as Germany's most celebrated economist. The German Confederation did not establish an all-German customs union, a common overseas trade policy, or a federal navy. Almost a half-century would pass before a united Germany acquired overseas colonies. Over his impassioned objections, the Zollverein of the 1830s and 1840s continued to have the most liberal tariffs in Europe. For decades the tide ran against the protectionism List advocated; his economic theories again become popular only in the 1870s.[61]

In the last years before his suicide in November 1846, List's prose reflected the romantic nationalist spirit of the era, especially in his references to maritime affairs: "The sea is the highway of the world. The sea is the parade ground of the nations. The sea is the playground of . . . the entrepreneurial spirit for all peoples of the earth and the cradle of their freedom. . . . He who has no part of the sea is cut off from the good things and honor of the world—he is our Lord God's stepchild."[62] Even though he did not live to see the outpouring of pro-navy sentiment that accompanied the German nationalism of 1848–49, List shaped this early navalism by helping to change the attitude toward the sea of many Germans who participated in various local or state elected bodies and later sat in the Frankfurt Parliament. Long before the revolution, in inland states such as Württemberg and Hesse-Darmstadt as well as in staunchly particularist Hanover, the state assemblies applauded List's ideas and urged their adoption.[63] Indeed, by the 1840s advocates of sea power included some of the most prominent people in Germany. Foreshadowing the "fleet professors" of the Tirpitz era, notables from the academic world—ranging from Jacob Grimm to the radical poet Georg Herwegh—held pro-navy sentiments. This phenomenon took on a greater importance later in the decade, when a significant number of professors (more than 120) were elected to the Frankfurt Parliament.[64]

Throughout the years 1815–48 a remarkable assortment of Prussian leaders favored the creation of some sort of navy. Kings Frederick William III and Frederick William IV, influential ministers such as Rother, Flottwell, and Bodelschwingh, and military men from Boyen to the less heralded Rauch and Reiche all supported the cause, and none of them opposed a Prussian navy. Thus it was equally remarkable that so little happened. The war and finance ministries and the Seehandlung dabbled in a variety of maritime projects, a Prussian prince joined leading intellectuals in promoting the naval cause, and yet it was not enough. The political structure of Germany made it essential for Prussia to take the lead in building a German navy, but in the twilight of the age of absolutism, Prussia and Germany were ill suited for action. Leaders of the bureaucratic Prussian state preferred to form committees whose reports could be easily ignored, while the Federal Diet avoided the navy question altogether.[65]

For a cause in need of a focusing crisis, the upheavals of 1848 more than sufficed, posing a threat to Germany that only a navy could counter. As an added bonus, the revolutions swept away the political structures that had been disinclined to act earlier. News of the February 1848 revolution in Paris touched off liberal and nationalist demonstrations in Germany. On 13 March the revolution reached Vienna, toppling Prince Metternich from power. Five days later the violence spread to Berlin; thereafter Frederick William IV saved himself by abandoning royal absolutism, appointing liberal opposition leader Ludolf Camphausen as his minister-president, and declaring Prussia to be "merged" with "Germany." It remained to be seen what this "merger" would mean, or what kind of "Germany" would emerge from the revolution. In Frankfurt, the Federal Diet suspended operations. In its place, a "pre-parliament" (*Vorparlament*) of five hundred members from state and local governments met to draft guidelines for elections to a German national assembly. But by the time the "German Constituent National Assembly" convened in the Paulskirche in mid-May, a crisis over Schleswig-Holstein had prompted Denmark to impose a naval blockade on the defenseless north German ports. The creation of a German navy would stand high on the agenda of the new Frankfurt Parliament.

REVOLUTION AND WAR

n January 1848 Frederick VII of Denmark proclaimed the integral union of the Danish possessions of Schleswig and Holstein with the remainder of his kingdom. Holstein, however, was a member of the German Confederation, and Schleswig also had a substantial German population. The duchies resisted, and patriotic indignation over their plight swept Germany, coinciding with the wave of liberal revolution. Volunteers flocked to Schleswig-Holstein to help the rebel provisional government defend its territory. After Danish troops routed the ragtag army of the duchies on 9 April, the Prussian army intervened in the conflict. Five days later, Denmark retaliated by seizing Prussian merchant ships in Danish waters. Denmark's formal declaration of a blockade of the German coast came on 29 April, one week after Prussian and German troops counterattacked across the Eider River into Schleswig.[1] The German-Danish war provided a crucial stimulus to the Prussian navy and gave rise, albeit briefly, to a Schleswig-Holstein navy. And because the Danish blockade became a symbol of the impotence of a divided Germany, the creation of a German navy went hand in hand with the Frankfurt Parliament's quest for national unity.

The Frankfurt Parliament and the German Navy of 1848

After the outbreak of war with Denmark, the north German governments initiated their own naval projects. The provisional government of Schleswig-Holstein formed a naval committee, and Prince Adalbert chaired a committee organizing Prussian coastal defenses. During May and

June of 1848 Hamburg armed four merchant ships for the defense of the Elbe estuary: the paddle steamers *Hamburg, Bremen,* and *Lübeck,* and the old sailing frigate *Deutschland.*[2] After convening on 18 May, the Frankfurt Parliament established a committee to study the naval question. General Joseph Maria von Radowitz of Prussia and Carl Ludwig Bruck of Austria dominated its proceedings, from the start focusing on the naval needs of a future united Germany rather than the immediate problems of coastal defense and the Danish blockade. On 8 June Radowitz presented a plan for a seagoing navy of two frigates, four corvettes, and two large and four small steamships. Another two hundred small gunboats were to protect north German coastal waters.[3]

During the debate that followed, the most serious opposition came from an Austrian representative who moved that half the money budgeted for a German navy should be directed toward the Adriatic to defend Trieste. The borders of the German Confederation included the ethnically Italian port; navies of hostile Italian states had blockaded it after Austria's predominantly Italian navy succumbed to desertions after the Venetian revolution of March 1848. The parliament ultimately ignored the Austrian objections and almost unanimously authorized 6 million thalers for the navy.[4] But in the planning for a German fleet, the Adriatic continued to be a factor that the Austrians themselves did not always have to promote. The ultranationalist Friedrich Ludwig Jahn, representing a town in Prussian Saxony, argued that Trieste would be essential to "the establishment of a German sea power in the Mediterranean Sea."[5] Few of his non-Austrian colleagues thought of "German" interests in such sweeping terms. Nevertheless, in those heady days the middle-class liberal nationalists of the Frankfurt Parliament showed signs of being more chauvinistic than any Prussian Junker. Many of them applauded the news that Austrian merchant steamers had put to sea from Trieste flying the new German flag, the horizontal black, red, and gold bars, at the time not recognized by any foreign country.[6]

Lacking powers of taxation, the Frankfurt Parliament could only ask the individual states to fund its navy. Austria received a request for 1.8 million thalers, double the usual annual budget of the pre-1848 Habsburg navy. While Prussia and the north German states did not challenge their assessments, Austria and three inland states—Bavaria, Saxony, and Luxembourg—refused to pay. Together, their boycott deprived the project of almost half its funding (more than 2.7 million thalers). Waging wars against revolutionary threats on several fronts, Austria could hardly afford to help finance the defense of the north German coast. Nevertheless, Vienna's refusal to contribute embarrassed Bruck and the other Austrians in the Frankfurt Parliament, but most of all Archduke John, recently chosen as imperial regent (*Reichsverweser*).[7]

In the autumn of 1848 the naval committee gave way to a technical naval commission (*Technische-Marine-Commission*) and a naval section (*Marine-Abteilung*), the latter under the new German ministry for trade. General Peucker of Prussia, German war minister in 1848–49, played no role in the fleet project despite his earlier involvement with the navy question; instead, the trade minister, Senator Arnold Duckwitz of Bremen, became administrative director of the navy. Leadership of the technical commission went to Prince Adalbert of Prussia, who had spent most of the past six months trying to prepare Prussian coastal defenses. Archduke John, a friend of the prince since 1837, had great faith in his abilities. Adalbert also enjoyed the reputation of being the most German-nationalist of the Hohenzollern princes; nevertheless, he accepted the post on the condition that he would not be placed in a position of ministerial responsibility vis-à-vis the parliament. The prince assumed his duties on 7 November. By then, some members of the original naval committee already had departed, including Bruck, who became trade minister under the new Austrian minister-president, Prince Felix zu Schwarzenberg. But Radowitz remained and, with Adalbert and Jan Schröder, represented Prussia on the commission. Members from smaller states included Captain Otto Donner of the Schleswig-Holstein navy and Saxon-born Captain Karl Rudolf Bromme (or Brommy), a veteran of Greek service.[8]

Adalbert and his colleagues could be thankful that the Armistice of Malmö, signed on 26 August 1848, had suspended hostilities between the German states and Denmark. The war, and the blockade, was to resume seven months later unless negotiations brought a settlement of the Schleswig-Holstein question. By the time Adalbert arrived in Frankfurt, the German navy acquired its first ships when Hamburg turned over the paddle steamers *Hamburg, Bremen,* and *Lübeck* and the worthless frigate *Deutschland*.[9] Over the summer of 1848 various shipyards on the Elbe, Ems, and Weser had begun work on small sailing gunboats that eventually belonged to the German navy; by early 1849 twenty-seven entered service.[10] In November 1848 Ludolf Camphausen, then Prussian plenipotentiary in Frankfurt, announced that Prussia would place its own navy at the disposal of the German fleet, to become a division of the "Marine des Reiches."[11] The offer meant little (at the time, the training corvette *Amazone* was still the only seagoing Prussian warship), but coming on the heels of Adalbert's appointment, it sealed a propaganda triumph for Prussia. Austria was slower to recognize the popularity of the naval cause.

Popular support for the creation of a navy swept through the German states in the spring of 1848, on the heels of the initial revolution. Outrage over the Danish blockade generated a pro-navy sentiment that went hand in hand with the broader desire for German unity. As far south as upper Bavaria, Salzburg, and the Tyrol, people clamored for a German fleet and offered to do their part. They formed self-appointed "fleet committees" and other pro-navy associations, and in virtually every major city a *Frauenverein* appeared, attracting the wives of leading citizens. Citing the arguments of List amid their appeals to patriotism, such groups raised money, mobilized opinion, and pressured the Frankfurt Parliament and state governments.[12] The navalists of 1848 at times were as chauvinistic as their counterparts a half-century later. Nevertheless, the groundswell of grassroots support for the fleet has prompted some historians to contrast this "constructive" liberal navalism with the later "destructive" imperialistic navalism of *Weltpolitik*.[13]

In their work over the winter of 1848–49, Adalbert and his commission refused to be bound by the plan Radowitz had presented the previous June. The prince had already published his own proposals for a navy in his *Denkschrift über die Bildung einer Deutschen Kriegsflotte*,[14] which postulated three scenarios. The "purely defensive" solution involved small coastal gunboats, steam tugs to tow them, and shore batteries. In contrast, "independent sea power" would require a sailing fleet of 20 ships of the line and 10 frigates, with 30 steamers and a coastal defense force of 120 gunboats. With such a navy, Germany would be "the fourth sea power of the first rank," trailing only Britain, France, and Russia, and have a greater alliance value in the balance of power. An intermediate solution, for "offensive protection" of the coast and defense of trade on the high seas, called for 6 sailing frigates, 12 steamers, and 120 coastal gunboats.[15]

The technical commission finally finished its work on 10 February 1849, presenting the Frankfurt Parliament with a much revised version of the "independent sea power" plan from Adalbert's *Denkschrift*. It called for a sailing fleet of 15 frigates and 5 schooners, a steam fleet of 5 frigates and 20 corvettes, and another 10 steamers to tow 80 small coastal gunboats. The report also cited the need for bases in both the Baltic and North Sea, and noted the "indispensability" of a canal across Holstein capable of handling seagoing warships.[16] A meandering waterway built by the Danes between

1777 and 1784 already linked Kiel on the Baltic with the Eider River, which flowed westward into the North Sea, but this so-called "Eider Canal" had an average depth of just 3.5 meters, which limited its use to light vessels.[17] A canal fitting the description of the one in the commission's report would not open until 1895 (the Kiel Canal). The construction of bases likewise had to be postponed while attentions turned to assembling ships, officers, and sailors. Austria had no intention of helping; after the commission produced its report, Schwarzenberg repeated his government's refusal to support a German navy.[18] Ironically, in the months that followed, the rebuilding Austrian navy became a competitor of the German in the quest to purchase warships and hire officers abroad.[19]

As early as his *Denkschrift* of 1848, Adalbert acknowledged that a German navy would have to depend upon foreign officers at least initially, until the establishment of a naval academy.[20] Before turning to European sources, the Germans first focused on the United States and took encouragement in American friendliness toward the provisional German government. Other than Belgium, the United States was the only country to extend formal recognition to the Frankfurt Parliament. After the Armistice of Malmö the new sailing frigate USS *St. Lawrence* docked at Bremerhaven, and its captain, Hiram Paulding, visited both Berlin and Frankfurt. When the *St. Lawrence* left Bremerhaven in late November for a winter cruise to warmer waters, its crew included four Prussian volunteer midshipmen. They would remain aboard the ship until the summer of 1849, when the resumption of the German-Danish war caused them to be returned.[21] Following this initial gesture of friendship, the United States sent Commodore Foxhall Parker on a secret mission to Germany in December 1848. After arriving in Frankfurt in late January 1849, Parker discussed the service of American officers in the German navy and his own appointment as its commander. But in the two months between Paulding's departure and Parker's arrival, the situation in Germany had changed dramatically. In Berlin the Prussian revolution had been crushed, while in Vienna the Schwarzenberg government had engineered the accession to the imperial throne of the young Francis Joseph. The forces of reaction were gaining strength at the expense of the Frankfurt Parliament, which had yet to complete the new German constitution.[22]

The head of the naval department of the trade ministry, Duckwitz, offered Parker command of the navy with the rank of rear admiral. He also asked for the services of another thirty-eight American officers, whose commissions would be for a term of nine months. But Duckwitz failed to consult the technical commission before making his overture to Parker. He soon heard objections from those among its members who aspired to hold active commands in the new navy. At the end of January 1849 Captain Donner of Schleswig-Holstein stated flatly that he would not serve under an American officer; Jan Schröder and Prince Adalbert likewise threatened to end their involvement with the German navy.[23] German-American negotiations soon collapsed, more because of Parker than the Germans. His reports home painted a grim picture of German prospects at sea, with the armistice due to expire on 26 March 1849 and the navy still in no shape to fight. Parker saw the tide turning against the Frankfurt Parliament and advised "that American officers have nothing to do with Germany until the central authority is definitively established."[24] Duckwitz subsequently offered the navy command to a member of the technical commission, Captain Ludwig Kudriaffsky of Austria, who also refused it.[25] An Austrian rear admiral, Baron August von Sourdeau, likewise turned down the job.[26] Thus, it went almost by default to Captain Brommy.

Brommy's naval career had begun in 1827 when, at the age of twenty-three, he entered Greek service. He fought in the Greek war for independence against the Turks, then served as chief of staff to Admiral Andreas Miaulis. In 1831, after Miaulis involved the navy in the assassination of pro-Russian president Ioannes Capodistrias, the Russian navy retaliated by destroying the Greek fleet. Brommy fled to Germany but returned in 1833, when Prince Otto of Bavaria became king of Greece. He served as a captain in the Royal Greek navy and, like other Germans serving under Otto, enjoyed close ties with the court in Athens. Eventually, however, the king's favoritism toward foreigners led to a xenophobic backlash, the "revolution of 1843," which compelled Otto to employ only Greeks in the highest ranks and offices. Brommy returned to Germany and in 1845 applied for the position of Prussian navigation director, which went to Jan Schröder instead. He then turned to writing, producing the handbook *Die Marine,* published in Berlin early in 1848.[27] In the summer of 1848 Brommy applied to the Austrian navy, but he did not receive a post.[28] That autumn, when Adalbert convened his commission in Frankfurt, Brommy accepted an offer to participate and thus placed himself in contention for the German command.

Contrary to legend, Brommy had no liberal convictions. Having been forced to flee Greece twice for political reasons, by 1848 he was scrupulously apolitical.[29] Over time he would be remembered for his professionalism and his loyalty to the authority that granted his commission, rather than for his political views. As he began to assemble an officer corps, he

Rudolf Brommy *Historische*
Sammlung der Marineschule
Mürwik

had to face the fact that American help would not be forthcoming. He finally hired six former Belgian officers at the rank of lieutenant. Other recruits included three with experience in the British navy and one renegade American, Francis Dallas, a twenty-five-year-old lieutenant from Massachusetts. Together these foreigners held ten of the fourteen highest ranks below Brommy.[30]

By March 1849 the provisional German government had assembled a fleet of eight paddle steamers converted for service as warships. All were anchored at Bremerhaven, the de facto main base of the fleet. The smallest were the original trio, *Hamburg, Bremen,* and *Lübeck* (displacing 380, 350, and 335 tons, respectively), from the Hamburg flotilla. The slightly larger *Grossherzog von Oldenburg* (415 tons) and *Frankfurt* (450 tons) had been purchased new from the Bristol shipyard of William Patterson for 110,000 thalers apiece and delivered over the winter of 1848–49. The 580-ton *Ernst August* also came from Patterson of Bristol, for 150,000 thalers. The largest vessels were the *Barbarossa* and *Erzherzog Johann,* 1,300-ton passenger liners that had served the Liverpool-Boston route since 1840. Purchased from the Cunard Line for £37,000 apiece, they arrived just before the armistice lapsed. All eight steamers carried British guns from the Woolwich Arsenal.[31]

Personnel problems left the German navy in no condition to take the offensive against the renewed Danish blockade. Under the foreigners who dominated the upper ranks of the officer corps, ship captains and boatswains from the German merchant marine served as auxiliary officers (*Hülfs-Offiziere*) or ensigns. Cadets accounted for the bottom 40 percent of the officer corps. Designated *Seejunker,* most came straight from the *Gymnasium* or *Realschule.* They ranged in age from fifteen to twenty and brought the navy far more patriotic enthusiasm than practical experience.[32] Brommy also lacked NCOs and seamen. Some came with the three steamers of the Hamburg flotilla, and through Duckwitz's efforts the navy received a company of men from the Bremen contingent of the German federal army. The rest of the seamen were German volunteers or foreigners who passed into the service by staying aboard the ships the Frankfurt Parliament purchased abroad; owing to the origin of five of the steamers, most of the foreign seamen were British. The Germans got along with their Belgian lieutenants, but relations with the British left much to be desired.[33] Some politicians in Frankfurt expected Brommy to put to sea as soon as the armistice lapsed, but he had no intention of risking his ships in battle until his personnel were properly trained. Impatient parliament members, including Jahn, favored the expedient of issuing letters of marque to privateers (a practice not outlawed until the Congress of Paris in 1856). When put to a vote, the measure attracted little support.[34]

Shortly after hostilities resumed, Brommy acquired another ship he could not man, thanks to the work of Schleswig-Holstein forces. On 5 April the Danes attacked the Schleswig port of Eckernförde with the 84-gun ship of the line *Christian VIII,* the 48-gun frigate *Gefion,* the 6-gun paddle steamers *Hekla* and *Geyser,* and three transport vessels carrying 250 troops. A ten-hour artillery duel between the warships and shore batteries ended in disaster for the Danes when a strong east wind carried the *Christian VIII* and *Gefion* too close to the shore and into the crossfire of two of the batteries. By dusk the *Christian VIII* fell victim to red-hot shot; it ran aground on the beach, a total loss. The *Gefion* surrendered to avoid a similar fate. The victors renamed the frigate *Eckernförde* and presented it to the German navy. It remained in the port as a harbor watch ship, commanded initially by Captain Donner (who passed into German service at this time)

The German fleet of 1848–52 *Historische Sammlung der Marineschule Mürwik*

and manned by a skeleton crew. In the battle the Danes lost 131 men killed, 80 wounded, and 943 taken prisoner; German losses were 4 dead and 17 wounded.[35]

Two months later Brommy took a squadron out of Bremerhaven on a North Sea sortie that ended in a more conventional naval encounter. On 4 June 1849 his flagship *Barbarossa* and its escorts *Hamburg* and *Lübeck* chased off the Danish vessels standing guard at the mouth of the Weser. Brommy soon succeeded in cutting off the *Valkyrien,* a sailing corvette that lagged behind the rest of the fleeing Danes. The steamers were moving in for the kill when the corvette headed for the safety of British territorial waters off Helgoland. After a British battery on the island fired a warning shot at Brommy's ships, they broke off the chase and returned to port. Archduke John protested to Britain but received no satisfaction. The Frankfurt Parliament's naval committee had designed a naval flag during the summer of 1848—the German banner of black, red, and gold bars, with a black double eagle on a gold field in the upper left-hand corner—but the countries that did not recognize the parliament, Britain included, naturally did not recognize the legitimacy of the navy's flag. Using an unfortunate choice of words in his response to John, the British foreign secretary, Lord Palmerston, called the German ensign a "pirate" flag.[36]

During the Tirpitz era, in the heat of the Anglo-German naval race, German naval historians characterized the action as a would-be victory foiled by British treachery. This interpretation was repeated in subsequent years until Nazi writers finally elevated Brommy to the status of folk hero. It also did not escape notice that the captains of two of the German steamers were Britons who allegedly showed little enthusiasm for the fight. In any event, in the summer of 1849 Frankfurt authorities had no desire to offend the British government; fearing another incident, they instructed Brommy to keep his ships in port. Before this order reached Bremerhaven he took the same three steamers out for another sortie. On 14 June the squadron chased off the paddle steamer *Hekla* and two frigates that had been blockading the Elbe. Brommy's forces then remained idle, awaiting further orders from Frankfurt that never came. Other than skirmishes involving small coastal gunboats, the two sorties of June 1849 were the only action the German fleet ever saw. A month later the Prusso-Danish Armistice of Berlin (19 July) brought a return to peace.[37] Ironically, the largest ship acquired by the German navy reached Bremerhaven after the end of hostilities. The 1,650-ton transatlantic paddle steamer *United States* was purchased in February 1849 from the Black Ball Line for $300,000. It finally left New York in May, steaming for Liverpool, where it was outfitted with cannon and turned over to Captain Donner and a German crew. The armistice allowed the ship, renamed *Hansa,* to proceed to Bremerhaven, where it anchored in mid-August.[38]

The brief resumption of warfare in 1849 coincided with the demise of the Frankfurt Parliament, which raised fresh questions about the future of Germany and the German navy. The parliament's draft constitution, completed in March 1849, gave the proposed central government exclusive rights in the area of sea power.[39] This provision would have brought the death of the Prussian and Austrian navies or perhaps their conversion into Baltic and Adriatic squadrons of the German fleet.[40] In late March, however, the rejection of Austrian counterproposals on the constitution prompted Vienna to recall its representatives from Frankfurt. The parliament then adopted a *kleindeutsch* solution to the German question, excluding the German Austrian provinces, and offered the German imperial crown to Frederick William IV of Prussia. After the king rejected the offer, Prussian delegates also left Frankfurt and the assembly sank into disarray. A rump parliament, no longer welcome in Frankfurt, reconvened in Stuttgart before disbanding in mid-June. Archduke John remained in Frankfurt as *Reichsverweser* and head of a provisional "central authority," pending the restoration of the German Confederation or implementation of some other solution to the German question. The remaining ministers of the provisional German government resigned. Duckwitz returned to Bremen, resuming duties as a senator. Prince Adalbert went home after the technical commission completed its work, to organize and command the Prussian navy. August Jochmus, a former Prussian general sympathetic toward the navy, assumed Duckwitz's naval responsibilities. After Jochmus resigned later in 1849, Brommy reported directly to Archduke John.[41]

By then the navy had become a pawn between Prussia and Austria in their battle for hegemony over Germany. Amid the disintegration of the Frankfurt Parliament, General Radowitz, in his capacity as Prussia's minister for German affairs, began a campaign for a union of German states under Prussian leadership. The project, launched in May 1849, soon included all but nine of the thirty-nine German governments. The Prussian Union had its maritime side as well: Radowitz's draft constitution included a clause on sea power identical to that of the final Frankfurt draft. In July, after the Armistice of Berlin, Prussia announced its intention to pay the Frankfurt Parliament's naval assessments for all of its allies, then expropriate the German fleet for the union.[42] Brommy, however, refused to turn over his ships and declared that he would take orders only from Archduke John, the heir to the authority that granted his commission. Prussian suspicions increased after Brommy remarked that his ships should spend the winter of 1849–50 on a warm-water cruise. He admitted that the flag question and a lack of funds would make the voyage impossible; nevertheless, his words provoked an uproar in the newly elected Prussian Landtag, which feared Brommy would take the fleet to the Adriatic and turn it over to the Austrians. He defused the conflict by staying at Bremerhaven for the winter.[43]

In September 1849 Prussia and Austria established a central commission (*Bundes-Central-Commission*) to replace Archduke John and the "central authority" left behind by the Frankfurt Parliament. The body was to handle federal affairs while the states negotiated the future German constitution.[44] But by the spring of 1850 the two German powers presided over rival federal diets, Austria at Frankfurt and Prussia at Erfurt, and the navy remained in limbo between the two groups. The Prussian Union suffered some defections but still included most of the north German states. The union also included most of the contributors to the fleet. Nevertheless, Brommy continued to obey Frankfurt, and the fact that Archduke John had promoted him to rear admiral before resigning as *Reichsverweser* only helped Austria in the contest for his loyalty.[45] Prussia could do little other than suspend its payments to the navy.

Amid the rising Austro-Prussian tensions, Prussia concluded peace with Denmark on behalf of all of Germany. By requiring the evacuation of German forces from Schleswig-Holstein waters, the Treaty of Berlin (2 July 1850) touched off a crisis over the fate of the frigate *Eckernförde*, the former Danish *Gefion*. The vessel had to leave the port of Eckernförde, amid a revival of the German flag question and bitter debate over the best way to move it to another German port. The Prussians, who had provided soldiers to guard the frigate, insisted that it sail under their flag. The Austrians objected, fearing the Prussians would seize the ship. A compromise allowed the *Eckernförde* to join the rest of Brommy's ships, moving under the Prussian flag but not with Prussian manpower. In late November 1850 the frigate arrived in Bremerhaven. Brommy elected to spend a second winter there, rather than propose a cruise to warmer waters and revive Prussian fears that the fleet would end up in the Adriatic, in Austrian hands.[46]

The ships remained at anchor throughout the ensuing crisis, which brought the two German powers to the brink of war. Austria and Prussia mobilized their armies, but a strong showing by the Habsburg military, bolstered by the diplomatic support of Russia, brought an end to plans for the Prussian Union. On 29 November 1850 the new Prussian minister-president, Otto von Manteuffel, signed the Olmütz agreement, committing Berlin to a peaceful reform of the German constitution. Conferences held at Dresden in midwinter brought only a restoration of the pre-1848 federal institutions. In May 1851 Prussia and its allies returned to the German Confederation.[47] Even though the German navy was 1.5 million thalers in debt by the end of 1850, during the Dresden negotiations Austria obtained a promise from Prussia to help fund it through the first half of 1851. After the first of July, the reconvened Federal Diet would control the fate of the fleet. Over the intervening months, proposals for the future included one by General Jochmus, Archduke John's navy minister for part of 1849, which called for a fleet of three separate squadrons: one in the Baltic under Prussia, another in the Adriatic under Austria, and a third in the North Sea under federal control. Schwarzenberg announced that if the Diet approved such a plan, Austria would place its entire fleet within the federal structure.[48] But after the Diet reconvened, no plan gained sufficient support. Over Prussia's objections, a majority of the state envoys granted the navy 532,000 gulden (309,000 thalers) to keep Brommy's fleet alive for the rest of 1851, postponing a decision on its ultimate fate.[49]

Within days of the vote, Count Otto von Bismarck became Prussia's en-

voy to the Diet. He quickly saw the hypocrisy in the Austrian position on
the navy question. Schwarzenberg considered the dissolution of the fleet
inevitable, but having finally recognized the popularity of the German
navy, he preferred to have Prussia appear responsible for killing it.[50] To justify its dissolution, minister-president Manteuffel and other Prussian
leaders called the navy the "illegitimate child" of the Frankfurt Parliament,
a ramshackle remnant of the upheaval of 1848–49.[51] After visiting Bremerhaven in August 1851, the Austrian ambassador to Berlin, Count Anton von
Prokesch, gave a far different account of the condition of the navy. Prokesch admitted to Schwarzenberg that he had expected to see "neglected,
half-useless vessels, rough officers, a rabble instead of seamen," a "woeful,
unmilitary service," and instead had found "the opposite." While he praised
the order and discipline of the fleet, Prokesch also advised Schwarzenberg
to guard Austria's interests and look into the purchase of some of its
ships.[52] In any case, the Prussians should be blocked from acquiring the
vessels, because a Prussian navy strong enough to defend German commerce overseas would strengthen the influence of the Zollverein. Prokesch
observed, prophetically, that "if Austria does not win the upper hand in
commercial-political relations," it would be "only a matter of time" before
Prussia won the contest for Germany.[53]

   In the autumn of 1851, Hanover took the lead in the quest to save the
German fleet, but a new commission only produced a variation of the
Jochmus plan—a tripartite navy of Prussian, Austrian, and federal
squadrons—which proved to be too ambitious for the Diet.[54] As Brommy's
navy prepared to spend its third winter anchored at Bremerhaven, Bismarck began to work for its conversion to a "Zollverein fleet," something
Prokesch had long suspected.[55] After even the Zollverein states refused to
support this scheme, Bismarck in January 1852 proposed disbanding the
navy without delay. He called for the sale of the ships to interested German
states, with their previous contributions to the fleet deducted from the cost
of the ships. But the following month Hanover again intervened to save the
navy, this time proposing a voluntary *Flottenverein* to support it.[56] Schwarzenberg kept the navy afloat through the first quarter of 1852 on money
borrowed from the Rothschilds of Frankfurt. The loan, contracted in the
name of the German Confederation, outraged Bismarck. At the same time,
however, Schwarzenberg agreed to contingency plans to liquidate the
fleet.[57] The Prussians put in a bid for the frigate *Eckernförde* and the navy's
best steamship, the *Barbarossa*. The Hanoverians found few volunteers for

the *Flottenverein* and on 2 April conceded defeat. The warships were put up for sale, and Brommy reluctantly turned over the *Barbarossa* and *Eckern-förde* to the Prussians.[58]

The Prussians could be pleased at having made a good bargain. They secured their two ships for a nominal sum plus Bismarck's claim against contributions made to the fleet between 1848 and 1851. Meanwhile, the Austrians, in disarray following the death of Schwarzenberg in early April, failed to secure any ships in return for their contributions from 1850–51. Laurenz Hannibal Fischer of Oldenburg, the minister in charge of selling the fleet, arranged for Bremen firms to purchase the *Hansa,* the *Erzherzog Johann,* and the old sailing frigate *Deutschland.* The General Steam Navigation Company of London bought the remaining six steamships.[59] In all, of the initial 6 million thalers appropriated for the navy, 3.8 million was actually collected. From 1848 through 1852, including the outlay to maintain the fleet after the restoration of the German Confederation, expenditure amounted to 5.4 million. Bismarck, magnanimous in victory, persuaded the Federal Diet to grant meager pensions to the defunct navy's officers.[60] Brommy finally struck his flag in March 1853, when the new owners claimed the *Hansa* and *Erzherzog Johann.*[61]

The Schleswig-Holstein Navy (1848–1851)

The brief life of the first German navy featured far more political action in Frankfurt than naval action in the Baltic and North Sea. But during the same years, frustrated German patriots could take heart in the performance of the tiny Schleswig-Holstein navy, a gallant force operating under David-versus-Goliath conditions. After the revolution of March 1848 and the onset of Danish-German hostilities the following month, the rebel provisional government of Schleswig-Holstein formed its own naval committee. At the end of June 1848 the Schleswig-Holstein assembly voted to create its own navy rather than wait for the Frankfurt Parliament to establish a fleet. Rebel forces at Altona on the Elbe seized two Danish warships, the schooner *Elbe* and the paddle steamer *Kiel,* and the shipyards of the duchies laid down several gunboats. The seven months of peace following the Armistice of Malmö (26 August 1848) allowed time for the completion of the gunboats and the overall organization of the navy.[62] The first Schleswig-Holstein war minister, Prince Friedrich von Noer, opposed the creation of a separate navy, but his successor, Friedrich Jacobsen, stepped up the effort after taking office in September 1848. The navy initially flew the blue-white-red flag of the duchies, but in October it adopted the black-red-gold flag of the Frankfurt Parliament and, in theory, became part of the German fleet.[63] To supplement the *Elbe,* the *Kiel,* and four gunboats constructed over the summer, Schleswig-Holstein purchased the paddle steamer *Christian VIII.* The vessel was renamed *Bonin* in honor of General Eduard von Bonin of Prussia, newly appointed head of the rebel army.[64]

The navy of Schleswig-Holstein, like the army, formed its initial cadre from men born in the two provinces who left Danish service at the onset of the revolution. *Kapitänleutnant* Otto Donner, commander of the Danish navy's customs service (including the schooner *Elbe* at Altona), was the highest-ranking sea officer among the defectors. The handful of Schleswig-Holstein vessels remained inactive, manned by skeleton crews, until it became clear that the Armistice of Malmö would lapse without a peace settlement being reached. In October 1848 Donner helped establish a cadet school (*Seekadettenschule*) in Kiel, which opened the 1848–49 term with twenty-eight students. The faculty included professors from the University of Kiel.[65] By February 1849 the provisional government had commissioned thirty officers. After representing the duchies on the technical commission in Frankfurt, Donner returned home to become commander of the navy with the rank of captain (*Kapitän zur See*).[66]

The Frankfurt Parliament and its successor "central authority" financed the Schleswig-Holstein navy, a modest commitment compared with the outlay for the much larger warships of Brommy's main fleet. Seven new gunboats were built to supplement the original four, while among the larger vessels, the paddle steamer *Löwe* and new propeller gunboat *Von der Tann* joined the *Elbe, Kiel,* and *Bonin.* The Hilbert'sche Werft in Kiel built the *Von der Tann,* the first warship constructed in Germany equipped with a screw propeller. The Kiel firm of Schweffel & Howaldt, founded just a decade earlier, provided its machinery.[67] The sixteen ships mounted a total of forty-one guns and employed almost eight hundred seamen. The force was tailored for conditions in Schleswig-Holstein. The schooners operated as autonomous warships along with the paddle steamers, but the latter also towed the gunboats to action in the coastal waters of the Baltic and North Sea, often using the Eider Canal in between.[68] Danish ships operating along the coasts of the duchies also had to contend with shore batteries and mines. Future industrialist Werner Siemens, a Prussian engineer officer in the first wave of volunteers, laid the minefield at Kiel.[69] The formidable Schleswig-Holstein batteries at Eckernförde sank the Danish ship of the line *Christian VIII* and forced the surrender of the frigate *Gefion* (renamed *Eckernförde*) on 5 April 1849.[70]

Because its own tiny navy had no use (and no manpower) for such a large ship, Schleswig-Holstein gladly presented the trophy to the Frankfurt authorities; the real loss came when Otto Donner assumed command of the frigate and transferred with it to the German navy. Lieutenant Johann Ernst Kjer succeeded him and subsequently commanded the Schleswig-Holstein navy in the most active phases of its brief history.[71] At the end of April 1849, Kjer took five gunboats through the Eider Canal from Kiel to the North Sea for successful operations against the North Frisian Islands. Early in May 1849 the Danes evacuated Sylt and Föhr. The gunboats remained in the islands through the summer and were joined by the steamer *Kiel* for autumn operations.[72] Meanwhile, the action also heated up on the Baltic coast. On 3 May 1849 the paddle steamers *Bonin* and *Löwe,* the schooner *Elbe,* and the propeller gunboat *Von der Tann* engaged the Danish paddle steamer *Hekla,* a frigate, and a brig in an inconclusive three-hour battle off the entrance to Kiel Harbor.[73] Eight days later the *Bonin,* with five gunboats in tow, exchanged shots with the same three Danish warships in an indecisive action off Bülk, halfway between Kiel and Eckernförde. On 19 June the *Bonin, Von der Tann,* and *Löwe,* the latter with four gunboats in tow, left on a sortie from Kiel northward to the mouth of the Schlei, where two gunboats were to be left on permanent watch. En route, off Bülk, the flotilla exchanged fire with the 84-gun ship of the line *Skjold,* then completed its mission unharmed. Four weeks later, on 17 July, the *Löwe* towed four gunboats out to meet the *Skjold* in another indecisive action off Bülk. After Prussia and Denmark concluded the Armistice of Berlin (19 July), the navy suspended its operations.[74]

After the Danes lifted their blockade, the Schleswig-Holstein navy almost completely demobilized. Furloughs idled 671 of 778 seamen over the winter of 1849–50, and just 7 officers remained on active duty. Meanwhile, the sea cadet school in Kiel remained open, its enrollment rising to 42 students for the 1849–50 school year. Almost half the boys were from outside Schleswig and Holstein, from states as far away as Bavaria, Württemberg, and Saxony. At least for them, the spirit of German nationalism remained alive months after the collapse of the Frankfurt Parliament and defeat of the various German revolutions.[75] During the first months of 1850 the navy refurbished its gunboats and prepared to resume the campaign against the Danes as soon as the weather cleared. Meanwhile, building upon the armistice of July 1849, Prussian and Danish diplomats worked on a definitive peace settlement. In early April 1850 Berlin ordered home all Prussian subjects still in Schleswig-Holstein service; the move had little effect on the navy but virtually crippled the army, which even lost its commander, General Bonin. After Prussia concluded the Treaty of Berlin (2 July 1850) with Denmark, the remaining non-native defenders withdrew, leaving the way open for the Danes to retake the duchies.[76]

The rebel provisional government resolved to continue resistance. In early July the navy returned to action, stationing the *Kiel* and three gunboats off Föhr in the North Sea and the remainder of the flotilla—the *Bonin, Löwe, Von der Tann, Elbe,* and eight gunboats—along the Baltic coast. Days later, in the first action east of the mouth of Kiel, two gunboats exchanged shots with four Danish gunboats off Heiligenhafen in a futile attempt to contest the occupation of the island of Fehmarn. The same gunboats remained in Heiligenhafen after the skirmish, coming out again two months later to duel with five small Danish warships.[77] The *Von der Tann* was not as lucky. On 22 July the Danish steamer *Hekla* and corvette *Valkyrien* cornered the propeller gunboat off the Holstein port of Neustadt, just north of Lübeck, and drove it aground. The entire crew abandoned ship safely, but the navy lost its most modern vessel.[78] In other Baltic action, on 21 July and again on 16 August the main body of the flotilla exchanged fire with Danes attempting to tighten the blockade off Kiel Harbor.[79]

Concurrent developments in the land campaign left the small North Sea contingent permanently cut off from the rest of the navy in the Baltic. Late in July 1850 Danish troops completed their conquest of Schleswig and occupied Tönning at the mouth of the Eider, blocking the river and canal connection to Kiel. The rebel vessels remained active, contesting the Danish reoccupation of the North Frisian Islands. On 17 September the three gunboats, towed by the *Kiel,* dueled with the Danish paddle steamer *Geyser* off the island of Amrum. Afterward they sought refuge at Büsum, a safe port south of the Eider.[80] Later that month the beleaguered rebel army counterattacked across the Eider in an attempt to retake Schleswig, focusing its offensive on Friedrichstadt. Although the city was only ten miles from the North Sea mouth of the Eider, the Danish occupation of Tönning prevented the warships at Büsum from entering the river to support the assault. Instead, the navy sent four gunboats from the Baltic all the way through the Eider Canal to Friedrichstadt. Their gunfire proved not to be decisive enough to turn the battle in favor of the rebels. In early October, the Schleswig-Holstein army gave up its offensive.[81]

The rebel army's bloody defeat at Friedrichstadt brought only light casualties to the gunboat crews. Indeed, throughout the campaigns of 1849 and 1850 the Schleswig-Holstein navy suffered negligible losses in personnel and, apart from the *Von der Tann*, none in materiel. It was a remarkable record considering that in their sorties the rebel warships always confronted far larger and more powerful Danish vessels. But the navy's luck ran out in early November 1850, when the North Sea contingent left Büsum for a winter sanctuary at Glückstadt on the Elbe. The move came amid stormy weather that sank one of the gunboats, drowning all forty-two men on board.[82]

When the boats reached Glückstadt, most of the North Sea personnel were discharged; during November and December 1850 the navy ordered a rendezvous at Kiel for most of its Baltic vessels, and their seamen, too, were sent home. The end of the year found Kiel again blockaded by the Danes. Desperate times called for desperate measures. On 18 December the firm of Schweffel & Howaldt, which had earlier provided the machinery for the *Von der Tann*, launched the *Brandtaucher*, a primitive submarine designed by Bavarian artilleryman Wilhelm Bauer. The vessel carried three men, two of whom operated its manual propeller while the third attached mines with "electric fuses" to enemy targets, an idea of Werner Siemens. They finally tested it on 1 February 1851, with near-disastrous results. The submarine sank but its crew of three was rescued.[83]

Even if the *Brandtaucher* had worked, it could not have saved Schleswig-Holstein from the Danes. Under diplomatic pressure from the great powers, on 11 January 1851 the provisional government agreed to give up its hopeless fight. In the surrender, the Danish navy received the paddle steamers *Bonin, Kiel,* and *Löwe,* the schooner *Elbe,* and the surviving ten gunboats. The Danes completed their clean sweep of the rebel navy by raising and repairing the wrecks of the two lost vessels: the *Von der Tann* and the eleventh gunboat. Not unlike the Frankfurt Parliament's fleet, the Schleswig-Holstein navy died a slow death. The sea cadet school at Kiel remained open until May 1851, the last officers served until November 1851, and the last ships were towed to Copenhagen in April 1852.[84]

The Schleswig-Holstein navy defended the duchies against great odds, with no small amount of ingenuity and no help at all from the rest of the German fleet. While Brommy saw most of his ships sold to the highest bidders, the Schleswig-Holstein veterans endured the surrender of their vessels to the enemy. But the memory of their efforts lived on. The disgraced commander of the stranded gunboat *Von der Tann*, Lieutenant Louis August Lange, lived long enough to be invited to the christening of the Imperial German navy's battle cruiser *Von der Tann* in Hamburg in 1909. Lange died two years later at the age of eighty-eight, the last surviving officer of the Schleswig-Holstein navy.[85]

The Prussian Navy (1848–1852)

The onset of the Schleswig-Holstein crisis in 1848 found Prussia virtually defenseless at sea. Besides the Danish threat, the Prussians feared naval action by Russia, because the installation of a liberal regime in Berlin had poisoned Prusso-Russian relations. The interim war minister, Major General Karl von Reyher, stating the obvious, informed the new finance minister, Adolph von Hansemann, that "not enough attention has been directed" to the security of Prussian harbors. Even before the onset of the Danish blockade, Pomeranian shipowners petitioned Camphausen, then minister-president, for protection. They cited their anxieties over "the current political situation of Prussia, and of the entire German Fatherland," and fears of "great losses" in "a war with Russia and Denmark."[86]

The shipowners asked the government to arm two postal paddle steamers—the *Preussicher Adler,* a 1,200-ton iron-hulled ship built in Britain in 1846–47, and the *Königin Elisabeth,* an older, smaller, wooden-hulled vessel—but the postmaster general rejected the notion because Prussia would have to break international postal treaties if the steamers became warships.[87] In April 1848, long before he became involved with the technical commission in Frankfurt, Prince Adalbert convened a committee charged with establishing a navy to defend Prussia's coast against the Danish threat. Members included Jan Schröder and army engineer officer Ludwig Bogun von Wangenheim.[88] Acting upon their advice, Frederick William IV authorized construction of thirty-six 40-ton and six 21-ton gunboats, the latter modeled after the two *Kanonenjollen* Prussia built in 1840–41. For larger vessels, Adalbert pursued offers of merchantmen that could be armed as warships. The Erich firm of Stralsund launched the *Strelasund,* the first of the 40-ton gunboats, just before the Malmö armistice (26 August) ended the first round of German-Danish warfare.[89]

In addition to its "official" naval committee, Prussia, like Schleswig-Holstein and other north German states, had its share of local, self-appointed naval committees in 1848. The group in Stralsund, chaired by the retired Colonel Longé, funded the *Strelasund,* which was launched with great fanfare as "the first Prussian gunboat for the German fleet." Local *Flottenvereine* in Halle, Rügen, and Greifswald paid for two of the *Strelasund*'s sister ships, the *Halle-Rügen* and the *Gryphia,* finally launched in 1849. The remaining thirty-three 40-ton boats were numbered rather than

named, as were most of the six new 21-ton boats. The navy distributed the
gunboat contracts among several small shipyards on the Baltic coast and
the various Prussian rivers. The greatest contributors were the Moegen-
burg firm of Kolberg (six boats), the Seehandlung's machine shop in Berlin
(four), Schüler of Grabow (four), and the machine shop of the Hamburg-
Magdeburg steamship company in Magdeburg (four). Fifteen other shipyards built one or two boats apiece.[90]

During the four months before the Armistice of Malmö, the Prussian
navy could do nothing to challenge the Danes. The *Amazone* had a *Kernmannschaft* of thirty at the time of the revolution, around sixty men short
of a full crew, and in any event its weak armament (twelve light Swedish
cannon) made Schröder doubt that it could outduel even a brig if it were
sent out to confront the Danish blockade. Thanks to a dozen infantrymen
and a dozen artillerymen on loan from the army, the *Amazone* finally took
up a station at the mouth of the Vistula, to help the shore batteries cover
the approaches to Danzig. None of the artillerymen had experience aboard
any kind of warship; when Schröder tried to secure the transfer of an artillery NCO veteran of the *Kanonenjollen* gunnery tests of the early 1840s, the
man threatened to quit the service rather than report to the *Amazone.* Fortunately, the corvette did not fire a shot during the summer of 1848, other
than in gunnery drills. The crew suffered its only casualty when rioters in
Danzig killed a sailor on shore leave.[91] Other than the *Amazone,* the only
Prussian vessel armed and manned before the armistice of 26 August was
the *Königin Elisabeth,* which the war ministry finally wrested from the
postal service. Carrying eight light guns and two dozen soldiers to supplement its civilian crew, the steamer patrolled the coast between Stettin
(Swinemünde) and Stralsund, never engaging the enemy. Meanwhile, the
blockading warships seized Prussian merchantmen with impunity. The
Danes even dispatched small craft to harass Prussian fishing boats operating in the bays and sounds along the coast. They impounded so many vessels that the hundreds of prisoners became a considerable burden. Some
were returned before the conclusion of the armistice.[92]

In November 1848, before joining Prince Adalbert on the technical commission in Frankfurt, Schröder, recently designated "commodore," commanded gunboat exercises in the Greifswalder Bodden, between the island
of Rügen and the Pomeranian coast. For most of the month, the *Strelasund*
and nine other new gunboats practiced maneuvering in the bay and firing
at a corvette-sized target on the shore near Putbus. The exercises involved
almost five hundred men, a mixture of volunteer seamen, army pioneers,

and artillerymen. Volunteer captains and boatswains from the merchant marine commanded the boats; the three lieutenants commissioned in May 1847 remained behind in Danzig, where Schröder left Jachmann in charge of the *Amazone*.[93] The corvette did not join in the exercises, mainly because of questions concerning its status vis-à-vis Frankfurt and the new German navy. In Frankfurt, Camphausen declared that the Prussian navy would become a division of the German navy, but in Berlin some of the ministers interpreted this pledge as covering only the new gunboats. They argued that they could hold back the *Amazone* on the grounds that it was a navigation school training ship; eventually, it could either be sold to the German navy, credited against Prussia's assessment for the German navy budget, or maintained as a Prussian warship. In December 1848 an impatient Duckwitz asked when the *Amazone* would be handed over, but the Prussians continued to stall.[94]

In February 1849, after the work of the technical commission in Frankfurt came to an end, Adalbert and Schröder returned to Prussia. The ambitious German fleet plan they had helped devise remained a dream. To make matters worse, all of the steamers being purchased for the German navy were going to Brommy at Bremerhaven, leaving Prussia no better defended at sea than before. With the Armistice of Malmö scheduled to lapse in late March, they set about the task of developing Prussia's own naval forces, leaving the question of their relationship to the German navy to be determined later. On 1 March 1849 Frederick William IV formalized the operational command structure, creating a High Command (*Oberkommando*) under Adalbert. The prince retained his army rank and position of General Inspector of Artillery. Naval administration would continue to be handled by the Naval Section (*Marine-Abteilung*) of the General War Department in the war ministry, established the previous year. Schröder served as the de facto operational commander and reported to Adalbert. The *Amazone* and the new gunboats were placed "in readiness . . . under the Prussian flag and Prussia's command." Meanwhile, in Frankfurt, Camphausen informed the provisional German government that Prussia—in defiance of the newly completed German constitution—would not renounce its right to build, arm, and maintain warships at its own cost.[95] Just as Frederick William IV soon would reject the German crown offered by the Frankfurt Parliament, reversing his own pro-nationalist rhetoric of the previous year, Camphausen's declaration contrasted sharply with his earlier support for a common German fleet. Prussia clearly was no longer willing to cast its lot entirely with "Germany" in naval affairs.

A flurry of activity followed as personnel and materiel were assembled for the upcoming campaign. Schröder established his command at Stettin, a better base than Danzig for operations against Denmark. On 29 March Frederick William IV issued orders laying the foundation for the Prussian navy officer corps: Jachmann and Schirmacher received promotions to first lieutenant, with the status of army captain (*Hauptmann*). By the end of the spring, the king commissioned another forty-four officers and cadets. All were Prussian subjects, relatively young (the oldest was thirty-four), with experience at sea as civilians. At least five had served aboard the *Amazone* on its prewar training cruises. Only two were noblemen, both of the lowest rank; they and three others were the only sons of army officers. Most in the group were not only merchant mariners, but sons of merchants or merchant mariners. In the emergency atmosphere, social status mattered little. When a young nobleman from the Berlin army cadet school applied for provisional naval cadet status, the king personally rejected him on the grounds that "he has never been to sea." Most of the men commissioned in the spring of 1849 made a career of the service, and six eventually became admirals. Their lack of social standing would cause trouble in later years, when class and bloodline mattered more than experience.[96]

By the end of March, Jachmann had arrived at Stettin with the *Amazone* and its reinforced cadre crew. By then the fleet included the requisitioned postal steamer *Preussischer Adler* and merchant paddle steamer *Danzig*, each manned by its civilian crew. The rest of the manpower of the tiny fleet, as in the gunboat exercises of November 1848, came from volunteer seamen and the ranks of the army. Throughout his effort to whip his forces into shape, Schröder lamented the shortage of senior officers (no one qualified for a rank above lieutenant) and experienced NCOs. Along with Adalbert, he urged the war ministry to consider hiring Dutchmen or Swedes to fill these gaps. The prince offered a captain's commission to Carl Siegmard Lous, the former navigation school director who had gone home to Sweden in 1842, but Lous declined to return to Prussian service.[97] Notwithstanding the civilian experience of the recently commissioned officers, their lack of naval experience made some operations (e.g., by several vessels in formation) a dangerous adventure. Both the *Danzig* and the *Königin Elisabeth* ran aground on the rocks in the Greifswalder Bodden, the latter sustaining such heavy damage that it had to be docked and disarmed.[98]

After hostilities resumed on 26 March 1849, the Danish navy focused its attentions on Brommy's fleet and the Schleswig-Holstein navy. In contrast to the close blockade of the entire Prussian coastline mounted in 1848, this time enemy warships stood farther to sea off the main ports. Under Schröder's command, on 27 June the *Preussischer Adler* ventured out to challenge the blockade. The steamer engaged the Danish brig *St. Croix* in an inconclusive five-hour artillery duel off Brüsterort. The navy saw no further action before Prussia and Denmark concluded the Armistice of Berlin, one month later. On the eve of demobilization, Adalbert and Schröder commanded four dozen officers and 1,753 men aboard three larger ships (*Preussischer Adler, Danzig, Amazone*), thirty-six 40-ton gunboats, and six 21-ton gunboats.[99]

Another year passed before Prussia, in the name of the German Confederation, concluded the Treaty of Berlin with Denmark (2 July 1850). The confederation was not restored until the spring of 1851, the German navy not liquidated until the spring of 1852; in the meantime, the climate of uncertainty left Adalbert and Schröder unable to plan for the long term. They fulfilled their primary goal, however, by keeping the Prussian navy alive in peacetime, preventing a return to the inaction and indecision of the years before 1848. They regularized procedures, acquired more warships and maintained those already on hand, and improved the quality of personnel and training. Schröder kept his *Marinekommando* headquarters at Stettin, which became home to a new "Marine Corps," two companies including a mixture of soldiers and seamen. During 1850 the navy segregated the seamen and soldiers into separate branches, soon redesignated the *Matrosencorps* (corps of sailors) and the *Seebataillon* (naval infantry), respectively. A third branch, the *Werftcorps* (corps of shipbuilders), was created later, organizing the workers of a new royal shipyard in Danzig along military lines. Most of the sailors still were volunteers with merchant marine experience, while the *Seebataillon*'s marines were conscripts serving a three-year term of active duty like infantry in the army. In 1851 the navy accepted its first seven one-year volunteers (*Einjährig-Freiwillige*); following the army's example, it used this practice to build up a cadre of reserve (*Seewehr*) officers and NCOs. A year later a machinist served as a one-year volunteer in the *Werftcorps,* setting an important precedent. The army soon acknowledged that such service fulfilled the universal military obligation.[100]

At the same time, the navy command continued to build up its officer corps. In late November 1849 Frederick William IV commissioned the four Prussians who had served as volunteer midshipmen aboard the USS *St. Lawrence.* Two of them, Carl Ferdinand Batsch and Wilhelm Berger, eventually became admirals in the Imperial German navy.[101] Over the next two months the navy commissioned another twenty-eight cadets. Socially more prestigious than the group of the previous spring, they included Count Alexander von Monts, who would end his career as chief of the Imperial German Admiralty, and eleven other noblemen. One-quarter were army cadets and *Gymnasium* students, who would have been rejected as "inexperienced" just a few months earlier. Clearly, the standards had changed. Adalbert and Schröder remedied the shortage of senior officers by securing the services of Captain Otto Donner from the German navy in April 1850; two years later, upon the demise of Brommy's fleet, he received a permanent Prussian commission. In January 1852, after three years of pondering various possibilities of hiring foreign officers, the king authorized commissions for three Swedes at captain's rank.[102]

While officers and NCOs from the Prussian army drilled the *Seebataillon* on land, Adalbert wanted to have the sailors of the *Matrosencorps* spend as much time as possible at sea. Unfortunately, demobilization brought the return of the three steamers requisitioned in 1848–49 to their former civilian roles. The postmaster general allowed the navy to operate the *Preussischer Adler* after it returned to postal service, but difficulties in maintaining military discipline in a civilian setting soon ended the experiment. Otherwise, the only seagoing warship was the 350-ton *Amazone,* which Schröder, as early as January 1848, had condemned as too small even for the training needs of the Danzig navigation school.[103] To remedy the problem, in March 1850 the navy bought the 660-ton Seehandlung ship *Mercur.* The corvette-sized vessel, launched three years earlier by Klawitter of Danzig, showed the strains of two voyages to the Far East and needed immediate repairs. Because no Prussian port had a dry dock at the time, the navy sent it to Karlskrona, Sweden, to have its hull recoppered. The Stralsund Marine Depot then installed its nominal armament of four cannon. Plans called for the *Mercur* and *Amazone* to go on a long training cruise over the winter of 1850–51, but during the summer of 1850 the *Amazone* collided with a merchant brig in the Baltic, raising doubts about its seaworthiness for the voyage. The *Mercur* set sail alone in November, under the command of Captain Donner. The ship cruised to Brazil via the Cape Verde Islands, then called at St. Helena en route back to Stettin. It arrived home in June 1851. Despite widespread illness only 2 of the crew of 155 died, and none deserted.[104] Because the *Mercur* was built as a merchantman, designed for maximum stability with a full cargo, it required an extraordinary amount of ballast even with a reduced amount of sail. Nevertheless, it held up so well that Schröder pressed it into service again in the autumn of 1851, for a Baltic cruise.[105]

The overseas training cruise of the *Mercur* did not signal the navy's abandonment of gunboats. Indeed, the influence of army artillerymen (including Adalbert himself) remained strong, and many within the war ministry still considered coastal defense the primary reason for having a navy. The Napoleonic-era gunboat strategies that Elbertzhagen had condemned in 1842 continued to have their share of proponents, as evidenced by the 1849 German translation of a 1808 Danish gunboat operations manual.[106] In September and October of 1849, Lieutenant Herrmann led exercises in the protected waters of the Stettin sound (Oder or Stettiner Haff) involving nine of the navy's forty-two gunboats, assisted by three rented tug steamers that towed the boats when they were not being sailed or rowed. Schröder observed from aboard the *Amazone,* which also participated in the artillery practice. Herrmann commanded exercises again in July 1850, in the Greifswalder Bodden, this time with twelve gunboats and three rented tugs. Jachmann led exercises in July and August 1851, with ten gunboats and two rented tugs, once more in the Greifswalder Bodden. Like the autumn 1848 exercises, those in the summer of 1850 and 1851 practiced firing at a corvette-sized target on the shore near Putbus. The training cruise of the *Mercur* may have been the main event of 1850–51, but far more naval personnel served aboard the gunboats. Seventeen officers and 441 men took part in the 1850 exercises, 13 officers and 401 men in 1851. In comparison, the *Mercur* cruised with a dozen officers and 155 men.[107]

Amid the continued uncertainty over the German navy question, Prussia hesitated to invest in new warships; nevertheless, during 1850 Adalbert secured permission to hire the English master shipbuilder Scott Russell to design three new paddle steamers. In August 1850 the royal shipyard in Danzig laid down the *Danzig,* a 1,450-ton wooden-hulled vessel to be powered with engines imported from the designer's own firm of Robinson & Russell. Meanwhile, in London, the Robinson & Russell shipyard began work on the 390-ton iron-hulled sister ships *Salamander* and *Nix.* It was an expensive arrangement. The *Danzig's* engines alone cost £20,000, as much as each of the smaller steamers. As part of the bargain, shipwrights from Danzig went to London to study under the British master, and an agent of Russell's firm supervised work on the *Danzig.*[108]

Delays plagued the construction of the *Danzig,* the first vessel built in the royal shipyard, in part because the shipyard itself was being constructed around the vessel. Workers actually laid the keel in a vacant lot next to the Vistula. Military convicts were supposed to start building the facilities in the autumn of 1850, but the Austro-Prussian war scare brought their reassignment to emergency fortification projects. They did not finish digging the slip between the ship and the river until November 1851, two weeks before the launching. To keep costs down, the navy tried to procure some of its materials from local Danzig suppliers: the Arnold firm for copper for the ship's hull, and the firms of Carl Steimmig and the Claassen Brothers for iron components. Ferdinand Schichau of Elbing supplied iron water tanks. Iron beams and bolts were ordered from Sabiou in Sweden, but after the ship carrying them to Danzig wrecked in the Baltic, replacements were imported from Britain. Steimmig likewise had to turn to Britain in order to fulfill his contract. Iron parts for a shipyard crane had to be imported from Britain in order for the imported British engines to be installed in the hull. The *Danzig*'s twelve heavy guns were ordered from Thomas & Charles Hood of London via the Woolwich Arsenal, which conducted the firing tests. Hailed as "the first genuine Prussian warship to be built in a Prussian shipyard," the *Danzig* showed just how far Prussia was from self-sufficiency in naval construction.[109]

The launching of the *Danzig* came several months after the *Salamander* and *Nix* entered service. Robinson & Russell completed the *Salamander* in December 1850 and the *Nix* in April 1851. The Woolwich Arsenal provided four heavy guns for each vessel. Because the Prussian navy had few personnel with steamship experience, British machinists were hired to serve aboard them. In the summer of 1851 Frederick William IV and Prince Adalbert went for brief cruises aboard the *Salamander*. The *Nix,* which ran aground off Swinemünde shortly after its arrival, saw much less duty but did visit Karlskrona in September. From the start both steamers suffered from engine-room fires, attributed to a flaw in their design.[110]

Under the patronage of Adalbert and the direction of Jan Schröder, the navy entered a period of postwar growth. Despite the prevailing uncertainties, over the years 1848, 1849, and 1850 Prussia spent 2.35 million thalers on naval defense, a far cry from the annual allocations of less than 3,000 thalers in the grim years of the 1830s. The new Prussian Landtag, elected on a restricted franchise under the conservative constitution of December 1848, sustained the momentum by granting the navy 487,000 thalers for 1851.[111] The fledgling navy remained insignificant as an armed force, the quality of its materiel and competence of its personnel leaving much to be desired, but clearly it would not return to the near-dormant status of the years before 1848.

. . .

In the spring of 1852, at the onset of the liquidation of the German navy, Jan Schröder led a contingent to Bremerhaven to take possession of the *Eckernförde* and *Barbarossa*. The 1,400-ton frigate and 1,300-ton paddle steamer instantly became the largest active warships in the Prussian navy.[112] In late May, in a gesture foreshadowing things to come, the king restored the frigate's original Danish name *Gefion*. With the spirit of counterrevolution well under way in Berlin, he preferred the Danish designation to one that commemorated a victory of the "revolutionary" German cause of 1848–49.[113] Prussian policy toward the personnel of Brommy's fleet reflected a similar mentality. Although sailors aboard the *Barbarossa* and *Eckernförde* were accepted into Prussian service along with their ships, the navy command would be far more selective in granting Prussian commissions to former German navy officers. Brommy's struggle to save his fleet left him with strong anti-Prussian sentiments; he remained inactive until 1857, when he accepted a rear admiral's commission in the Austrian navy. He served only four months, as a "technical advisor," before poor health forced him to retire. Brommy died in January 1860, at the age of fifty-five. At his request, he was buried with the black-red-gold banner of his old flagship *Barbarossa* covering his casket.[114]

A PEACEFUL INTERLUDE

hrough the rest of the 1850s, Adalbert and Schröder continued to direct the Prussian navy on its course of modest growth. The interlude of more than a decade of peace would be a mixed blessing. The navy further regularized recruiting standards and training procedures, but at least until the end of the decade, the lack of an imminent threat to the maritime interests of Germany kept the naval cause from attracting public attention on the scale of 1848–49. It did not help that many leading spokesmen of navalism during the revolution had been liberals, who were silenced (or silenced themselves) during the conservative 1850s. Disagreement over whether Prussia should claim overseas colonies divided the navy leadership as well as the Prussian cabinet, neutralizing a potential argument for naval expansion. The Prussian fleet grew steadily but remained inferior even to the Danish navy.

Personnel and Policies

Throughout the formative years of 1848–52, the Prussian navy had suffered from a shortage of trained officers. The overall failure of the first attempts to groom junior officers had made the problem worse; of the twenty-eight cadets appointed in the winter of 1849–50, only eleven served long enough to become lieutenants. But just as the death of the German navy of 1848–52 gave the Prussian navy its two largest ships along with their seamen, the pool of unemployed veterans of Brommy's officer corps promised to solve the officer shortage. Applications from German navy officers far outnumbered openings in the Prussian navy, enabling Adalbert and Schröder to be selective. They took only junior officers and cadets; of the ten accepted, only one, Reinhold Werner, qualified as a lieutenant. The others became cadets. Two applicants from the Schleswig-Holstein flotilla also received commissions as lieutenants. The navy met the rest of its needs by making permanent most of the temporary commissions granted to merchant mariners in 1849.[1] Meanwhile, at the top of the *Rangliste,* Otto Donner received a permanent Prussian commission as captain (*Kapitän zur See*) in June 1852, after his release from German service. After the appointment, he outranked every sea officer but Schröder. Below him, the three Swedes hired in 1852 served at the rank of captain (*Korvettenkapitän*).[2] Ironically, a greater share of former German navy officers—including, briefly, Brommy himself—ended up in the Austrian navy than in the Prussian. Of the eighty-nine sea officers and cadets serving under Brommy as of May 1850, sixteen ultimately received Habsburg commissions. The Austrians also commissioned one veteran of the Schleswig-Holstein navy. The Habsburg fleet, which had lost two-thirds of its officers in the Venetian revolution of 1848, was rebuilding with a German language of command and accepted any qualified German-speaking officer. The Austrian flexibility contrasted sharply with the Prussians' strong preference for commissioning their own subjects.[3]

Indeed, the fact that eight of the former German officers to receive Prussian commissions were Prussian subjects reflects the navy leadership's desire to build a Prussian rather than a "German" service. Schröder and the four captains commissioned in 1852 were not Prussians, but for such senior appointments, Adalbert preferred non-Prussians with experience in a navy over Prussians from the merchant marine. When the Seehandlung liquidated its fleet of armed merchantmen, the agency's directors sent the navy résumés of its five active ship captains—all Prussian subjects—with the observation that "the Prussian flag has been shown with honor by them in the most distant oceans of the world." The navy refused to consider any of them. Thus, the goal of the early 1840s—in the words of Hermann von Boyen, to create "the cadre of a navy" in the merchant marine—came to fruition only in a limited way. Most of the common seamen got their start aboard merchantmen, as had most of the officers commissioned in 1849. But Adalbert acquiesced in the officers' appointments only reluctantly, reflecting his belief that few men could make the transition from merchant marine to navy officer.[4]

In the autumn of 1853 the navy established its first permanent officer training school, the Sea Cadet Institute in Stettin. In designing the four-year program of study, the Prussians consulted foreign models, including the curriculum of the new United States Naval Academy in Annapolis, Maryland. Qualifying exams for lieutenant second class followed graduation. When possible, students shipped out for an extended cruise after their third year at the school; depending upon the length of the voyage, this practice could delay the final term of studies by a year or more. Other disruptions stemmed from the school's frequent moves in its early years: to Danzig for the 1854–55 term, then to Berlin. From the start, faculty included army officers. In 1855, F. B. Haller von Hallerstein of the Guard Artillery started an eleven-year term as school director.[5] In the mid-1850s more than half the students were sons of army officers or civil servants; few were merchants' sons, and none were sons of merchant mariners. Reflecting the trend toward social exclusivity, almost half the cadets held noble titles. Unfortunately, the institute suffered from a high attrition rate, as reflected in the distribution of the forty-five students of 1858–59: seventeen in the first year of study, fourteen in the second, six in the third, and eight in the fourth. The institute alone could not meet the growing need for officers, and in any event, a curriculum designed for teenagers was inappropriate for older officer candidates. Between the early 1850s and early 1860s, Adalbert placed six such men with the British navy and two with the Dutch; after two-year tours of duty, they were offered Prussian navy commissions.[6] A few army officers entered the navy after initial duty in the *Seebataillon* commanding marines. In one case, a German nobleman entered the British navy on his own initiative, then applied to Adalbert for a commission. Prince William of Hessen-Philippsthal-Barchfeld transferred to the Prussian navy in 1854 as a lieutenant and served for five years, rising to captain's rank. In 1856 another prince, Hugo of Schwarzburg-Sondershausen, entered as an ensign; in a dozen years with the navy, he likewise rose to captain.[7]

To free as many sea officers as possible for duty at sea, the navy used army officers to fill most of its posts on land. In addition to faculty at the Sea Cadet Institute, these included administrators in Berlin and the coastal depots, as well as the officers of the *Seebataillon* and an artillery company created for the navy in 1858. Especially in the naval infantry and artillery, most rotated through on short tours of duty, but some remained with the navy for years at a time and served it with dedication. They faced a painful dilemma when their sailors and marines, eager to defend the honor of the junior service, engaged in brawls with soldiers stationed in the same cities. In the early 1850s, when Stettin was home to the *Marinekommando* as well as the army's 2nd and 9th Infantry regiments, such "*Schlägereien*" became serious enough to cause concern for Adalbert and Schröder.[8]

In 1853, after the commissioning of the former German navy officers and the Swedes, the corps (from Adalbert through the rank of sea cadet first class) included fifty men. By 1862 the number of sea officers (down to ensign or *Fähnrich zur See,* after 1855 the equivalent of sea cadet first class) had grown to sixty-four. During the same years, the land-based branches experienced a more dramatic expansion. In 1853 ten officers served in the *Seebataillon* and five army officers in other capacities; those rated as officials (*Beamte*) rather than officers included four medical doctors and thirteen administrators. In 1862 the *Seebataillon* employed twenty-four officers and the naval artillery (created in 1858) six, with eight army officers serving in other capacities. The *Beamte* included twenty medical doctors, a dozen engineers (a branch created in 1858), and twenty-one administrators.[9]

Despite the relatively slow growth of their corps, sea officers enjoyed rapid advancement throughout the decade, thanks to early retirements in the upper echelons. Two of the three Swedish captains left Prussian service in 1855; Schröder, promoted to rear admiral in 1854 and vice admiral four years later, retired in 1860 at the age of sixty. Donner retired in 1862, at fifty-three, and the last Swedish captain, Henrik Sundewall, would leave service on the eve of the War of 1864, at forty-nine. Of the three original lieutenants commissioned in 1847, Jachmann ultimately emerged as the star, receiving promotions to *Korvettenkapitän* in 1855 and *Kapitän zur See* in 1859. Schirmacher quit the navy in 1855, as a lieutenant first class, the same rank Herrmann held at the time of his death in 1861. Thus Adalbert topped the *Rangliste* of 1863, followed by Sundewall and Jachmann. The next seven men in seniority, occupying the remainder of the captain's ranks, included six commissioned in 1849; like Jachmann, they had seen their first sea duty in the merchant marine. They would hold the navy's key commands during Bismarck's wars of German unification.[10]

In 1854 the navy recognized the separate status of its deck officers (*Deckoffiziere*), who constituted an intermediate layer between officers and NCOs. Numbering only a dozen at the time (compared with thirty-six sea officers), their ranks would swell to more than a thousand by the onset of the Tirpitz era in 1897—more than the sea officers and engineer officers combined. Aboard ship they assumed many roles filled in other navies by senior petty officers. It was a tradition in the German merchant marine for the line between officers and the ranking members of their crews to be somewhat blurry, and as a group deck officers personified this line. By custom they enjoyed some perquisites of officers, but in other ways they were treated as NCOs. Their numbers grew dramatically when technological changes created entirely new skilled positions aboard ship, jobs that the Prussian (and later German) navy rated with the deck officers. At least initially, in a time when common seamen and NCOs still could rise to sea officer status, the navy did not bar deck officers from such advancement. Once the officer corps evolved into an exclusive body and promotion from below became impossible, the "half-caste" status of the deck officers generated much controversy. As early as 1862, Adalbert considered deck officer rank proper for all merchant captains and boatswains entering the navy. He would rather expand the number of deck officers and their responsibilities (to include command of "small gunboats") than let more merchant mariners into the officer corps.[11]

The conscription districts of the I (Pomeranian) and II (West and East Prussian) Army Corps sent the navy most of its common manpower. Those with experience as sailors or fishermen went to the corps of sailors, while the *Werftcorps* received the carpenters, sail and rope makers, chainsmiths, machinists, and machine builders. The *Seebataillon* drafted men from the same districts with no special skills or experience that would send them to either of the other two branches.[12] The navy's volunteer apprentice seamen (*Schiffsjungen*), like the cadets of the sea officer corps, entered the service between the ages of fourteen and sixteen. They received three years of training, which they paid for with another six years of service. This time did not count toward the standard three-year universal service obligatory for all young men in Prussia; thus, the *Schiffsjungen* had to serve at least twelve years.[13] Ironically, the service exemption for merchant seamen, which dated from the 1820s, kept the navy from getting many experienced sailors. Nevertheless, by the early 1860s the peacetime manpower numbered just over a thousand men, including deck officers and NCOs.[14]

Despite the clear progress of the 1850s, it remained to be seen whether the navy's personnel would ever gel into a competent fighting force. Writing early in 1862, Adalbert lamented that his officer corps remained "a collection of diverse elements." He acknowledged that "almost without exception" the foreigners and former merchant mariners receiving commissions in 1849 and the early 1850s proved to be good officers. But he wanted the navy officer corps to be a "union of professional and social comrades (*Vereinigung von Berufs- und Standes-Genossen*)," recruited from "elements imbued with the spirit of the army." He considered sons of army officers the best navy officer candidates.[15] Thus, decades before the largely bourgeois corps of the Wilhelmine era slavishly imitated its more prestigious army counterpart, the navy leadership itself set the tone for things to come. In this regard, the service faced a dilemma. Without the patronage of Adalbert and the interest of other army leaders, the navy would never have grown and expanded in the first place; but because their formative experiences were in the Prussian army, they considered its standards and practices to be the ideal for the navy. Unfortunately, their attitude constrained the navy's ability to develop its own spirit and traditions, and helped give it an inferiority complex that future experience only reinforced. Efforts to "prussianize" the fleet facilitated the adoption of the worst aspects of the outlook and mentality of Prussian militarism.

Growing Pains: Prussian Naval Operations (1852–1860)

The demise of the Frankfurt Parliament's German navy put Prussia in a position to lead the further development of German sea power. Within the cabinet in Berlin, Baron August von der Heydt, trade minister from 1848 to 1862, welcomed the opportunity. He considered the Prussian navy a potential "instrument of Prussia's *Zollvereinpolitik.*"[16] As early as 1851 he supported a strong fleet, arguing that "the objection, that the country in addition to covering the military budget could not bear . . . the costs of maintaining a fleet, in my opinion is not tenable."[17] At the same time, peace brought a boom in German overseas commerce, strengthening the case for a role for the Prussian navy in defending it. Hamburg reestablished itself as the leading port for Prussian trade, as it had been in the days of the Seehandlung fleet, and the trading interests of Prussia continued to be linked to those of Germany as a whole. But with the Seehandlung divested of its own fleet, the focus shifted to new private companies based in Hamburg. In 1852 the sailing ships of the fledgling Hamburg-Amerika Line carried forty-seven hundred passengers from Hamburg to New York, a fourfold increase since 1849. Other companies operating under sail included August Bolten's line between Hamburg and South America, founded in 1852. Meanwhile, in 1850, Robert Sloman initiated a steamship line between Hamburg and New York.[18]

The navy's ships were soon to show the flag in American waters, but at least for its three steamships, the cruises of 1852–53 were limited to the Baltic. In July 1852 the *Barbarossa* steamed from Bremerhaven to Swinemünde, where it joined the *Nix* to salute the visiting Tsar Nicholas I of Russia. It marked the first time that a foreign head of state had ever reviewed Prussian warships. In August the *Nix* escorted Frederick William IV from

Danzig to the island of Rügen and back. That autumn the *Barbarossa* moved on to winter quarters at Danzig. The *Salamander* spent all of 1852 docked at Stralsund, but the following year it was the only steamer activated, escorting the king on his annual August trip to Rügen. Other than one gunboat activated in August 1852 for use by marines of the *Seebataillon,* none of the forty-two vessels of the gunboat flotilla saw action in 1852–53. The navy never again held gunboat exercises, although the boats remained on hand and would be used again in the next war with Denmark.[19]

The limited operations in the Baltic reflected Adalbert's desire to shepherd resources for a cruise in 1852–53 by a squadron of his largest ships. Like the old armed merchantmen of the Seehandlung, they were to investigate opportunities for trade.[20] In preparation for the mission, the Stettin Marine Depot renovated the *Amazone* in 1850–52 and the *Mercur* in 1851–52. The royal Dutch shipyard in Vlissingen overhauled the former German navy frigate *Gefion* after Schröder took possession of it at Bremerhaven. The *Amazone* met the *Gefion* at Vlissingen in November 1852, and the two ships departed for the South Atlantic. The *Mercur* followed later, loaded with supplies. Other than Jachmann, all of the navy's original officers were involved: Schröder aboard the flagship *Gefion,* Schirmacher as commander of the *Amazone,* and Herrmann as commander of the *Mercur.*[21] After calling at Monrovia, Liberia, in January 1853, the *Gefion* and *Amazone* crossed the South Atlantic for visits to Rio de Janeiro, Montevideo, and Buenos Aires. In the South American ports they lost enough men to desertion for Schröder to forbid further shore leave. The *Mercur* joined the squadron in Montevideo in March, delivering supplies. The three ships cruised the coast of Brazil until May, when the *Mercur* left for home. The *Gefion* and *Amazone* went on to call at several Caribbean ports before proceeding to Norfolk, Virginia. According to the Prussian minister in Washington, "the appearance of a royal squadron in the United States left a favorable impression, with the government as well as the great number of Prussian businessmen and Prussian merchant captains."[22] During July 1853 the ships crossed the Atlantic to Portsmouth, where Prince Adalbert awaited them. The British welcoming ceremonies featured an inspection of the *Gefion* and *Amazone* by Queen Victoria and her consort Prince Albert. Afterward, the queen invited Schröder to a reception at Osborne House.[23]

By the time Schröder's ships reached Britain, the Russo-Turkish crisis that led to the Crimean War was already brewing. Determined to be represented in the Near East along with the other great powers, Prussia sent the paddle steamer *Danzig* straight to the Mediterranean after its commissioning in June 1853. The ship picked up its twelve cannon in Britain en route to its destination. After returning from the Americas, Schröder's flagship *Gefion* and the *Mercur* likewise headed for the Eastern Mediterranean. The two ships arrived off the Turkish coast in December 1853. With a large Anglo-French fleet assembled at the Dardanelles in support of the Turks, the Prussian squadron, like the Austrian fleet, operated out of Smyrna (Izmir), a safe distance from the war zone. Other ports of call included Alexandria, where all three warships docked in February 1854. In the spring the *Gefion* and *Mercur* returned home, followed later by the *Danzig*.[24]

In 1854 and again in 1855, the British and French deployed large fleets in the Baltic during the summer months, but the Russian fleet refused to venture out of its base at Kronstadt. Apart from the capture of Bomarsund in the Aaland Islands in August 1854 and the bombardment of Sweaborg in August 1855, the allies limited themselves to capturing the handful of Russian merchantmen bold enough to challenge their blockade.[25] Adalbert secured assignments for Prussian cadets aboard ships of the British fleet, following his precedent of placing cadets with the United States navy in 1848–49.[26] Otherwise, the navy did nothing to compromise Prussian neutrality. Baltic training cruises continued throughout the war. During the summer of 1854 a reactivated *Amazone,* commanded by the Prince of Hessen, joined the *Gefion* on a visit to Karlskrona. The *Salamander* entered service only briefly but the *Nix* remained on active duty all summer, escorting Frederick William IV on his annual August trip to Rügen. During August the king inspected all active warships at Swinemünde.[27] In 1855 the Baltic cruise lasted from May to October, with the burden carried by the *Mercur* and the newly acquired frigate *Thetis*. Prussia secured the 1,500-ton sailing ship from the British navy in exchange for the seldom-used 390-ton *Salamander* and *Nix*. While German naval historians have criticized this trade of steamships for a sailing frigate, at the time the *Thetis* was a godsend. By the mid-1850s only steam-powered vessels were valued as warships, but all navies still used sailing ships as training vessels. The growing Prussian navy desperately needed a frigate, especially with the *Gefion* laid up indefinitely for repairs following two years (1852–54) of continuous service. The two small steamers, meanwhile, had been of little use to Prussia. Vessels of their type were best suited to serve as dispatch boats in large fleet operations or, if properly outfitted (which the *Nix* and *Salamander* were not), as steam yachts for dignitaries. After consummating the deal with the British, Adalbert negotiated with Sweden for yet another sailing frigate, an initiative that ended in failure later in 1855.[28]

Unfortunately, the trade of January 1855 left Prussia temporarily with no steamships in active service, owing to serious problems with the *Barbarossa* and *Danzig*. Built in 1839–40, the *Barbarossa* was hardly in fighting trim when it came over from the defunct German navy. After the ship arrived in Danzig in November 1852, an inspection committee concluded that repairs would be too expensive. It remained in Danzig as permanent harbor watch. At the same time, the brand-new *Danzig* succumbed to severe dry rot. This problem afflicted most wooden-hulled steamers, owing to the heat generated by their engines. Dry rot also resulted when ships spent long periods of time in fresh water, as the *Danzig* had while riding at anchor on the Vistula from its launching in November 1851 until it finally left port in July 1853.[29] Except for a six-month reactivation of the *Danzig* during 1856, the embarrassing hiatus in steamer operations lasted until June 1858; meanwhile, dozens of otherwise valuable naval personnel were idled. In April 1855, three months after the exchange of ships, the captain of the *Thetis* reported that his crew still included twenty-one machinists and stokers from the *Nix* and *Salamander*—men with nothing to do aboard a sailing frigate.[30]

During the American and Mediterranean cruises of 1852–54, Adalbert and his staff in Berlin focused their attentions on negotiating administrative changes with the king and the war ministry. In November 1853 Frederick William IV formally freed the navy from the control of the army. The Naval Section (*Marine-Abteilung*) of the Prussian war ministry, since 1850 under the direction of Colonel Bogun von Wangenheim, gave way to an independent "Prussian Admiralty." Just as Adalbert's status as a royal prince had prevented him from assuming ministerial responsibility before the Frankfurt Parliament for the German navy in 1848, he could not now appear before the Landtag in Berlin as a minister speaking for the Prussian navy. The plan recognized him as "supreme commander (*Oberbefehlshaber*)" in charge of naval operations, while the Prussian minister-president became nominal chief of the Admiralty, entrusted with representing the navy in the legislature. In other changes, Adalbert abolished the Stettin *Marinekommando* in favor of a Baltic station headquartered at Danzig. Upon his return to Prussia in May 1854, Schröder received command of the station with a promotion to rear admiral. That same spring, Adalbert finally relinquished his post of General Inspector of Artillery and received the awkward rank "Admiral of the Prussian Coasts." Unless special circumstances made general's dress more appropriate, from now on he wore an admiral's uniform.[31]

Traditional accounts blame Frederick William IV for Adalbert's unique new rank. According to legend, he refused to make the prince "Admiral of the Fleet" on the grounds that "we do not have a fleet." This episode, often cited to emphasize the pathetic state of German sea power at the time,[32] belies the fact that in the 1850s the condition of the navy improved, although at a slow pace. The 270-ton schooners *Hela* and *Frauenlob* entered service in March 1854 and May 1856, respectively. The former had been laid down in 1852 and the latter even earlier, in 1849, funded by donations from a *Frauenverein* formed in Berlin in the pro-navy atmosphere of 1848. They were activated annually for training cruises, usually limited to the Baltic and North Sea; in 1860 (the same year the *Frauenlob* sank in a storm) the *Hela* was rerigged as a brig. During 1855 the navy also laid down its first two ships with screw propulsion, the 1,900-ton corvettes *Arcona* and *Gazelle*, at the royal shipyard in Danzig.[33] These and three similar ships built over the next decade ultimately were the only tangible results of a new fleet plan drafted by Adalbert. Sanctioned by the king in April 1855, the program called for a fleet of nine ships of the line, three frigates, and six corvettes, all steam-powered with screw propellers, to be built at a cost of 12 million thalers. Adalbert consigned paddle steamers and sailing ships to auxiliary roles. Such a fleet would be more than a match for the Danish navy. The plan accounted for the transition from the paddle wheel to the screw, but it did not foresee the revolutionary impact of armor plate, first affixed to French floating batteries in the Black Sea during the Crimean War. The timetable of the plan—extended over fifteen years, at 800,000 thalers per year—ensured that it would fall victim to technological change.[34]

During the Crimean conflict, as plans were made to establish the Baltic station at Danzig, Prussia laid the groundwork for a future naval base on the North Sea. In July 1853 Oldenburg sold Prussia the village of Heppens and adjacent land at the mouth of the Jade, the future site of Wilhelmshaven. In November 1854, in their last appearance under the Prussian flag, the paddle steamers *Salamander* and *Nix* represented the navy at a ceremony in which Frederick William IV and Prince Adalbert formally took possession of the territory. The Prussians paid 500,000 thalers for the land and pledged to spend 400,000 thalers on its development over the next three years (1854–56); otherwise, it would revert to Oldenburg. Prussia assumed responsibility for the defense of Oldenburg's coastline and seagoing trade. In return, Oldenburg gave Prussia the right to construct a railway linking

the new base to the Prussian fortress town of Minden in northern Westphalia. The initial harbor developers were plagued by ice in winter, floods
in spring, and malaria in summer. Wood-boring worms even threatened a
temporary dam that protected workers from the tides. As long as the fleet
grew only slowly, there was no rush to complete the base. In 1855 the corvette *Amazone* spent the summer in the Jade as a harbor watch ship; in
subsequent years the navy's presence continued to be largely symbolic.
Nevertheless, Prussia fulfilled the terms of the agreement regarding the development of the harbor. The same could not be said for the railway project. Because Oldenburg had no border with Prussia, in order to reach
Westphalia the line had to cross a strip of Hanoverian land. To thwart
Prussia's ambitions, Hanover blocked its construction. The railway would
finally be completed when Prussia annexed Hanover after the War of
1866.[35]

Ironically, both Oldenburg and Hanover had joined the Zollverein in
1851, the first of the German coastal states to do so. Their diametric views
of Prussian sea power demonstrate that for the smaller states, acceptance
of Prussian economic leadership did not necessarily bring acceptance of
broader Prussian hegemony. Some north German states hoped to balance
Prussian domination of their trade with Austrian political and diplomatic
support, even at sea. Under the leadership of Emperor Francis Joseph's
brother, Archduke Ferdinand Max, after 1854 the Habsburg navy expanded
dramatically. At least among the officers, Germans became the dominant
nationality, and because German Austria alone could not meet the demand for German-speaking officers, Vienna turned to the rest of Germany
to fill the void. Besides the sixteen veterans of Brommy's fleet who entered
Habsburg service, during the 1850s and 1860s another thirty non-Austrian
Germans received commissions in the Austrian navy. Hanover accounted
for roughly one-fourth of them; others hailed from Mecklenburg, Hesse,
Nassau, Saxony, Bavaria, Württemberg, Baden, and even Prussia. The
Prussian navy could not boast of a similar representation. When Austria
sent the screw frigate *Radetzky* on a goodwill cruise to the North Sea in
1856, it received a warm welcome in the German ports it visited.[36]

Despite the tense political climate, non-Prussian north German entre-
preneurs did not hesitate to follow where Prussians took the lead. In 1854, a
year after Schröder visited Liberia with the *Gefion* and *Amazone*, Carl
Woermann of Hamburg established his first African trading post there. He
extended his operations to Gabon in 1862 and eventually to Cameroon as
well.[37] Later in the 1850s Bremen's Vietor brothers, two merchants and a

pastor, established trading posts and mission churches in Togo.[38] The modest German presence in West Africa, the first since the failure of Brandenburg-Prussia's Guinea colony 140 years earlier, laid the foundation for Imperial Germany's later interest in annexing West African territory. Schröder's 1853 account of conditions in the Caribbean likewise had an impact on future German activity, only deterring rather than encouraging involvement. Leaders of the Berlin-based Colonization Society for Central America had asked for detailed reports of the coast of Colombia, where they proposed to settle German emigrants. Schröder's grim depiction of conditions there helped change their minds.[39]

The end of the Crimean War returned the Prussian navy to its peacetime regimen of training cruises and showing the flag overseas. In June 1856 Prince Adalbert left Danzig with a squadron consisting of the paddle steamer *Danzig*, the frigate *Thetis*, the corvettes *Amazone* and *Mercur*, and the schooner *Frauenlob*, the largest single group of Prussian warships assembled since the days of the Great Elector. A collision with the *Danzig* forced the *Mercur* to drop out almost immediately. The *Amazone*, manned in part by cadets, accompanied the other ships on calls at Cherbourg and Plymouth before turning back at Madeira. From there the *Thetis* and *Frauenlob* went on a mission to South American waters, which lasted into 1857. Adalbert and the *Danzig* went on to the Mediterranean.[40]

Before entering the Mediterranean the *Danzig* steamed to the coast of Morocco, where local pirates had plundered the Stettin merchant brig *Flora* after it ran aground in 1852. After learning of the attack, Adalbert had proposed a punitive mission against the Moroccans, but the Crimean War and a lack of funds had forced postponement of his plans. Four years after the fact, the actual perpetrators of the earlier offense could not be found and punished; Adalbert hoped instead for a confrontation that would deter future acts of piracy. The actions of other minor naval powers in the past quarter-century served as precedents: after Austria launched an operation against Morocco in 1828–30, Sardinia-Piedmont and Naples against Tunis in 1833, and Naples against Morocco in 1834, the North African pirate states had been compelled to respect their ships on the high seas.[41]

On 7 August 1856 the *Danzig* anchored off Cape Tres Forcas and Adalbert led a landing party ashore. In four and a half hours of skirmishing with local Moroccans, the Prussians suffered two dozen casualties—more than one-third of the landing party—including seven killed. Adalbert sustained a minor leg wound. Contemporary Prussian accounts did not call the action at Tres Forcas a victory, but in the later heyday of gunboat diplomacy some writers considered it a baptism of fire for the navy. After the landing party reembarked, the *Danzig* proceeded to Gibraltar, where the British allowed the Prussians to bury their dead. The steamer assumed its duties in the Mediterranean and finally returned home in November.[42] The episode proved to the Prussians that a lone warship would not always suffice to command respect, even from local adversaries along the coasts of Africa.

During the summer of 1857 the *Amazone* took cadets on a cruise in the Baltic and North Sea, while the *Thetis,* only recently returned from South America, went on a cruise of the Mediterranean. The latter deployment continued the navy's unfortunate policy of driving its newest acquisitions into a state of disrepair (e.g. the *Mercur* in 1850–51, the *Gefion* in 1852–54). The durable *Thetis* remained in the Mediterranean through the spring of 1858. The *Mercur* was scheduled to take over cadet ship duties from the *Amazone* for the summer cruise of 1858, but its questionable seaworthiness prompted Adalbert to activate the *Gefion* instead. The frigate had spent the past four years in port, and its commander, Captain Donner, the past seven years in posts on land. After leaving Danzig in July, the *Gefion* joined the *Thetis* on a visit to the Jade, where Prince Adalbert conducted an inspection, then assumed overall command. His squadron included a third ship, the new 350-ton yacht *Grille,* the navy's first steamer equipped with a screw propeller rather than paddle wheels. Built by the Le Havre firm of A. Normand, with British engines from Penn & Sons of Greenwich, the *Grille* received its commission in June 1858; it would serve as the royal (later imperial) yacht for much of the next three decades. On its maiden cruise, it accompanied the two sailing frigates to Falmouth, Brest, and Spithead. Adalbert, the *Grille,* and the *Thetis* returned home in October, while Donner's *Gefion* underwent repairs at Portsmouth, then continued in December 1858 on a cruise to the Caribbean. It returned home in the summer of 1859, after a forgettable final stop in Norfolk, Virginia, where four men deserted and force alone prevented others from jumping ship. Donner lamented that the *Gefion's* apprentice seamen showed a "predisposition to desert" and required constant supervision. The unpleasant experience was Donner's last at sea. The veteran of four navies spent the rest of his career as interim chief of the Baltic station, retiring in 1862.[43]

In the late 1850s the fleet continued to expand. Except for the *Grille* the Prussians built all new warships at home, but dependence on foreign industry continued. The royal shipyard in Danzig launched the screw corvette *Arcona* in May 1858, its sister ship *Gazelle* in December 1859, and one last paddle steamer, the 430-ton *Loreley*, in May 1859. Engines for the *Arcona* came from John Cockerill of Belgium; for the *Loreley*, from the Seehandlung's Berlin machine shop; and for the *Gazelle*, from A.G. Vulcan of Stettin. The *Loreley*, the navy's first vessel equipped with German-built engines, became Prussian station ship at Constantinople shortly after receiving its commission. Unfortunately, the *Gazelle's* engines never performed up to expectations, and for years to come the navy would trust German machine shops to build engines only for the smallest warships.[44] Amid the flurry of new projects, in 1858 the navy wisely declined an offer from Scott Russell, the original architect of the *Danzig*, to dismantle the rotted paddle steamer and rebuild it with an iron hull in his own London shipyard; it would have been obsolete even with a sound hull, thanks to the recent widespread application of the screw propeller to larger warships. Unfortunately, the *Danzig's* expensive (£20,000) engines could not be adapted to turn a screw.[45] The most dramatic example of reliance on foreign producers came in the area of artillery, where the navy shunned Alfred Krupp of Essen (who already supplied some foreign navies) and other Prussian producers in favor of Swedish foundries. In 1855 Finspong received a contract for forty-eight guns for the *Thetis* and the schooners *Frauenlob* and *Hela*. Three years later Åker won a contract for ninety guns for the *Gefion* and the new *Arcona*. Upon completion, the *Gazelle* also received Swedish artillery.[46]

Even more so than the Prussian navy, the leading companies of the German merchant marine took a dim view of the capabilities of domestic industry. Although the Hamburg-Amerika Line had ordered its original sailing ships in Bremerhaven and Hamburg, once it switched to steamships it turned to British shipyards. The North German Lloyd, founded in 1857 to serve the Bremen–New York route, patronized one firm almost exclusively, ordering twenty-five of its first twenty-seven transatlantic steamers from Caird of Greenock. The Lloyd eventually trusted German shipyards to build its tugs and smaller steamers but waited almost thirty years before ordering a seagoing liner from a domestic builder. Just as the Danish war of 1848–49 had plagued the Hamburg-Amerika Line's initial efforts, the worldwide economic slump that started in the United States during 1857 cast a shadow over the birth of the North German Lloyd. The following year, the line began service to British ports and New York.[47]

In the autumn of 1858 the king's brother, William, assumed the duties of prince regent. Sweeping changes in Berlin soon affected the navy leadership. William replaced the reactionary minister-president Otto von Manteuffel with the more moderate Prince Karl Anton of Hohenzollern, a member of the south German branch of the royal family. Rather than continue the arrangement of 1853, which called for the minister-president to serve as nominal head of the Admiralty, Hohenzollern brought Schröder to Berlin from Danzig to fill the ministerial role. In May 1859 the prince regent approved the prince's plan to subdivide the Admiralty. Schröder headed the Naval Administration (*Marineverwaltung*) as "a chief with the powers and responsibility of a minister," representing the navy with other ministries and before the Landtag. He received a promotion to vice admiral but not a seat in the cabinet. Meanwhile, Adalbert directed naval operations as head of the High Command (*Oberkommando der Marine*), with the clumsy "Prussian coasts" wording finally dropped from his admiral's title.[48]

Shortly after the implementation of the reform, war between Austria and an alliance of France and Sardinia-Piedmont provoked a general European war scare. While the Prussian army mobilized in the west for possible action against France, the navy feared hostilities with France, Denmark, and even Russia. By July 1859 Adalbert had every warship in service except the new *Arcona*, kept out of harm's way in Danzig, and the old *Barbarossa*, which had been converted to an accommodation hulk after several years as Danzig harbor watch. The onset of the war scare caught the *Gefion* on the last leg of its American cruise. To be on the safe side, Donner took a northern route home, around Scotland, rather than via the English Channel, where the sailing frigate could easily fall victim to the French navy. In July the *Gefion*, the *Thetis*, and the leaky *Danzig*—the navy's three largest active warships—participated in artillery exercises in the Baltic. Adalbert even ordered full armament for the schooners *Hela* and *Frauenlob*, which were normally only nominally armed. He canceled mobilization orders for the tiny wooden gunboats of 1848–49 vintage only after Austria's defeat brought a quick end to the war.[49]

The division of responsibilities between Adalbert and Schröder worked well enough during the mobilization of 1859, but a clash over which ships to activate for the summer of 1860 escalated until it poisoned their relationship beyond repair. The argument involved the unseaworthy *Danzig*, which Schröder wanted to employ for artillery exercises off Danzig, and the new screw corvette *Gazelle*, launched in December 1859, which Adalbert wanted to press into service as quickly as possible. The prince considered the *Danzig* "not passable as a training ship," while the vice admiral contended that the *Gazelle*, owing to problems with its German-made engines, could not possibly be readied for service during 1860. Adalbert threatened to engineer a cutoff of funds if Schröder persisted with plans to use the *Danzig,* and for an officer arguing with a Hohenzollern prince, Schröder responded in remarkably strong language. In April 1860 Adalbert sought to break the impasse by appealing directly to the prince regent. William confirmed that the fitting out of the *Gazelle* was a top priority, and that because of the Far Eastern cruise then under way (see below), summer training exercises in the Baltic should involve a bare minimum of vessels. After the stubborn Schröder chose to fill this quota with the *Danzig* (along with the *Amazone* and *Hela*), his relationship with the prince reached a breaking point.[50]

It did not help matters that during the same months, the two men were on opposite sides of a debate over whether Prussia should pursue the acquisition of colonies. Adalbert, minister-president Hohenzollern, and foreign minister Alexander von Schleinitz favored a colonial policy, over the objections of Schröder and trade minister Heydt. Schröder, sixty years old in 1860, retired, and in April 1861 a new navy ministry took over the naval administration. General Albrecht von Roon, war minister since December 1859, also became minister of the navy. Adalbert again remained operational commander, with the additional title "General Inspector of the Navy."[51] Despite its acrimonious end, the command partnership of Adalbert and Schröder, in various forms since 1848, had served the navy well. Amid the initial upheavals of the revolutionary year, the *Amazone* and two *Kanonenjollen* were their only warships; a dozen years later, Prussia stood on the verge of respectability in the second rank of Europe's sea powers.

The Revival of the German Navy Question (1859–1862)

"With a Prussian fleet, Germany will achieve its rightful place among the neighboring sea powers, and only in this way will the unresolved conflict with Denmark be brought to a final settlement."[52] Count Helmuth von Moltke, chief of the Prussian general staff, used these stirring words in January 1860 to assure the prince regent of his support for naval expansion. During the war scare of the previous year, fears of a blockade swept the North Sea and Baltic port cities, reviving the German navy question. Some scenarios involved the French or Russian navies, but the Danes alone could have shut down German overseas commerce. The crisis forced Prussian and German leaders to recognize just how little had been done during the 1850s to avoid a repetition of the humiliation of 1848–49.[53]

Over the tense summer months of 1859, both Hamburg and Mecklenburg appealed to Prussia to help organize a common coastal defense. Leaders in Berlin recognized that they could revive the navy question and turn it to Prussia's advantage in the contest with Austria for hegemony over Germany. In October 1859 the prince regent appointed a commission on coastal defense, including Moltke and three other generals. Schröder, not yet retired, represented the navy along with Adalbert. In December the commission proposed a unified coastal defense system for all of northern Germany and called for negotiations with the smaller coastal states. Meanwhile, representatives from the kingdom of Saxony, the Saxon duchies, Bavaria, Nassau, Württemberg, Hesse-Darmstadt, and Mecklenburg met in Würzburg to discuss coastal defense. Other than Mecklenburg all were landlocked, making the conference an important test of the willingness of the interior states to contribute to the common cause. In December 1859 the "Würzburg bloc" members proposed that the German Confederation take up the problem. Advocates of a stronger confederation, led by Saxon minister-president Friedrich Ferdinand von Beust, hoped to use the popular naval issue to build support for the much maligned Bund. Beust made it clear that Saxony would not contribute to a Prussian-led navy organized outside the German federal framework. The news from Würzburg discouraged Prussia, which did not want a navy or coastal defense system to be under federal control. Furthermore, contrary to Prussian interests, the mere referral of the question to the Federal Diet ensured that it would become bound up in broader efforts to strengthen the confederation.

Prussia resolved to keep the initiative from passing to Frankfurt. In January 1860 representatives from Mecklenburg, Oldenburg, Hamburg, Bremen, and Lübeck attended a conference on coastal defense in Berlin; other than Mecklenburg, none had participated in the Würzburg conference. Fearing that these states would join Prussia in an extra-federal solution, the Diet in Frankfurt invited Berlin to propose a unified coastal defense system of its own to the confederation. The Prussian scheme, born in the meeting of Adalbert, Schröder, and the generals the previous autumn, called for 110 small gunboats to be based at coastal stations in East Prussia, Mecklenburg, and Prussia's Jade territory. Strategic railways would link the bases to the interior. Three infantry *Küstenkorps*—two along the North Sea coast and one on the Baltic—would be on hand to defend against landings. The non-Prussian participants in the system would provide fifty of the gunboats and the two North Sea *Küstenkorps*, but Prussia would have overall command.

The prospect of such Prussian domination caused uneasiness in Hanover and the other northern states. To make matters worse, in a separate initiative begun in January 1860, war minister Roon revived an old plan that would place the federal army corps of the smaller north German states under Prussian command, conceding the south Germans to Austrian command. The coastal system and Roon's military plan appeared to be components of a broad Prussian initiative to dominate all of northern Germany—which, indeed, they were. When the Diet considered the Prussian coastal defense plan in July 1860, it attracted lukewarm support from Hamburg, Lübeck, and Mecklenburg. No other state would accept it without considerable revisions.

The matter then lay dormant until early in 1861, when signs of Danish rearmament sparked a reaction throughout northern Germany. Should Denmark choose to reopen the Schleswig-Holstein question, the German ports would be almost as helpless as they had been in 1848. Roon, Moltke, trade minister Heydt, the newly crowned King William I, and Crown Prince Frederick William all declared their support for a Prussian navy at least as strong as the Danish. In Hamburg, Bremen, and Lübeck the press and public opinion clamored for the construction of a German fleet. Over the summer of 1861 the pro-navy movement spread inland, reaching proportions reminiscent of 1848. This time, however, the phenomenon had a distinctly Prussian tone and was hardly spontaneous. The government encouraged local fleet committees and fund drives throughout Prussia, from Saarbrücken to Breslau. The Nationalverein, founded in 1859 to promote a Prussian-led German Reich, orchestrated the agitation outside of Prussia. Beyond the three Hanseatic cities, it aroused little sympathy.[54]

In May and June 1861 both Hamburg and Bremen entered secret negotiations with Prussia on the navy question, with Arnold Duckwitz leading the way for Bremen. The former German trade and navy minister of 1848, now serving as mayor of Bremen,[55] called for the construction of blockade-running steamers and relegated gunboats to a secondary role. The Prussians accepted this modification but winced at Duckwitz's other proposals, which reflected the old liberal nationalism of the Frankfurt Parliament. He felt the fleet should be recognized as a federal institution, include Hanoverians as participants, and fly the black-red-gold flag of 1848. Roon hoped that public opinion would pressure the Hanseatic leaders to adopt views more acceptable to Prussia. Toward this end he sent Prince Adalbert to Hamburg, Bremen, and Lübeck just as the pro-Prussian, pro-navy agitation reached its peak. The visits, in August and September, were timed to coincide with appearances by the Prussian summer squadron, led by the corvette *Amazone* and the brig *Hela*. The prince and the navy received a warm reception in each city, with Bremen showing the greatest enthusiasm.

In the autumn of 1861 Hanover proposed its own plan for a federal flotilla of fifty gunboats to defend the non-Prussian North Sea coast.[56] The Austrians also entered the fray, reviving the Jochmus plan of 1851, which would have created a German fleet of three squadrons, operated by Prussia in the Baltic, Austria in the Adriatic, and the remaining states in the North Sea. The proposal won even less support than it had a decade earlier. Among the landlocked states only Saxony supported the Austrian scheme. Beust qualified his support with the condition "that the Bund really administered the fleet."[57] Losing all hope in the confederation, in October 1861 Bremen suggested a Prussian-led German navy organized on the model of the Zollverein. Rather than build its own vessels to contribute to the fleet, Bremen offered simply to pay an annual sum to Prussia to defend it from blockades and protect its merchantmen on the high seas. Other states could be invited to do likewise, or be given the option of contributing their own ships rather than money. This proposal raised hopes in Berlin, but a more detailed version of it, drafted in December 1861 by Duckwitz, included provisions Prussia could not accept: an annual contribution by Bremen of just 50,000 thalers, a guarantee of a certain level of naval spending by Prussia, and federal control over the fleet if the Diet in Frankfurt declared a federal German war. The biggest problem, of course, was that Duckwitz and his Bremen colleagues wanted a genuine German fleet constructed in the spirit of 1848; they were willing to accept an expanded Prussian navy as a stepping stone to this German fleet. In contrast, Prussia wanted to use the issue of coastal defense to strengthen its overall influence in northern Germany. In a last effort to salvage an agreement with Bremen, in February 1862 the Prussians included Duckwitz's "German ideas" in a preamble to a new draft of their earlier proposal for a coastal defense system. The final gasp came during the spring in Hamburg, where Moltke chaired a conference of representatives from all federal states. Austria backed recalcitrant Hanover, and Prussia had full support only from the tiny Thuringian enclave states. It irritated the Prussians most of all that the hosts showed so little enthusiasm for their ideas. Though Hamburg continued to serve as the primary port for Prussian overseas trade, the city remained staunchly anglophile and suspicious of Prussia.[58]

Apart from the weak attempt to revive the three-squadron scheme in the autumn of 1861, Austria stood aloof from this round of the German navy debate. Habsburg foreign minister Count Johann von Rechberg sought a partnership with Prussia in Germany and, unlike Schwarzenberg in 1849–52, had no desire to exploit the navy question. From the time of his appointment late in 1859 until the early months of 1862, Rechberg consistently took the position that Austria was doing its part for the defense of German maritime interests by maintaining a fleet in the Adriatic. Prussia and the north German states should be responsible for the Baltic and North Sea.[59] The early 1860s found Austria in a naval race with the new kingdom of Italy and unable to support naval projects in the north. Ironically, the failure of the Baltic and North Sea plans, coinciding with the unprecedented Habsburg naval buildup in the Adriatic, made Austria the unquestioned defender of Germany in European waters. Rechberg himself would agree to send Austrian warships to the North Sea in 1864, during the next German-Danish war.

The breakdown of German navy negotiations in 1862 disappointed the leaders of the Prussian navy, but they could take heart in the fact that the rekindling of the debate had led to an unforeseen expansion of their own forces. Twenty-three screw-powered gunboats, a category of vessel not even in Adalbert's fleet plan of 1855, were built or begun during the years 1859–62. The royal shipyard in Danzig built eight 350-ton gunboats, each armed with three cannon: the *Camäleon, Comet, Cyclop, Delphin, Blitz, Basilisk, Meteor,* and *Drache.* The first four were laid down in 1859 and launched in the late summer of 1860; the rest were not begun until 1861. The remaining fifteen gunboats, armed with two cannon and displacing only 240 tons, were laid down in 1859 by private shipyards and launched between January and April 1860. The first six boats were in service in time to accompany the *Amazone* and *Hela* on their tour of the Hanseatic ports in the late summer of 1861. Unfortunately, because they had been designed to fit the abortive coastal defense scheme, the gunboats were practically useless in the long run. The navy decommissioned some of them as early as 1867.[60] The enduring significance of the screw gunboat program came in the business it provided for private German shipbuilders and machine shops. Discounting the construction of the tiny sailing gunboats in 1848, it marked the first widespread use of private domestic industry to serve the needs of the fleet, a clear attempt to break with the policies of the 1850s. For the fifteen smaller gunboats not constructed in the royal shipyard, the navy awarded two contracts apiece to the shipbuilders Klawitter of Danzig, Keier & Devrient of Danzig, Mitzlaff of Elbing, Lübke of Wolgast, Zieske of Stettin, Domcke of Grabow, and A. E. Nüscke of Grabow. Liegnitz of Grabow built the remaining boat. All twenty-three gunboats had German-built engines, purchased from A.G. Vulcan of Stettin, Möller & Hollberg of Stettin, Ferdinand Schichau of Elbing, and Borsig of Berlin, winners in an open competition for the contracts.[61] Two of these four firms—Vulcan and Schichau—eventually would construct both ships and engines for the navy. It was a modest beginning for what would become a massive naval-industrial complex.[62]

Amid the naval discussions of the late 1850s and early 1860s, the fleet plan of 1855 fell hopelessly behind schedule. A revised program of February 1859 retained the fifteen-year construction timetable, only for the years 1860–75 rather than the initial 1855–70. Other changes included the new screw gunboats—a projected fifty-two by 1875—and five screw frigates instead of three. The draft of February 1859 still included six ships of the line, but a revision six months later called for only five. The plan's projected cost of 31.5 million thalers was more than double the estimate of 1855. In March 1861, just before the formal creation of the new navy ministry, Roon revised the plan yet again. His screw-propelled fleet included six ships of the line and six frigates (all with postponed target dates for completion), six large and six small corvettes, and the gunboat program.[63]

The ongoing ironclad revolution soon required further revisions in the fleet plan. The trend that began with armored floating batteries off the Crimea in 1855 led to the launching of the French navy's *Gloire,* an armor-plated wooden frigate, in November 1859. The British responded with the *Warrior,* an iron-hulled armored frigate launched the following year. During 1861 the launching of the Italian *Terribile,* the Austrian *Salamander,* and the Russian *Pervenez* made Prussia the only great power without an iron-clad. In December 1861, in response to a new Danish fleet plan, an Admiralty Council including Adalbert and Roon rewrote the program again. The ships of the line and unarmored frigates were replaced by four large and four small armored frigates. The wooden-hulled screw gunboats not yet constructed gave way to eight armored and fifty-seven unarmored iron-hulled gunboats. The twelve wooden-hulled screw corvettes remained in the program. The council resolved to order two of the smaller armored frigates in Britain "as soon as possible," along with the first two iron-hulled gunboats. The royal shipyard in Danzig, expanded by two new slips, was to continue work on the corvettes, but their engines would be imported from Britain.[64]

Of course, other than the completed screw corvettes and gunboats, the fleet continued to exist only on the drawing board. The lack of progress on the fleet plan, coinciding with Prussia's failed German coastal defense initiatives, made the years 1859–62 frustrating for the navy. During this time, however, Prussia took a decisive step toward becoming the leading representative of German interests overseas. In August 1859, shortly after the revival of the navy question, the Austrian frigate *Novara* returned to Trieste from a two-year cruise around the world. More than just an exercise in showing the flag, as a scientific expedition it ranked with Charles Darwin's earlier voyage aboard the HMS *Beagle*. In the mood of the moment, the Austrian effort received favorable publicity throughout Germany.[65] Prussia felt compelled to undertake an expedition of its own without delay, to show its own resolve to be taken seriously as a factor overseas.

In the autumn of 1859 the new screw corvette *Arcona*, the frigate *Thetis*, and the schooner *Frauenlob* were fitted out for a mission to East Asia, to conclude trade treaties and investigate commercial opportunities.[66] The Swedish captain Sundewall commanded the squadron, with the *Arcona* as his flagship; Jachmann received command of the *Thetis* after its captain, the Prince of Hessen, retired on the eve of the expedition. The navy recruited a zoologist, a botanist, and a geologist to provide a scientific dimension. After Adalbert condemned the *Amazone* and *Mercur* as too unseaworthy for the long voyage, in December 1859 the navy purchased the 740-ton clipper ship *Columba* from a Hamburg firm. It served as the fourth ship in the squadron, under the name *Elbe*.[67]

At the start of the mission a North Sea storm caused heavy damage to the *Arcona*, forcing it to dock in Britain for repairs. For the sake of staying together, all four ships spent the winter in Southampton, but in the spring of 1860 the *Elbe* sailed directly for Singapore while the others made a slower passage to the Far East via Rio de Janeiro and Capetown. Prussia's diplomatic plenipotentiary, Count Friedrich zu Eulenburg, joined the mission at Singapore in August 1860; one month later the *Arcona* led the squadron into Tokyo Bay. After months of negotiations with their reluctant Japanese hosts, in January 1861 the Prussians finally left with a trade treaty. The squadron went on to China, and in September 1861 Eulenburg concluded the Treaty of Tientsin (Tianjin) with the Chinese Empire. The squadron reassembled at Bangkok in December 1861, and the next month Eulenburg concluded a trade treaty with Siam. The ships did not stay together on their way home. The *Elbe* reached Danzig in May 1862, the *Thetis* and *Arcona* in October.[68]

The expedition left Prussia's colonial ambitions unfulfilled. Before departing for the Far East, Count Eulenburg visited Paris and received Na-

The Prussian East Asian Squadron, 1860: screw corvette *Arcona,* frigate *Thetis,*
schooner *Frauenlob.* Clipper *Elbe* not shown. *Historische Sammlung der
Marineschule Mürwik*

poleon III's blessing for a Prussian annexation of Taiwan. In March 1860
the prince regent authorized the acquisition of colonies, and afterward the
Prussian press speculated that Sundewall and his squadron would claim
Taiwan. The officers on the mission recognized the impossibility of securing an island of that size with the resources at their disposal. Eulenburg
abandoned the project after concluding the trade treaty with China, on the
grounds that an attempt to annex Taiwan would jeopardize Prusso-Chi-
nese relations. On the journey home, Jachmann sidestepped orders to explore the coast of Patagonia as a site for a colony, citing the poor condition
of his ship *Thetis* and its crew.[69]

Remarkably, the Far Eastern cruise had little bearing on the fate of Prussia's concurrent initiative for a north German coastal defense system. Even
though the other Zollverein members, Mecklenburg, and the Hanseatic
cities permitted Eulenburg to conclude trade treaties on their behalf, none
felt any special obligation to support Prussia's naval schemes in home
waters. Nevertheless, in the words of one historian, "in the competition
with Austria, Prussia . . . had made itself the spokesman of the rest of Germany in East Asia."[70] The cruise of 1859–62 also paid dividends for the officer corps, serving as a common formative experience. Of the fifty-one offi-

cers and cadets involved, twenty eventually became admirals.[71] The benefits came at a heavy price, as all of the ships fell victim to severe weather. In 1860, just months after the *Arcona* sustained damage in the North Sea, a storm raked the *Elbe* off South Africa. On the return voyage in 1862 the *Thetis* suffered serious damage and had to put in at Bahia, Brazil, for repairs. Worst of all, in September 1860 the *Frauenlob* sank in a typhoon off the coast of Japan. The disaster claimed the lives of all 44 men on board. In all, more than 100 of the squadron's 800 men died during the cruise, with disease claiming those not killed in the mishaps.[72]

The navy could ill afford such heavy losses in personnel, especially since in November 1861 the tragic loss of the corvette *Amazone* had claimed just as many lives. The oldest active Prussian warship, fresh from its triumphant calls at the Hanseatic ports, sank in a storm in the North Sea while en route to Iberian waters to join the *Hela* for a winter training cruise. None of the 114 men on board survived. Besides the commander, Robert Herrmann—one of the original lieutenants of 1847—the dead included 4 officers and 19 cadets. Of these 23 young men, 13 were from noble families, including 2 counts and 3 barons.[73] Prussians mourned the sinking as a great national tragedy, but if the Landtag and public had known of the contents of the navy's own files, it might have been an equally great scandal. Two years before the disaster, Adalbert admitted that the *Amazone* "appears less seaworthy from year to year." The revised fleet plan of 1859 called for its replacement before 1865.[74]

·   ·   ·

By the early 1860s, Prussia's small fleet was well on its way to becoming the world's most accident-prone navy. One may debate whether the cause was bad seamanship, bad luck, or a combination of both. In the area of personnel, the prevailing peace of the previous decade allowed improvements in training, even if most cruises were aboard obsolete sailing ships. Unfortunately, the human losses of 1859–62 offset much of the progress. In materiel, the fleet grew in size but had no active steamers other than the *Danzig* for three and a half years (1855–58), during which dry rot idled the *Danzig* for all but six months. With steam technology revolutionizing naval service worldwide, the failure to acquire another steamship promptly was inexcusable. Given the material weaknesses of the fleet already on hand, the goals of the fleet plans of 1855, 1859, and 1861 seemed almost hopelessly ambitious. The frequent revisions in the Prussian program were prompted, in part, by changes in technology, a factor that would loom even larger in the 1860s. Apart from the yacht *Grille,* Prussia's first wooden warship with screw propulsion was the corvette *Arcona,* which received its commission in 1859, the same year France launched its first armored frigate, the *Gloire.* If Prussia intended to be serious about sea power, its navy could not afford to lag so far behind other European fleets.

With Roon heading both the war and navy ministries after 1861, the navy, though technically independent, fell under the administrative leadership of a general. In 1867 William I would appoint a sea officer to serve under Roon as de facto navy minister, but in the meantime Major General August von Rieben, an aging old-school Prussian with little knowledge of naval affairs, served as director of the navy ministry. Even though Roon appreciated sea power and in the future would fight for a larger and stronger navy, his concurrent army reform proposals made him the most unpopular minister before the Landtag. Adalbert soon regretted his own role in bringing about Schröder's retirement.[75] Complicating matters, in September 1862 the crisis over Roon's army bill led William I to appoint Otto von Bismarck minister-president and foreign minister. Over the next nine years the navy would face the challenge, and burden, of supporting an ambitious foreign policy in the era of German unification.

THE ERA OF GERMAN UNIFICATION

etween the autumn of 1862 and the first weeks of 1871, Otto von Bismarck made Prussia and its army the catalyst for the unification of Germany. Unity came from above, sanctioned by William I, engineered by Bismarck, and secured by Moltke's victories in three wars, rather than from below, manifesting the popular liberal nationalism of 1848. During the same nine years, the Royal Prussian navy became the federal navy (*Bundesmarine*) of the North German Confederation, and finally the Imperial German navy. The emergence of a German fleet, like national unity, came from above rather than from below. In the new Second Reich, it would be an instrument of state power emulating the army's example, not a "people's navy" capitalizing on the earlier popularity of the naval cause. To make matters worse, the army's leading role in the achievement of national unity, and the navy's negligible role in it, would haunt the junior service for years to come.

To the Danish War (1862–1864)

The constitutional crisis that led to Bismarck's appointment as Prussian minister-president concerned the expansion and reorganization of the army, but money for the navy was also involved. The political stalemate over the army thus made it difficult for the fleet to continue to grow. The conflict arose when William I and Roon sought funds to expand the regular army, at the expense of the reserve *Landwehr*. Liberals and the newly organized Progressive party opposed the reforms in the Landtag, but the government implemented them anyway. Late in 1861 and again in the spring of

1862, new elections reaffirmed the Liberal-Progressive majority, and in mid-September 1862 the Landtag rejected the army budget by an overwhelming margin. William pondered abdication before deciding to turn to a new strongman as head of the cabinet. On 22 September, Bismarck returned home from his ambassador's post in Paris to become minister-president.[1]

The crisis over army reform doomed the plan for naval expansion formulated by the Admiralty Council in December 1861. The failure came in spite of Roon's efforts and strong backing from William I. In a January 1862 speech before the Landtag, the king made his first declaration of support for naval expansion and announced that the government would submit a new fleet plan to the legislature.[2] Liberal and Progressive legislators in Berlin, including several veterans of the Frankfurt Parliament, had far greater sympathies for the navy than the army; indeed, just one year earlier many of them had lobbied for the navy through the Nationalverein. But in the political climate of the autumn of 1862, such sentiments counted for little. When Roon presented the program to the Landtag, the majority were consistent in their constitutional principles (and dislike of Roon) and refused to fund it. In this instance the navy clearly suffered from the legislators' inability to separate Roon the war minister from Roon the navy minister.[3]

Like the army, the navy continued to operate without a legal budget. The service received 2.1 million thalers in 1862 and 3.1 million in 1863 (compared with an annual budget of less than half a million in the early 1850s) but hardly prospered. Army expansion received priority, forcing postponement of important navy projects including the purchase of the first two armored warships from Britain, expansion of the royal shipyard in Danzig, and construction of a new Baltic base on the island of Rügen.[4] The fleet plan became a dead letter at the worst possible time. In November 1863 a new Danish king, Christian IX, approved a constitution incorporating Schleswig into his kingdom. This bold act revived the Schleswig-Holstein question and put Denmark on a collision course with Germany.

The new crisis found the Prussian navy still vastly inferior to its Danish rival, despite recent improvements in materiel. The fleet of screw-propelled warships included the 1,900-ton corvettes *Arcona* and *Gazelle* (the latter finally commissioned in May 1862), the 1,100-ton corvette *Nymphe* (commissioned in November 1863), the yacht *Grille*, and twenty-one of the twenty-three gunboats laid down after 1859. Other than the *Loreley*, the only paddle steamer with any value as a warship was the *Preussischer Adler*, which the navy purchased from the postal service in July 1862 to replace the decommissioned *Danzig*.[5] Among the sailing ships, the navy sold the *Mercur* in 1860 and its replacement, the clipper *Elbe*, after the Far Eastern cruise in 1862. With the *Amazone* and *Frauenlob* lost at sea and the *Gefion* and *Thetis* slated to become artillery school ships, only the tiny brig *Hela* remained for training cruises. Prussia turned to Britain to remedy the shortage, purchasing the 1,300-ton frigate *Niobe* (launched 1849) and the 510-ton brigs *Musquito* (1851) and *Rover* (1853). All three vessels arrived in Danzig late in 1862.[6] Other foreign purchases of the early 1860s included guns and engines. Owing to the *Gazelle*'s problems with its domestic machinery, the *Nymphe* received engines imported from Penn & Sons of Greenwich.[7] Most of the armament for the new additions to the fleet came from Finspong of Sweden, although the navy ordered a few rifled guns from the Spandau royal foundry.[8]

With its armored frigate projects on hold for financial reasons, Prussia developed a keen interest in smaller, less expensive ironclad types deployed by the Union navy in the American Civil War. After the Prussian ambassador in Washington, Carl Ferdinand von Gerolt, praised the "extraordinary successes" of James B. Eads's gunboats on the Cumberland and Tennessee Rivers in February 1862, Eads provided a description of his armor-plated wooden gunboat *Benton*. But by the time Eads's report reached Berlin, the Battle of Hampton Roads (8–9 March) had focused Europe's attention on John Ericsson's *Monitor*. The Prussian press hailed monitors as an inexpensive solution to the ironclad question; one commentator concluded that "for the money that the [armored frigate] *Warrior* has cost the English nation, twenty [ironclads] could be built on the model of the *Monitor*."[9] But in the early 1860s no Prussian or German shipyard was capable of building an ironclad, even one as small as a monitor, and the ongoing financial crisis prevented the ordering of armored warships abroad. In any event, in December 1862, when Roon convened an Admiralty Council to discuss another revision of the fleet plan, Adalbert and navy captains showed a strong preference for larger ironclads. They agreed on a goal of ten armored frigates and persuaded a skeptical Roon that such vessels should receive top priority when funds became available.[10] In the meantime, Denmark took steps to add ironclads of all types. During 1862 the Danes commissioned two small armored schooners built by the Thames Iron Works, then ordered Europe's first monitor, the 1,350-ton twin-turreted *Rolf Krake*, from Napier & Sons of Glasgow. The Copenhagen navy yard also began converting the wooden ship of the line *Dannebrog* into a 3,100-ton armored frigate. The *Rolf Krake* arrived in Copenhagen in July

1863, just eleven months after it was ordered, reinforcing Denmark's margin of superiority.[11]

The onset of the Danish crisis found the *Preussischer Adler* on duty in the Levant with the screw gunboats *Blitz* and *Basilisk.*[12] The 350-ton gunboats, initially intended for coastal defense in home waters, hardly cut an imposing figure; Captain Wilhelm von Tegetthoff of the Austrian navy remarked that they were "insignificant little ships, hardly bigger than our Lake Garda boats."[13] In other prewar operations, the new *Gazelle* made a brief maiden voyage in the summer of 1862, then left Danzig again in November 1862, accompanied by the *Gefion.* The two ships parted at Plymouth; the *Gazelle* went on to the Far East, while the *Gefion,* with cadets and apprentice seamen aboard, cruised to Madeira and the West Indies. The last mission of the old sailing frigate lasted until June 1863. By then the *Niobe* was ready to take over as cadet ship.[14] The navy's future annual routine would include winter cruises by the *Niobe* to the West Indies with the cadets and by the training brigs *Rover* and *Musquito* to Iberian waters with the apprentice seamen. In 1863–64, however, the tensions with Denmark disrupted their initial voyages. Citing "current political conditions," Bismarck advised the navy to recall all three ships to Danzig.[15]

The Schleswig-Holstein crisis escalated to the brink of war too fast for any last-ditch attempts to improve Prussian readiness at sea. German federal troops entered Holstein and, just before the New Year, occupied Kiel. On 16 January 1864 Bismarck and Count Rechberg bypassed the Federal Diet in Frankfurt and submitted a joint Austro-Prussian ultimatum to Denmark, demanding the withdrawal of the new constitution. After the Danes refused to capitulate, a joint Austro-Prussian force assembled in Holstein and, in early February, moved on into Schleswig. Denmark responded as it had in 1848–49, with a blockade. At the outbreak of war the Danish navy had an armored force of the monitor *Rolf Krake* and two schooners. The *Dannebrog* was completed in March 1864, while a fifth ironclad, the 3,400-ton frigate *Peder Skram,* remained under construction. The Danes also purchased a 4,800-ton armored frigate from Thomsons of Glasgow. The ship, later named *Danmark,* had been laid down for the Confederate States of America, which by 1864 no longer could afford to pay for such projects. Fortunately for Prussia, it did not arrive in Copenhagen until shortly after the end of the war. Denmark's wooden-hulled screw fleet included one ship of the line, four frigates, three corvettes, and ten schooners, supplemented by eight paddle steamers.[16] In contrast, Prussia had only its unarmored screw-propelled fleet of three corvettes, one yacht, and twenty-one gunboats, supplemented by two paddle steamers. Of the three corvettes and two gunboats under construction in Danzig, only the 2,100-ton corvette *Vineta* (commissioned in March 1864) would be ready in time to see action. The tiny wooden gunboats (*Kanonenjollen*) were activated for the first time since 1851, but these, along with the sailing ships, had no value as warships.[17] The bleak situation prompted navy leaders to consider repurchasing the rotted, leaky paddle steamer *Danzig,* deactivated in 1862 and finally sold to a British firm early in 1864. They finally came to their senses and dropped the project.[18] For the German allies the Austrian navy held the balance, with its five armored frigates and an unarmored screw-propelled fleet roughly equal to the Danish: one ship of the line, five frigates, two corvettes, and twenty-one gunboats.[19]

At the onset of war, the state of the Prussian navy's personnel left much to be desired. The losses aboard the *Amazone* and the ships of the Far Eastern expedition still had not been made good, and the *Amazone* disaster in particular had a devastating effect on recruiting. In 1862, even after lowering standards, the navy enrolled the smallest cadet class in years. By the 1862–63 school year the routine of the Sea Cadet Institute in Berlin had broken down entirely. More than a dozen cadets assigned to the Far Eastern expedition returned three years behind in their course of study and had to be graduated after a special short course. Below them, a class was virtually missing, thanks to the *Amazone* disaster. At the bottom, a small first year left little margin for the usual attrition. The war and mobilization only exacerbated the problem. At the end of February 1864 the boys of the second class, who began their studies only in the autumn of 1862, were mustered out and commissioned. The oldest boys of the first-year class likewise received emergency promotions. Some very recent graduates commanded their own warships in 1864; the youngest of these, future admiral Eduard Heusner, received the 240-ton screw gunboat *Wespe* shortly after his twenty-first birthday. When the influx of inexperienced junior officers failed to remedy the shortage, for the first time since 1849 the navy granted temporary commissions to merchant captains and boatswains. More than sixty of them accepted the rank of sublieutenant (*Hülfs-Unter-leutnant*) in the activated *Seewehr.*[20]

Adalbert, the navy's only admiral, spent the war on the Baltic, but Jachmann, as senior captain, became "squadron chief" and operational commander, raising his flag aboard the *Arcona*. With their blockade in the North Sea initially unopposed, the Danes deployed most of their fleet in the Baltic, bottling up the Prussian navy and closing the major ports. The armored frigate *Dannebrog* and five other steamers blockaded Danzig, where the royal shipyard was completing the *Vineta*. The ship of the line *Skjold* and five smaller steamers blockaded the mouth of the Oder, closing the port of Stettin and trapping the *Arcona* and *Nymphe* at Swindemünde. The fourth Prussian corvette, the *Gazelle*, was out of harm's way in the Far East, where it seized four Danish merchantmen during the war. Meanwhile, the *Rolf Krake* and the two Danish armored schooners patrolled the Schleswig and Jutland coast, guarding against Austro-Prussian attempts to ferry troops from the mainland to the island of Sjaelland (Zealand) and the capital, Copenhagen.[21]

The Italian threat in the Adriatic limited the number of warships the Austrian navy could deploy against the Danes. Nevertheless, in February 1864 Captain Tegetthoff was sent to the North Sea with the screw frigates *Schwarzenberg* and *Radetzky* and gunboat *Seehund*. Rear Admiral Bernhard von Wüllerstorf followed later with the main Austrian force, consisting of two armored frigates, one paddle steamer, and a screw-propelled contingent of one ship of the line, one corvette, and one gunboat. Britain's strong pro-Danish posture failed to deter the Austrians from sending ships to the war zone, but during a coaling stop a mysterious "mistake" by a British harbor pilot caused the *Seehund* to run aground, forcing Tegetthoff to proceed with just his two frigates.[22]

While the Austrian warships were still en route to northern waters, the Prussian navy initiated the only action of the war in the Baltic. On 17 March 1864 Jachmann took his flagship *Arcona* with the *Nymphe* (*Kapitänleutnant* Reinhold Werner), the *Loreley* (Lieutenant Count Alexander von Monts) and six screw gunboats on a sortie against the blockade off the mouth of the Oder. Rounding the island of Rügen, they encountered the Danes off Jasmund: the ship of the line *Skjold* with two frigates and three smaller steamers. Hopelessly outgunned, the Prussians still managed to fire more than 250 shots before and during their retreat to Swinemünde. Neither side lost a ship, but Werner's *Nymphe* suffered serious damage and thirteen casualties.[23] The Danes reimposed the blockade of Swinemünde, and Jachmann did not venture out again. In April, in the war's only action off Danzig, the Danes foiled a breakout by Captain Johann Köhler and the new corvette *Vineta*.[24] Two sorties during April by Prince Adalbert with the yacht *Grille*, the fastest steamer in the navy, provided the only further excitement in the Baltic.[25]

After that the focus shifted to the North Sea, where warships enforcing the Danish blockade had captured nineteen German merchantmen early

Paddle steamer *Loreley* (left) and screw corvette *Arcona* (center) at Battle of Jasmund, 17 March 1864 *Historische Sammlung der Marineschule Mürwik*

in the war, effectively closing Hamburg and Bremen for German-flagged shipping.[26] The blockade went unchallenged until early May, when Tegett- hoff's frigates *Schwarzenberg* and *Radetzky* finally arrived. The Prussian Mediterranean squadron—the *Preussischer Adler* and the gunboats *Blitz* and *Basilisk*—soon joined them. On 9 May they ventured out of Cuxhaven to meet the Danes off Helgoland. The three small Prussian vessels contrib- uted little to the allied effort; the Austrian frigates bore the brunt of the fighting against a Danish force of two frigates and one corvette. The rivals exchanged shots at a distance for several hours, but neither side attempted to close. In the late afternoon the allies returned to Cuxhaven; the Danes ultimately withdrew all the way to the Skagerrak. The Austrians lost 138 men killed and wounded, and both of their ships were badly scarred. The Danes suffered roughly half as many casualties, and their flagship *Niels Juel* sustained moderate damage. The Prussians lost no men, and their vessels emerged completely unscathed. Tegetthoff called the battle a draw, but the Danes, despite giving up their North Sea blockade, claimed victory.[27]

With the war still under way, each of the allied monarchs rewarded his squadron commander in the same manner: while William I promoted Jachmann to rear admiral for his efforts at Jasmund, Francis Joseph promoted Tegetthoff to rear admiral as a reward for Helgoland.[28] Meanwhile, the main body of the Austrian fleet under Rear Admiral Wüllerstorf arrived in the North Sea in late May, long after the Battle of Helgoland and the end of the Danish blockade in the North Sea. Moltke and other Prussian army leaders hoped he would move against Copenhagen itself or into the Baltic Sea. Fearing British intervention if they pressed the naval war that far, the Austrians kept all of their warships in the North Sea. Apart from two summer sorties, by the *Rolf Krake* in the Baltic and *Dannebrog* in the North Sea, the Danish navy made no further efforts to engage the allies.[29] No longer in command of the sea or under the illusion that the British would intervene to save them, the Danes sued for peace. In October 1864 Denmark formally ceded Schleswig-Holstein to the joint control of Austria and Prussia.[30] Amid the postwar uncertainties over the ultimate fate of the duchies, the Prussian navy kept four corvettes in service throughout the winter of 1864–65. The *Niobe, Rover,* and *Musquito* left for their training cruises, but William I cited "political grounds" in ordering that they range "not too far" from home. In March 1865 the navy finally returned to a peacetime footing. The squadron commander, Rear Admiral Jachmann, became head of the Baltic station.[31]

When the *Seewehr* demobilized at the end of the war, Adalbert reluctantly agreed to grant permanent commissions to the most promising auxiliary sublieutenants. In the summer of 1865, seventeen of them completed a special term at the Sea Cadet Institute and entered the officer corps. The program did nothing to enhance the social standing of the corps, and to make matters worse, once on duty the new officers did not command much respect. Tirpitz, who entered service in 1865, later recalled that everyone ridiculed the "auxiliary barons (*Hilfsbarone*)" and that their "authority [was] often not recognized" even by the sailors. Nevertheless, fearing that the shortage of officers would only worsen, the navy left the door open for merchant mariners to enter the corps in the future. A policy statement drafted in 1864 reaffirmed that "every Prussian seaman may advance to officer in the royal navy" by taking the route of one-year volunteer (*Einjährig-Freiwillige*), then passing the examinations required of all other officer candidates.[32]

A wartime decree by William I brought dramatic changes to Prussian naval education after 1864. The program of the Sea Cadet Institute, roughly paralleling the last four years of a *Realschule* curriculum, gave way to a new routine including more sea duty and a shorter curriculum of naval-related courses. Young men would graduate from a *Gymnasium* or *Realschule,* then enter the navy in their late teens. New cadets would ship out aboard the training frigate *Niobe* for a year at sea, followed by another two years aboard warships of the fleet and just one year in the classroom, at a new Navy School (*Marineschule*) in Kiel. Assuming an average entry age of seventeen, cadets would be twenty by the time they entered the school. This fact alone rallied most officers behind the change. They shared Captain Köhler's conclusion that educating "twenty-year-old people would be easier than ... boys of thirteen to fourteen." The system remained in effect until 1918, with some alterations. The first cohort boarded the *Niobe* in 1865, giving the navy plenty of time to phase out the institute in Berlin before establishing the new school in Kiel. Haller von Hallerstein abridged the curriculum for the boys who had entered in 1863 and 1864, guaranteeing that all would graduate in time for the school to close in the spring of 1866. This target date, set in the autumn of 1864, fell on the eve of Prussia's next war.[33]

To the German War (1864–1866)

The allied victory in the Danish war became an important milestone on the route to Bismarck's unification of Germany. The bilateral Austro-Prussian approach to the Schleswig-Holstein crisis had been a risky course for Count Rechberg, who broke with Austria's traditional insistence on using the German Confederation as the framework for dealing with German problems. His policy poisoned Austria's relations with many of the smaller states while failing to genuinely improve relations with Prussia.[34] After his resignation in October 1864, his successor, Count Alexander von Mensdorff, conducted negotiations leading to the Gastein Convention (14 August 1865), which preserved joint Austro-Prussian sovereignty over the duchies, with Prussia administering Schleswig and the Austrians Holstein. Austria thus gained a detached possession it neither needed nor wanted, while Prussia received free access across Holstein to Schleswig, the right to construct a Baltic–North Sea canal across Holstein, and a naval base at Kiel.[35]

The future needs of the Prussian navy figured prominently in the negotiations leading up to the Gastein Convention. As early as February 1865 Bismarck and Mensdorff discussed the Holstein canal project, and on 5 April Roon caused a sensation by revealing to the Landtag the navy's intention to build its new Baltic base at Kiel rather than on Rügen.[36] With a long, deep harbor similar to a Scandinavian fjord, Kiel offered great advantages over the shallow harbors of Königsberg, Danzig, Stettin-Swinemünde, and the Jade. Unfortunately, the weather there was just as bad; on the day Roon announced Kiel would be the new home of the Baltic station, Jachmann reported that the harbor there was *"fest mit Eis,"* completely frozen over by an early April cold snap.[37] Even before the Gastein Convention formalized Prussia's rights to Kiel, Jachmann already had most of the warships, training ships, and hulks anchored there. Indeed, the move from Danzig to Kiel became the navy's primary activity of the summer of 1865. Work on the base started immediately, and two years later construction began on the royal (later imperial) shipyard.[38]

In anticipation of a longer war against Denmark, Prussia purchased two ironclads and two screw corvettes while the conflict was under way. None arrived in time to see action. L'Arman Frères of Bordeaux provided three former Confederate projects for 1.75 million thalers: the 1,400-ton ram *Cheops* and the 1,800-ton corvettes *Augusta* and *Victoria.* Shortly after a French crew brought the *Cheops* to Danzig in May 1865, William I ordered it renamed *Prinz Adalbert.*[39] It missed being the navy's first armored warship by a matter of days. This honor went to the *Arminius,* a 1,600-ton twin-turreted monitor laid down in 1863 as a speculation job by Samuda Brothers of London. A wartime funding drive in Prussia and other north German states raised three-quarters of its purchase price of 629,000 thalers. A Prussian crew brought the ship to Kiel in early May. Navy leaders were pleased with the *Arminius* and looked forward to doing more business with Samuda in the future.[40] In contrast, problems plagued the *Prinz Adalbert* throughout its brief career, from the time it ran aground off Danzig on its first sea trial in June 1865. Unlike the *Arminius,* which had an armor-plated iron hull, the *Prinz Adalbert* was an armor-plated vessel of less durable composite (wood and iron) construction. The engines of the three French-built warships, provided by Mazeline of Le Havre, likewise disappointed. For ships originally designed as blockade runners, the *Augusta* and *Victoria* were remarkably slow.[41] Alongside the foreign purchases, domestic construction projects continued. The screw corvettes *Hertha* (2,100 tons) and *Medusa* (1,100 tons), launched in October 1864 in Danzig, were identical sisters of the *Vineta* and *Nymphe,* respectively, right down to their imported Penn & Sons engines. The *Hertha* finally entered service in November 1865, the *Medusa* in April 1867.[42] The war against Denmark and the various warship projects drove Prussian naval spending for 1864 to just over 6 million thalers, almost double the total for 1863.[43]

The continuing reliance on foreign shipyards and machine shops naturally discouraged the growth of domestic industries needed to serve the cause of future naval expansion. Thus far, the private gunboat and engine contracts granted in 1859–61 were practically the only exceptions to the rule of building ships in the state-owned shipyard with imported engines, or importing the entire ship. The introduction of ironclads only extended the dependence. In the 1860s no Prussian or German foundries could produce even the primitive wrought-iron armor used to plate the first generation of armored warships. In November 1862 Alfred Krupp informed Roon that he had "succeeded in producing specimens of forged plates . . . which I at present consider suitable for the purpose of armor," but tests proved him wrong. In February 1865 he conceded defeat, at least for the present: "I cannot help admitting . . . that the product of the English factories . . . at present makes better plates for such purposes."[44] Even if there had been a domestic armor supplier, Prussian and other German shipbuilders lacked the facilities and the expertise to build their own ironclads. They stood behind even Austria, where the Trieste firm of Giuseppe Tonello (the Cantiere Navale Adriatico) by 1866 built seven armored frigates for the Austrian navy. In October 1864 Tonello offered his services to the Prussians, but Roon rejected the overture because Tonello, at the time, built only armor-plated wooden ships.[45]

On 5 April 1865, in the same speech that revealed the navy's plans for Kiel, Roon presented a new fleet plan to the Landtag calling for ten armored frigates, ten monitors for coastal defense, fourteen screw corvettes, eight paddle steamers to serve as dispatch boats, and other steamers and sailing ships for auxiliary and training purposes, all to be in service within twelve years.[46] Roon gave priority to the completion of the Jade base, soon to be named Wilhelmshaven, the new base at Kiel, and acquisition of the first two armored frigates.[47] He justified the buildup, costing an estimated 34.6 million thalers over the next twelve years, in these terms: "For Prussia there are two important and urgent reasons to enter the ranks of the sea powers: first, in order to protect the overseas trade of Prussia and Germany and defend the Baltic and North Sea coasts, and second, in order to maintain for the future its European influence against such lands which may only be reached by sea."[48] He observed that Prussia was "for now, in no condition" to build a first-rate navy. "The present plan focuses only on the establishment of such a navy for the Fatherland" capable of defeating "sea powers of the second and third rank."[49]

Bismarck saw the navy bill as his best chance to break the constitutional logjam in the Landtag. Although the 1862 navy plan had failed to entice the Liberals and Progressives into voting for a government bill, Prussia's embarrassing impotence at sea in 1864 and the continued expansion of the

Danish navy gave him reason to hope for a different outcome this time. Once again, navy legislation presented the majority of the Landtag with a dilemma: either vote for a government bill against their constitutional convictions, or vote against a stronger navy. The majority failed to take the bait. A frustrated Bismarck noted that victories by the army had followed the Landtag's anti-army votes in the Danish war; he anticipated, with no lack of sarcasm, that in the wake of the anti-navy vote "a Prussian fleet will emerge."[50] In June 1865, before the session ended, a Liberal representative prompted another tirade by Bismarck by contending that "Prussia is too weak" to shoulder the burden of defending Prussian and German trade on the high seas. Bismarck responded: "There is no question in the last twenty years that has so unanimously interested public opinion in Germany as the fleet question. We have seen . . . the *Vereine*, the press, and the Landtag express their sympathies. . . . I would not have believed that the maritime ambition of the Prussian Liberals would be so far reduced."[51] Thus the navy, like the army, continued to receive funding outside the framework of the constitution. In November 1865 William I finally authorized the foreign orders for two armored frigates, almost four years after the Admiralty Council first proposed the projects. In January 1866 Roon signed the contracts with Samuda Brothers of London and the Forges et Chantiers de la Méditerranée of La Seyne, near Toulon.[52]

Along with the foreign firms, the Krupp works finally secured a navy contract in 1865, for artillery rather than armor plate. For years an apostle of steel cannon, Alfred Krupp had met with rejection from Prussian generals and admirals who placed their faith in traditional brass guns and, in any event, were distrustful of any domestic product. Earlier, his first Prussian army order came only after he had secured foreign gun contracts first. The initial navy order included more than one hundred guns, most of which replaced Swedish ordnance aboard the unarmored screw-propelled ships.[53]

Austro-Prussian tensions over the fate of Schleswig-Holstein and, generally, over the future of Germany did not abate after the Gastein Convention. As early as March 1866 both German powers prepared for war, and in April, in clear violation of the Federal Act of 1815, Prussia concluded an alliance with Italy against Austria. On 9 June Prussian troops occupied Holstein; later that week, Prussia seceded from the confederation and Bismarck invited the smaller states to join a new federal union excluding Austria. The Austro-Prussian conflict erupted into a German civil war, with Hamburg, Bremen, Lübeck, Oldenburg, Mecklenburg, and most of the tiny Thuringian states siding with Prussia while Hanover, Saxony, and the south German states supported Austria. In late June, the Prussians invaded Bohemia and the Italians Venetia. While the Austrians defeated the Italians on 24 June at Custoza, the Prussian armies easily advanced onto Austrian soil.

Prince Adalbert's decision to spend the summer with the army, in the Bohemian field headquarters of Crown Prince Frederick William, reflected the fact that the navy had little to do during the war.[54] Most of the Austrian fleet had returned to the Adriatic after the War of 1864, but the corvette *Erzherzog Friedrich* remained in Kiel until 20 March 1866, when it left to avoid possible capture.[55] On its way to the Adriatic, it almost crossed paths in the English Channel with the Prussian *Niobe,* hurrying back to the Baltic from a transatlantic training cruise with the latest class of cadets.[56] The only other Prussian warships caught far from home by the outbreak of war were the corvette *Nymphe* and gunboat *Delphin,* sent to the Mediterranean in August 1865, and the corvette *Vineta,* sent to the Far East in November 1865.[57] The *Vineta* was out of danger, but in the spring of 1866 the *Nymphe* and *Delphin* took center stage in a comic opera of mishap and indecision. The *Nymphe* was scheduled to call at Trieste in April 1866 to receive supplies sent overland from home, but Bismarck advised Roon not to have the ship dock there. Given Prussia's ongoing alliance talks with Italy, he considered La Spezia "safer" than the Austrian port. The *Nymphe* docked in La Spezia along with the *Delphin,* only to learn that its supplies had been sent to Trieste. The *Nymphe* then remained in La Spezia while the *Delphin* raced home to pick up provisions for itself and a replacement shipment for the *Nymphe's* missent supplies. Late in April, while attempting a shortcut across Holstein through the old Eider Canal, the *Delphin* ran aground just west of Kiel. The 350-ton gunboat, too large to use the shallow waterway in any event, remained stranded for two days before being refloated to continue its mission. Leaking from a damaged hull, the *Delphin* finally returned to La Spezia in mid-May. By then the *Nymphe's* original supplies had been located in Athens, where they had been sent from Trieste. Bismarck finally advised Roon to recall both ships. The *Delphin's* leaky hull slowed their progress and delayed their arrival home until July.[58]

In the meantime, William I had ordered the navy onto a war footing as of 15 May. The ships activated at Kiel included the corvettes *Arcona, Gazelle, Hertha, Augusta,* and *Victoria,* the ironclads *Arminius* and *Prinz Adalbert,* and several of the screw gunboats. As in 1864, Jachmann served as squadron commander.[59] With no rivals at sea and Mecklenburg, Olden-

burg, and the Hanseatic cities already in the Prussian fold, the navy focused on supporting the army's campaign against Hanover. In late June,
operations on the Elbe, Weser, and Ems helped secure the surrender of
Emden, Stade, and other cities. Hanoverian shore batteries likewise capitulated with little resistance. The appearance of the *Arminius* prompted most
of the surrenders. At the onset of hostilities, the ironclad had raced from
Danzig through the Kattegat and Skagerrak to Hamburg, a distance of 940
sea miles, in 100 hours, at the time an impressive feat for an armored warship under steam. The *Arminius* and a flotilla of screw gunboats operated
out of Geestemünde (Bremerhaven) during the campaign, and the flotilla
commander, Reinhold Werner, led most of the landing parties. Other
duties included ferrying troops across the Elbe for the occupation of Hanover; in one ten-hour operation on 15 June, some 13,500 men crossed the
river at Altona. The *Prinz Adalbert* and the screw corvettes remained in the
Baltic throughout the war.[60] The real naval action in 1866 came in the Adriatic, where Tegetthoff's fleet defeated its stronger Italian rival at Lissa on 20
July. By then the Prussian army had defeated the Austrians at Königgrätz to
decide the outcome of the war.[61]

When the navy mobilized in 1866, it recalled less than half the available
Seewehr sublieutenants and granted permanent commissions to only two
of them. Navy leaders resolved that expansion would come from below
and placed great hopes in their revamped officer education program. Unfortunately, the first class, shipped out aboard the *Niobe* in 1865–66, had
left much to be desired. Adalbert hoped for a cohort of "at least twenty,"
and when only eleven of twenty-six boys (including sixteen-year-old Alfred Tirpitz) passed the entrance examinations, the prince enrolled eight of
the failures, eliminating only the hopeless cases.[62] The Navy School opened
at Kiel in the autumn of 1866, under the direction of Colonel Christian
Amynt Liebe. With Tirpitz's class not due for their studies in Kiel until
1868–69, the school spent its first two years remedying the educational deficiencies of junior officers whose earlier studies had been cut short by the
War of 1864 or the closing of the institute at Berlin. The group for 1866–67
had both potential and actual social status, including Baron Gustav von
Senden-Bibran, eventual chief of William II's Navy Cabinet in the Tirpitz
era, five other noblemen, and four other future admirals. But they gave
Liebe more than his share of headaches. Early in the term the director informed Berlin that "more than 25 percent" of the students had reported to
the school's infirmary suffering from syphilis, and "the station chief himself," Rear Admiral Jachmann, had to be called in to admonish the young

men for their "moral negligence."[63] The navy could only hope that Prussia's territorial gains of 1866 and the ensuing creation of the North German Confederation would increase the pool of potential officers.

The North German *Bundesmarine* and the French War (1866–1871)

Prussia took no territory from Austria in the peace settlement of 1866, but a number of northern and central German states paid dearly for their anti-Prussian stance. Prussia annexed Hesse-Cassel, Frankfurt, and Hanover; the latter acquisition, along with the absorption of Schleswig-Holstein, sealed the Prussian grip on the North Sea coast. The south German states were quickly forgiven for siding with Austria and offered alliances that made Prussia their protector against future threats from France. Meanwhile, within Prussia, elections held on the day of Königgrätz reduced the Landtag's Liberal-Progressive majority, paving the way for a postwar indemnity bill retroactively legalizing appropriations made during the constitutional crisis. The navy's share of the four illegal budgets amounted to 14.4 million thalers.[64]

It took Bismarck almost a year to formally establish the new North German Confederation, which included most of Germany north of the Main River. Its structure mirrored that of the old German Confederation, only with Prussia playing the leading role, holding absolute control over the federal foreign policy and armed forces. In the spring of 1867 a constituent North German Reichstag approved a new constitution that took effect on 1 July 1867. A concurrent renegotiation of the Zollverein treaties brought all members of the confederation into the customs union except for Hamburg and Bremen, which joined later.[65] During the initial Reichstag debate over the constitution, Bremen renewed its earlier support for a Prussian-led German navy. H. H. Meier, a director of the North German Lloyd, argued for a strong federal navy, citing the need to project "great power status" as well as to defend trade overseas.[66] Article 53 of the new constitution affirmed the federal status of the navy, under Prussian command, and named Kiel and Wilhelmshaven as the two naval bases. Article 54 provided for a unified North German merchant marine, and Article 55 specified the colors black, white, and red for the flags of the navy and merchant marine. Effective 1 October 1867, warships flew the new naval ensign in place of the traditional Prussian black eagle on a white field.[67]

Whereas the Prussian army retained its identity within the North German federal army, as it would from 1871 through World War I within the Imperial German army, the Prussian navy simply became the North Ger-

man *Bundesmarine.* The change generated considerable confusion, personified in Roon. As Prussian war minister he remained responsible for the
Prussian army, but as Prussian navy minister he answered to the Reichstag
for the *Bundesmarine* through the federal chancellor, Bismarck. A ruling in
1869 finally confirmed that navy administrators were federal officials, but
the ministry and the minister himself remained "Prussian." Prince Adalbert remained supreme commander, responsible to William I for the operational readiness of the fleet. In August 1867 Rear Admiral Jachmann became director of the Prussian navy ministry under Roon, replacing the
retiring General Rieben. Jachmann served as "federal plenipotentiary for
naval affairs" and de facto federal navy minister, representing the navy for
Bismarck before the Bundesrat and Reichstag. The arrangement worked
largely because Roon and Jachmann were good friends. Roon admitted the
limits of his naval expertise, and Jachmann was not jealous of Roon's ministerial status.[68] The creation of the North German Confederation also
united the German merchant marine under one flag. Because all of the
coastal states were members, for the merchant fleet the unification of Germany occurred in 1867. While the navy remained well down the list of sea
powers, the unified merchant marine instantly became one of the world's
largest. By 1869 the North German Confederation ranked third in commercial tonnage, trailing only Britain and the United States.[69]

In October 1867 Jachmann presented a new fleet plan to the Reichstag.
The ten-year program called for sixteen armored warships, twenty unarmored corvettes, and eight dispatch boats. The plan also mentioned the
twenty-two gunboats, sailing ships for training purposes, and other auxiliary vessels already in service. In sharp contrast to the Prussian Landtag's
rejection of Roon's plans of 1862 and 1865, the new Reichstag approved the
program with no reductions.[70] The 1867 plan confirmed the navy's desire
to have both a battle fleet in home waters and a cruiser fleet to show the
flag worldwide, but the cruiser fleet now received more attention. Compared with the 1865 proposals, there were four fewer ironclads and six more
unarmored corvettes. Prince Adalbert disapproved of the changes despite
his pro-colonial views; he observed that only the Far East saw enough German-flagged visitors to justify much of a cruiser presence, and felt the battle fleet should receive priority. But Jachmann, though personally ambivalent on the colonial question, recognized that the larger number of
corvettes was needed to attract colonialists to the navy's cause. Prophetically, Adalbert warned that overseas missions would strain the resources of
manpower and materiel, hampering the development of the battle fleet.[71]

At least initially, the transformation of the Royal Prussian navy into the North German *Bundesmarine* did not make it any less Prussian. Above the cadets' ranks, the officer corps of 1868 was still overwhelmingly Prussian: just over 85 percent of the sea officers (121 of 142) had been born within the kingdom's pre-1866 borders. Despite its defeat in 1866 and elimination from German affairs, Austria, in 1868, still had more German naval officers from other states (twenty-seven) than the North German navy had from places other than Prussia (twenty-one).[72] A few officers transferred from the Austrian navy to the North German, but the overwhelming majority of north Germans in Habsburg naval service chose to remain there. In a promising sign, the forty new cadets entering the navy in 1869 included thirteen born outside the pre-1866 Prussian borders.[73] Of course, for an officer corps already having problems integrating officers from the merchant marine, additional diversity would be a mixed blessing.

The navy's evolution from Prussian to North German had a more immediate impact for the common seamen than for their officers. Under the new Federal Military Law of 1867, the three-year term of active duty for army conscripts also applied to the navy. The fleet received all young men who had served at least one year in the merchant marine or aboard fishing vessels. This brought many men from the Hanseatic cities (which produced almost no officers) and Mecklenburg into the fleet, alongside those from the expanded kingdom of Prussia. In the age of steam the navy also needed men competent to work with machinery, whatever their familiarity with the sea. A census of December 1867, showing more than 15,000 Prussian subjects liable for naval service, included more than 1,000 locomotive machinists and stokers from the railways.[74] The navy had always had three-year conscripts serving alongside its cadre of twelve-year apprentice seamen, but the influx of conscripts after 1867 made them an overwhelming majority. Training practices geared toward volunteers serving the much longer term would have to change.

The new uncertainties in personnel came at a time when the navy was already taking great strides toward achieving its goals in materiel. Before the approval of the new constitution, a tamed Prussian Landtag granted the navy almost 8.5 million thalers for 1867. The outlay included 4.1 million for the new armored frigates ordered in January 1866 in La Seyne (the 6,000-ton *Friedrich Carl*) and London (the 5,800-ton *Kronprinz*), and the down payment for a third armored frigate, soon named *König Wilhelm*.[75] The latter was a 9,800-ton giant laid down in 1865 by the Thames Iron Works of Blackwall. The Turkish navy had placed the original order, then defaulted on the contract. Prussia stepped in early in 1867 and assumed responsibility for the ship. Thus, the navy continued to rely upon foreign firms to build its ironclads, while Krupp received the gun contracts.[76]

The acquisition of the battleships came at a time of great confusion in armored warship construction. All three were armored frigates like the original seagoing ironclads, the French *Gloire* and the British *Warrior*, with guns arranged in broadside batteries. Smaller ironclads tended to be turret ships or "monitors," after the model of the first such vessel constructed, the *Monitor* of the United States Navy; these included Prussia's *Arminius*. While the armored frigate dominated the first generation of European ironclads, the turret ship was the design of choice in the United States. Experimental cruises by large American turret ships in the late 1860s demonstrated that they could function as oceangoing vessels. Their low freeboard left their decks awash much of the time, however, and they were in danger of sinking in heavy seas. The *Monitor* itself had perished in this manner off Cape Hatteras not long after the Battle of Hampton Roads in 1862. The most tragic loss of a turret ship came in September 1870, when the *Captain*, an experimental British design, capsized in a storm off Cape Finisterre. A fully-rigged twin-turreted vessel of nearly 7,000 tons, the *Captain* sank with almost five hundred men aboard.[77]

Armored frigate *König Wilhelm* (laid down 1865; launched April 1868).
Courtesy of Conway Maritime Press, from Steam, Steel and Shellfire:
The Steam Warship, 1815–1905. © *1992 Conway Maritime Press*

To answer the complaints against the broadside design, avoid the problems of turret ships, and accommodate heavier guns and thicker armor, in the late 1860s European navies began to build their larger ironclads as casemate ships. Instead of having two or three dozen guns mounted in side batteries for its entire length, the casemate ship had no more than a dozen heavier guns, mounted in a heavily armored central battery or casemate. Owing to the arrangement of guns, some navies—most notably the British—called them "central battery ships." The lines of the hull were modified so that the guns nearest the bow could pivot, firing forward or to the side. Guns at the rear of the casemate were often given a similar ability to fire aft. To compensate for their heavy plating amidships, most casemate ships had little or no armor at the bow and stern. This made the design controversial, but its advocates pointed to many positive features: a high freeboard ensured its seaworthiness; the central casemate protected the engines and all of the heavy guns; and the lack of armor fore and aft saved weight and improved speed. Apart from the embrasures in their hulls—recessed to allow the end guns to fire forward or to the rear—casemate ships had the same general appearance as broadside armored frigates. Their masts and yards also gave them the ability to sail, like most ironclad warships built before the late 1880s. The casemate ship marked an important step away from the broadside ironclads of the earlier 1860s. The design remained in fashion until turrets again became common in the 1880s and 1890s.[78]

Following an Admiralty Council meeting in October 1867, Jachmann ordered the first armored warship ever built in Germany. The following year, the royal shipyard in Danzig laid down the 3,950-ton casemate ship *Hansa*. The vessel mounted eight guns in its casemate, of which two could fire forward, two aft, and four to each side. The navy saved money on the *Hansa* by limiting its size and ordering its engines from A.G. Vulcan of Stettin. Its composite wood-and-iron construction was also much cheaper (and would be much less durable) than the all-iron construction of the three foreign-built armored frigates. The guns were ordered from Krupp, but the armor had to be imported from Britain.[79]

While the navy focused on increasing its armored strength, the inventory of unarmored ships continued to grow. The 2,500-ton *Elisabeth,* the last of five large wooden-hulled screw corvettes constructed in the royal shipyard in Danzig, received its commission in September 1869, after the installation of engines imported from Maudslay Sons & Field of London.[80] Thereafter the Danzig shipyard focused on the construction of the *Hansa* and a number of unarmored projects: the 1,700-ton screw corvettes *Ariadne,* laid down in 1869, and *Luise,* delayed until 1871; the 710-ton screw gunboats *Albatross* and *Nautilus,* laid down in 1869 and 1870, respectively; and the 600-ton brig *Undine.* The *Undine* received its commission as a training vessel in 1871, the last sailing ship added to the fleet.[81] The navy also bought the British screw ship of the line *Renown,* for use in artillery training.[82]

In the years between the German and French wars, the navy increased the pace of its peacetime activity, but not without problems and disappointments. For the winter of 1866–67 Prussia reestablished the Mediterranean station with the corvette *Gazelle* and gunboat *Blitz.* They made an even less impressive showing than their predecessors. In February 1867 the *Gazelle* collided with a merchant steamer in Constantinople harbor, and later the same month the *Blitz* ran into a merchant steamer at Malta.[83] An investigation of the *Gazelle*'s accident revealed that its first officer, *Kapitänleutnant* Johannes Weickhmann, had been responsible, and that his commander, Captain Ludwig Henk, had been asleep at the time of the collision. In spite of their negligence, both men rose to prominent positions in the years that followed. In the wake of the accident the *Gazelle*'s head machinist recited a litany of problems, some related to the collision. In April the navy recalled the ship, leaving the less heavily damaged *Blitz* alone on the station.[84]

A "training squadron" for European waters, formally proposed in the fleet plan of 1867, actually would have debuted in 1866 if not for the war. In February 1866 the king authorized the activation of four warships for summer exercises in the Baltic and North Sea; the subsequent general mobilization superseded the order. Jachmann assigned four corvettes to the inaugural "*Lehr- und Uebungs-Geschwader*" in 1867. Unfortunately, the *Gazelle* required extensive repairs after its return from the Mediterranean, and a boiler problem crippled another of the quartet, the *Nymphe,* for the entire summer. Ultimately, Jachmann's flagship *Hertha* and the small corvette *Medusa* cruised in the Baltic in July and August of 1867. The king named Jachmann "squadron commander," but the frustrated rear admiral observed that "two ships do not constitute a squadron."[85] In the late summer the navy sent the *Hertha* and *Medusa* to join the *Blitz* in the Mediterranean. En route to their station, they dropped off crews in Britain and France for the armored frigates *Kronprinz* and *Friedrich Carl.* The two new ironclads then steamed to Kiel, where they remained out of service pending delivery of their Krupp guns. The corvettes returned home in the spring of 1868, again leaving the *Blitz* alone in the Mediterranean.[86]

The reduction of the Mediterranean station was part of an overall austerity program ordered by the king in April 1868. Despite approving the fleet plan the previous autumn, the new Reichstag gave the navy less money for 1868 (24.2 million marks, or just under 8.1 million thalers) than the Prussian Landtag had for 1867. The cost of the three armored frigates and their artillery made the budget for operations very tight in the first place. The failure of a test-firing of a Krupp gun in March fueled a near-panic at the navy ministry, raising the possibility that their ordnance would have to be ordered at a greater cost from the Woolwich Arsenal. Some nine hundred seamen were furloughed, and apart from vessels far overseas at the time, operations ground to a virtual halt. The overreaction saved enough money for William I to cancel the order less than two months later, in mid-June, prompting a terse comment from Jachmann's office that the king should be informed of "the difficulty of recalling the furloughed 900 sailors in the present year." The navy's activities for the remainder of 1868 were makeshift at best. On the bright side, by autumn the Krupp cannon crisis appeared to be resolved, with delivery promised by early 1869.[87]

A North German navy crew took possession of the *König Wilhelm* in February 1869, ten months after its launching. It remained in British waters for extensive sea trials, which were uneventful except for an explosion in a coal bunker the first week out. In May the ship arrived in Kiel. During the same month the navy activated the *Kronprinz* and *Friedrich Carl*. The three frigates were scheduled to form an "armored squadron" for four or five months during 1869, for a cruise to the West Indies, but Jachmann had to cancel all plans when Krupp failed to deliver their guns as scheduled. The *Kronprinz* and *Friedrich Carl* finally received their artillery (sixteen 8.25-inch guns apiece) in July, but the *König Wilhelm*'s battery (eighteen 9.4-inch and five 8.25-inch guns) was still incomplete in September. Apart from an August cruise to Britain by the *Kronprinz*, to have its hull cleaned in the Portsmouth dry dock, the armored frigates remained in the Baltic all summer.[88] The navy wanted the ships present to open the new North Sea base at Wilhelmshaven, but the festivities took place as scheduled without them. On 16 June 1869 William I presided over the dedication ceremony, accompanied by Bismarck, Roon, and Adalbert. A visiting British squadron, including the impressive five-masted armored frigate *Minotaur*, dwarfed a makeshift host squadron led by the screw corvette *Arcona*. When the armored squadron finally made it to Wilhelmshaven in September, Crown Prince Frederick William inspected the ships. His ten-year-old son, the future Emperor William II, was profoundly impressed by his first tour of a warship, aboard the *König Wilhelm*.[89]

In November 1869 the crown prince attended the opening of the Suez Canal. His entourage included Major General Albrecht von Stosch, future navy commander.[90] The North German contingent at the canal ceremonies included the corvettes *Hertha*, *Arcona*, and *Elisabeth*, gunboat *Delphin*, and yacht *Grille*. The crown prince went through the waterway aboard the *Grille*.[91] His party used the *Elisabeth* for the return trip to Italy. In early December the ship put in at La Spezia while the crown prince called on King Victor Emmanuel II. He reboarded the *Elisabeth* to cruise from La Spezia to Villafranca, where he met his family for Christmas.[92] The brief Riviera holiday included a tour of the *Elisabeth* and *Hertha* by his sons William and Henry. The younger son, then just seven years old, went to the top of the *Elisabeth*'s rigging in the company of the ship's officers; William's crippled left arm prevented him from joining his brother in the climb. Before leaving for Paris, the family also visited the French navy base at Toulon.[93] The English-born crown princess, Victoria, hoped such tours of ships and naval bases would balance her sons' overexposure to the army and the parade grounds of Berlin and Potsdam. She also allowed William to supplement his English lessons with sea stories written for an adolescent audience; his early favorite was *Masterman Ready*, by the popular adventure novelist Frederick Marryat.[94] It is no small irony that Victoria—who naturally hoped for cordial Anglo-German relations—nurtured in William the naval enthusiasm that later helped put the two countries on a collision course.

En route home to Berlin, Frederick William called on Napoleon III in Paris.[95] The crown prince's next visit to France, the following summer, came at the head of an invading army in the Franco-Prussian War. The origins of the conflict are well known: the crisis over the Hohenzollern candidacy for the vacant Spanish throne peaked in Bismarck's skillful editing of the infamous Ems Dispatch, which the French interpreted as a serious affront to their national honor. On 19 July 1870 France declared war on Prussia. The North German federal states soon joined the Prussian mobilization, along with Baden, Württemberg, and Bavaria, whose Prussian alliances were activated by the French threat.[96]

Early in 1870, before the onset of the crisis, William I authorized the mobilization of the *König Wilhelm, Kronprinz,* and *Friedrich Carl* for a six-month training cruise that would range as far as Lisbon and Madeira, under the personal command of Adalbert. The ram *Prinz Adalbert* temporarily left watch duties at Altona on the Elbe to join the squadron. After the *Friedrich Carl* ran aground off Kiel in May, breaking its propeller, the *Kronprinz* towed it to Britain for repairs. In early June Adalbert raised his flag aboard the *König Wilhelm* for his first sea voyage since the War of 1864. The flagship and the *Prinz Adalbert* steamed to Britain, where the entire squadron finally assembled at Plymouth. From the start engine trouble plagued the *König Wilhelm,* prompting plans to have its machinery (manufactured by Maudslay Sons & Field) repaired in Britain before the cruise progressed any further. But in Plymouth, Adalbert received a telegram from Bismarck warning of imminent hostilities with France. The ships left for home, with the *König Wilhelm*'s engines still not repaired and the *Friedrich Carl*'s repairs untested. On 16 July, just three days before the war began, they put in safely at Wilhelmshaven.[97]

After the *Arminius* arrived in the Jade, the North Sea station became home to all of the navy's ironclads for the duration of the war. Meanwhile, most of the unarmored fleet was dispersed to defend the Baltic coast. The *Elisabeth,* which had returned home from the Mediterranean early in the year, stood guard at Kiel, the *Nymphe* at Danzig, and the *Vineta* at Swinemünde, while the yacht *Grille* and three screw gunboats—also based at Swinemünde—patrolled the waters around Rügen. As for the remaining corvettes, the onset of war found the *Hertha, Medusa,* and *Arcona* overseas (see section below) and the *Gazelle, Augusta,* and *Victoria* in Danzig for repairs. The *Victoria* remained laid up throughout the war, but the *Gazelle* and *Augusta* were ready for action by late July.[98] The navy also bought the iron-hulled paddle steamers *Pommerania* and *Falke,* and converted the Hamburg-Amerika liners *Cuxhaven* and *Helgoland* for service as scout cruisers. The latter were returned after the war.[99] On the eve of the conflict the corps of sea officers included 162 officers and more than 200 cadets. Common manpower numbered over 3,000, but full mobilization increased the force to 6,500.[100]

The French fleet enjoyed a great superiority over the North German navy. Its four hundred warships included thirty-four ironclads, of which half were seagoing frigates in the same class with the *König Wilhelm, Friedrich Carl,* and *Kronprinz.* French navy war plans called for attacks on Wilhelmshaven and Kiel, the destruction of merchant shipping, and cooperation with the army in landing troops on the north German coast. But the navy and army had done little prewar planning for amphibious assaults, and the fleet included too few of the small vessels needed for close coastal operations. In any event, French navy leaders concluded that they could execute a successful landing only on the beaches of the Baltic, an undertaking unthinkable without a Danish alliance. The Prussian army's invasion of France days after the war began left Copenhagen in a strictly neutral mood.[101]

The fleet steamed into action anyway, for what one historian has called "one of the most useless demonstrations in French naval history."[102] The Northern Squadron moved from Cherbourg into the Baltic, where it stood watch for more than five weeks, while the Mediterranean Squadron relocated to northern waters, maintaining a porous blockade of the German North Sea ports for almost a month.[103] The French seized enough merchantmen early in the war to deter German-flagged vessels from venturing out. The ports remained open only because British merchantmen continued to call and the French did not dare stop them, for fear of provoking British intervention in the war. At the onset of bad weather, the French squadrons withdrew to Cherbourg. By then the defeat of Napoleon III at Sedan (2 September) had decided the outcome of the war. After the imperial government gave way to a republic, some of the fleet's men and guns were put to use ashore, in the defense of Paris and other cities. After the French gave up the blockade, their ships continued a sporadic surveillance of the North German navy and patrolled the English Channel. The French republic pursued the war for five more months, sustained in part by American arms shipments that the North German navy could do nothing to stop.[104]

Throughout the war, the navy at best annoyed the French. Adalbert himself underscored the irrelevance of sea power in the Prussian-German strategy by spending the war with the army, as he had in 1866. He fulfilled his wish to see action; at Gravelotte on 18 August, he even had a horse shot out from under him.[105] In the absence of the prince, the navy ministry absorbed the functions of the High Command (*Oberkommando der Marine*) and the navy went through the war with a divided command structure. Jachmann, since 1868 a vice admiral, exchanged his duties in Berlin for command of the armored squadron in Wilhelmshaven. Rear Admiral Eduard Heldt, Jachmann's successor as chief of the Baltic station, headed all forces in the Baltic but was not subordinate to Jachmann. Meanwhile, Rear Admiral Hans Kuhn replaced Jachmann as administrative chief in Berlin.

Captain Carl Ferdinand Batsch, chief of staff of the High Command under
Adalbert since 1867, headed a new operations section (*Kommandoabtei-
lung*) in the navy ministry and coordinated the operations of the autonomous commanders.[106]

At the end of the first week of August 1870, Jachmann took the *König
Wilhelm, Kronprinz, Friedrich Carl,* and *Arminius* on a sortie all the way to
the Dogger Bank. He encountered no French warships. The French made
their first appearance in the North Sea, off the Jade, shortly after Jachmann
returned to port. Thereafter, the *Kronprinz* (Captain Werner) and *Arminius* (Captain Otto Livonius) ventured out of Wilhelmshaven periodically
to exchange shots with the French; the durable little *Arminius* went out on
more than forty sorties during the war. Meanwhile, the *König Wilhelm*
(Captain Henk) and *Friedrich Carl* (Captain Eduard Klatt) continued to
suffer from their prewar engine troubles, and the port had no facilities to
repair their machinery. Both William I and Moltke agreed that the navy
should adopt a defensive posture, but from the start Jachmann came under
criticism for the fleet's relative inactivity. He finally managed to get all
three armored frigates running well enough for a second squadron sortie,
but by then (11 September) the French had already left for home.[107] The
North German contingent in the Baltic fared no better. In mid-August
Captain Count Franz von Waldersee took the yacht *Grille* and three gunboats out of Swindemünde and exchanged shots with French ironclads off
Rügen.[108] Later in August the *Nymphe,* under Captain Weickhmann, left
Danzig for a sortie against the 5,800-ton armored frigate *Surveillante* and
the 3,700-ton armored corvette *Thétis.* The enemy ironclads soon chased
the 1,100-ton wooden corvette back into port.[109]

In late July 1870, just days after the declaration of war, William I approved the creation of a "volunteer *Seewehr*" of merchant mariners. The
navy invited shipowners to turn over their vessels and crews for the duration of the war, in exchange for a charter fee and prize money for any
French warships they sank. The navy promised armament for the ships,
compensation for vessels lost, and postwar pensions for officers and crews.
Officers with "excellent" service records would be considered for regular
commissions after the war. References to the volunteer fleet as the "offensive torpedo service (*Offensiv-Torpedo-Dienst*)" suggest that the proposed
service amounted to a suicide mission against the French blockade. Few
shipowners were willing to take the risk. Eventually some volunteers were
mobilized on the new North Sea station, where they only added to the

force already blockaded in Wilhelmshaven. As an attempt to tap the re-sources of the merchant marine while keeping merchant mariners apart from the regular navy, the scheme was ingenious, and a miserable failure.[110]

At the start of the war Bismarck refused to authorize a commerce raid-ing strategy against the French merchant marine, but after the French navy seized a number of German merchant ships he changed his mind.[111] In November 1870, after most of the French navy had returned home, Weickhmann took the corvette *Augusta* out of Danzig, through the Skager-rak, and around the northern tip of Scotland into the Atlantic. After coal-ing off Ireland at Christmas, the ship went on to the Atlantic coast of France. Early in January 1871 the *Augusta* caught three French supply ships off the mouth of the Gironde, burning one and sending the other two to Wilhelmshaven with prize crews. The attack caused alarm in nearby Bor-deaux, the temporary capital of France. With several French armored frig-ates bearing down on him, Weickhmann took the *Augusta* to the safety of Vigo in neutral Spain, where it remained blockaded until the war ended.[112]

The three ships taken by the *Augusta* were the only French merchant-men claimed in the war. In comparison, the French navy captured no Ger-man warships but seized more than two hundred merchantmen, paralyz-ing German overseas trade for more than half a year. Of the leading shippers the North German Lloyd took the most risks, completing a total of fourteen Bremen–New York voyages during the war. Its ships steamed northward around Scotland to avoid the French gauntlet in the English Channel. Few firms pursued such a bold course. The Hamburg-Amerika Line suspended transatlantic operations altogether, canceling one-third of its scheduled departures in 1870.[113]

After the war Weickhmann received the iron cross, but only after con-siderable lobbying by Adalbert. Count Waldersee won the same honor for his sortie aboard the *Grille*. Adalbert likewise received an iron cross, along with his aide, Captain Baron Paul von Reibnitz, who also spent the war with the army. The poor showing of the armored squadron precluded honors for any of its officers. In a deliberate slight, the navy was allowed a representation of just twenty-two officers and seamen in a massive postwar victory parade in Berlin. In May 1871 a Reichstag member from Stettin even questioned whether all naval personnel should receive the commem-orative medals (*Kriegs-Gedenkmünze*) given to all veterans of the conflict. The seamen got their medals, but it embarrassed the navy that the matter had even been raised.[114]

The Expansion of German Overseas Interests (1862–1871)

During the era of unification, the most dramatic expansion of German overseas interests came in the South Pacific. The Hamburg firm of J. C. Godeffroy & Sohn, whose interest in the Samoan group dated from 1857, expanded its operations to other Polynesian islands during the 1860s. Copra (for coconut oil) became the most lucrative export from the region. Other German businesses active in the South Pacific included the firm of Ruge, Hedemann & Company of Hamburg, based on Fiji.[115] Despite the growing German commercial interest, none of the Prussian warships that cruised to the Far East visited the South Pacific islands; the squadron of 1859–62 came no closer than Singapore, and vessels sent after that also concentrated on East Asian waters. The highlight of the mission of the corvette *Gazelle* (1862–65) was the 1864 ratification ceremony for a new Prusso-Japanese trade treaty, held aboard the ship in Tokyo Bay.[116] The *Vineta* succeeded the *Gazelle* on the East Asian station, in the process completing the navy's first circumnavigation of the globe (1865–68). But its route across the Pacific, which included a stop at Honolulu, went far to the north of Samoa and the South Pacific islands.[117]

After the departure of the *Vineta,* the East Asian station remained unoccupied until the arrival of the *Medusa* in March 1869. From then until 1914 at least one German warship would be in the Far East at any given time. For almost thirty years Yokohama would be the focal point of their operations; in 1868 the North German minister to Japan, Max von Brandt, purchased land there for a naval hospital. During 1869 the *Medusa* participated in a demonstration off Yokohama, where conditions for foreigners remained uncertain after the Meiji Restoration.[118] Prince Adalbert tried to revive the earlier project of annexing Taiwan, but in January 1870 Bismarck promised Anson Burlingame, an American diplomat serving as roving ambassador for the Chinese Empire, that he would respect the territorial integrity of China. Nevertheless, after the *Hertha* joined the *Medusa* on the station early in 1870, its captain reported to Adalbert on sites for bases in Shanghai, Hong Kong, and Amoy, as well as Nagasaki, Japan. Speculation about colonial acquisitions in the Far East flared up again that autumn, after the initial defeat of France.[119]

The regular presence in the Far East developed at a time when the navy's warships rarely visited the waters of Latin America. In 1865–66 a brief naval war matching Spain against Peru and Chile underscored the weakness of Prussia's position. When many of the great powers sent ships to the war zone to guard their interests, the Prussians had none to spare. During a Spanish bombardment of Valparaiso, defenseless German merchants incurred losses of 2.5 million pesos.[120] At the same time, the tight Union navy blockade of Confederate ports toward the end of the American Civil War disrupted German trade in the Caribbean and Gulf of Mexico. The unrest in Mexico during the French intervention and brief reign of Emperor Maximilian only made matters worse. With the return of regional stability in 1867, the Hamburg-Amerika Line opened service to New Orleans via Havana. Two years later, the North German Lloyd inaugurated a Bremen–Havana–New Orleans route.[121] At Bismarck's request, the corvette *Augusta* spent most of 1868 showing the flag in the Caribbean. On the personal urging of Adalbert and without the approval of Bismarck, the *Augusta*'s Captain Franz Kinderling negotiated with the president of Costa Rica for a base at Puerto Limón. Bismarck repudiated the overture, to avoid a challenge to the Monroe Doctrine. His desire not to offend the United States also led him to reject a Dutch offer of a base at Curaçao off the Venezuelan coast.[122] In 1869 the corvette *Victoria* visited the West Indies, calling at Norfolk on its way home.[123] Although plans to send the armored squadron to the Caribbean in 1869 had to be dropped, by the following year complaints of German businessmen in Haiti and Venezuela brought a stronger naval presence to the West Indies. In the spring of 1870 the screw gunboat *Meteor* and training frigate *Niobe* visited the region. Engine trouble delayed a third ship, the corvette *Arcona,* en route from the Suez Canal, where it had participated in the festivities late in 1869.[124]

The onset of the Franco-Prussian crisis of 1870 caught three of the navy's nine screw corvettes overseas: the *Medusa* and *Hertha* in the Far East, and the *Arcona* en route home from the Caribbean via New York. The *Medusa* and *Hertha* put in at Yokohama, where they remained blockaded by the French East Asian squadron.[125] The *Arcona,* in the middle of the Atlantic at the outbreak of war, faced a less certain fate. Its captain, Baron Georg von Schleinitz, lacked confidence in his ship's shaky machinery and lingered in the Azores from July through November, dogged by French warships. In mid-November he even declined a direct challenge from the French *Bellone,* a screw corvette similar to the *Arcona* in size and armament. In December, Schleinitz received orders to either run for home via the northern route, around Scotland, or disarm in a neutral port. The *Arcona* left the Azores at the end of 1870 and headed for Portugal, pursued by French frigates. It remained blockaded in Lisbon until being freed by the preliminary peace in February.[126]

Of the navy's smaller vessels caught overseas by the French war, only the tiny (350-ton) gunboat *Meteor* engaged an enemy ship. Its captain, Eduard Knorr, broke off his patrol of the Caribbean early in the war and steamed to Key West, where he hoped to transfer his crew and guns to a larger, faster vessel more suitable for commerce raiding. After strict American neutrality foiled his plans, he returned to sea and eventually moved on to Cuban waters, where he challenged the captain of the 800-ton French dispatch steamer *Bouvet* to a battle off Havana. The engagement occurred on 9 November 1870, just outside the three-mile limit, with a Spanish navy corvette and gunboat standing by to guard against a violation of neutral Spanish waters. The duel of almost two hours damaged both vessels but disabled neither. Two seamen were killed and one wounded aboard the *Meteor* before the *Bouvet* broke off the action. Knorr took his ship into Havana for repairs, then had to remain there for the duration of the war after other French steamers arrived to reinforce the *Bouvet*. The *Meteor* finally returned home via New York and Halifax in May 1871. Knorr and four of his men received iron crosses, accounting for more than half of the total number won by the navy during the war.[127]

After the Prussian victory at Sedan, pro-colonial groups bombarded Bismarck with demands that French colonies be ceded to Germany in the postwar settlement.[128] He ignored all of them and in February 1871, at the onset of peace negotiations, reassured Britain and the United States that Germany would not accept colonies or warships from France as part of the settlement.[129] Thus, the German Empire began its life as a great power with a conscious decision by its founder not to be a player in the colonial game. By the time Bismarck changed his mind a dozen years later, there would be much less left to claim.

·   ·   ·

In the era of German unification, the navy participated in victorious wars against Denmark, Austria's north German allies, and France. It lost no ships and very few men, and played a negligible role in the outcome of the three conflicts. Indeed, in human and material terms, the preceding peacetime decade (in which the navy suffered two ships sunk, several others damaged, and losses of more than two hundred men) had been far more costly. The contrasts did not end there. The decade before the era of German unification had featured an emphasis on training and personnel development, while the lack of a focusing crisis caused progress in materiel to lag behind. Then, the wars of German unification sparked the resolve that gave Germany, by 1870–71, a fleet that included five ironclads, but expan-

sion in materiel, especially the addition of large armored warships, increased the strain on personnel, especially the demand for sea officers.
Doubts about the competence and cohesion of the officer corps continued,
casting a shadow over the first years of the Imperial German navy.

The navy's relative inactivity in 1870 left deep scars on the younger generation of the officer corps. The frustrated young men included Lieutenant
Alfred Tirpitz, then twenty-one years old, who spent most of the war at anchor in Wilhelmshaven aboard the *König Wilhelm*. Several gave up on the
navy. By the summer of 1872 twelve men at the ranks of *Unterleutnant* and
cadet (including nine noblemen) transferred to the army, more than
would normally do so in a decade. For Tirpitz, the humiliating formative
experience of 1870 helped shape his later conviction that Germany must
have a fleet capable of offensive action.[130]

SERVING THE NEW REICH

The transition from the North German Confederation to the German Empire brought little constitutional change. The empire had the same structure as the confederation, only enlarged to include members from the south German states. Just as Article 53 of the North German constitution had granted federal status to the navy, Article 53 of the constitution of April 1871 granted it imperial status. Thus the *Bundesmarine* became the *Kaiserliche Marine*, the designation it retained through 1918.[1]

In addition to refusing French colonies, Bismarck would not accept French warships as a part of the postwar spoils.[2] But when it came to spending the French reparations money, the chancellor did not deny the navy its share. Compared with the Tirpitz era the sum was modest, but contemporary observers considered it a dramatic windfall. More money bought more warships but could not buy unity for the officer corps or purchase a secure place for the growing fleet in German grand strategy.

Reorganization and *Reinigungswerk*: Stosch Transforms the Navy (to 1878)

On 15 June 1871 William I formalized the wartime measure that subordinated the navy's operational command to the navy ministry: effective 1 January 1872 the ministry would become the Imperial Admiralty, with its chief serving as both operational and administrative commander. For Roon (then sixty-eight) and Adalbert (sixty), age and poor health helped justify the change. Roon stayed on as war minister until his retirement in

October 1873. After giving up the operational command he had held since 1849, Adalbert remained "General Inspector of the Navy" until he died of a heart attack in June 1873.[3] Jachmann, the ranking sea officer after Adalbert, expected to become chief of the Imperial Admiralty. Instead, the appointment went to Lieutenant General Albrecht von Stosch.

Eventually, in September 1875, when Stosch was promoted from lieutenant general to general, he also received the equivalent navy rank of admiral. Nevertheless, William I, Bismarck, and his peers in the military and political realm all continued to call him "General von Stosch." Navy officers naturally did not accept him as one of their own; most gave him "dutiful obedience but not exactly responsive support." His own oversized ego would limit his effectiveness. An old friend, liberal publicist Gustav Freytag, conceded that Stosch "never could bring himself to acknowledge that anything he undertook was ever near being a failure." He surrounded himself with sycophants eager to echo his own ideas and conclusions: "Everything was to be looked upon as excellent, and of course there were people ready to think anything originated by the new minister a success."[4] Even Tirpitz, whose rise to prominence began under Stosch, later criticized his mentor for "his not always favorable choice of advisors. . . . There were too many orders and not enough questions asked."[5] Despite the problems, some sea officers welcomed his campaign to transform the navy. Captain Karl Paschen, a Mecklenburger who had transferred over from the Austrian navy in 1867, praised the *Reinigungswerk,* the "cleaning up" of the navy under Stosch's "strong hand."[6]

The son of a Prussian general, Stosch entered the army in 1835, at the age of seventeen. He showed an interest in naval matters as early as 1841, the year of his first posting to Danzig. His artillery background led him to study coastal fortifications; eventually, he published an article on "our coasts in a war with France."[7] Subsequent appointments sent him to the Guard Artillery in Berlin and to the general staff. Stosch's acquaintance with Adalbert dated from 1847, but his friendship with Crown Prince Frederick William had a much greater impact on his rise to prominence. Stosch met the crown prince in 1865 and a year later served under him as quartermaster general in the Prussian Second Army, during the war against Austria. After the victory he negotiated a military convention between Prussia and Saxony that laid the groundwork for the overall military structure of the North German Confederation; Bismarck's criticism of these negotiations marked the beginning of their stormy relationship. From 1866 to 1870 Stosch directed the Military Economic Department of the war ministry.

Albrecht von Stosch *Historische Sammlung der Marineschule Mürwik*

After streamlining the army's procurement process in peacetime, he earned praise as commissary general in the war against France. During the siege of Paris, Stosch directed an army nominally commanded by the Grand Duke of Mecklenburg-Schwerin and helped keep newly formed republican armies from relieving the French capital. Stosch's mutual antagonism with Bismarck continued during armistice talks, when he drafted the terms under which the army occupied parts of France. After the war Stosch became chief of staff to Field Marshal Edwin von Manteuffel, head of the occupying army. The offer to take over the navy reached him at Manteuffel's headquarters in Nancy.[8]

Other than his connections at court, Stosch's greatest assets were his energy and organizing skills. Their strong points aside, neither Adalbert nor Jachmann had provided consistent energetic leadership for the navy or shown special talent as administrators.[9] In 1869, while accompanying Frederick William to the Suez Canal opening, Stosch impressed the crown prince with his interest in naval affairs.[10] Two years later, Frederick William lobbied for Stosch to receive the Admiralty post, and Bismarck formally proposed his name to the emperor. To a regime determined to place a general in command of its navy, he was the most logical candidate. In November 1871 Bismarck and Roon formally defined his future powers. Official word of the appointment followed in early December.[11]

The constitutional position of the head of the navy, while not as muddled as it had been under the kingdom of Prussia or the North German Confederation, still left plenty of room for a renewal of friction between Stosch and Bismarck. As administrative head, the chief of the Admiralty was responsible to the chancellor, but as operational commander, he reported directly to the emperor.[12] It did not help matters that his connections with the crown prince made Stosch a likely candidate for chancellor, especially after William I's death. Many insiders considered Stosch a liberal alternative to Bismarck—including Bismarck himself, who would privately accuse him of plotting to form a "Gladstone cabinet."[13] Stosch's Freemasonry compounded Bismarck's suspicions. He considered it the key to his rival's influence with the aging emperor, who was also a Mason.[14] In the short term, Stosch sought the post of war minister and viewed the inheritance of Roon's naval responsibilities as a stepping stone to his army portfolio. For his part, Bismarck considered the Admiralty a sidetrack for Stosch's career, removing him from the line of succession to the war ministry. He proved to be right, at least on the question of Roon's immediate successor. In 1873, General Georg von Kameke became war minister.[15]

Under the arrangement that took effect in January 1872, Jachmann remained a member of the Admiralty Council and "commander of all active naval forces (*Befehlshaber der sämtlichen in Dienst gestellten Seestreitkräfte*)," confirming that he would have functioned as operational head of the navy in case of war. But Stosch rarely convened the Admiralty Council, and Jachmann received even less consideration after the death of Adalbert and retirement of Roon eliminated his most influential friends. In February 1874 he finally retired, just short of his fifty-second birthday.[16] Jachmann's origins as a common seaman and lack of formal higher education left him out of place in a navy officer corps the new chief sought to reshape on the model of the Prussian army officer corps. He soon had plenty of company in retirement. Of the twenty most senior officers (admirals and captains) of 1872, ten were gone by 1878. All had served in the merchant marine, and none held noble titles, hereditary or acquired. Captain Johannes Weickhmann was typical of the casualties; he had received an iron cross for his role as commander of the raider *Augusta* in 1870–71, but in the end this mattered less than his humble origins and the fact that he was "somewhat rough in form." For Stosch, practical experience—even bravery in wartime—failed to outweigh factors such as inferior social background, poor education, and the stigma of onetime civilian sea service. Too many of the senior officers Stosch inherited were not the sort of role models he wanted for the young men who would lead the navy in the future.[17] The chief did not limit his purge of "undesirables" to the senior ranks of the officer corps. By the spring of 1873 he retired six lower-ranking captains and lieutenants who had first entered the navy as auxiliary officers from the merchant marine. During the early 1870s he removed all former auxiliary officers from the rolls of the reserve *Seewehr*. The future *Seewehr* officer corps would consist of junior officers from the regular navy (lieutenants and cadets) requesting or accepting transfer to inactive status. Thus, even in an emergency, the navy would not have to use officers with merchant marine backgrounds.[18]

For his second-in-command Stosch chose Ludwig Henk, a senior officer whose limitations made him no threat to his boss. Indeed, Henk embodied many qualities that marked others for dismissal: he was a former merchant mariner, son of a merchant mariner, with a dubious record as ship commander. He received a promotion to rear admiral in 1871 and to vice admiral six years later; in 1878 he was the first navy officer to be ennobled for his service. Henk moved to Berlin early in 1872 to become "director of the Admiralty," with responsibilities similar to those of Rieben and Jachmann in the old navy ministry of the 1860s. After 1874, however, Stosch limited the director's authority to "technical" matters such as shipbuilding, ordnance, and supply. The chief of staff of the Admiralty, Captain Batsch, received jurisdiction over "military" matters, including operations and personnel.[19] Batsch, who began his career in 1848–49 as one of the cadets placed by Adalbert aboard the USS *St. Lawrence*, first rose to prominence in 1867 as chief of staff of the High Command. He became Stosch's protégé and heir apparent.

In other administrative moves, Stosch in 1872 created the Machine Engineer Corps alongside the corps of sea officers, thus setting the precedent for a formal "separate but equal" status for the technical branches of the service. In 1873 he granted the same status to medical officers. Two years later he established an Admiralty Staff (*Admiralstab*), a planning group within the Admiralty (not to be confused with the later *Admiralstab* established in 1899). Stosch also founded a Navy Staff (*Marinestab*) to explore technical questions, but it lacked the prestige of the Admiralty Staff and would be perennially short of applicants.[20] Junior staff officers, the best and brightest in the corps, were to receive their training in the two-year curriculum of the Naval Academy (*Marineakademie*), established in 1872 at Kiel. It was the world's first naval war college, founded a dozen years before the next-oldest such school, established by the United States Navy in Newport, Rhode Island. Stosch intended the Naval Academy to be a counterpart to the army's War Academy (*Kriegsakademie*), which produced staff officers for the army, but in future years navy officers received staff positions without completing the program at Kiel.[21]

Meanwhile, the course of training and study prescribed in 1864 for entering officers underwent only minor revisions. The four-year routine (one year aboard the training frigate *Niobe,* two years in the fleet, and a final year at the Navy School in Kiel) was lengthened in 1873 by a six-month preparatory course (*Vorbereitungscursus*) at the Navy School, inserted in the program after the first six months aboard the *Niobe.* The change raised the average age for promotion to *Unterleutnant* (received upon graduation) to twenty-two—too old, in the opinion of most navy leaders. A compromise retained the new lengthened program but granted the rank of *Unterleutnant* at the beginning of the final year of studies at the Navy School instead of at the end. As time went on, the academic caliber of officer candidates improved, enabling the navy, in turn, to raise its standards. In 1872 the emperor even raised the age limit for entry to nineteen for applicants holding the *Abitur,* signifying the completion of the exams that qualified one for university admission.[22] The higher academic expectations, which required the entering cadet to have spent his teenage years in school, all but closed the sea officer corps to young men from the merchant marine or those who had started their navy careers as common sailors. Other discouragements included the requirements for clothing and personal effects, which posed an economic barrier to candidates from other than rich families. Under standards reaffirmed in 1874, even entering cadets were required to bring with them 131 separate clothing and toiletry articles, including 18 white dress shirts. Though the policy of 1864 (affirming access to a permanent commission via the *Einjährig-Freiwillige* option) technically remained in effect, only eleven men followed this route after Stosch took command, the last in 1881. The new chief's desire to introduce a social exclusivity to the navy even spilled over into the corps of engineers, a group he wanted to keep inferior to the sea officer corps. At the same time that language standards were reduced for the sea officers, in the new Machine Engineer Corps candidates for promotion to *Maschinen-Unter-Ingenieur* had to demonstrate competence in both English and French. Stosch used this device to prevent common machinists from advancing to engineer officer status.[23]

While Stosch's policies effectively barred the advancement of the least socially desirable, at the opposite end of the spectrum the corps of sea officers failed to attract even as many noblemen as it had in previous years. In the five classes, or "crews" as they were known, entering before the Franco-Prussian War (1866 through 1870), an average of 28 percent of the cadets held noble titles; for the eleven classes entering under Stosch (1872 through 1882), the figure fell to 17 percent. The "crew" of 1881 included an all-time low of just one noble cadet in a group of thirty-four. The war of 1870–71 cast a shadow over recruiting efforts throughout the following decade, making a career at sea appear less attractive especially for candidates from the nobility.[24]

While the academic preparation of sea officer candidates changed for the better under Stosch, some aspects of their training remained firmly rooted in the past. Like their peers in other navies, German cadets continued to see their first duty aboard sailing ships. The *Niobe* and the training brigs remained in service until the 1880s; as late as the winter of 1885–86, the *Musquito* would sail all the way to the West Indies. In general terms, however, Stosch had little regard for the preservation of naval tradition; indeed, he sought to make the navy officer corps as much like its army counterpart as possible. The officers of the Baltic and North Sea stations were organized along the lines of the officers of army regiments, down to their officer's mess and courts of honor.[25] But according to Freytag, the "prussianization" of the sea officer corps brought "the blind worship of everything that emanates from 'superior authority.'"[26] The new mindset caught on quickly among junior officers, stifling any last hope of the navy establishing a healthier mentality of its own. Tirpitz later recalled its effect on virtually every aspect of daily naval routine. "Strict guard duty, in the military sense, was introduced to the ships and consumed time and energy" that could have been put to better use. Prussian army spit and polish went to ridiculous lengths. Stosch relaxed his strict dress code for tropical stations only after an officer collapsed from the heat in his formal *Waffenrock* and sash.[27]

In navy folklore, Stosch is best remembered for his introduction of infantry drill in the training routine of sailors. After the Federal Military Law of 1867 was applied to the German Empire in 1871, the navy continued to receive conscripts whose skills were relevant to the needs of the service. Men from nonmaritime backgrounds also could opt for the navy, but Stosch required these "volunteers" to serve an additional year beyond the customary three. The problem for the navy became how to train its conscripts in such a short time, and how to maintain discipline amid the rapid turnover of personnel. Stosch emphasized discipline and introduced extensive infantry drill to maintain it, sacrificing time badly needed for actual naval training. Army drill sergeants supervised the process. Thanks to Stosch's overall militarization of the corps of seamen, the naval infantrymen of the *Seebataillon* gradually lost their special functions. After 1880 they no longer served aboard overseas corvettes; eventually, after 1895, none served aboard battleships.[28]

It would be easy to characterize Stosch's changes in personnel and training as one egotistical general's heavy-handed attempt to militarize the navy. Yet his philosophy regarding the officer corps and officer candidates differed little, if at all, from the vision articulated by Adalbert in 1862: that the corps should reflect "the spirit of the army," united by social homogeneity as well as a high degree of professionalism.[29] But Adalbert knew better than to introduce army practices that had no relevance to the navy. Indeed, the prince had strictly prohibited infantry drill for seamen.[30] Stosch's relative ignorance of naval affairs, combined with his self-confidence, would have fateful consequences.

"*Die Geldmittel Flossen Reichlich*": Fleet Expansion under Stosch

"I do not believe that we are called . . . to compete with states that have already developed large fleets."[31] With these words, four months after his appointment, Stosch reassured the Reichstag that German naval ambitions would be kept within limits, at least on his watch. He made it clear that "as a soldier" he believed "the *Hauptaccent* of German power lies with the land army." His remarks drew cheers, evidence of the navy's low political standing after the war of 1870–71. Few would have predicted that within a decade Stosch would lead Germany from last place to third in ironclad tonnage among the powers of Europe, trailing only Britain and France.

Shortly after assuming command, Stosch measured the navy's progress in materiel against the fleet plan of 1867. Of the prescribed sixteen armored warships, five had been commissioned: the armored frigates *König Wilhelm, Friedrich Carl,* and *Kronprinz* and the much smaller *Arminius* and *Prinz Adalbert.* Another six ironclad projects were under way. The royal/imperial shipyard in Danzig would launch the casemate ship *Hansa* in October 1872. The navy's next trio of battleships were 6,800-ton vessels of all-iron construction. Originally projected as casemate ships, they were built with a lower freeboard and four heavy 10.25-inch Krupp guns paired in two turrets on deck amidships. In 1869 the new royal/imperial shipyard at Wilhelmshaven laid down the *Grosser Kurfürst*.[32] After further delays caused by the war, during 1871 the royal/imperial shipyard in Kiel began work on the *Friedrich der Grosse*. The same year, the *Preussen* was laid down by A.G. Vulcan of Stettin, the first private German firm to receive a contract for a large warship. Domestic machine shops received the engine orders: A.G. Vulcan for the *Preussen* and F. A. Egells of Berlin for its sister ships.[33] Like the *Hansa* before them, all three of the warships were plated with wrought-iron armor imported from Britain. Although domestic foundries produced other components for the navy's iron-hulled projects, even the Krupp works continued to fail in its attempts to produce armor plate.[34] The two remaining ironclads were 7,600-ton casemate ships being built by Samuda Brothers of London: the *Kaiser* (laid down in 1871) and *Deutschland* (1872), both of all-iron construction. The contracts were signed shortly after the conclusion of peace, in anticipation of an early French war of revenge.[35]

When Stosch took stock of the 1867 fleet plan, ten of the projected twenty unarmored corvettes were already in service, including the new *Ariadne* (commissioned in 1872). Another two corvettes, the 1,700-ton *Luise* (laid down in 1871) and 2,000-ton *Freya* (1872), were under construction at the imperial shipyard in Danzig.[36] The navy had already reached the goals for transports, coastal gunboats, and training ships, but in these categories the numbers in the program for the most part reflected vessels already on hand in 1867. Other than the 710-ton *Albatross* (commissioned in 1871) and *Nautilus* (1873), the gunboats were survivors from the smaller class laid down in the years 1859–61.[37]

To meet the goals of the 1867 plan, another five armored warships and eight unarmored corvettes would have to be ordered, built, and commissioned by 1877. As early as the spring of 1872, Stosch concluded that this could not be done. In proposing a new plan to Bismarck in November 1872, he argued that the fleet should "not . . . have the task to proceed offensively against the great European states, but . . . extend our power only where we have to represent lesser interests and where we cannot otherwise bring to bear the actual power of our state, our power on land." Bismarck added in the margin of the report: "We must surpass all sea powers of the second rank." Stosch presented his plan to the Reichstag in April 1873, with his budget estimates for 1874.[38] It called for an armored fleet of twenty-three warships rather than sixteen, but only fourteen of Stosch's ironclads would be high seas battleships (eight "frigates" and six "corvettes"). The remaining nine armored vessels—seven monitors and two floating batteries—

were to defend the coast. The change reflected Stosch's opinion of large armored warships: "I consider larger battleships still inappropriate or superfluous for our circumstances," he informed his friend Freytag, because
Germany would not call upon its navy "to win a sea battle" anytime soon.
The core of the unarmored fleet remained at twenty corvettes, consistent
with Stosch's view that the navy "should be able to provide security for the
German merchant marine" and have unarmored ships available for "police
actions (*Polizeizwecken*) in distant waters."[39]

Besides the corvettes, the unarmored ships of the fleet plan of 1873 included six dispatch boats, two fewer than the 1867 plan. A reduction of
gunboats from twenty-two to eighteen came after Stosch decided to scrap
more of the navy's old wooden-hulled screw gunboats. The program also
included twenty-eight torpedo boats, a new category since the 1867 plan,
reflecting the impact of the introduction of the self-propelled torpedo. Invented by Johann Luppis, an Austro-Hungarian navy officer, and manufactured by Robert Whitehead, a British expatriate living in Rijeka, the torpedoes were reliable enough to be adopted by the Habsburg navy in 1868.
Other navies quickly followed suit.[40] The German navy added six small
torpedo boats during 1872, but all were equipped with old-fashioned spar
torpedoes; in 1873 a new torpedo commission ordered one hundred self-
propelled torpedoes from Whitehead.[41] Stosch also renewed the appeal for
a new canal from Kiel on the Baltic across Holstein to the North Sea. In addition to the strategic motive, there was a strong economic argument for
the project: more than five thousand commercial vessels still crossed Holstein every year via the outdated Eider Canal, by then almost a century old.
Nevertheless, the Kiel Canal remained on the drawing board for another
dozen years.[42]

Stosch's fleet plan was to be completed in ten years at a cost of just
under 219 million marks (73 million thalers), including 54 million marks
from the French indemnity fund. In the federal upper house (Bundesrat),
representatives of the state governments gave it their unanimous endorsement, but it never received the "approval" of the Reichstag. Stosch merely
presented it to the legislators along with his budget estimates as a point of
information. Nevertheless, from the start the Reichstag never gave Stosch
much trouble over the funding of the plan. It helped considerably that no
controversial ideology of *Weltpolitik* accompanied this naval buildup, and
that no one yet saw the fleet as a rival of the army for funding. Many conservatives supported the plan as if it were a supplementary military expenditure. Stosch's friendships with leaders of the National Liberal party se-

cured another flank. His opposition to Bismarck's *Kulturkampf* endeared him to the Catholic Center party, albeit at the risk of alienating some of his Liberal supporters, whose strong anticlerical views led them to support the anti-Catholic campaign.[43]

The fleet plan of 1873 remained the yardstick for the progress of the navy for years to come. Compared with its own recent Prussian and North German past, the Imperial German fleet mushroomed in size, the beneficiary of a massive infusion of money. The French money alone included tens of millions beyond the sum earmarked for warship construction; ultimately the fleet received 95.8 million marks from the total French indemnity of 4.2 billion marks (5 billion francs). Stosch's program appears ridiculously unambitious if measured against the Tirpitz plan of a quarter-century later. But a history of the navy published in the early 1890s hailed the plan of 1873 as a great watershed, after which "*die Geldmittel flossen reichlich.*"[44]

To ensure continued funding for his program, Stosch became the first navy commander to court the favor of politicians and industrialists.[45] In the spring of 1873, in the first occasion of its kind, several members of the Reichstag visited Wilhelmshaven. Even the Progressive leader Eugen Richter, no great friend of defense spending, went along. After touring the harbor aboard a chartered North German Lloyd steamer, they were treated to a banquet aboard the *König Wilhelm*.[46] Stosch had an easier time developing good relations with key industrialists. According to Freytag, he "expressed his determination to have everything that the German navy required procured in Germany." He had no sympathy for the practical concerns of "many officers of high rank in the navy who placed faith only in English engines."[47] When it came to gun contracts, Stosch patronized the Krupp works exclusively. At the middle of the decade a satisfied Alfred Krupp remarked to William I that "though at first [the navy] was prejudiced against my product and was notoriously an admirer of British ordnance, I have since enjoyed its unvarying recognition and confidence."[48] Stosch also encouraged the use of German rather than imported English coal.[49] Within the officer corps, even his detractors conceded that he freed the navy from its dependence on foreign builders and suppliers.[50]

On good terms with the emperor, the crown prince, and leading politicians and industrialists, Stosch faced opposition only from the chancellor. From the beginning he was too independent for Bismarck and the Reich Chancellery staff. In the spring of 1872 he did not seek the chancellor's permission to decommission the obsolete wooden gunboats or establish the

Naval Academy, nor did he inform Bismarck before announcing the reorganization of the naval administration.[51] He clashed with the chancellor again late that summer, when a strike at the imperial shipyard in Danzig threatened to delay the launching of the casemate ship *Hansa*. Stosch shocked Bismarck by meeting with the strikers and agreeing to raise wages, in return for an immediate end to the walkout and the workers' acceptance of longer hours.[52] In November 1872 Stosch began to promote the creation of an imperial ministry for overseas trade (*Handelsmarineministerium* or *Oberseebehörde*), a radical notion at a time when the Reich Chancellor's Office and Admiralty were the only central administrative bodies in the German Empire. He pressed his campaign through his ill-defined position as chairman of the Bundesrat's committee for maritime affairs. In January 1874 Stosch's activity drew a sharp rebuke from Bismarck, along with a reminder that the Admiralty had no jurisdiction over the merchant marine.[53]

The stormy relationship took a turn for the worse in December 1875. For months Stosch had resisted Bismarck's appeals for a reduction in the navy budget requests, but when the chancellor's archenemy, Richter, raised the same question in the Reichstag budget committee, Stosch agreed to a compromise. The agreement, mediated by his National Liberal friend, Heinrich Rickert of Danzig, reduced the budget figure for fiscal year 1876–77.[54] This incident led to a terse exchange of letters between Bismarck and Stosch, and even worse relations in the new year. Early in 1876 Bismarck tried to get the Imperial Justice Office to indict Stosch for treason for his role five years earlier in the postwar occupation of France. Bismarck alleged that Stosch had secretly conspired with the French to draft occupation terms unfavorable to Germany; at least in his private correspondence, he alleged that Stosch had been bribed by Adolphe Thiers. After the Justice Office refused to indict Stosch, Bismarck dropped the campaign.[55] The conflict over the budget for 1876–77 became public only in March 1877, when Bismarck, in the Reichstag, rebutted criticism from Richter by referring to the events of December 1875, with the obvious intention of questioning Stosch's conduct as minister. The timing of the chancellor's remarks—made moments after Stosch had left the hall—increased their impact. In protest, Stosch presented his resignation to the emperor. Bismarck assumed that he would finally be rid of his rival, but William I refused to accept the resignation.[56] Instead, he gave Stosch a strong vote of confidence, with praise for "the great progress which the navy has made."[57] The emperor also would not let Bismarck retire over the matter. The crisis ended with both men still in office but Bismarck weakened by the failure of his public attempt to force out

Stosch.[58] In April 1877 the crown prince reaffirmed his support for Stosch, visiting Kiel with him on the occasion of his son Henry's entry into naval service. The fourteen-year-old prince joined other cadets for a cruise aboard the old training frigate *Niobe*. He became the first Hohenzollern after Adalbert to wear the navy's uniform.[59]

At this stage the problems with Bismarck did not threaten Stosch's fleet plan. In the category of larger battleships classified as "frigates," the goal of eight was reached by the spring of 1878, as the three old battery ships *Kronprinz, Friedrich Carl,* and *König Wilhelm* were joined by the casemate ships *Kaiser* (commissioned February 1875) and *Deutschland* (July 1875) and the three turret ships *Preussen* (July 1876), *Friedrich der Grosse* (November 1877), and *Grosser Kurfürst* (May 1878). Because of the size of the casemate ship *Hansa* (May 1875), Stosch classified it as an armored corvette, leaving another five "corvettes" to be constructed by 1883. Four of these were laid down early in Stosch's tenure: the imperial shipyard in Kiel started work on the *Bayern* during 1874 and the *Baden* in 1876, while A.G. Vulcan of Stettin began the *Sachsen* in 1875 and the *Württemberg* in 1876. Designated "sortie corvettes (*Ausfallkorvetten*)," these 7,600-ton battleships actually were larger than all of the armored frigates except the *König Wilhelm*.

Designed for the conditions of the Baltic Sea, the "sortie corvettes" were to serve as part of an integrated coastal defense system, the outlines of which owed much to the 1859 project drafted by Adalbert, Schröder, and army generals. Not unlike the host of gunboats in the earlier scheme, the new battleships were to operate out of fortified bases linked to the interior by strategic railways, which would transport troops to the coastline in case of an enemy landing. A contemporary account outlined the basic characteristics of the *Ausfallkorvetten*: "moderately light draught" to enable them "to run into any of the principal harbors along the Prussian seaboard on the Baltic; . . . heavy armor-plating and armament [for] great defensive power"; and "great offensive power in order that they might engage any hostile armor-clad squadron in the Baltic." The first German battleships built without masts or yards, they also had only "moderate coal-carrying capacity," because by staying close to their bases, they "could . . . easily replenish their supply." The unique ships had their drawbacks, however. Even those who accepted the rationale behind their design would find little to praise in the finished product.[60]

In the category of smaller ironclads, the navy had to start from scratch. In October 1871 the *Prinz Adalbert* had to be decommissioned, its wooden interior rotten after less than a decade in service. The following year the

Arminius became a school ship.[61] Stosch's plan called for seven new monitors and two floating batteries, but in their place the navy ultimately built eleven 1,100-ton coastal gunboats, each armed with a single 12-inch gun. A.G. Weser of Bremen built all eleven of the vessels, which were often called the "insect" class because of their names. The first of the class, the *Wespe,* laid down in 1875, entered service in November 1876; the last, the *Hummel,* was begun in 1879 and commissioned in August 1881. As an integral part of Stosch's coastal defense system, the armored gunboats were to operate in the shallow Baltic coastal waters, in support of the "sortie corvettes." Built at a cost of just over 1 million marks apiece, they generated less controversy than the *Ausfallkorvetten* but were equally ill conceived and spent little time in active service.[62]

The navy made fewer mistakes in completing the unarmored portion of Stosch's program. The remaining eight corvettes were laid down in the years 1874–78 and received their commissions between June 1877 and October 1880. The imperial shipyard in Danzig built two of the vessels, A.G. Vulcan of Stettin constructed four, and the Norddeutsche Schiffbau A.G. of Kiel the remaining two. Like the navy's first dozen corvettes, they were fully-rigged screw-propelled ships; unlike their predecessors, they were built of iron rather than wood. The two largest vessels, at 4,000 tons, would have been classified as frigates in any other navy. At just under 2,900 tons, the remaining six still were larger than any of the old wooden-hulled corvettes. While most of the corvettes already in service were named either for mythological characters or for women of the house of Hohenzollern, the new warships had distinctly Prussian names that gave equal honor to the Napoleonic era and to contemporary times. The larger pair were named after great victories, *Leipzig* and *Sedan.* Among the smaller six, the *Blücher, Gneisenau,* and *Stein* were matched by the *Moltke, Bismarck,* and *Stosch.* The navy went against international custom in naming the latter trio after persons still living, an honor normally reserved for members of royal families. After the *Stosch* entered service in March 1878, the chief of the Admiralty became the world's only active navy commander with a warship named after himself. Until the early 1890s, when they gave way to more modern cruisers, these ships shouldered most of the burden of showing the flag and representing German interests overseas. To ease this largely peaceful mission, in 1878 the *Sedan* was redesignated *Prinz Adalbert,* taking the name of the decommissioned ironclad. Its officers had found the original name a source of awkwardness in encounters with French vessels, whose captains declined to exchange the courtesy visits customary between warships on overseas stations.[63] Meanwhile, the retirement of more of the wooden-hulled screw gunboats of 1859–61 vintage led Stosch to order three new 490-ton gunboats. The *Wolf* (completed in 1878) and *Hyäne* (1879) were built in Wilhelmshaven, the *Iltis* (1880) in Danzig. Like the newest corvettes, they were fully-rigged vessels of iron construction. Despite their small size, the navy often employed them on extended overseas missions as a supplement to the larger cruisers.[64]

Owing to the prevailing confusion over the design and tactical role of torpedo boats, only six of the projected twenty-eight were built by 1878. Between 1874 and 1876 the navy also added four "torpedo steamers," the largest displacing 370 tons. These relatively slow vessels, like the original half-dozen torpedo boats, were designed to deliver their torpedoes with a bow spar. After 1876 torpedo experiments centered around the dispatch boat *Zieten,* a 1,000-ton iron-hulled screw steamer built in 1875–76 by the Thames Iron Works in London. The *Zieten* had the graceful lines of a sailing ship, but its two masts carried only nominal rigging. Engines from Penn & Sons of Greenwich gave it a top speed of sixteen knots, faster than any other ship in the fleet. It had two firing tubes for self-propelled torpedoes. Despite the modest scope of the navy's torpedo operations, Stosch considered the German version of the new technology a secret worth guarding. On his orders, a French navy engineer visiting Kiel in 1876 received "only very general impressions" of "everything related to *Torpedowesen.*" Later that year, Stosch ordered "*all* torpedo materiel" excluded from future tours by foreign officers.[65]

The *Zieten* bore witness to the fact that the navy still spent a significant share of its construction budget abroad, despite Stosch's rule of patronizing domestic industries as much as possible. In addition to the cost of the *Kaiser* and *Deutschland,* ordered before Stosch came to the Admiralty, the outlay for armor plate for the battleships built in Germany still went to British firms. Not all of the most expensive navy projects involved warships. Stosch enlarged or improved the three imperial shipyards, as well as the Baltic and North Sea bases.[66] In all, the navy had few budget worries in the 1870s; reductions, such as the one for 1876–77, came only with Stosch's consent. In the five fiscal years 1868 through 1872, the outlay had averaged 24.5 million marks per year; in Stosch's first budget (for 1873), it more than doubled to 54.2 million. The sums declined after that, before rebounding to a record 58.8 million for the 1878–79 fiscal year.[67] Stosch would be unable to sustain the momentum during the remainder of his time at the Admiralty.

Overseas Stations and Gunboat Diplomacy

Stosch's program of 1873 projected five overseas stations: those already established for the Mediterranean, East Asia, and West Indies, plus "West America" (the Pacific coast of the Americas) and Australia.[68] The creation of an Australian station reflected Germany's growing commercial interests in the nearby South Pacific. Indeed, economic considerations could hardly be ignored in the navy's planning. In 1872 the total value of the German Empire's imports and exports stood at 5.9 billion marks, up from 3.6 billion marks (1.2 billion thalers) for Prussia and the Zollverein states in 1860.[69] A boom in merchant shipping coinciding with the founding of the Reich promised to drive the figures even higher. Older firms such as the North German Lloyd of Bremen and the Hamburg-Amerika Line, Woermann Line, and Bolton Line of Hamburg were joined by the Hamburg-Südamerikanische Dampfschiffahrts-Gesellschaft, or "Hamburg-Süd," serving South America (1871); the Kosmos Line of Hamburg, also with routes to South America (1872); and the Deutsch-Australische Line (1874), serving Australia.[70]

After rejecting the appeals for the annexation of French colonies in 1870–71, Bismarck rebuffed an 1871 request from the firm of Godeffroy of Hamburg for a protectorate over Samoa, the focal point of German interests in the South Pacific. In 1872, fifteen years after Godeffroy's initial arrival, the corvette *Nymphe* became the first German warship to visit the island group. After that, Samoa became a regular stop for warships on world cruises or detached from the Australian station.[71] From its Samoan foothold, the Godeffroy company expanded far to the northwest, first to the Gilbert and Ellice Islands, then to the Marshall Islands. From there the web of operations spread quickly to the northwest (the Marianas), the west (the Carolines), and the southwest (New Britain, the future Bismarck Archipelago). By the mid-1870s Godeffroy also had expanded as far east as Tahiti. The firm's vessels visited the network of trading posts once or twice a year, collecting copra and other tropical products and delivering manufactured goods, all through the central depot at Apia Bay in Samoa. Other German firms competed with and complemented the Godeffroy empire, most notably the Hernsheim brothers, who in 1874 opened a post at Palau, on the western fringe of the Carolines, and then expanded their trade to the Marshalls, Gilberts, and New Britain. The late 1870s have been called "the golden age of German commerce in the Pacific." In 1877 the value of products exported from the South and Western Pacific islands by German firms exceeded 6 million marks, and Germans controlled 87 percent of the export trade of Samoa and Tonga.[72] As the decade went on, however, Berlin received a growing volume of complaints from German merchants being squeezed out of Pacific island markets by the subjects of other great powers. In addition to the British, French, and Americans, even the Spanish got into the act, restricting the commercial activities of Germans in the Carolines.[73] Bismarck demanded that Stosch send warships to show that Germany was serious about defending its interests. As the navy increased its strength overseas, most vessels went to the Far East or South Pacific. In 1874, three of four ships went to these two stations; in 1875, five of six; in 1876, eight of ten; in 1877, eight of nine; and in 1878, seven of nine.[74] Warships in the Far East continued to use Yokohama, site of the German naval hospital, as an informal base. The connection retained its importance until the turn of the century, when the Germans developed their Chinese base at Tsingtao (Qingdao). The hospital remained open until 1911.[75]

The unprecedented eight warships in the Pacific in 1876 included four corvettes and two gunboats in East Asian waters. The senior officer on the station, Captain Alexander von Monts of the corvette *Vineta,* had almost fourteen hundred seamen under his command. Monts's ships supported the assertive diplomacy of Max von Brandt, appointed German ambassador to China in 1875 after thirteen years as envoy to Japan. Britain supported Germany's efforts to combat piracy in the China Sea; their joint show of force also coerced China into granting further trading concessions to both countries, formalized in the Convention of Chefoo (Yantai) in September 1876.[76] During 1876 the *Hertha,* under Captain Eduard Knorr, visited Tonga and Samoa. The ship was present when the king of Tonga signed a friendship pact granting Germany most-favored-nation trading status, and when rival parties in Samoa formally recognized German property as "neutral" in their conflict.[77] Afterward, Germany became increasingly involved in Samoan affairs. While circumnavigating the globe in the years 1877–79, the *Ariadne* visited Samoa four times between June 1878 and May 1879.[78] In January 1879 the *Ariadne* and the gunboat *Albatross* witnessed the signing of a German-Samoan friendship treaty, in which the Samoans conceded the same trading rights the Tongans had granted earlier.[79]

While the navy focused on defending the interests of German trade in the Pacific, the leading shipping companies continued to expand their Caribbean and Latin American interests. Compared with the Pacific, far fewer German warships visited these waters, but under Stosch the most dramatic cases of gunboat pressure came in Latin America. During the deliberations that led to Stosch's appointment to the Admiralty, the navy was already stepping up its activity in the region. In the autumn of 1871, on the first leg of its world cruise, the *Nymphe* put in at Rio de Janeiro to support a German merchant and protest the Brazilian government's behavior toward the local German consul.[80] Over the winter of 1871–72 the *Vineta* cruised off Brazil, while the corvette *Gazelle* and training frigate *Niobe* patrolled the West Indies. The *Gazelle* also visited Venezuela, where debts owed to Germans had gone unpaid for two years and conditions were becoming "increasingly threatening" for German nationals.[81] The *Vineta* left Brazilian waters in March 1872 to join the *Gazelle* in the Caribbean for the summer; Captain Batsch of the *Vineta,* as senior officer, took command of the station. After Haiti reneged on a promise to pay a claim of £3,000 (20,000 thalers) to a Hamburg merchant, Batsch took his ships to Port-au-Prince in June 1872. In a daring nighttime operation, a landing party led by Lieutenant Friedrich Hollmann stormed the town, while others seized two Haitian navy paddle steamers anchored in the harbor. They suffered no casualties, and the debt was promptly paid.[82]

Batsch's ships returned to the West Indies in the autumn to join a squadron consisting of the armored frigate *Friedrich Carl,* corvette *Elisabeth,* and gunboat *Albatross,* under the command of Reinhold Werner. The warships first went to Colombia, where a Bremen firm had built a railway but had not been paid a government subsidy promised years earlier. When it received word of Werner's approach, the Colombian regime paid the subsidy. During the winter of 1872–73 a change in orders left just the *Albatross* in the West Indies while the remaining vessels returned to European waters. Werner subsequently took the *Friedrich Carl* and *Elisabeth* to Spanish waters, where controversy awaited him in 1873.[83] In 1872 the five German warships active in the Caribbean outnumbered those sent to East Asia (two), but it marked the last year until 1886 in which at least half the navy's active overseas cruisers were not assigned to the Pacific. Nevertheless, Germany continued to maintain a presence in the West Indies. The corvette *Augusta* visited the islands, and also Brazil, in 1874–75, followed in 1875–76 by the corvette *Victoria.*[84]

The next great display of gunboat diplomacy in Latin American waters came in March 1878, after Germany demanded reparations of $30,000 (120,000 marks) for alleged ill treatment of the German consul in Nicaragua. When Managua refused to pay, the corvettes *Leipzig, Elisabeth,* and *Ariadne* blockaded the Nicaraguan coastline on the Pacific side, the corvette *Medusa* the Atlantic side. The government in Managua remained defiant until it learned that German agents had leased a number of oxcarts to carry supplies for an inland march by a large landing party. Payment of the debt and a Nicaraguan salute to the German flag brought a quick end to the crisis.[85] For the navy, the elaborate choreography behind the demonstration made the outcome anticlimactic. The new orders had caught the *Ariadne* on a westward circumnavigation of the globe; after leaving Nicaraguan waters, it continued across the Pacific. The *Elisabeth* had been in East Asian waters on a scientific mission, as part of an eastward circumnavigation; afterward, it rounded Cape Horn and returned home later in 1878.[86] The *Leipzig*, in Japan on a scheduled westward circumnavigation, had to double back across the Pacific to join the demonstration; the ship even had Japanese cadets on board, who were put ashore temporarily in Panama.[87]

At the turn of the century, the Nicaraguan demonstration of 1878 was still being hailed as a classic example of gunboat diplomacy.[88] Nevertheless, the makeshift nature of the operation supported the argument that the navy should maintain a permanent "flying squadron" of overseas cruisers, available at all times for such emergencies. The idea had been raised as early as 1872, when Stosch sided with his second-in-command, Henk, in rejecting it as too extravagant (*"kostspielig"*). Henk also contended that a "flying squadron" would exhaust the navy's wooden corvettes; ironically, cruises by individual warships and the need for ad hoc squadrons for gunboat diplomacy eventually would wear out even the newer, iron-hulled corvettes. In the short term, the requirement of showing the flag overseas and the resulting arguments over which ships to send where and when only exacerbated Stosch's conflict with Bismarck.[89] Adalbert had predicted such a problem in 1867, when the fleet plan of that year had included so many corvettes for overseas duty.

Projecting Power: The Navy in European and Mediterranean Waters (1872–1878)

In rejecting the "flying squadron" concept in 1872, Henk also argued that the scheme would take too many men away from duty in European waters on armored warships, "the real battleships" of the fleet. Citing the Russian navy's example, Henk called for annual summer exercises by an armored squadron.[90] Besides the need for training aboard battleships, foreign policy considerations helped make the squadron in European waters a part of the navy's annual routine in the 1870s. In the mid-1860s Roon had called for a navy that would enable Prussia to "maintain . . . its European influence against such lands which may only be reached by sea."[91] For a generation of leaders that thought of Prussian-German interests in continental terms, such language referred not to Britain but to other areas of interest on the periphery of Europe: the Iberian peninsula, the Mediterranean littoral and Levant. Because German military might could not be brought to bear in these areas, the navy would have to shoulder the burden.

In the afterglow of victory over France and national unification, Germany gave little thought to Spain and the abortive Hohenzollern candidacy to the Spanish throne, the diplomatic issue that had precipitated the Franco-Prussian crisis of 1870. At the end of 1870 the Spanish crown went to Prince Amadeo of Savoy, whose brief reign in Madrid ended in February 1873. A fragile republican government replaced the monarchy, and the great powers dispatched warships to the Spanish coast to protect their interests. Germany sent Reinhold Werner with the armored frigate *Friedrich Carl,* corvette *Elisabeth,* and gunboat *Delphin.* After their arrival in June, the German warships joined a British patrol of the southern coast of Spain. Because Werner had seniority over the ranking British officer on the station, maritime custom gave him overall command of the force. He soon faced the challenge of dealing with vessels of the Spanish navy operated by a rebel faction. After the frigate *Almansa* and ironclad *Victoria* were observed shelling Spanish coastal cities, the Anglo-German squadron pursued them into the harbor of Cartagena. Werner's command decisions included seizing a Spanish dispatch ship, temporarily blockading Cartagena, and holding a captured rebel leader aboard the *Friedrich Carl.* Upon receiving this news, Bismarck relieved Werner of his command. The captain left the *Friedrich Carl* in Gibraltar and returned home to face a court-martial, charged with exceeding his orders.[92]

Bismarck, wishing to appease foreign critics of Germany's Spanish policy, called for Werner to receive a prison sentence. In contrast, the emperor and crown prince applauded the captain's boldness and wanted him freed. Stosch agreed with Bismarck that Werner had overstepped his instructions but pushed for a light punishment. Ultimately the captain was "exiled" to jobs on land; he directed the imperial shipyard in Wilhelmshaven for just over a year, then moved on to Kiel to become chief of the Baltic station.[93] Meanwhile, in February 1874 Stosch disbanded the squadron.[94] Werner, a supporter of Stosch in his first years at the Admiralty, blamed the commander for his disgrace and never forgave him. He went to his grave defending his actions off the coast of Spain; in a book published a quarter-century later he contended that he had received five hundred letters of thanks from residents of the city of Malaga, whose bombardment he had prevented.[95]

The manpower requirements of the Spanish operation and various overseas cruises changed the agenda for the scheduled summer maneuvers of 1873. Henk took command of a squadron consisting of the corvettes *Hertha*, *Vineta*, *Ariadne*, and *Arcona*, escorted by the gunboat *Nautilus*. The navy mobilized no armored warships other than the *Friedrich Carl* for Spanish waters. The squadron first cruised from Wilhelmshaven to Kiel, practicing tactical formations devised by the late Prince Adalbert. After that they visited Trontheim and Christiania (Oslo) for the social events of the summer, Oscar II's coronations as king of Sweden and Norway. The yacht *Grille* brought Crown Prince Frederick William to Sweden as the emperor's representative, and the squadron escorted him to the second ceremony, in Norway. In September, Henk's ships demobilized in Kiel.[96]

For the summer of 1874 the squadron included two ironclads—the *Friedrich Carl*, back from its Spanish mission, and the *Kronprinz*—along with the *Ariadne* and gunboat *Albatross*. Again, Henk commanded the force, and for the second year in a row the focal point was a state visit by the crown prince, this time to Britain. The squadron left Kiel in June for a rendezvous off Plymouth in early July with the yacht *Hohenzollern*, which brought Frederick William from Bremerhaven. After a review at Cowes, the three larger warships conducted cruises in the Atlantic, while the *Albatross* remained behind at the disposal of the crown prince. A flare-up in the Spanish crisis subsequently sent the *Albatross* directly from Britain to Spain with the *Nautilus*. After the prince's visit ended, the armored frigates and the *Ariadne* returned to the Baltic. In September, final exercises simulated actions against a blockade off Danzig and a Russian landing at Kolberg.[97]

After arriving in Iberian waters in the late summer of 1874, the *Nautilus* and *Albatross* showed the flag along the northern coast of Spain, in defense of local German interests. The *Nautilus* moved on to Moroccan waters but returned to visit the same Spanish ports again in 1876, en route home to Germany. By that time unrest in Spain had died down, a consequence of the Bourbon restoration of 1875. Coming on the heels of the "Werner Case," the navy's Spanish operations of 1874–75 led to a bitter clash between Bismarck and Stosch over the availability of ships for foreign stations and the channel of command for orders to their captains. Bismarck questioned the readiness of the fleet, and Stosch complained that German diplomacy placed unreasonable demands on the navy.[98]

After the exercises of 1874, Henk lamented that the *Kronprinz,* in reserve since the war of 1870–71, clearly had suffered from its years of inactivity. He also reported the difficulties of maneuvering a mixed squadron of armored and unarmored warships, a common problem in an ongoing era of transition in warship design. Stosch responded by giving Henk an unprecedented four armored warships for the summer squadron of 1875: the *König Wilhelm* (in reserve since 1870–71), the *Kronprinz,* and the new casemate ships *Kaiser* and *Hansa.* The squadron spent the entire summer in the Baltic, its operations plagued by mechanical problems aboard the new warships. The British-built *Kaiser,* completed by Samuda Brothers only in February, was soon running smoothly, but the *Hansa,* built at Danzig, spent very little time at sea. In July a German crew took possession of the *Deutschland,* just completed by Samuda Brothers, but the warship arrived from Britain too late to join the squadron. Henk's itinerary included no foreign visits, but in September, William I reviewed his ships at Warnemünde (Rostock).[99]

For 1876 Stosch again made the squadron command a sort of summer holiday for one of his high subordinates. This time Henk remained in Berlin while the chief of staff, Rear Admiral Batsch, took command. Batsch raised his flag aboard the *Kaiser;* the new *Deutschland,* the *Kronprinz,* and the *Friedrich Carl* rounded out the force. A foreign policy crisis sent the squadron straight to the Mediterranean: the murder of the German consul in Salonika. In June 1876 Batsch arrived off Salonika, where three smaller unarmored warships reinforced him. Fears of further attacks on German residents of the Ottoman Empire proved unfounded, and in August the demonstration ended.[100] Batsch returned home with the *Kaiser* and *Deutschland,* leaving behind the *Kronprinz* and *Friedrich Carl.* The latter stayed on until March 1877. It returned to Wilhelmshaven for repairs and a change of crews, then went back to the Mediterranean with the next summer squadron.[101]

During 1877 Batsch again left Berlin to command the squadron. The *Friedrich Carl* was joined by the *Kaiser,* the *Deutschland,* and the new turret ship *Preussen,* completed at Stettin in July 1876. Responding to reports of anti-foreign and anti-Christian violence in the Ottoman Empire, in July 1877 Batsch put in at Haifa and Jaffa. The prevailing calm ashore gave him little reason to stay, however, and the squadron spent the rest of the summer cruising in the Mediterranean before returning home in October. The Russo-Turkish war, which broke out in the spring of 1877, brought an increased international naval presence in the Eastern Mediterranean, but

Bismarck and Stosch decided not to keep ironclads in southern waters for a second winter in a row. Instead, Captain Franz Kinderling headed a makeshift "Mediterranean squadron" including the corvettes *Gazelle* and *Hertha* and three smaller warships. The force disbanded in the spring of 1878.[102]

Over the winter, fears of a Turkish collapse prompted the British to send a fleet to the Dardanelles. The Russians and Turks concluded peace in March 1878, but ongoing instability in the Balkans left the situation uncertain. Ultimately Bismarck would invite the statesmen of Europe to resolve their differences at the Congress of Berlin; meanwhile, he could not decide whether the armored squadron's summer itinerary again should include the Mediterranean. The Admiralty and Foreign Office finally agreed that Batsch would take the squadron as far as Gibraltar, then await further orders.[103] If circumstances did not warrant an appearance in the Mediterranean, the ships would cruise in the Atlantic. Given the good showings of the past two years, no one would have predicted that disaster would prevent the armored squadron of 1878 from ever reaching its destination.

•   •   •

During the 1870s, Bismarck came to appreciate the fleet as a unique asset to the German Empire. The navy demonstrated its usefulness from the coast of Spain and the Levant to the waters of Latin America and East Asia. The chancellor still considered Germany a continental power, and still shunned the acquisition of colonies; nevertheless, he recognized that a respectable navy, even of the second rank, gave Germany influence in places where it would otherwise have none. But in their use of the fleet, Bismarck and his Foreign Office at times resembled children uncertain of how to play with an unfamiliar new toy. Indecision and reversals of course in Berlin exacerbated the headaches normally attending the activation, maintenance, and deactivation of warships. It certainly did not help matters that a general, not an admiral, served as chief of the Admiralty—and not just any general, but the one Bismarck considered his greatest political rival.

In a simpler age of small sailing ships or wooden steamers, the navy had experienced more than its share of accidents and mishaps. In comparison, the deployment of squadrons of armored battleships on an annual basis, not just in the Baltic and North Sea but in the Mediterranean as well, placed far greater demands on the personnel of the navy. Eventually the new strains were bound to expose the weaknesses of Stosch's system: deficiencies in the training of conscripted manpower, the incompetence of many officers, and above all the practice of sending someone normally employed in an administrative job to command the squadron every summer. Rear Admiral Batsch, appointed chief of the North Sea station in April 1878, received command of the squadron for the third year in a row. His ships included the *Preussen*, the *König Wilhelm* (out of service since 1875), and the *Preussen*'s new sister ships *Friedrich der Grosse* (commissioned in November 1877) and *Grosser Kurfürst* (commissioned on 6 May 1878). The *Grosser Kurfürst* was barely ready in time to join the squadron, but as Batsch assumed command his attentions focused on the *Friedrich der Grosse*, which had been plagued with mechanical problems. On 22 May the ship ran aground off Nyborg while en route from Kiel to Wilhelmshaven; serious hull damage, combined with doubts about its engines, compelled Stosch to order it back to Kiel for repairs.[104] The remaining three ships left Wilhelmshaven on 29 May. Two days later, in broad daylight and clear weather, the *König Wilhelm* collided with the *Grosser Kurfürst* and sent it to the bottom of the English Channel with 276 men still aboard.

6

DISASTER AND DISARRAY

The *Grosser Kurfürst* Affair

he armored squadron of 1878 left Wilhelmshaven on the evening of 29 May. The *König Wilhelm, Preussen,* and *Grosser Kurfürst,* with the dispatch vessel *Falke,* proceeded to the English Channel en route to Gibraltar, where Batsch was to receive further orders regarding the summer's itinerary. On the morning of the thirty-first, after passing Dover, Batsch ordered the ships to conduct a variety of close-order maneuvers. The battleships were steaming westward in formation—the flagship *König Wilhelm* leading the way, followed by the *Grosser Kurfürst* less than one hundred meters behind, with the *Preussen* a distant third—when they sighted a merchant brig and bark off Folkestone. The two merchantmen, though still well ahead, were on a collision course with the squadron, prompting the battleships to execute a turn-away to starboard. But the *König Wilhelm* turned in a sharper turning circle than the *Grosser Kurfürst,* placing the two vessels on a collision course of their own.

Batsch, his flag captain Heinrich Kühne, and the *König Wilhelm*'s first officer, Captain Baron Georg von Hollen, looked on while the watch officer, *Kapitänleutnant* Oskar Klausa, directed the man at the helm of the 9,800-ton flagship: Otto Rantzau, a nineteen-year-old *Einjährig-Freiwillige.* As the ships drew nearer, Klausa barked a string of orders to the nervous Rantzau, to turn slightly to "port (*backbord*)" or "starboard (*steuerbord*)." The *Grosser Kurfürst* appeared to be on a course to cross the bow of the *König Wilhelm* by the narrowest of margins; if the flagship had continued on its sharper starboard circle, at the worst its bow would have clipped the stern of the passing ship. But amid the flurry of "ports" and "starboards," Klausa inserted an emphatic "the other way! (*den anderen Weg!*)," causing a fatal split second of confusion for Rantzau just as the *Grosser Kurfürst* crossed the *König Wilhelm*'s bow. Before the *Grosser Kurfürst* was completely clear, the flagship turned suddenly to port and back into the *Grosser Kurfürst,* ripping a hole in its port side, near the stern.[1]

The wounded battleship pulled clear of the *König Wilhelm,* then slowed to a halt, listing badly to port. It sank stern first, disappearing completely in just fifteen minutes. The prevailing conditions—broad daylight, clear weather—eased rescue efforts, but despite the best efforts of the rest of the squadron and fishing boats from Folkestone, 276 of the 500 men on board the *Grosser Kurfürst* were lost, including 7 officers. Survivors pulled from the cold waters of the channel included the ship's captain, Count Alexander von Monts. When nothing more could be done at the site of the accident, Batsch took the squadron to Portsmouth. Immediately after the collision, the officers and crew of the *König Wilhelm* feared they, too, would go under, but the sturdy flagship remained seaworthy, although leaking from its damaged bow. When the ship arrived in Portsmouth, British navy officials made a dry dock available for emergency repairs. On 3 June, Stosch ordered Batsch and his staff to return immediately to Wilhelmshaven with the *Preussen* and the dispatch steamer *Falke.* The *König Wilhelm* followed upon completion of its repairs. Under the circumstances, assembling a replacement squadron would have been difficult. Within days the Reich Chancellery informed Stosch that "the appearance of our ships in Turkish waters in this summer" was "not necessary."[2]

The sinking of the *Grosser Kurfürst* precipitated the greatest crisis of the Stosch era. Initial word of the disaster reached the chief at his summer home in the Rheingau. He hastened to Berlin, arriving on 2 June. Fortunately for both Stosch and the navy, other events distracted attention away from the *Grosser Kurfürst*'s sinking. On the day of Stosch's return to the capital, William I was wounded in an assassination attempt. Coming just three weeks after the emperor had escaped an earlier shooting unscathed, the incident outraged the public and preoccupied the press. After the first attempt on William's life, Bismarck had failed to get the Reichstag to pass an antisocialist law; following the second shooting, he secured a dissolution of the Reichstag and fresh elections. In late July, German voters gave the chancellor a more conservative legislature, which in October would pass a bill severely restricting the activities of the Social Democrats. Meanwhile, coinciding with the election campaign, Bismarck hosted the

Alexander von Monts
Historische Sammlung der Marine-
schule Mürwik

leading European statesmen at the Congress of Berlin, which sorted out the Balkan and Near Eastern crises.[3] Under normal circumstances the accidental sinking of a brand-new battleship that had cost some 7.3 million marks to build, not to mention the great loss of life, would have been front-page news. Thanks to the distractions of the summer of 1878, Stosch could initiate the navy's inquiry of the *Grosser Kurfürst* disaster out of the limelight of public and political scrutiny.

Rear Admiral Werner, the chief of the Baltic station, chaired an investigating commission consisting of three captains. A week after the sinking of the *Grosser Kurfürst*, Stosch lamented that his protégé, Batsch, "will bear most of the burden of guilt." The report of Werner's commission, filed on 21 July, confirmed his fears. Testimony revealed that Monts, the captain of the *Grosser Kurfürst*, had told Batsch before their departure that he had not had time to familiarize himself with his newly commissioned ship or its crew, most of whom were conscripts who had never been to sea and, under Stosch's training regimen, had spent much of the previous winter drilling as infantrymen. When Monts argued that the mobilization process should last four to six weeks, Batsch agreed. Indeed, Batsch himself had complained to Stosch the day before the squadron departed that "a great number of shipyard workers" would still be on board the *Grosser Kurfürst* on the morning of 29 May, working on its engines, boiler, and rudder mechanism. Nevertheless, he took the squadron out as scheduled. Witnesses also criticized Batsch for holding the close-order maneuver so early in the cruise, before the officers knew the capabilities of their men and ships. Batsch attempted to shift the blame by arguing that the *Grosser Kurfürst* had been out of position before the accident, but his estimates of the distances between the ships conflicted with the testimony of all other witnesses. Werner and the captains concluded that "Rear Admiral Batsch bears the responsibility for the mishap." They exonerated Monts, who "maneuvered the *Grosser Kurfürst* correctly and did everything possible to avoid the collision and to save his ship and crew."[4]

The condemnation of Batsch dismayed Stosch, but not as much as the criticism Monts and other officers had leveled against his own policies, especially the timetable for placing vessels in service. From 1872 onward, Stosch had insisted that all warships be ready for duty within days of their commissioning. The regulation went against conventional naval wisdom, which called for extensive sea trials of new vessels. Tirpitz later characterized Stosch's requirements as "mobilization on the model of the army." The chief of the Admiralty viewed a new ship not as a "complicated microcosm of technology" but as a regiment of the service that should be able to leave

Preussen, sister ship of *Grosser Kurfürst,* with *Hansa* in background
Historische Sammlung der Marineschule Mürwik

its base in a matter of days.[5] It was a hard blow to Stosch that an admiral as respected as Werner had allowed the inquiry to become a forum for Monts and other officers to question his policies. The tone of their testimony demonstrated both the degree to which senior officers still considered Stosch an outsider and their lack of appreciation for his political efforts on behalf of the fleet. Feeling betrayed by his subordinates, Stosch confided to his friend, Freytag, that "if it would not be so terribly cowardly to leave the navy now, I would gladly do so."[6]

But Stosch quickly returned to form, rejecting the criticism and accusing all of his critics of treachery. He reserved his harshest words for Werner. In a letter to William I on 19 August, Stosch argued that the Baltic station chief had unfairly focused blame "on Admiral Batsch and on the system" under which ships were placed in service. In defense of his protégé, he praised Batsch's service as commander of the maneuvers of 1876 and 1877. Hoping for a different verdict, Stosch asked for courts-martial for the four officers with central roles in the *Grosser Kurfürst* sinking: Batsch, the squadron commander; Kühne, his flag captain aboard the *König Wilhelm;* Klausa, the flagship's watch officer; and Monts, captain of the *Grosser Kurfürst.*[7]

William I submitted the case to an honor court of the Baltic station. Meanwhile, Stosch launched his own campaign to drive Werner out of the navy. On the surface, the two processes appeared motivated merely by a desire for vengeance on the part of Stosch; in fact, the rehabilitation of Batsch and ouster of Werner were essential to the fulfillment of the chief's long-term plans. Other than Henk, only Werner had seniority over Batsch; when the time came for Stosch to retire, Henk would go easily, leaving Werner as the main obstacle to Batsch becoming the next chief of the Admiralty. But in targeting Werner, Stosch declared war on a rather unique officer. Widely respected within the corps, he was also well known as an author and publicist. A native of Prussian Saxony, Werner had entered Prussian service in 1852, at the age of twenty-two, following three years in Brommy's German fleet. After commanding the *Elbe* on the East Asian mission of 1859–62 he wrote his first book, an account of the expedition.[8] He captained ships with distinction in the three subsequent wars, but his controversial conduct off Spain in 1873 ended his career as a seagoing commander. After that, Werner gained an avid supporter within the Hohenzollern family: his best-seller, *Das Buch von der deutschen Flotte* (1874), became the favorite book of the future William II, reinforcing the prince's fascination with the cause of German sea power. It appeared the year William went to Cassel as a *Gymnasium* student; he recalled later that "this book never left me so long as I was in Cassel. . . . I often read aloud from it to my comrades, in order to inspire them with my own enthusiasm; and, eventually, I knew it by heart."[9] Of course, the admiration of the teenaged prince did not help Werner in 1878. And even though both the emperor and the crown prince had admired his boldness in the Spanish affair, their soldier mentality prevented them from supporting Werner against his commanding officer. Once it became clear that Stosch wanted to force him out, he had no choice; he "requested retirement" on 15 October.[10] He would live on until 1909, writing in support of German navalism. Freed from the constraints of officer status, he also continued his battle with Stosch.

By the time Stosch eliminated Werner as a focal point of criticism within the officer corps, the *Grosser Kurfürst* disaster had become a scandal of major proportions. In September 1878 the monthly *Deutsche Revue* published an "expert elucidation on the catastrophe of the German armored ship *Grosser Kurfürst*" by an anonymous "former sea officer." The author was the retired Vice Admiral Jachmann, still bitter at being passed over in favor of Stosch seven years earlier. Jachmann contended that "the underlying causes of the terrible mishap are to be found in the system followed by our navy." He alleged that Stosch's training practices emphasized "theory and pure military principle" rather than "practical seaman's experience, which . . . in our navy is often considered superfluous."[11] In response, Stosch stood by his "system" of training, blaming external factors for any lack of preparedness. The rapid expansion of the fleet during the 1870s, the short service term of conscripted seamen, and the demands for more vessels for overseas stations all combined to strain manpower.[12] The figures supported his argument. For example, at one time in 1876, 6,851 seamen had been serving aboard German warships either in European or more distant waters. Just five years earlier, when fully mobilized for the war with France, the entire navy had not had so many sailors on active duty.[13] Stosch's contempt for his critics only grew as the affair dragged on. In a letter to Freytag shortly after Jachmann's anonymous article appeared, he characterized "the whole uproar" as "nothing more than a manifestation of the feelings of the older officers," whose "faulty education and training" stood in the way of the further development of the navy.[14]

As the autumn weeks passed, the *Grosser Kurfürst* affair became linked to Stosch's old rivalry with Bismarck. In November 1878, after Stosch drove him out of the service, Werner visited the chancellor at his home in Friedrichsruh. The two men were far from friends (five years earlier, Bismarck had been disappointed when Werner did not go to prison for his behavior off Spain), but their mutual hatred of Stosch warmed the atmosphere of their meeting. Over the winter of 1878–79 Werner gave a delighted Bismarck plenty of ammunition for his own war against Stosch. Reports of the divisions within the Admiralty and internal criticism of the commander began to appear in the newspapers, courtesy of the press office of the Prussian ministry. In March 1879, almost two years to the day since his first offer to resign, Stosch again submitted his resignation to the emperor. William I rejected it, assuring him of continued imperial support. An emboldened Stosch soon dumped his administrative second-in-command, Henk, on the grounds that he had agreed with Werner on the question of Batsch's responsibility for the *Grosser Kurfürst* disaster. Henk, ennobled for his service just the year before, appealed to the emperor, but William I upheld Stosch's decision and made Henk retire.[15]

Things did not go Stosch's way in the concurrent courts-martial. The court of the Baltic station, meeting in November 1878, included Major General Liebe, director of the Navy School; recently retired Vice Admiral Klatt, Batsch's predecessor as chief of the North Sea station; and Jachmann. The navy had to put two retired admirals and its only general on the court because Batsch, a rear admiral, was one of the defendants and could not be judged by a body composed entirely of officers of inferior rank. Jachmann, at this stage still not identified as the author of the anonymous piece in the *Deutsche Revue*, did not disqualify himself despite his obvious prejudices in the case. The court unearthed a great deal more evidence than the Werner commission. Key testimony came from the first officer of the *König Wilhelm*, Captain Hollen (in an unenviable position, as Stosch's son-in-law), and the *Einjährig-Freiwillige* Rantzau, the man at the helm of the *König Wilhelm* when it struck the *Grosser Kurfürst*. Both Rantzau and Klausa, the watch officer instructing him at the time of the collision, acknowledged that amid orders to turn to "port" and "starboard," Klausa's unfortunate command "the other way!" had confused the novice helmsman just as the *Grosser Kurfürst* crossed the *König Wilhelm*'s bow. The new revelations did nothing to change the verdict. The court ruled that Batsch bore the ultimate responsibility for the accident but did not recommend a punishment.[16]

In early December, Batsch protested to Stosch that Jachmann and Klatt had been less than objective as judges. Stosch appealed to William I for another court-martial in a new venue. In January 1879 the emperor agreed to a retrial for all four officers under the auspices of the *Garde-Korps* in

Berlin.[17] A month later the second court-martial found Batsch and Kühne innocent, but sentenced Klausa to a prison term of one month and one day and Monts to one month and two days. The emperor declined to implement the sentences, prompting a third trial, again under the *Garde-Korps.* This time the court found Kühne and Monts innocent, and Batsch and Klausa guilty. The latter again received a light sentence (one month imprisonment), while Batsch was given six months. On 15 June, a week after the sentences were handed down, Batsch appealed to William I to overturn his conviction. The emperor upheld his sentence, then commuted it; Batsch ended up serving two months in the fortress prison at Magdeburg. Stosch, disappointed at his protégé's fate, turned his attentions to securing a conviction for Monts, too. Though the June trial had acquitted the captain, it produced fresh evidence that the *Grosser Kurfürst*'s watertight doors were open at the time of the collision; thus, Monts could be held at least partially responsible for the sinking and loss of life. Despite the new argument, in August 1879 a fourth court-martial—again under the *Garde-Korps,* this time with Monts as the lone defendant—found Monts not guilty.[18]

Though William I's appreciation for discipline compelled him to support Stosch's efforts to "suppress the opposition" within the officer corps, he had the good sense to refuse to let him fire a captain acquitted by three courts-martial. The fact that Monts's father and uncle were Prussian army generals no doubt helped secure his position. The emperor also found it difficult to accept the argument that Monts was incompetent. In an evaluation written six months before the *Grosser Kurfürst* disaster, Stosch himself had called Monts "a man of character," a "good comrade," and "suitable for promotion." Indeed, as a nobleman from an army family, Monts matched the profile Stosch had set for the ideal officer. In Stosch's own words, "he represents a very valuable . . . element in the officer corps."[19] In September 1879, after the emperor sanctioned the verdict of the fourth court-martial, Stosch gave up his campaign against Monts.[20] In all, Monts had been acquitted by Werner's commission of inquiry and three of four courts-martial, and served no time in prison. Batsch had been found guilty by the commission and two of three courts-martial, and had his record tainted by the two months in the Magdeburg fortress.

In December 1879, William I issued an imperial order intended to end the turmoil and encourage the sea officer corps to mend its wounds. The document reflected the wisdom of his eighty-two years, but in language that revealed his inability to understand the navy in terms different from the army. He lamented the *Grosser Kurfürst* disaster and the loss of so many "good soldiers (*brave Soldaten*)," but noted that "a soldier must never look backwards, only forward; he should learn from the past but his energy must belong to the future." Comparing the navy with an infantry unit that had suffered "losses in the field," he appealed to the officers to "close ranks" behind Stosch. Perhaps most important of all, he reassured the corps that "this incident has in no way shaken my firm trust in the further successful development of the navy."[21]

Bloodied but far from beaten, Stosch emerged firmly in charge at the Admiralty, still with the ability to make or break most careers. He brought Batsch to Berlin shortly after his release from prison, to take Henk's old job as director of the Admiralty. Rear Admiral Wilhelm Berger, a friend of Batsch's ever since their days as cadets aboard the USS *St. Lawrence* in 1848–49, succeeded Batsch as chief of the North Sea station. Rear Admiral Franz Kinderling, a supporter of Stosch throughout the crisis of 1878–79, took Werner's old post as chief of the Baltic station. In February 1880 Batsch received a promotion to vice admiral, and in January 1881, after Kinderling retired, he became chief of the Baltic station. In April 1881 Monts received a promotion to rear admiral, but he would hold no positions of responsibility until after Stosch left the Admiralty. The other defendants of 1878–79, Kühne and Klausa, were denied ship commands as long as Stosch remained in charge, but in 1881 Kühne became director of the imperial shipyard in Kiel. Both men later became admirals.[22]

As for the *Grosser Kurfürst* itself, as late as 1903 the German navy was still considering projects to salvage the wreck.[23] Ironically, the five proceedings of 1878–79 had focused so completely on the guilt or innocence of key individuals that no one ever questioned the soundness of the ship itself. Because everyone agreed that the steering error had been made aboard the *König Wilhelm*, no one ever questioned the steering of the *Grosser Kurfürst*. The record shows that shipyard personnel were still working on the new vessel's rudder the day before it left Wilhelmshaven. Since the collision occurred after the two ships had executed turns-away with uneven turning circles, a rudder problem of even the slightest degree would have contributed to the disaster. Such mechanical quirks could be discovered only in extensive sea trials; with the abandonment of Stosch's timetable for activating warships, these again became the norm. The next new battleship, the "sortie corvette" *Sachsen*, did not join the squadron until nineteen months after its commissioning in October 1878. In another consequence

of the disaster, the navy corrected a glaring oversight by requiring all officer candidates to certify their ability to swim. In future years, junior officers were responsible for ensuring that all seamen knew how to swim.[24]

As the navy began a difficult healing process, Bismarck stepped up his
own effort to use the *Grosser Kurfürst* disaster to weaken Stosch politically.
In a case of strange bedfellows, in March 1880 he supported efforts by the
Progressive leader, Albert Hänel of Kiel, to get a vote of no confidence
against Stosch in the Reichstag. But powerful friends of the crown prince
and the navy, including Georg von Bunsen of the National Liberals and industrialist Wilhelm von Kardorff of the Free Conservatives, led the defense
of Stosch, and the measure failed.[25] Bismarck then tried to revive the post
of general inspector of the navy, dormant since the death of Prince Adalbert in 1873. The idea had appeal as a way to check Stosch's power without
removing him from office; H. H. Meier of Bremen, National Liberal politician and director of the North German Lloyd, had first proposed it in the
autumn of 1878. But Bismarck's choice of candidates hardly helped his
case. First he suggested Prince Frederick Charles, a Hohenzollern with
naval interests for whom the armored frigate *Friedrich Carl* was named,
then Prince Ernst zu Leiningen, a relative of the British royal family and
honorary British admiral who had once commanded Queen Victoria's
yacht. Their dubious credentials caused the scheme to fail altogether.[26]

Afterward, Bismarck tried to place a trusted high-ranking naval officer
in the Reichstag as a nemesis to Stosch. He chose Rear Admiral Otto Livonius, recently named director of the Admiralty after Batsch's appointment
to head the Baltic station. A former director of the imperial shipyard in
Danzig, Livonius contested the Danzig seat held by Stosch's old friend
Rickert. Unfortunately for the chancellor, in the Reichstag election of October 1881 he lost to Rickert by a wide margin. Stosch naturally considered
his bid for a political career to be an act of insubordination and personal
disloyalty.[27] Nevertheless, Livonius remained on active duty after the episode. Protected by Bismarck, he kept his post as Admiralty director until
1883.[28]

Meanwhile, William I remained confident in Stosch. As a token of his
continuing support, in September 1881 he awarded him the Order of the
Black Eagle. At the same time, however, William I's age and the crown
prince's increased wavering and indecision left Stosch politically far less secure than before.[29] It only made matters worse that many of his friends in
the Reichstag, even those who stood by him in 1878, deserted him as the
Grosser Kurfürst affair dragged on. During the remainder of Stosch's time

at the Admiralty, the declining naval outlay reflected his ineffectiveness with the politicians. The most dramatic fall, from the peak of 58.8 million marks in 1878–79 to 48.5 million in 1879–80, came while the courts-martial were still under way. By 1882–83, expenditure amounted to just 40.6 million marks.[30]

Expansion amid Technological Change: A Mixed Blessing in Materiel (1878–1883)

In sheer numbers of warships, the material progress of the Stosch era was impressive enough. In 1872 the German navy ranked last in size among the fleets of the six European great powers, but four years later it passed the Austro-Hungarian navy in total tonnage of warships in commission. In 1880 Germany passed Italy in total tonnage, and by 1882 it trailed only Britain and France in armored tonnage.[31] But the German navy's rapid rise came because of projects Stosch inherited in 1872 or initiated between then and 1879. Amid the declining budgets of his last years in office, Germany laid down no armored warships at all between 1879 and 1883. In Stosch's last years at the helm, the only vessels begun were a handful of torpedo boats and six small unarmored warships designed for overseas duty.

After the *Grosser Kurfürst* disaster, Stosch's detractors focused criticism not just on his leadership and methods but on the materiel of the fleet as well, pointing to the fact that the collection of warships left much to be desired. The seven armored "frigates," the oldest of which had already been in service for fifteen years, were of five different designs and vastly differing capabilities. The casemate "corvette" *Hansa* was such a disappointment that it would be relegated to harbor watch duties at Kiel in 1884, after hardly being used in its nine years with the fleet. The "sortie corvettes" provided even more grist for the mill of Stosch's critics, a consequence of the host of problems that plagued them from the time they entered service: the *Sachsen* in October 1878, the *Württemberg* in May 1881, and the *Bayern* in August 1881. Attempts to correct design flaws delayed the commissioning of the fourth "sortie corvette," the *Baden*, until September 1883, six months after Stosch retired. A projected fifth sister ship ultimately bore little resemblance to the others: in 1883, A.G. Vulcan laid down the *Oldenburg* as a 5,200-ton casemate ship.[32]

Contemporary critics of the *Ausfallkorvetten* noted that their "flat bottoms" caused them to "roll so frightfully at sea, that it is out of the question to expect anything like accuracy from their heavy guns." Their primary armament of six 10.25-inch Krupps was arranged in open turrets (barbettes) on deck that were only lightly armored. On the question of armor in general the ships were a disaster. Caught in the technological transition from wrought iron to compound iron-and-steel plates (invented in Britain in 1876–77), designers plated them with so-called "sandwich" armor of alternating wrought iron and teak. Unlike the four older German-built ironclads, which carried imported British plates, the "sortie corvettes" received their sandwich armor from Karl Stumm's foundry at Dillingen on the Saar.[33] Stosch ordered their engines from the Märkisch-Schlesische firm of Berlin (formerly F. A. Egells). Although the same firm had provided engines for earlier battleships, the results were not good and the *Ausfallkorvetten* ended up being slower than most of the navy's armored frigates: "As regards speed . . . they leave much to be desired . . . while they still have such a heavy draught that the idea of their running into the harbors on the [Baltic] coast seems highly problematical." Their unconventional appearance only underscored their lack of speed and maneuverability. They belched smoke from four funnels arranged at points of a square instead of in customary line-ahead fashion, prompting critics to nickname them "cement factories."[34]

The eleven small armored gunboats commissioned in the years 1876–81 likewise became targets of criticism. The 1,100-ton vessels were designed "to defend the mouths of rivers and entrances to harbors" in support of the efforts of the *Ausfallkorvetten,* but one critic observed that they "roll and pitch to such a degree that only chance hits from their guns could be reckoned upon" and "could, therefore, be only employed in perfectly calm weather." They carried obsolete wrought-iron armor—British for the first five boats, domestic Dillinger plate for the remaining six—which made them heavy for vessels of their dimensions; indeed, their speed was "so slight that they cannot possibly risk an encounter with larger hostile vessels." Just as the last of the *Ausfallkorvetten* took a different form from its predecessors, a final pair of armored gunboats—the *Brummer* and *Bremse,* laid down by A.G. Weser of Bremen in 1883—were lighter (at 870 tons), faster, and less heavily armed than the earlier eleven. They were the first German warships equipped with compound (iron and steel) armor, which Stumm began producing at Dillingen in 1880, after securing a license to manufacture plates on the British model.[35]

As for the unarmored vessels, by the late 1870s the question arose of replacing the fleet's twelve older corvettes. Some of these wooden-hulled screw ships had already been in service for twenty years, and almost all remained in commission throughout the Stosch era, deployed on overseas

Sachsen-class battleship, pictured in 1895   *Naval Historical Center, Basic Collection*

missions. Another half-dozen new corvettes eased their burden. The 2,100-ton *Carola, Olga, Sophie,* and *Marie,* laid down in 1879–80, received their commissions in 1881 and 1882. The 2,400-ton *Alexandrine* and *Arcona,* begun in 1881, finally entered service five years later. Constructed of iron and steel, these vessels still carried a full set of masts and yards. Again Stosch divided the contracts between private and government shipyards: A.G. Vulcan of Stettin built two of the corvettes, the imperial shipyard in Danzig two, Reiherstieg of Hamburg and the imperial shipyard in Kiel one apiece.[36] Reiherstieg's *Marie* was the first German navy vessel built in Hamburg, where the shipyards had previously shown little interest in building warships; at least for the upcoming decade they would profit little from the connection, because many Hamburg shipwrights still resisted the change from wood to iron and steel construction.[37] To supplement these larger cruisers the navy added another three overseas gunboats. In 1878–80 Schichau of Elbing completed the 840-ton *Habicht* and *Möve,* and in 1882 the imperial shipyard in Kiel laid down the 880-ton *Adler.*[38]

At the end of Stosch's tenure the navy still had only its original six torpedo boats in service, but another seven were under construction, ordered in 1882 from A.G. Weser of Bremen. By then the Admiralty had already taken a decisive step in the development of the torpedo branch, ordering Germany's first pair of modern unrigged steel cruisers in 1881. Classified as dispatch boats, they were equipped with torpedo tubes that would enable them to serve as flotilla leaders for torpedo boats. The 1,400-ton *Blitz,* built by the Norddeutsche Werft of Kiel, and its sister ship *Pfeil*, built by the imperial shipyard in Wilhelmshaven, received their commissions in 1883. Their Märkisch-Schlesische engines were capable of sixteen knots, putting their speed in the same league with the older torpedo ship *Zieten*.[39] Stosch could be proud that his fleet included steel warships at such an early date. The British navy had launched its first vessels of steel construction only in the late 1870s.[40]

In the wake of the antisocialist law of October 1878, the government expected navy leaders to take a vigilant stand against Social Democratic influences within the fleet and especially at the state-owned shipyards in Danzig, Wilhelmshaven, and Kiel. Late in 1879 the Prussian interior ministry warned Stosch of widespread socialist sympathies among the twenty-five hundred workers at the imperial shipyard in Kiel. The police estimated that "75 percent of the metalworkers and carpenters" were socialists and identified suspected Social Democratic ringleaders among those working on the *Bayern* and other key projects. Early in 1880 Stosch admitted that the antisocialist law had done nothing to change the political sympathies of the workforce in Kiel: "As before, the overwhelming majority of workers employed by the imperial shipyard support socialism." Captain Baron von der Goltz, shipyard director from 1878 to 1881, fired Social Democratic agitators, but in such cases the navy's standard of proof was more stringent than that of the police. Skilled metalworkers and machine builders were not easily replaced and thus not dismissed without very good cause. At least for the time being, only those foolish enough to proselytize in the workplace lost their jobs. In the atmosphere of economic insecurity following the great depression of 1873, few workers were willing to take the risk.[41]

At the end of the 1870s, the effects of the depression were still being felt by the firms that formed the navy's domestic industrial base. The leading companies did not suffer as much as the smaller ones, but even Krupp had to curtail operations.[42] Successful as a gun manufacturer but frustrated in his experiments with armor production, Alfred Krupp became increasingly outspoken in his view that the gun would inevitably triumph over armor. In the wake of the *Grosser Kurfürst* sinking he pointed to the costly disaster as an example of the vulnerability of big battleships. Germany's interests would be better served by gunboats, unarmored or lightly armored, equipped with his latest weapon, the 12-inch pivot gun. In February 1879 he argued that in an attack by ten of his boats against an armored warship, "the big ship is in ten times more danger, and if the small one is actually hit and sunk, the loss in material and in human lives is only one tenth as much."[43] In some ways Krupp foreshadowed the thinking of the French *Jeune École* of the 1880s, only with gunboats, rather than torpedo boats and cruisers, spelling the end for battleships.

While Stosch believed in the utility of small coast defenders—his own armored gunboats attested to that—he did not agree with the view that the seagoing battleship was obsolete. No doubt offended by Krupp's attempt to exploit the *Grosser Kurfürst* disaster, he rejected the gunboat scheme. In January 1880, in a letter to Crown Prince Frederick William, Krupp noted that "the General [Stosch] does not yet approve of my new system for a ship [*sic*] with a pivot gun, and has given me some very frank expressions of opinion about it. . . . But I shall not give in to my last hour. This ship must rule the seas in the future."[44] By 1881 the concept had evolved from a small gunboat to an unpowered floating battery, still armed with a single powerful gun, which would be towed into place offshore and anchored. A line of these artificial "islands," as Krupp called them, could provide a first line of defense, engaging enemy warships before they steamed close enough to bombard the German coast. Even if an "island" were lost in battle, "we can still buoy the spot, so that later, when peace has been restored, the gun can be lifted again."[45] Of course Krupp thought first of the gun, overlooking the fact that in a combat situation his "islands" would be worse than sitting ducks and that duty aboard them would be tantamount to a suicide mission. By the end of 1882 he had abandoned the "island" concept, revived the notion of "small pivot boats," and conceded the utility of larger, albeit unarmored, warships. Ironically, within a decade the Krupp firm would be not only involved in the armor business but on the verge of monopolizing the German market and establishing itself as world leader of the industry. Alfred Krupp did not live to see it.[46]

Stosch's strained relationship with the aging Krupp stood in sharp contrast to the warm ties he enjoyed with most industrialists, as his friend Gustav Freytag noted on the occasion of his retirement: "Amidst the flood of adulation which greeted the departing administrator, nothing was more flattering than the address presented to him by the great industries which he had employed in the reconstruction of the navy. . . . Nothing excited their admiration more than the energy with which he had elaborated and carried out his idea that all work and material for the service of the navy should be forthcoming within the German Empire itself."[47] In 1872 Stosch had taken command of a navy that was still importing all of its armor plate, many of its engines, and some entire vessels from Britain. In 1883

German steel mills, machine shops, and shipyards were filling the navy's orders. While his critics could cite "the fact that many things procured in Germany cost three or four times as much as similar [imported] articles of better quality,"[48] Stosch laid the foundation of the naval-industrial complex that helped make Germany a first-class sea power after the turn of the century.

European and Mediterranean Operations: New Alliances and New War Plans (1878–1883)

Within a week of the *Grosser Kurfürst* sinking, the navy disbanded the summer squadron of 1878 and canceled maneuvers. Other than the casemate ship *Hansa,* sent to the West Indies for the winter of 1878–79, unarmored vessels overseas were the only active warships for the remainder of the year. A full year passed before the navy assembled another armored squadron, in May 1879, under Rear Admiral Kinderling. It included the *Grosser Kurfürst's* surviving sister ships *Friedrich der Grosse* and *Preussen,* and the old armored frigates *Friedrich Carl* and *Kronprinz.* Kinderling took his ships out of the Baltic only for a June cruise to the coast of Norway. He conducted close-order maneuvers similar to those that had led to the *Grosser Kurfürst* disaster, only this time in the Skagerrak, where a sudden onset of fog almost caused another catastrophe. The squadron demobilized in September at Kiel, where Kinderling resumed his duties as chief of the Baltic station.[49]

For the summer of 1880 a former Austrian navy officer, the Mecklenburger Wilhelm von Wickede, succeeded Kinderling as squadron commander. The *Sachsen,* the first of the "sortie corvettes" to be commissioned, replaced the *Kronprinz* in the quartet of active battleships. Apart from a cruise in August to Wilhelmshaven and Cuxhaven, the squadron again spent the entire summer in the Baltic. During June, Wickede played host to the captain of the Italian frigate *Cristoforo Colombo* at Kiel. That same month, a group of steam pinnaces and cutters simulated a torpedo attack against the flagship *Friedrich Carl,* which deployed an experimental floating torpedo boom for defense. In September, Stosch inspected the squadron at Eckernförde and spent two nights aboard the *Friedrich Carl.* The *Sachsen* was the greatest disappointment of the summer. Although the new battleship had already been in commission for a year and a half, engine trouble kept it from leaving Kiel with the squadron at the onset of exercises in May; the following month it sustained minor damage in a collision with a British merchant schooner at the mouth of Kiel Harbor.[50] In

July the crown prince and his son, Prince William, met the squadron off Rügen aboard the yacht *Hohenzollern*. They went on to Kiel to witness an exercise in which Captain Alfred Tirpitz's torpedo ship *Zieten* torpedoed and sank the old paddle steamer *Barbarossa*. A leading advocate of torpedoes and torpedo boats at this early stage of his career, Tirpitz later boasted that the success of such displays of the latest technology bolstered Stosch's position in the wake of the *Grosser Kurfürst* disaster.[51]

Early in 1881 the corvette *Victoria* represented Germany in an international demonstration against the Turks that ultimately forced the Ottoman Empire to cede the Adriatic port of Dulcigno (Ulcinj) to Montenegro. This token contribution—a wooden-hulled, fully-rigged screw steamer—contrasted sharply with the armored presence Stosch had deployed in the Eastern Mediterranean during the crises of 1876 and 1877.[52] The 1881 summer squadron, again under Wickede's command, included the battleships *Friedrich Carl, Kronprinz, Friedrich der Grosse*, and *Preussen*. For the third year in a row, the squadron spent most of its time in the Baltic; in August, a two-week North Sea cruise again visited Cuxhaven and Wilhelmshaven. In July the ships anchored at Kiel to welcome the British reserve squadron, commanded by the Duke of Edinburgh. The visiting force of eight battleships included the original British ironclad *Warrior*, by then more than twenty years old. Princes Henry and William presided at the festivities for their imperial grandfather.[53] In September the German squadron's visit to Danzig coincided with a meeting between William I and Tsar Alexander III, who arrived with his entourage aboard the imperial Russian yacht *Derjawa*. Later in the month, the emperor observed torpedo exercises and mock landings to storm the forts guarding Kiel Harbor. Afterward, he gave Stosch his Order of the Black Eagle and promoted Wickede to rear admiral.[54]

Alexander III's visit followed the revival of the Three Emperors' League, a loose alignment of Germany, Russia, and Austria-Hungary originally formed in 1873. Bismarck took pride in the diplomatic breakthrough, but by the spring of 1882 a variety of factors threatened the Russo-German relationship, including a spy scandal in which a career German navy NCO was accused of passing secrets to the Russians.[55] During Stosch's last years at the Admiralty the navy's first efforts at war planning focused on a theoretical threat from Russia in the Baltic. Captain Eduard Heusner drafted the Admiralty's initial Russian plan. In its final form, dated August 1882, it assumed that the superiority of the German navy over the Russian Baltic fleet in armored warships would keep the Russians in a defensive posture.

Russian mines and torpedoes would make a German offensive in the Baltic risky, but Heusner believed it should be undertaken anyway. His plan called for most of the armored warships of the fleet to assemble in Danzig or Memel and steam for the Gulf of Finland, where they would seek battle with the Russians, if necessary luring them out of Kronstadt by bombarding Russian coastal cities.[56]

The 1882 summer squadron, again commanded by Wickede, included the same ships as the previous year. After mobilizing in Wilhelmshaven in May, the ships went to the Baltic, where they spent the rest of the summer. In a simulation at the close of maneuvers in September, Wickede's battleships played the squadron of an "eastern power" attacking Kiel from the direction of Danzig; the defending force, under Tirpitz, included the corvettes *Luise* and *Blücher,* simulating German battleships, and four torpedo boats. The so-called "Battle of Fehmarn Sound," on the night of 10–11 September, ended in a victory for the torpedo forces against the "enemy" battleships. The squadron then cruised to Wilhelmshaven, where it demobilized at the close of the exercises.[57] Two months later, a plan for a war against both France and Russia, formulated by Captain Otto von Diederichs, then a staff officer in the Admiralty, gave a prominent place to the new torpedo technology. Like Heusner in his earlier draft, Diederichs recommended an offensive against the Russian navy in the Baltic. For the North Sea, he assumed that the French, as in 1870, would deploy a superior blockading force against which a defensive force based at Wilhelmshaven would launch occasional sorties. Diederichs assumed that torpedo boats would bear much of the burden of disrupting a French blockade.[58]

Given the growing German interest in the torpedo, it is ironic that Stosch did little to cultivate relations with the navy of Austria-Hungary, Germany's closest ally and a pioneer in torpedoes and torpedo tactics. A rare exception came in May 1877, when Stosch sent Captains Heusner and Tirpitz to Rijeka to visit the Whitehead torpedo factory.[59] But the conclusion of the Dual Alliance of October 1879 and the Triple Alliance of May 1882 did not increase contact between the German and Austrian navies.[60] In 1882, when Stosch sent the first naval attachés to German embassies abroad, they went to Washington and London; years would pass before the navy assigned permanent attachés to Vienna or Rome.[61] Nevertheless, the navy did import torpedoes from Austria-Hungary and was dependent upon Whitehead until its German licensee, Schwartzkopf, began producing torpedoes in Berlin.[62]

Although the Triple Alliance became one of the longest-running in the history of European diplomacy, the initial treaty had a term of five years. Its terms committed Germany and Italy to help each other in case either fell victim to an attack by France. Austria-Hungary would join Italy and Germany against France if France attacked Italy, but not if France attacked Germany. Should an alliance member be attacked by two or more non-members, the other members were bound to intervene. If a member attacked a nonmember, the others were to observe a benevolent neutrality toward their ally. All terms were secret, to be renewed in 1887. After signing the treaty, Italy insisted upon an exchange of notes affirming that it was not directed against Britain.[63]

Although all three of the allies objected to the subsequent British occupation of Egypt, they were careful not to show their disapproval at sea. The four German battleships mobilized for the 1882 summer maneuvers remained in northern waters, where their exercises would run no risk of offending the British. Captain Baron von der Goltz commanded a special "Mediterranean squadron," a motley collection of unarmored vessels including the corvettes *Gneisenau* and *Nymphe,* the torpedo ship *Zieten,* the old paddle steamer *Loreley,* and a screw gunboat. During the British bombardment of Alexandria, sailors from the squadron guarded the German consulate and a German hospital.[64] The navy's response could hardly have been meeker.

The operational plans drafted during 1882 did not reflect a thorough consideration of the diplomatic context of the time. As such, they suggest a broader problem facing the navy during the Stosch era: the overriding goal was expansion for the sake of fulfilling the fleet plan of 1873, a program that, like earlier fleet plans, had few direct connections to the strategic needs of the state. In his last months as chief of the Admiralty, Stosch finally articulated the link between the fleet and Germany's international position, contending that "in a major war against a power with superior naval strength" Germany would have to hold its own at sea; otherwise "Germany can have no value for maritime allies." The argument that a navy enhanced Germany's alliance value echoed the position taken by Prince Adalbert a quarter-century earlier, in his *Denkschrift* of 1848.[65] But Stosch never resolved the problem of having to maintain two different navies, an armored battle fleet in home waters and unarmored warships for overseas duty. In the future, as the navy became more serious about strategic and operational planning, the problem only grew worse.

From Samoa to Saltpeter: Overseas Operations
on the Eve of Colonialism

In the last years of Stosch's command, the East Asian and Australian (or South Pacific) stations continued to be the destinations of most overseas cruises. In 1879 the navy assigned eight of twelve active cruisers to the Pacific; in 1880, ten of twelve; in 1881, eight of eleven; in 1882, seven of ten; and in 1883, seven of twelve.[66] Activity in the South Pacific continued to center around Samoa, where warring factions posed an increasing danger to foreign trading interests. Elsewhere such conditions led to the establishment of protectorates and colonies, but Samoa remained independent because the three leading competitors for influence there—Britain, Germany, and the United States—each feared an annexation attempt by the others. In 1878 and 1879 the three powers concluded their own treaties with the local regime to safeguard their interests and attempted, individually, to mediate an end to the Samoan civil war. In 1879 Captain Karl Deinhard arrived with the corvette *Bismarck* but failed to impose peace. In 1881 an American attempt fared better, and the rivals signed a treaty aboard the USS *Lackawanna.* Unfortunately for Germany, the pact confirmed the claim to the Samoan throne of a pro-British king.[67]

Ironically, German commercial predominance in the region collapsed some five years before Germany ever claimed a Pacific colony. In December 1879 J. C. Godeffroy & Sohn went bankrupt. Bismarck coordinated an effort by financiers Adolph von Hansemann and Gerson von Bleichröder to purchase the company's holdings, but the Reichstag balked when the bankers insisted that the government guarantee dividends to investors. The defeat of the chancellor's controversial "Samoa bill" in April 1880 reflected a political climate still divided on the subject of colonialism. A new Hamburg firm, the Deutsche Handels- und Plantagen-Gesellschaft der Südsee (DHPG), inherited the German Samoan holdings, but a French company headquartered on Tahiti bought most other Godeffroy properties. The DHPG struggled from the start, thanks largely to new regulations on British-controlled islands that disrupted German sources of island labor. The annexation of German Pacific colonies in the mid-1880s would come, in part, to prevent further losses in the markets for both trade and labor.[68]

Meanwhile, in East Asia, German attentions turned at least temporarily from China and Japan to Korea. In the spring of 1882, after Berlin learned that the United States had signed a trade treaty with the isolationist king-

dom, the Germans resolved to secure similar concessions. Brandt, the ambassador to China, conducted the negotiations; the corvette *Stosch* ferried
him to Korea and remained offshore with the gunboat *Wolf* until he
achieved his goal. The German-Korean trade treaty was signed in June
1882.[69] As the leading German diplomat in the Far East, Brandt often pursued policies more aggressive than those advocated by Bismarck. For example, during 1882 he twice called upon ships of the East Asian station for
shore parties to support the claims of German merchants involved in very
minor disputes with the Chinese.[70] Bismarck showed his displeasure for
these actions early in 1883 by temporarily recalling Brandt. But no one
could fault the ambassador's record of successfully defending German
firms long involved in the China trade. He also promoted the interests of
those seeking to penetrate the market, including pillars of the growing
naval-industrial complex. Starting in the 1880s, Krupp profited hand-
somely from the arming of China, securing artillery contracts worth millions of marks. Meanwhile, in 1881 the Chinese government contracted
with A.G. Vulcan of Stettin to build the *Ting Yuen,* a modified version of
the German navy's 7,600-ton "sortie corvette." The first larger foreign warship built by a German firm, it had Dillinger compound armor, a great im-
provement over the sandwich armor of its German counterparts. A year
later A.G. Vulcan began work on a sister ship, the *Chen Yuen,* and later in
the decade completed three more warships for China: the armored corvettes *King Yuen* and *Lai Yuen* and the protected cruiser *Tsi Yuen.* For the
firms involved, these orders helped compensate for the dearth of German
navy contracts in the early and mid-1880s.[71] In contrast, during the same
period German firms did little business with the Japanese navy. In Stosch's
last years, the largest order for Japan consisted of fifty Schwartzkopf torpedoes.[72]

In the wake of the Nicaraguan affair of 1878, Latin American waters remained the most active theater of German gunboat diplomacy after the
Far East and South Pacific. In 1879 the outbreak of the Saltpeter War, pit-
ting Chile against Peru and Bolivia, drew foreign warships to the western
coast of South America. Twenty-five Hamburg firms petitioned Berlin for
a German squadron to protect their interests in the region. Bismarck refused to act until one of the belligerents actually seized a German ship. After Peru interned the Hamburg merchant steamer *Luxor,* which had delivered Krupp guns to Chile, Bismarck dispatched the corvette *Freya* to the
war zone. The *Hansa,* in the West Indies on a rare voyage beyond European
waters, steamed for Peru to strengthen the German hand. Unfortunately,

its poor construction and underpowered engines left it in no shape for a high-speed dash around Cape Horn. In the words of a contemporary critic, the *Hansa* took "twice as long getting [to Peru] as an ordinary merchant steamship." Its commander, Captain Heusner, subsequently deterred the Chilean navy from bombarding Callao, Peru. After the war ended the ship limped home to Germany, never to see distant waters again.[73] The navy continued to maintain its "West American" station until 1885, but after the Saltpeter War only one ship at a time cruised the Pacific coast of South America.[74]

Though Germany soon would claim colonies of its own in Africa, the navy saw only limited duty in African waters. In March 1881, after local inhabitants looted a German ship stranded on the beach at Nanakru, Liberia, a landing party from the corvette *Vineta,* en route home from the Far East, recovered the lost cargo and destroyed a village in retaliation. The following year the corvette *Hertha,* also returning home from the East Asian station, responded to a similar incident on the coast of Dahomey but managed to settle it peacefully.[75] In the early 1880s, leading Hamburg merchants clamored for an aggressive colonial policy; among them, Adolph Woermann became a leading advocate of annexations in West Africa. After inheriting his family's Woermann Line in 1880, he increased its stake in the Hamburg–West African route by inaugurating regular steamer service to Cameroon. The imperialist camp included far fewer members from Bremen. Thanks to the North German Lloyd, the overseas trade of Germany's second-largest port remained tied to the Americas, especially the United States.[76] In any event, after the colonial annexations of 1884–85, individual ships cruising to or from other stations would no longer suffice to safeguard German interests in Africa. In the Pacific as well as in African waters, the new overseas empire would place unprecedented strains on the navy.

The End of the Stosch Era

After weathering so many political storms, Stosch left office over a dispute that in no way concerned the navy. In February 1883, during a Reichstag debate over a new military pension law, war minister Kameke agreed with opposition leaders seeking to eliminate a traditional tax exemption on the private income of officers. His rivals within the military hierarchy urged William I to fire Kameke; leading the campaign were General Emil von Albedyll, chief of the emperor's military cabinet, and General Count Alfred von Waldersee, Moltke's deputy (and eventual successor) in the general staff. Sensing that he had lost the confidence of the emperor, Kameke yielded without a fight. General Paul Bronsart von Schellendorf replaced him. The archconservative Bronsart did not oppose efforts by the military cabinet and general staff to become completely independent alongside the war ministry. The change did not enhance efficiency; in the future, the heads of the three agencies would bicker incessantly over their ill-defined powers and prerogatives.[77] Because the changes of 1883 further removed the military from constitutional accountability, Kameke's resignation has been characterized as "another victory for reactionary conservatism" in Germany.[78]

Stosch agreed with Kameke on the income tax question and also felt a general empathy toward him. In the past, Bismarck had scolded both of them for dealing with Reichstag deputies directly rather than through his office, as proper procedure dictated. After the *Grosser Kurfürst* disaster, Kameke had defended Stosch's efforts to purge his critics from the corps of sea officers; in contrast, Albedyll had opposed him, most notably in the case of Monts. Furthermore, Stosch could not envision working with Bronsart, a man ideologically far to his right, who privately had branded him a "republican." After Kameke was forced out, Stosch professed solidarity with him and submitted his own resignation.[79]

Stosch had submitted resignations before, and William I had never accepted them. This time Stosch cited his health, which at age sixty-five was starting to fail him. In a letter to Albedyll the same day, he outlined his political reasons for leaving. He defended Kameke and fired a last broadside at Bismarck, who "over the last few years has slowly robbed me of almost every prerogative of my office."[80] The emperor refused to accept the resignation, no doubt assuming that Stosch, as before, merely wanted a fresh vote of confidence. He assured the chief that "the results which you have achieved for my navy surpass by far my expectations." He promised Stosch as much leave time as he would need to recover his health.[81] This time, however, Stosch really wanted to go. In a second letter to William I, he emphasized his political principles rather than his health. Repeating his support for Kameke in the matter of the pension law, he criticized the government's rejection of the changes for the harm it did to "the better elements in the Reichstag." He defended the parliament as a unifying force in Germany, and observed that "the army and the Reichstag are the two strongest bulwarks against . . . revolutionary elements."[82] By putting the legislature on a par with the military in its importance to the stability of the regime, Stosch ensured that the emperor would finally accept his resignation. On 20 March his long tenure at the Admiralty officially ended.[83]

Through fiscal year 1882–83, the Reichstag had appropriated 212.2 million marks for Stosch's fleet plan of 1873. In nearly all categories, he had fulfilled or surpassed his construction goals. Counting warships still being built, the armored fleet consisted of thirteen battleships (seven "frigates" and six "corvettes") and thirteen gunboats. If not for the sinking of the *Grosser Kurfürst*, the number of battleships would have been the requisite fourteen. For the gunboats, the thirteen took the place of the seven monitors and two floating batteries proposed in 1873. In the unarmored fleet, most of Stosch's projections of 1873 (twenty corvettes, eight dispatch boats, eighteen gunboats) had been met. Eleven of the twelve wooden corvettes he inherited still were in service, while another fourteen iron-hulled corvettes had been built or were nearing completion. Only two small wooden-hulled screw gunboats were still in service in 1883, but Stosch had added eight larger gunboats, mostly of iron construction. Initially the navy classified the torpedo ships *Zieten*, *Blitz*, and *Pfeil* as dispatch boats, but at least for the latter pair, future duties would involve leading torpedo flotillas rather than serving as messengers. Stosch let other navies take the lead in developing torpedo technology and tactics; in 1879 he created a "Torpedo Engineer Corps," but the fleet of 1883 had only three useless torpedo boats, with another seven on order.[84] Dramatic expansion in the number of light vessels was just around the corner, however, as the influence of the French *Jeune École* prompted Germany, and most other naval powers, to build dozens of torpedo boats by the end of the 1880s.

· · ·

The sinking of the *Grosser Kurfürst* had touched off the most heated political debate in the history of the Imperial German navy, at least until the Tirpitz era. Afterward, a decade of lower appropriations reflected the public loss of confidence in the fleet. There would be no *Marinepolitik*, no long-range program promoted by a navy leader, until the late 1890s. With some justification Stosch could boast that he left the German navy stronger than any except the British and French, but the actual fighting value of the fleet remained in doubt. The armored vessels included the much maligned *Ausfallkorvetten* and coastal gunboats, along with battery frigates that were clearly obsolete. The unarmored fleet now had a core of iron-hulled corvettes to show the flag overseas, but many wooden-hulled screw steamers remained in service. To his credit, Stosch had decommissioned most of the sailing ships and paddle steamers, deeming them unfit even for training duty.

In materiel, as in personnel matters, Stosch never admitted failure. He refused to concede that some ship designs he supported had been ill conceived, but his posturing fooled no one. In an 1884 piece acknowledging the problems of the "sortie corvettes" and coastal gunboats, Freytag observed that "the retirement of General von Stosch cannot be dissociated from these repeated disappointments."[85] His successor, General Leo von Caprivi, inherited a mixed legacy and an office with more than its share of problems.

7

CAPRIVI

ike Albrecht von Stosch, Leo von Caprivi came to the post of chief of the Admiralty with the reputation of being a talented general with excellent administrative skills. In contrast to his predecessor, who faded from the limelight after leaving the Admiralty, Caprivi would go on to succeed Bismarck as German chancellor. Caprivi's brief term as head of the navy witnessed its substantial role in the annexation of the first German overseas colonies since the days of the Great Elector. He also faced the strategic and tactical chaos generated by the French *Jeune École,* and ordered the first operational planning after the conclusion of the Triple Alliance. Caprivi, like Stosch before him, also had to cope with life as a general assigned to command a navy whose officers were demoralized by the very fact that an outsider had been brought in to lead them.

A Tranquil Transition: From Stosch to Caprivi (1883–1884)

Caprivi, fifty-two at the time of his appointment, had entered the Prussian army in 1849. Rising through the officer corps, he served as a major in the general staff in 1866 and as chief of staff of the X Corps in the war against France. During the years Stosch led the Admiralty, Caprivi served first as a section head in the war ministry, then as a brigade and division commander.[1] The ideal chief of the Admiralty would have had the skills of both an admiral and a politician. Caprivi was not an admiral and never pretended to be one; furthermore, he lacked basic political skills. Coming after the arrogant, politically ambitious Stosch, the modest and remarkably apolitical Caprivi should have been welcomed as a breath of fresh air. Ironically, he would be just as unpopular with navy officers and never feel comfortable as their commander.[2] In his relationship with the officer corps, Caprivi suffered not so much from his army background but from the fact that, again, the emperor and army leaders had concluded that the navy needed a general at the helm. In some cases, sea officers who had acquiesced in the appointment of Stosch balked at serving under yet another general. Captain Paschen, for the most part a supporter of Stosch, called Caprivi's appointment a "hard blow" for the officer corps.[3]

But the navy could present no plausible alternative of its own. Even in the wake of the *Grosser Kurfürst* disaster, Stosch continued to do everything possible to secure Batsch's position as heir apparent. Batsch had served in all of the most prominent positions both in Berlin and on the coast: chief of staff, director of the Admiralty, chief of the North Sea station, and, since 1881, chief of the Baltic station. The forced retirements of Henk and Werner made him the senior sea officer under Stosch, and after his most recent promotion, in 1880, also the only vice admiral. Despite Bismarck's bitter rivalry with Stosch, the chancellor considered Batsch the logical choice for chief of the Admiralty, and Batsch himself expected to receive the post. But the emperor and military leaders could not overlook the *Grosser Kurfürst* disaster and its aftermath. Batsch's conviction by two of three courts-martial, and the brief term he had served in prison, made his appointment out of the question. Thanks to Stosch's persistent effort to eliminate all of Batsch's competitors, William I had to give the job to a general.[4]

Caprivi had almost two years less service as a lieutenant general than Batsch had in the equivalent rank of vice admiral, but upon giving Caprivi the Admiralty post, William I backdated his seniority in rank to 2 February 1880, one day before Batsch became vice admiral. The snub ensured that Batsch would not try to stay on, as Jachmann had after Stosch became chief. He retired in July 1883, along with his friend Berger, the senior rear admiral. Their departure left Rear Admiral Livonius, the Admiralty director, as ranking sea officer, but he, too, retired by the end of the year. Monts and Wickede, next in seniority, succeeded Berger and Batsch as chiefs of the North Sea and Baltic stations. Baron von der Goltz, one of six captains promoted to rear admiral during 1883, succeeded Livonius.[5]

Unlike Stosch, Caprivi never received an admiral's rank or wore a navy uniform, choosing instead to remain a soldier in form and appearance. While the corps of sea officers, in particular the junior officers, found it disheartening to look up to a Prussian general as their commander, the fact

Leo von Caprivi *Historische Sammlung
der Marineschule Mürwik*

that Caprivi did not pretend to be a navy man actually helped ease his relations with senior officers. Whereas Stosch felt that he could learn nothing
from his admirals, Caprivi went to the opposite extreme of actively seeking
their opinions.[6] The new chief could be remarkably inconsistent in his
openness, but even when an officer's actions offended him, he did not hold
a grudge. For example, in October 1883, when Captain Alfred Stenzel, director of the imperial shipyard in Wilhelmshaven, suggested that he convene an Admiralty Council, he considered it an act bordering on insubordination; nevertheless, when he convened an Admiralty Council in
January 1884, he invited Stenzel and three other captains to participate
along with Rear Admirals Monts, Wickede, Louis von Blanc, and Eduard
Knorr.[7] Such moves reflected the fact that Caprivi had more confidence in
his officers than Stosch, who had waited seven years to convene his first
Admiralty Council, and then never called another. By the end of his tenure,
Caprivi would consider the officer corps the navy's greatest asset.[8]

Under Caprivi, the corps increased its social prestige and educational
standards. Whereas just over one-sixth of the cadets in the eleven "crews"
to enter under Stosch held noble titles, for the six to enter under Caprivi
(1883 through 1888) the figure topped one-quarter. Most were still from the
lowest nobility, but the average entering class under Caprivi included more
than twice as many barons and counts than the average class under
Stosch.[9] At the same time, the number of new cadets holding the *Abitur*

continued to rise, to a record fifteen in 1883. Rear Admiral Baron von Reibnitz (the first sea officer to direct the Navy School, in the years 1881–86) expressed dismay over the fact that half were older than the official *Abitur* age
limit of nineteen, but Caprivi ultimately increased the age limit for all entering cadets.[10] Unlike Stosch, he took no deliberate steps to enhance the
exclusivity of the corps; in contrast, he led the way in reducing the financial
burdens on an officer's career. In January 1884 he ordered cuts in the list of
clothing and personal items required of every cadet; the number of white
dress shirts, for example, fell from eighteen to only twelve. Supporters of
the initiative included Monts—a count and the son of a Prussian general—
who predicted that a reduction in the "*Kostspieligkeit*" of a sea officer's career "would increase the cohort of good and suitable officer aspirants."[11]

Because Caprivi's appointment came shortly after the Reichstag had
passed the budget for 1883–84, he did not have to face the politicians until
March 1884, when they debated the 1884–85 estimates. In contrast to the
stormy receptions Stosch received during his last years in office, support
for the new chief and the navy echoed from all quarters. Sympathetic
speakers included Progressive leaders Rickert of Danzig and Hänel of Kiel,
and the aging H. H. Meier of Bremen from the National Liberals.[12] Caprivi
was just as ill at ease with politicians as with admirals; nevertheless, he
managed to get off to a tranquil start. It helped matters considerably that
Caprivi presented the Reichstag with no expensive grand designs. He announced the fulfillment of Stosch's fleet plan of 1873 and made known his
intention to focus on short-term goals rather than propose another long-
term plan. From the start, Caprivi also benefited from Bismarck's decision
that Germany should claim overseas colonies, a quest in which the navy
would play a central role. The chancellor reversed his anticolonial position
in the spring of 1884, ensuring that the German colonial lobby would support the new chief of the Admiralty at budget time.

Establishing the Colonial Empire (1884–1888)

The popularity of Bismarck's anticolonial stance had been waning ever
since the Franco-Prussian War, and in the mid-1880s many Germans hailed
his conversion to the colonial cause. The protracted depression that set in
after 1873 shook Europe's faith in free trade, and almost forty years after the
death of Friedrich List, the neomercantilist philosophy of trade again was
in vogue. The argument that colonies were needed, both as secure sources
of raw materials and as markets for goods, gained general acceptance. List's
appeal for settler colonies likewise experienced a revival, joining the eco-

nomic argument to bolster the overall case. Patriotic Germans considered it a national disgrace that the wave of emigration then under way took so many of their countrymen to places where they would eventually lose their German identity. Most went to the United States, where, by 1890, some 2.8 million people—almost 5 percent of the population—were German-born.[13] In Germany, as in other countries, there was also the mixture of humanitarian, religious, and racist motives of the "white man's burden," espoused by the most vocal proponents of the new imperialism. These included Friedrich Fabri, a publicist with roots in the evangelical missionary camp who later founded the Allgemeiner Deutscher Verband, forerunner of the Pan-German League. Among academicians, colonialists included the historian Leopold von Ranke, author in 1879 of an appeal for German colonies in Africa.[14]

The first sign of Bismarck's new colonial policy came in April 1884, when he agreed to declare a German protectorate in Southwest Africa. Adolf Lüderitz of Bremen had purchased land between the Orange River and Portuguese Angola from a local chief for two hundred rifles and two thousand marks. He then founded a trading post at Angra Pequeña, on the bay that ultimately bore his name. In June 1884 Bismarck ordered the corvette *Elisabeth* to the waters off Lüderitz's new lands; two months later the corvette *Leipzig* and gunboat *Wolf* joined it in a cruise along the coast, formally staking Germany's claim to the territory.[15] Meanwhile, Bismarck named colonial enthusiast Gustav Nachtigal imperial commissioner for West Africa, with broad powers to promote and protect German interests. Backed by the gunboat *Möve*, Nachtigal established a protectorate in Togo in July 1884, and in Cameroon shortly thereafter.[16]

That autumn, Rear Admiral Knorr arrived in West African waters with the corvettes *Bismarck, Gneisenau, Olga,* and *Ariadne* for a show of force designed to impress both Europeans and Africans who might oppose German ambitions.[17] From the start, the navy did not hesitate to destroy villages and inflict heavy African casualties in the quest to enforce German rule. When the pro-German king of Cameroon was threatened by his own subjects in December 1884, Knorr sent a landing party ashore to crush the revolt. In an operation typical of the times, the contingent of 350 men routed thousands of African warriors, in the process suffering casualties of only 1 dead and 8 wounded. Lieutenant Reinhard Scheer, later commander of the High Seas Fleet during World War I, distinguished himself in leading the first landing party from the *Bismarck*.[18]

During 1885 Germany's African interests focused on the east coast of the continent, where historian and colonialist Carl Peters had laid the ground-work for empire the previous autumn. Peters negotiated with local rulers on behalf of his own colonial society and purchased land for German set-tlers between the Pangani and Kingani Rivers. In February 1885, upon re-turning to Germany, he received sweeping powers to administer a colony vaguely defined as "west of the lands of the sultan of Zanzibar."[19] The Ger-mans traditionally enjoyed good relations with Zanzibar; as early as 1859 the Hanseatic cities had concluded a trade treaty with the sultanate, and within fifteen years Germany's trade there outpaced Britain's by three to one.[20] But Zanzibar claimed the East African hinterland as its own, and in 1885 Sultan Said Bargasch deployed troops along the coast to block the German occupation. Bismarck promptly sent Karl Paschen to Zanzibar with the corvettes *Prinz Adalbert, Stosch, Gneisenau,* and *Elisabeth* for a demonstration. Knorr subsequently reinforced him with the *Bismarck* and the gunboats *Möve* and *Hyäne.* At the end of 1885 the sultan recognized the German protectorate over East Africa, including the port of Dar es Salaam. The longest, largest overseas demonstration yet undertaken by the German navy finally ended in January 1886, after costing 1.6 million marks.[21]

Caprivi did not intend to maintain so many ships in African waters on a regular basis. In 1885 he formally established stations for East and West Af-rica, each covered by two gunboats, to be reinforced during times of crisis by larger warships. It became customary to make African waters the last station for veteran gunboats; they remained on duty as long as they re-mained seaworthy and returned home only to be scrapped.[22] In January 1886 Caprivi extended this station concept worldwide, at the same time implementing the "flying squadron" proposal Stosch and Henk had re-jected fourteen years earlier. Henceforth, stations had fewer warships but could be reinforced on short notice by an overseas cruiser squadron. Ad hoc deployments and ridiculously long zigzag cruises, such as the five-and-a-half-year circumnavigation by the 490-ton gunboat *Hyäne* in 1882–87, became a thing of the past. The initial cruiser squadron consisted of ships already at sea for the African activities of 1885, including the *Bismarck* with Rear Admiral Knorr, who became the first commander. The utility of the force became clear later in 1886. Knorr was cruising in the Pacific when he learned that an agent of Carl Peters's society, Karl Jühlke, had been mur-dered. The flagship *Bismarck,* with the corvettes *Olga, Sophie,* and *Carola,* raced back to East Africa and anchored at Zanzibar until the sultan paid reparations.[23]

Coinciding with the annexation of its first African colonies, Germany also established a colonial presence in the Pacific Ocean. In November 1884 the corvette *Elisabeth* and gunboat *Hyäne* enforced a German claim to the islands subsequently known as the Bismarck Archipelago. Later that month, landing parties from the *Hyäne* and the corvette *Sophie* extended German sovereignty to the adjacent mainland of northeastern New Guinea, which they claimed as "Kaiser Wilhelmsland."[24] The British responded promptly, dispatching a warship to Port Moresby to claim southeastern New Guinea. Early in 1885, fears that Britain would dispute the German claims prompted Berlin to order Paschen, then in Hong Kong with the *Stosch*, to proceed to the Australian station and defend the New Guinea colony. Paschen received the corvette *Marie* and gunboat *Hyäne* as reinforcement but received a friendly reception when visiting Australian ports. He reported no trace of Anglo-Australian resolve to challenge the German annexations.[25]

In 1885 a landing party from a German gunboat raised the flag on the island of Yap, in an attempt to claim the Carolines. Spain, which had claimed the islands for centuries, protested the move. The Spanish press fanned anti-German opinion at home, and thirty thousand Spaniards attended a protest rally in Madrid that degenerated into a mob action against the German embassy. Bismarck agreed to papal arbitration to resolve the crisis. Spain retained sovereignty over the Carolines but granted Germany a coaling station and trading rights. Germany purchased the islands in 1899.[26] The Marshall Islands came under German rule in October 1885, when the king of Jaluit concluded a treaty with Captain Fritz Rötger of the gunboat *Nautilus,* placing his archipelago under German protection. In April 1886 an Anglo-German treaty provided for the Solomon Islands to be annexed to German New Guinea; two years later Germany claimed the island of Nauru, south of the Marshalls and west of the Gilberts.[27] From the Marshalls the Germans secured a lucrative source of copra, while Nauru had valuable deposits of phosphate. The Bismarck Archipelago and the Solomons provided labor for the plantations of Samoa.[28] In 1886 Captain Count Friedrich von Baudissin took the gunboat *Albatross* on the first of many punitive expeditions against coastal villages in New Guinea, defending the interests of the Berlin-based Neuguinea Compagnie.[29]

The new colonial ventures in the western Pacific paled in comparison to the German stake in Samoa, where the ongoing competition with Britain and the United States continued to preoccupy the navy. In November 1884 the presence of the corvette *Marie* and gunboat *Albatross* enabled agents of the Deutsche Handels- und Plantagen-Gesellschaft der Südsee (DHPG) to force the king of Samoa to give their company control over his treasury and police force.[30] Aggressive consular personnel, backing German merchants, gave Bismarck constant headaches; wary of provoking the British and Americans, he refused to sanction their actions. Navy captains were often caught in the middle, because a warship anchored offshore had to support a German consul who claimed to be in distress. After the *Marie* departed, the Samoan king appealed for British help, and the *Albatross* alone did not suffice to coerce him back into the German camp. In April 1886 Knorr arrived with the four corvettes of the new cruiser squadron, but as soon as these ships departed a maverick U.S. consul in Samoa proclaimed an American protectorate. The U.S. government disavowed the move, but German-American mistrust grew.[31] In the summer of 1887 the cruiser squadron, now under Captain Eduard Heusner, returned to Samoa for an extensive stay. In August the four corvettes joined the gunboat *Adler* of the Australian station in a punitive expedition. A landing party of seven hundred helped install a pro-German king.[32] Backed by the navy, DHPG agents controlled Samoa for the following year. By the summer of 1888 the squadron had moved on, leaving only the *Adler* to defend German interests.[33] The next crisis over Samoa would come with William II reigning in Berlin and Caprivi no longer at the Admiralty.

Leading German shipping companies expected a boom to follow the establishment of the colonial empire in the Pacific. In 1885 the North German Lloyd accepted a postal subsidy to open new lines to East Asia and Australia. The former route included stops at Colombo (Ceylon), Singapore, Hong Kong, and Shanghai; the latter, at Adelaide, Melbourne, and Sydney. The expansion put the Bremen firm in direct competition with two Hamburg-based firms, the Kingsin Line (the Deutsche Dampfschiffs-Reederei) in East Asian trade and the Sloman Line in Australian waters. The Lloyd added connecting service from Hong Kong to Nagasaki and Yokohama, and from Sydney to Tonga and Samoa.[34] The Lloyd's expansion opened new markets for Bremen, which traditionally had focused on trade with the Americas. Yet, contrary to expectations, in the late 1880s German business in the Pacific was mediocre at best. In 1888 the oldest surviving German trading company in Polynesia, Ruge & Company, went bankrupt and liquidated its assets in Samoa and Tonga.[35] The ongoing chaos in the Samoan group placed all German interests there at great risk, and the Lloyd's line to Tonga and Samoa lost money from the start. It would be eliminated in 1893 in favor of a new branch from Singapore to New Guinea.[36]

All together, in 1884 nine of seventeen overseas cruisers served in the Far East and South Pacific, and in 1885, seven of fourteen. With the creation of the new cruiser squadron in 1886, the primacy of the East Asian station ended; a decade would pass before Germany again deployed so many warships in the Far East. Besides the vessels in Knorr's force, in 1886 the navy maintained two ships on each of five stations: the East Asian, Australian, "East American" (western Atlantic and Caribbean), East African, and West African. In 1887, for the second year in a row, the East Asian and Australian stations accounted for just four of thirteen overseas cruisers; in 1888, five of fifteen.[37]

Whereas Stosch had argued with Bismarck over matters such as when ships were to be sent where and on whose orders, Caprivi focused on the sheer number of ships required for overseas stations and the share of the navy's manpower they consumed. During the colonial annexations of 1884 Caprivi had observed that such missions left "the best part of our personnel" occupied by essentially nonmilitary service.[38] He also felt a distinct discomfort with the navy's involvement in skirmishes against Africans and Pacific islanders; in January 1885, shortly after the first African colonies were claimed, he even questioned the constitutionality of such operations, asking if the emperor could legally "enter into a state of warfare against Blacks (*gegen Schwarze*)" without the approval of the Bundesrat.[39] The cruises provided years of experience on the high seas for officers and seamen, and the claiming of colonies brought many of them under fire for the only time in their careers, but Caprivi lamented that overseas duty on lightly armed, fully-rigged vessels did little to prepare personnel for wartime service in a modern battle fleet. As a navy leader he served, rather than shaped, Germany's stumbling debut as a world power. There was no grand design behind it, no *Weltpolitik*, and it certainly did not occur on the navy's terms.

Germany and the *Jeune École*: Continuity, Confusion, and Change

During his first year at the Admiralty, Caprivi became convinced that Germany must take a cautious attitude toward naval construction. With the concepts of the *Jeune École* challenging the conventional wisdom of naval strategy, promoting cruiser warfare and torpedo boats over the armored battle fleet, he hesitated to commit the navy to either the old path or the new. Sitting squarely on the fence, Caprivi made vague pledges to strengthen the battle fleet, along with more specific proposals to build torpedo boats. After reviewing the conclusions of the Admiralty Council of

January 1884, he opted not to develop a capacity for high seas cruiser warfare; in case of war such a strategy would harm neither of Germany's most likely adversaries, Russia and France, sufficiently to justify the construction of the necessary cruisers.[40] With the political-economic side of navalist thinking in its infancy, most pro-navy politicians did not yet view naval expenditure as a source of employment and income for their constituents. In the prevailing climate, less expensive proposals were much easier to support. Thus, the navy's friends in the Reichstag hoped that the light unarmored craft central to the *Jeune École* strategy would spell the end of expensive battleship projects. Almost unanimously, they hailed the torpedo as a panacea and applauded Caprivi's pledge to expand the torpedo arm.[41]

The "young school" of naval strategy that emerged in France during the 1880s ultimately caused a philosophical schism within every navy, wreaking havoc with fleet plans and construction programs. Admiral Hyacinthe-Laurent-Théophile Aube, the founding father of the *Jeune École,* actually belonged to the older generation; indeed, he was five years older than Caprivi. Almost forty years of service on overseas stations left Aube with a strategic outlook that focused on the defense of worldwide interests and, in wartime, a *guerre de course* attacking enemy commerce.[42] Aube took a dim view of ironclads from the time of their introduction.[43] His "discovery" of the torpedo boat in 1883, upon returning to home waters, confirmed his view that large battleships were worthless. That same year he invited journalist Gabriel Charmes to observe maneuvers with the French Mediterranean fleet. During the exercises two 46-ton torpedo boats rode out a heavy storm better than some of the larger vessels, prompting Charmes, as Aube's mouthpiece, to write several articles arguing that torpedo boats could be used as autonomous seagoing warships within a *guerre de course* strategy.[44] According to Aube and Charmes, torpedo boats would join cruisers in a campaign of commerce raiding to cripple an enemy's economy. The new strategic school of thought quickly gained the support of younger French officers, and of all those who saw Britain as their country's most likely enemy. Aube and the *Jeune École* felt the perfection of the torpedo neutralized Britain's lead over France in battleships. They were also aware of the traditional British faith in a seagoing deterrent and disinclination to invest in coastal defenses. Surprise torpedo attacks on ports and indiscriminate shelling of the enemy coastline thus found their place in Aube's strategy, alongside commerce raiding.[45]

In the area of coastal defense, Aube ironically copied freely from Stosch's strategies. Apparently unaware of the problems that the German "sortie corvettes" and small armored gunboats experienced after entering service, Aube advocated the construction of ironclads of these types rather than larger battleships. Aube's equivalents of the *Ausfallkorvetten,* dispersed in fortified coastal bases, were to conduct sorties to break an enemy blockade. Along with armored gunboats, they would prevent or delay enemy attempts to land troops on the coast. As in Germany, telegraph and semaphore stations would link the naval bases and provide an early warning network for the army inland. But the *Jeune École* also maintained that such a coastal defense could be a springboard for offensive operations. The telegraph would work against a blockading fleet, facilitating coordinated feints and breakouts from many ports that would confuse blockaders and enable commerce-raiding cruisers to slip out to open sea. Aube believed that whole squadrons of armored "sortie corvettes" could break out in the same manner, rendezvous at sea, and enjoy temporary superiority over the enemy fleet.[46] This assumed that the "sortie corvettes" would be able to operate on the high seas and fight on equal terms with enemy battleships, tasks few German navy men believed Stosch's *Ausfallkorvetten* could perform.

For a majority of Aube's critics, the most controversial aspect of the *Jeune École* strategy was the appeal for ruthless commerce raiding, ultimately for an unrestricted torpedo-boat warfare against all enemy shipping. Aube declared that "war is the negation of law. . . . Everything is therefore not only permissible but legitimate against the enemy."[47] In France, the heyday of the *Jeune École* came in 1886 and 1887, when Aube served as navy minister. Despite protests over the immorality of the strategy, his ideas had a profound and immediate effect on all navies. Shipyards came alive with the construction of torpedo boats, and doubts about the battleship could be heard from every corner. In June 1886, during a debate in Britain over the funding of the 12,000-ton *Nile* and *Trafalgar,* Lord Northbrook, the First Lord of the Admiralty, conceded that these battleships probably would be the last of their size ever added to any navy.[48] Though Caprivi rejected the *Jeune École*'s cruiser warfare doctrines as irrelevant to the German strategic situation, he endorsed Aube's view of the torpedo as the decisive factor in future naval warfare, a weapon that held special promise for defense against the attacking fleet of a superior enemy. As a result, Caprivi proceeded with great energy in adding torpedo boats to the fleet, while adopting a wait-and-see attitude regarding the construction of larger warships.[49]

Under Caprivi, the navy's annual maneuvers only gradually came to reflect the growing importance of the torpedo arm. He had no voice in structuring the exercises of 1883, which began just two months after his appointment to the Admiralty; nevertheless, he spent several days at sea and cruised from Wilhelmshaven to Kiel with the squadron, which Wickede commanded for the fourth summer in a row. Activities centered around the battleships *Friedrich Carl, Kronprinz, Deutschland,* and *Kaiser.* The latter pair, in service for the first time in six years, experienced engine trouble; Wickede also complained about the fitness of his personnel, citing the "many people sick with syphilis" aboard his ships. A confused itinerary took the squadron from the North Sea to the Baltic, then back to the North Sea, before finishing in Kiel. Four torpedo boats accompanied the battleships for the summer, but they used the Eider Canal rather than the Kattegat and Skagerrak when passing from one sea to the other. The biggest innovation in 1883 was a decision not to equip the battleships with sails; in previous summers the navy had wasted much time testing the sailing capabilities of the fully-rigged ironclads. Simulations included a landing on the Mecklenburg coast and a "battle" off Zoppot, near Danzig.[50]

The maneuvers of 1884 reflected Caprivi's desire to test the armored warships as well as the torpedo boats. The exercises were the first to feature a homogeneous squadron of four armored sister ships: the controversial "sortie corvettes." The newest of them, the *Baden,* served as flagship of the rehabilitated Rear Admiral Monts, commander of the maneuvers. The *Baden* just received its commission the previous autumn, but the others had already spent years in reserve: the *Sachsen* entered service in 1878 but had been activated only for a problem-plagued stint in the squadron of 1880, and the *Bayern* and *Württemberg,* commissioned in 1881, had yet to see active duty. The much maligned ships were accompanied by four of the equally controversial 1,100-ton armored gunboats, commissioned late in the Stosch era but making their first appearance with the fleet. A division of six new torpedo boats, under the command of Captain Tirpitz, also participated. The three components operated separately in the Baltic until late June, when they joined other warships off Zoppot for a week of combined maneuvers. In this largest collection ever of German warships, the "sortie corvettes" were designated the I Division, the armored gunboats the II Division, and the torpedo boats the V Division. The III Division (a "steam corvette division") included the iron-hulled *Sophie,* the old wooden *Nymphe,* and the armored *Hansa;* the IV Division (the "sailing ship division") included the old frigate *Niobe* and the brigs *Undine* and *Rover.* The marines of the *Seebataillon* were also involved, defending the coast against simulated landings. Before disbanding the fleet, Caprivi treated Prince Henry and Prince William to a review. Years later, William II recalled how impressed he had been to see this display of "every vessel in the service down to the training brig." Days after witnessing the spectacle, he named his newborn third son Adalbert, in honor of the late prince-admiral.[51]

The 1885 maneuvers brought further changes. The "sortie corvette" *Bayern* joined the old armored frigate *Friedrich Carl* and the casemate corvette *Hansa* in an armored division, while the dispatch boat *Pfeil* joined the *Stein, Olga,* and *Sophie*—corvettes normally used for overseas missions— in an unarmored division. A torpedo flotilla, under the command of Tirpitz, included a total of fifteen torpedo boats with the dispatch boat *Blitz* and armored gunboat *Brummer* serving as division leaders. Rear Admiral Blanc commanded the armored division and the overall exercises. As in 1884, the divisions first cruised separately; in June, Blanc took the armored warships from Kiel to Ålesund, Norway, before returning to the Baltic. Inaugurating a practice followed in subsequent years, the divisions combined only for the months of August and September, for exercises that the navy called "autumn maneuvers" even though they usually ended around the first day of autumn. Owing to the patchwork nature of the armored squadron of 1885 and the dubious fighting value of the unarmored cor-

Torpedo boat with *Sachsen* and rigged warships in background
Naval Historical Center, Basic Collection

vettes, attentions focused on Tirpitz's torpedo boats. After the demobilization, the *Stein* and *Sophie* remained on active duty and were joined by the corvettes *Moltke* and *Ariadne* in a training squadron (*Schulgeschwader*) for the winter months. Under the command of Captain Stenzel, between October 1885 and March 1886 the ships visited Madeira, the Cape Verde Islands, the West Indies, and Venezuela before returning home via the Azores. In 1886 and subsequent years, the ships of the training squadron served as a division of the fleet for summer and autumn maneuvers. On their winter cruises with cadets, apprentice seamen, and four-year volunteers, they filled the former roles of the *Niobe* and the old training brigs, which long ago outlived their usefulness.[52]

The armored division (I Division) for 1886 included the new casemate ship *Oldenburg* along with the "sortie corvettes" *Baden, Württemberg,* and *Sachsen.* While engine troubles plagued the latter two ships, the new vessel performed well. The *Hansa,* which spent the winter months as harbor watch at Kiel, joined the unarmored corvettes of the training squadron in July for a Baltic cruise, then stayed with them in the II Division for autumn maneuvers. Tirpitz headed a torpedo flotilla including the *Blitz, Brummer,* and thirteen torpedo boats, which exercised on its own from March through July before joining maneuvers as the III Division. The main exercise simulated a blockade of the entire coast of East Prussia. Additional older and smaller warships were activated to fill the roles of blockade runners. Wickede, now a vice admiral, commanded maneuvers for the last time; he would retire in the spring of 1887. An opponent of the *Jeune École* and initially skeptical of the utility of torpedo boats, Wickede joined Caprivi in praising their performance in 1886. Besides the extensive operations in the Baltic, the navy mobilized four of its small armored gunboats (designated the "reserve division" of the North Sea) at Wilhelmshaven for a month of maneuvers. In the winter of 1886–87 the training squadron again included four unarmored corvettes. They cruised to the West Indies, visiting Lisbon en route to the Caribbean and British ports on the way home.[53]

While the exercises of the mid-1880s never included more than fifteen torpedo boats at a time, the navy purchased dozens of them, most of which joined the inactive reserve after their initial sea trials. The seven boats ordered by Stosch from A.G. Weser in Bremen entered service in 1883; Caprivi ordered another sixty-five, all of which were commissioned by 1888. Because of their size (none of the various designs displaced more than 150 tons) the boats were inexpensive and could be built in a matter of months. Those joining the fleet in 1884 included another six from A.G. Weser, ten from A.G. Vulcan of Stettin, six from Schichau of Elbing, two imported from Thornycroft of Britain, and one from Yarrow of Britain. In September 1884, after that year's maneuvers, German torpedo boats rode out a heavy storm in the North Sea. Just as a similar experience had fired the imagination of Aube and Charmes during the French maneuvers of the previous summer, on this occasion the durability of the boats impressed Tirpitz. They happened to be the Schichau boats, which in many ways (including their speed of up to twenty-three knots) were superior to the others. From 1885 onward the navy patronized Schichau almost exclusively; in all, forty-two of the sixty-five torpedo boats built under Caprivi came from the Elbing firm. In 1887 Schichau received a contract for six larger torpedo boats, displacing from 250 to 400 tons, to serve as torpedo division leaders. Meanwhile, in 1884 the navy decommissioned the original six torpedo boats built in 1872 under Stosch.[54]

In 1886 Caprivi established the Torpedo Inspection in Kiel, with Tirpitz as its head. The following year he created two torpedo divisions, one based in Kiel, the other in Wilhelmshaven. At a time when the future of the battleship appeared in doubt, the torpedo service attracted the brightest junior officers in the German navy and even developed a measure of prestige. In 1887, after accelerated promotions made him a captain (*Korvettenkapitän*) at the age of twenty-five, Prince Henry chose the First Torpedo Division as his initial command assignment.[55] In a partial reversal of the trend toward greater employment of private industry, under Caprivi the navy established its own torpedo factory, at Friedrichsort near Kiel, thus freeing the service from dependence upon Whitehead or its German licensee, Schwartzkopf of Berlin.[56]

During 1886 Caprivi's growing concern over the expansion of the Russian Baltic fleet prompted him to sound out Bismarck regarding possible German responses. Though Russia and France were not yet allies, Bismarck, like Caprivi, assumed that France would intervene in any future German-Russian war, and agreed that Germany should measure its defensive needs, naval as well as military, against the strength of France and Russia.[57] Strategic considerations supported further naval expansion, and Bismarck expressed sympathy for the cause, but the systematic buildup initiated by Tirpitz eleven years later had no chance of starting here because the chief of the Admiralty himself rejected the idea. As a soldier, Caprivi could not support a program that would drain resources away from the army, the key to Germany's fate in wartime. His view of the division of German resources was reflected in the often-cited remark he made after leaving the Admiralty: that the question should be one of "how small our fleet can be, not how large."[58]

Attentions thus focused not on creating a larger fleet but on improving the smaller navy's chances against larger, potential rivals, especially the Franco-Russian combination Caprivi dreaded. In 1883 he revived a plan for a canal across Holstein on the Kiel-Rendsburg-Brunsbüttel route; it gained Reichstag approval in 1886.[59] Caprivi acknowledged the need for new armored warships but wanted to avoid the mistakes of Stosch's designs. Unlike the armored gunboats, they should have armor and armament heavy enough to undertake offensive operations against larger enemy battleships; unlike the "sortie corvettes," they should be sufficiently seaworthy to operate in the North Sea in any season or on occasional overseas missions.[60] The ships Caprivi proposed reflected these concerns. Eventually classified as "fourth-class armored ships," they could be described either as miniature battleships, painfully slow armored cruisers, or very large armored gunboats. The 3,500-ton design carried three 9.4-inch Krupp guns, two paired in a forward turret and one aft in a turret of its own. The gun mountings, also from Krupp, were the first to turn on ball bearings rather than wheels. The ships were much smaller and less heavily armed than the most recent German battleships, the "sortie corvettes" of the *Sachsen* class (7,600 tons, six 10.25-inch guns) and the casemate ship *Oldenburg* (5,200 tons, eight 9.4-inch guns), but with a top speed of fourteen knots they were just as slow. Caprivi requested ten of these ships, the first of which would be included in the budget for the 1887–88 fiscal year.[61] The Germaniawerft of Kiel (the former Norddeutsche Werft) received the contract for the *Siegfried*, the first vessel of the program.[62] The onset of construction on the *Siegfried*, in 1888, ended a hiatus in the armored warship program; from 1868 until A.G. Vulcan of Stettin launched the *Oldenburg* at the end of 1884, the navy always had at least one battleship under construction.

For a shipbuilding industry that had grown to depend upon the navy for its most lucrative contracts, the appointment of Caprivi and the popularity of the *Jeune École* had been nothing short of disastrous. By 1884 the private shipyards of Germany employed only 13,000 workers, down sharply from 24,500 the previous year. For shipyard workers, the government offered no better prospects than the private sector. The imperial shipyard in Kiel, which had a payroll of 3,000 men while building two of Stosch's four *Ausfallkorvetten,* by 1884 employed 1,600.[63] The prospect of new armored warship contracts, even for vessels as small as the *Siegfried*s, encouraged the shipbuilders as well as related industries whose goodwill the navy had largely lost since Stosch's departure. The *Oldenburg* had been the first battleship built entirely of German steel. Like the tiny *Brummer* and *Bremse,* it was plated with Dillinger compound armor. After its launching, the *Siegfried* also received Dillinger compound plates. In 1887, the year of Alfred Krupp's death, his firm conducted tests of its own compound armor, but the navy would not encourage the Krupp works to compete for armor contracts until after the accession of William II.[64]

In the area of unarmored warships, the German navy of the 1880s, like every other fleet, had a motley collection of old and newer cruisers, with the only common characteristic being that all were unarmored and lightly armed, with very little fighting value. Caprivi, however, believed that all warships should be genuine warships. He called for all new German cruisers—even those destined for overseas stations—to be designed with consideration for their utility in wartime.[65] Nevertheless, the cruisers commissioned under Caprivi were a mixture of old and new designs. The imperial shipyards completed six fully-rigged vessels of iron construction, three of which had been laid down under Stosch: the 2,400-ton corvettes *Alexandrine* (built in Kiel in 1881–86) and *Arcona* (Danzig, 1881–86); the 880-ton gunboat *Adler* (Kiel, 1882–84); the 3,300-ton corvette *Charlotte* (Wilhelmshaven, 1883–86); the 1,800-ton corvette *Nixe* (Danzig, 1883–86); and the 580-ton gunboat *Eber* (Kiel, 1886–87). Meanwhile, private shipyards secured contracts for five unrigged steel cruisers of modern design. A.G. Vulcan of Stettin built the 4,300-ton *Irene* in 1886–88; A.G. Weser of Bremen constructed the 1,200-ton vessels *Wacht* in 1886–88 and *Jagd* in 1887–89; and the Germaniawerft of Kiel built the 2,000-ton *Greif* in 1885–87 and the *Irene*'s 4,300-ton sister *Prinzess Wilhelm* in 1886–89. All five were capable of at least eighteen knots, in the same league with the speed of the newest ocean liners of the time. Except for the *Greif,* all had armored decks, armored conning towers, and torpedo tubes. Designers gave the *Irene* and *Prinzess Wilhelm* fourteen 5.9-inch guns, further enhancing their fighting capabilities. The last cruisers laid down under Caprivi, the 1,100-ton *Schwalbe* and *Sperber,* were of composite steel-and-wood construction. Designed for overseas service, they carried nominal rigging. The imperial shipyard in Wilhelmshaven built both vessels, the *Schwalbe* in 1887–88 and *Sperber* in 1888–89.[66]

Under Caprivi the navy also reclassified all of its cruisers, mixing old and new labels. The larger fully-rigged corvettes became "cruiser-frigates (*Kreuzerfregatten*)." These included the 4,000-ton *Leipzig* and *Prinz Adalbert,* the 2,900-ton *Bismarck* and its five sister ships, and the new *Charlotte.*

Siegfried-class battleship, in early 1890s   *Naval Historical Center, Basic Collection*

Meanwhile, the new *Alexandrine* and *Arcona* and all smaller corvettes became "cruiser-corvettes (*Kreuzerkorvetten*)." The same labels were given rather arbitrarily to the unrigged steel cruisers that joined the fleet under Caprivi, generating considerable confusion. For example, the new *Irene* and *Prinzess Wilhelm* were called "cruiser-corvettes" even though they were larger than all of the "cruiser-frigates." Among the remaining unarmored vessels, the nominally-rigged light cruisers *Schwalbe* and *Sperber*, along with the smaller, fully-rigged gunboats *Habicht*, *Möve*, and *Adler*, were simply designated "cruisers," while the designation "gunboat" was reserved for gunboats of less than 800 tons. The dispatch boats (*Avisos*) included a variety of vessels ranging from the old yacht *Grille* to the new light cruisers *Greif*, *Wacht*, and *Jagd*.[67]

The addition of so many new cruisers enabled Caprivi to retire five of the eleven wooden-hulled screw corvettes he inherited from Stosch.[68] A sixth corvette, the *Augusta*, sank in June 1885 in a storm in the Gulf of Aden, between the Red Sea and the Indian Ocean, while en route to the Australian station. Other than the sinking of the *Grosser Kurfürst*, it was the greatest peacetime disaster in German naval history; all 223 men aboard were lost.[69] Overall, the navy's accident record did not improve under Caprivi. Other losses included the torpedo boat *V-3*, which sank at the close of the maneuvers of 1885 after a collision with the *V-8* in Kiel Harbor, and the training brig *Undine,* slated for retirement in another year or two, which wrecked on the west coast of Denmark in October 1884. One sailor died in the *Undine* sinking; there was no loss of life aboard the *V-3*.[70]

The strategy of the *Jeune École* disrupted the construction programs of all navies, but the German navy suffered more confusion than most. Caprivi's torpedo boat program, along with the navy's involvement in claiming the German colonial empire, pushed expenditure for 1884–85 to a record 61.4 million marks, a sum that would not be topped until the early 1890s. In other years, cruiser construction, along with the expense of the more extensive annual maneuvers, helped sustain a steadier rise in the naval outlay: 48.4 million marks in 1885–86, 53.1 million in 1886–87, and 54.2 million in 1887–88, compared with 45 million for fiscal year 1883–84, the last budget submitted by Stosch. But the types of ships being built provided neither the numbers of jobs nor the stimulus for domestic industry that larger armored projects had in the past, or would in the future. During these years, the navy's standing also declined among the fleets of Europe. When Caprivi took office at the Admiralty, Germany trailed only Britain and France in tonnage of armored warships in commission. In overall warship tonnage the German navy ranked fourth, behind Britain, France, and Russia. In 1885 Italy again surpassed Germany in armored tonnage, and the following year, in overall tonnage as well. Germany held on to fourth place in armored strength and fifth in overall tonnage for the remainder of the Caprivi era. Nevertheless, Caprivi's failure to respond to a Russian battleship buildup in the 1880s with anything more than the *Siegfried* class would be felt in the near future. When the Russians, in 1892, passed the Germans again in armored tonnage for the first time in a decade, Germany, in both armored and total strength, ranked ahead of only Austria-Hungary among the naval powers of Europe.[71]

The Navy, the Triple Alliance, and Grand Strategy

"We are worthless as an ally at sea, if we cannot appear on the high seas with a battle fleet." With these words, in 1884, Caprivi embraced Stosch's argument of the previous year (and Prince Adalbert's of 1848) regarding the potential alliance value of the navy.[72] His identification with such a position, at the same time that his construction policies were weakening the armored fleet for a decade to come, reflected the contradictions in his own mind. While Caprivi did not want Germany to have a navy that would divert resources from the army, he wanted the fleet to be large and strong enough to support the efforts of the army and of Germany's allies in wartime.

The war plans drafted under Stosch's direction during 1882, for contingencies against Russia or a Franco-Russian combination, discussed naval activity almost in a vacuum, with only passing references to action on land and little explanation of how proposed sea campaigns would contribute to the overall German war effort. In 1883, shortly after arriving at the Admiralty, Caprivi pressed for elaboration. Captain Knorr, chief of staff at the time, pursued the matter and found the army general staff receptive to interservice cooperation on war planning against Russia. Discussions centered around the navy's role in securing Riga and other Baltic harbors as supply bases for a German army advancing into Russia. Knorr also proposed Narva and Reval as potential sites for amphibious landings.[73] For the time being, army-navy cooperation did not extend to planning against France or a Franco-Russian coalition.

The year 1884 found the Admiralty and Foreign Office preoccupied with the annexation of the first German colonies, as Bismarck, in an election year, suddenly abandoned his anticolonial convictions. His entry into the colonial game threatened Anglo-German relations, fortunately at a time when Franco-German relations were as cordial as they would be anytime between 1871 and 1914. In conversation with the French ambassador in Berlin, Bismarck even referred to the need for a "balance of power at sea" and raised the prospect of a continental naval bloc against Britain.[74] During the so-called Congo Conference, which met in Berlin from November 1884 through February 1885, Germany and France stood together against Britain and ultimately secured a free trade agreement covering the Congo and Niger basins.[75]

The autumn of 1885 brought Bulgaria's annexation of Eastern Rumelia, an increase in Austro-Russian tensions, and the virtual collapse of the Three Emperors' League. In the winter of 1885–86, with the Bulgarian crisis still unresolved, a war scare between Greece and Turkey added more fuel to the fire. In January 1886 Britain demanded that the Greeks demobilize. When they refused, the British took the lead in organizing an international naval demonstration in Greek waters. All of the great powers except France supported the British demobilization demand and contributed warships. After a demonstration by one armored ship from each of the five powers off Piraeus failed to intimidate the Greeks, in May 1886 the British, Italian, and Austrian contingents each blockaded part of the coast. In June the Greeks capitulated to the demands of the powers and demobilized their army. Germany's contribution to the demonstration, the armored frigate *Friedrich Carl*, at 6,000 tons was the largest ship present other than those

of the British navy. At nineteen years of age, it was also one of the most obsolete.[76] Though Russia had aligned itself with the Triple Alliance and Britain rather than with France during the Greek crisis, the deteriorating international situation of 1885–86 heightened Caprivi's fears over how his navy
would fare in a war against Russia or a Franco-Russian combination. These
concerns for the future motivated his decision in the summer of 1886 to
ask the Reichstag to fund the armored warships of the *Siegfried* class starting in the 1887–88 fiscal year. Ironically, late in 1886 Bismarck's son Herbert,
recently appointed foreign secretary, approved a sale of Schwartzkopf torpedoes to the Russians, informing Caprivi that he saw "no reason" for
blocking the sale. Krupp likewise continued its long-standing business
with Russia.[77]

While the German-Russian relationship remained ambivalent, the suc-
cessful blockade of Greece demonstrated to Britain the possibilities of
Mediterranean cooperation with Italy and Austria-Hungary. With Bis-
marck's encouragement, British prime minister Lord Salisbury concluded
an agreement with Italy in February 1887 to maintain the status quo in the
Mediterranean. In March the British exchanged similar notes with the
Austrians, including special references to the Black Sea and the Aegean.
Spain entered the picture in May via a separate agreement, pledging not to
collaborate with France in partitioning unclaimed lands in North Africa.
At the end of the year a more specific exchange of notes among Austria-
Hungary, Italy, and Britain pledged the three powers to defend Turkey
against Russian aggression. They asserted their right to intervene "either
jointly or separately" to preserve Ottoman territorial integrity and uphold
existing treaties.[78]

These so-called Mediterranean Agreements did not include Germany
but formed a valuable part of Bismarck's system of alliances at the confus-
ing zenith of his diplomacy. Along with other arrangements made during
the first half of 1887—the renewal of the Triple Alliance in February and
the conclusion of the secret Russo-German "Reinsurance Treaty" in June—
the agreements joined the often contradictory web of commitments and
obligations that had as their common goal the continued isolation of
France. In an addendum to the renewed Triple Alliance, the Italians secured a pledge of German support in case of Franco-Italian war not just if
France attacked Italy proper, but if Italy went to war with France because
of a French move to annex Tripoli or Morocco.[79] Although the new commitment raised the theoretical possibility of direct German involvement in
North Africa, which the navy would have to facilitate, at this stage Italy

valued Germany for the diplomatic pressure it could bring to bear. In the late 1880s the Italians had the world's third-largest navy and expected no help from the Germans at sea.

In June 1887, as the period of intense diplomatic activity ended, the navy held dedication ceremonies for the Kiel Canal project. The festivities included eight battleships: the armored frigates *Friedrich Carl* and *König Wilhelm* and the casemate ships *Hansa* and *Oldenburg,* all of which went on to autumn maneuvers, and the four "sortie corvettes," which had been laid up in Kiel as the Baltic "reserve division." The training squadron, consisting of the unarmored corvettes *Prinz Adalbert, Moltke, Stein,* and *Gneisenau,* also participated, along with the *Blücher,* the older wooden-hulled school ships, and several torpedo boats.[80] Later in June, a naval review at Cowes celebrating the fiftieth jubilee of Queen Victoria gave the great powers an opportunity to show off their newest or best ships. To represent Germany, however, Caprivi sent torpedo boats under the command of Prince Henry. Prince William accompanied him aboard the flotilla leader *Blitz,* a vessel captained by Alfred Tirpitz. While in Britain, William met Lord Charles Beresford, sea officer and member of parliament, a leading advocate of the *Jeune École.* Beresford's praise of the German torpedo boats filled the prince with pride. The visit was William's first abroad in naval uniform; at the Kiel Canal dedication the emperor had appointed him an officer *à la suite* in the naval infantry. From the time of the visit onward, much to the chagrin of army leaders, the future emperor preferred wearing the navy's uniform.[81]

In late August and early September 1887, after the close of the ceremonial activities, Rear Admiral Paschen commanded three weeks of fleet exercises. The aging *König Wilhelm*—active for the first time since 1878, when it collided with the *Grosser Kurfürst*—joined the casemate ships *Kaiser* and *Oldenburg* in the armored I Division. The four corvettes of the training squadron became the II Division, while four of the armored gunboats from the North Sea "reserve squadron" constituted the III Division. Tirpitz's torpedo flotilla, consisting of the *Blitz* and fourteen torpedo boats, formed the IV Division. Vice Admiral Blanc, Wickede's successor as chief of the Baltic station, commanded a separate "Baltic squadron" including the *Sachsen, Friedrich Carl,* and *Hansa,* the latter making its last appearance before being converted to an accommodation ship. The combined operations of the other divisions also focused on the Baltic, but for eight days in September the fleet conducted "tactical exercises" in the North Sea. During that time Vice Admiral Monts, the station chief in Wilhelmshaven, assumed overall command. The maneuvers set new records in numbers of ships and men involved. Reserve officers, machinists, and seamen had to be recalled in order for all of the vessels to be fully manned.[82] Nevertheless, the mixture of warships attested to the tactical and strategic confusion that reigned under Caprivi: obsolete battleships, fully-rigged unarmored cruisers, worthless armored coastal gunboats, and modern torpedo vessels.

The itinerary of the training squadron for the winter of 1887–88, to the Western Mediterranean rather than the West Indies, reflected Germany's interest in supporting the new Mediterranean Agreements. In August 1887 the francophobe colonialist Francesco Crispi became prime minister of Italy, and Franco-Italian relations began to deteriorate. In November, as a gesture of support to Italy, Rear Admiral Philipp von Kall took the *Prinz Adalbert, Moltke, Stein,* and *Gneisenau* to Genoa, La Spezia, and Naples. At their La Spezia base, the Italian navy hosted a "sumptuous dinner" for the Germans; the local German consul noted the good impression made by the visitors, praising the "exemplary conduct" of sailors on shore leave. The squadron was scheduled to go on to Morocco, but at the last minute foreign secretary Herbert von Bismarck asked Caprivi to cancel the visit, on the grounds that it would only heighten tensions with the French. The ships called at Gibraltar, then cruised to Madeira while Franco-Italian tensions neared a boiling point. In February 1888 the French fleet at Toulon tested a new system of mobilization, coincidentally just as France broke off negotiations for a trade agreement with Italy. Crispi concluded that the French were preparing for a preemptive strike and asked Bismarck for support. The chancellor did not consider sending the winter training squadron back to an Italian port. The quartet of fully-rigged cruisers would not send a very strong diplomatic message, and in case of war they would be easy prey for the French fleet. Instead, Bismarck joined Crispi in appealing to Lord Salisbury for a show of solidarity with the Italians. The prime minister responded by ordering a squadron of British battleships to visit Genoa.[83] Even after the crisis passed, Caprivi kept the training squadron on a short leash. After the cancellation of the Moroccan visit, he also dropped plans to send the four ships down the coast of West Africa, because "the crews of the training squadron" might be needed "for the war-readiness of the navy at home." The ships ended up cruising in the waters around Madeira and the Cape Verde Islands, then visited Southampton before returning to Wilhelmshaven in April 1888.[84] After being caught with no armored warships in the Mediterranean during the winter, Bismarck requested one to represent Germany at the opening ceremonies of the Barcelona World's

Fair in May 1888. Caprivi sent the casemate ship *Kaiser,* which participated in a naval review held as a display of friendship for the parties to the Mediterranean Agreements. The Spanish welcomed large British, Italian, and Austro-Hungarian squadrons, leaving the *Kaiser* lost in the shuffle of activity.[85]

During the tense winter of 1887–88, Caprivi personally drafted four memoranda outlining the navy's position in almost every conceivable war scenario. His plan for a Franco-German war in the North Sea called for the fleet to seek a decisive battle to prevent a French blockade of the coast; if the French forces were too strong, persistent sorties would be undertaken to weaken their blockade gradually.[86] In a general Franco-German naval war, the navy's main task would be to attack the French northern fleet before the Mediterranean fleet could reinforce it. In this scenario Caprivi considered the armored fleet expendable and was willing to trade losses with the French in battleships. He also raised the possibility of commerce raiding and attacks against French fishing fleets off Iceland and Newfoundland; the latter had been taken seriously enough as economic targets to prompt an unusual North Atlantic scouting cruise to those waters by the corvette *Moltke* in 1885. Caprivi concluded, however, that the fishing grounds would not be worth attacking, that France could never be starved out by a naval blockade and could always receive arms overland through neutral neighbors. Overall, the plan rejected the cruiser warfare of the *Jeune École* while embracing the strategy's emphasis on torpedo boats, which Caprivi thought would play a decisive role in an attack on Cherbourg at the start of the war.[87] His Baltic war plan called for a defensive deployment at Danzig, where the fleet would wait for the Russians to appear; Caprivi rejected an attack on the base at Kronstadt as too risky. In a war against both Russia and Denmark, the navy would deploy from Kiel with the goal of intercepting and defeating each of the enemy fleets before they could join forces. For a war against France and Denmark, Caprivi envisioned a defensive posture in both the Baltic and the North Sea. Because a Franco-Russian combination against Germany would activate the Triple Alliance, Caprivi assumed that in such a war the French would focus on the Mediterranean, where the Austrian and Italian navies could join forces against them, leaving few French ships to support the Russians in northern waters.[88]

A plan dated 15 November 1887, the only one of the four actually sent to the emperor and Bismarck, anticipated a conflict between the Triple Alliance and a Franco-Russian coalition. It called for an Austro-Italian fleet in the Western Mediterranean to compel the French to reinforce their Mediterranean fleet at Toulon with Atlantic forces from Brest, leaving only the French Channel forces at Cherbourg to face an attack from the German fleet. The scheme envisioned only a defensive posture against Russia's Baltic fleet and did not consider the Black Sea fleet at all. Caprivi placed little hope in Austro-Italian cooperation but assumed that if Britain sided with the Triple Alliance, the Austrian and Italian fleets would eagerly join forces with the British Mediterranean squadron.[89]

Not surprisingly, the generals brought in to head the Admiralty from 1872 to 1888 abandoned the traditional "liberal" commercial raison d'être for German sea power and sought to reshape the navy as a "military" service designed to meet the strategic needs of the state. Yet by the time the Mediterranean Agreements were concluded, Bismarck's decision to involve Germany in building a colonial empire created new missions for the navy far beyond Europe. The central role of the fleet in claiming and defending the overseas empire rallied colonialists behind the naval cause and revived the commercial argument for future fleet expansion. But these supporters wanted a navy to show the flag worldwide, while Caprivi recognized the need for a fleet to serve as an extension of German power in Europe and the Mediterranean. The navy had yet to produce a leader from its own ranks, a Tirpitz, capable of formulating persuasive arguments for a battle fleet concentrated in European waters that would also serve the needs of German world power.

·   ·   ·

Whereas Stosch had focused on formulating and fulfilling the goals of his fleet plan, in the process paying little attention to how the ships would be used, Caprivi considered operations and war planning to be the central question and offered no fleet plan of his own. Caprivi's failure to act upon Bismarck's green light for a larger fleet in 1886 is intriguing as a possible missed opportunity, especially considering the subsequent victory of the liberal-conservative "Cartel" in the Reichstag elections of 1887, which provided a majority more amenable to naval expansion. German industry also stood poised to support a more ambitious program. The *Oldenburg,* which joined the fleet in 1886, was the first battleship built entirely of domestic steel, the Krupp works remained a world leader in naval ordnance, and by 1887 Krupp was on the verge of joining Dillinger in manufacturing state-of-the-art compound armor. But the *Jeune École* left the German navy, like all others, divided over which course to pursue and what types of ships to build. Caprivi himself reflected the confusion. Although he rejected many of the premises of *Jeune École* strategy, he ordered dozens of torpedo boats, in his view a quick, inexpensive way to prepare for the two-front war against France and Russia he felt could come anytime.

The events of 1888 set Germany on the course that led to the formulation of the Tirpitz plan and the construction of the High Seas Fleet. The navy unwittingly played a role in bringing on the "Year of the Three Kaisers," as festivities in Kiel provided two occasions for the aging William I to fall ill. In June 1887 he presided at the dedication ceremony at the onset of construction on the Kiel Canal; it was a windy day and the ninety-year-old emperor caught cold. That September, after his health rallied, he returned to Kiel to review the fleet. Determined that the sailors should see their monarch, he stood on the deck of a ship in raw weather and afterward fell seriously ill. He never fully recovered and on 9 March 1888 died of pneumonia, just before his ninety-first birthday.[90] Crown Prince Frederick William, already terminally ill with throat cancer, became Emperor Frederick III. Upon his death on 15 June 1888, William II inherited the throne.

"WASTED" YEARS?

he decade between the accession of William II and the passage of Tirpitz's First Navy Law has been characterized as "the wasted ten years,"[1] a depiction fostered by Tirpitz himself.[2] But there were good reasons why the great fleet plan emerged in 1898 rather than a decade earlier. The new emperor initially was unsure of why he wanted a larger navy.[3] Just as his officers remained divided between proponents of battleships and cruisers, a legacy of the *Jeune École,* William II for years wavered between the two schools of thought, even after reading Alfred Thayer Mahan's *The Influence of Sea Power upon History* (1890), which became the bible of battle fleet proponents. To make matters worse, within a year of taking the throne the emperor reorganized the navy leadership on the model of the divided army command, creating new cliques and rivalries in an officer corps that had spent the Caprivi years recovering from the *Grosser Kurfürst* affair. The industrial infrastructure essential to naval expansion already existed in 1888, but with some key exceptions: Krupp, for instance, had not even begun to experiment with its revolutionary nickel-steel armor. In politics, the fall of Bismarck brought new uncertainties, making it difficult for navy leaders to gauge the mood of the Reichstag. Most important of all, in the international arena the Franco-Russian threat preoccupied German strategists, and even ardent navalists conceded that a war against the continental powers would be decided on land. The cause needed a catalyst, which came in the dramatic souring of relations with Britain in the winter of 1895–96, following the Transvaal crisis in South Africa.

The Navy in Transition: William II and the End
of the Caprivi Era (1888–1890)

Almost immediately after his accession to the throne, William II announced his intention to separate the operational and administrative commands of the navy, which had been united in the post of chief of the Admiralty ever since the end of 1871. On 26 June 1888 Caprivi let it be known that
he would rather resign than accept reduced powers. Wary of keeping the
general in office as an unhappy lame duck, on 5 July the emperor replaced
him with Vice Admiral Count von Monts. Caprivi returned to the army as
commanding general of the X Corps. Twenty months later, he succeeded
Bismarck as chancellor.[4]

Monts, the first genuine navy man ever to command the service, took
office just before his fifty-sixth birthday. A veteran of thirty-nine years of
naval service, he had been the officer corps's first count, first son of a Prussian general, and (in 1849) first cadet to enter from a *Gymnasium* rather
than the merchant marine. Monts always enjoyed the respect of his peers
within the service, but he had the great misfortune of being captain of the
Grosser Kurfürst at the time of its sinking. After surviving four courts-martial and Stosch's attempts to drive him from the service, he enjoyed quieter
times under Caprivi. In August 1883 he became chief of the North Sea station and in September 1884 received a promotion to vice admiral.[5] From
the time of his arrival in Berlin, Monts accepted the fact that he held both
the operational and administrative commands only temporarily, pending
the reorganization of the naval hierarchy.[6] Meanwhile, Baron von der
Goltz, Admiralty director since the end of 1883, succeeded Monts as head of
the North Sea station, with a promotion to vice admiral. Captain Eduard
Heusner, most recently commander of the overseas cruiser squadron, replaced Goltz in Berlin.[7]

William II spent part of the first summer of his reign with the navy, setting the tone for his future annual routine. In July 1888, one month after
taking the throne, he boarded the imperial yacht *Hohenzollern* for a Baltic
tour. His escort, commanded by Rear Admiral Knorr, included the battleships *Baden, Bayern, Kaiser,* and *Friedrich der Grosse,* the four corvettes of
the training squadron, and the dispatch vessels *Blitz* and *Zieten.* The seven-
teen-day cruise included stops in St. Petersburg, Stockholm, and Copenhagen. Tsar Alexander III and King Oscar II of Sweden inspected the ships
and decorated the leading officers. Even though Knorr's flagship *Baden* ran

William II *U.S. Naval Institute Photographic Collection*

aground in the harbors of Stockholm and Copenhagen, William II informed Monts of his "sincere satisfaction" with the cruise.[8]

Knorr went on to command the newly designated "maneuver fleet" in the exercises for 1888. As usual, the battleships formed the I Division, the training squadron the II Division. The *Blitz* and fourteen torpedo boats formed the III Division. Although the small armored gunboats of the North Sea "reserve squadron" were not designated as a division, they participated in exercises held in September, after the rest of the fleet arrived from the Baltic. Simulations included a torpedo boat attack on the main body of warships as they approached Wilhelmshaven, and a mock battle in the North Sea that Monts attended as an observer.[9] After the close of maneuvers, Rear Admiral Friedrich Hollmann commanded the training squadron on an Eastern Mediterranean itinerary during the winter of 1888–89. In November the Germans received a warm welcome from their Austro-Hungarian allies in Trieste, Pola, and Rijeka. The following month they visited Greek and Turkish ports.[10]

At least in European waters, the imperial itinerary often influenced the operations of the navy. After his first winter on the throne, William II's annual routine usually included a Mediterranean winter cruise of some sort. From 1889 until his "Kruger telegram" of 1896 soured Anglo-German relations, the emperor cruised to Britain every summer, timing his visit to include the Cowes regatta off the Isle of Wight. Shortly before his visit of August 1889, Queen Victoria gave her imperial grandson the honorary rank of admiral of the fleet. At the Cowes regatta and naval review, William II proudly wore British admiral's dress. The *Hohenzollern*'s escort again included two divisions of warships. Kall, just promoted to vice admiral, commanded the I Division, consisting of the "sortie corvettes" *Sachsen* and *Baden,* the casemate ship *Oldenburg,* and the new cruiser *Irene,* captained by Prince Henry. The II Division, under Hollmann, included four old battleships instead of the customary corvettes: *Kaiser, Deutschland, Friedrich der Grosse,* and *Preussen.* The seven battleships were the most ever to represent Germany on a single occasion abroad. Subsequent maneuvers, under Kall's supervision, included the same two divisions, along with the torpedo flotilla and the North Sea armored gunboats.[11]

The four old battleships of Hollmann's division went on to become the training squadron for the winter of 1889–90, marking the beginning of year-round battleship operations for the German navy. The ships went to the Mediterranean with the emperor's yacht *Hohenzollern,* Prince Henry's *Irene,* and the light cruiser *Wacht.* William II met them at Genoa in October, for an itinerary that included state visits to Turkey and Italy, and the wedding, in Athens, of his sister Sophie and the crown prince of Greece. In November he disembarked at Venice and returned overland to Berlin. The squadron remained in the Mediterranean until April 1890.[12]

The maneuvers of 1888 and 1889 reflected no clear departure from the tactical and strategic confusion of the Caprivi era, and construction policies remained equally unfocused. In August 1888 William II instructed Monts to include the first installments for four battleships in the budget for 1889–90. The new chief, a battle fleet proponent, soon settled on a program of 10,000-ton battleships, to be built instead of the last four of Caprivi's ten 3,500-ton *Siegfried*-class coast defenders.[13] The design included six 11-inch guns paired in three turrets, fore, aft, and amidships. Foreshadowing the "all big-gun" dreadnought of later years, their secondary armament (eight 4.1-inch guns) was much lighter.[14] Along with the new battleships, the navy proposed additional coast defenders, seven medium-sized and four small cruisers, two dispatch vessels, and two large torpedo boats, all to be laid down by 1893.[15] The battleships were merely the most important, and most expensive, element of a catchall program including something for everyone.

Heusner, as Admiralty director under Monts, piloted the proposal through the Reichstag with the rest of the budget for 1889–90. In February 1889 the legislators almost unanimously approved initial funding for the first of the battleships, the *Brandenburg,* but the first installments for the remaining three faced significant opposition. The Catholic Center party wanted the navy to complete the *Brandenburg* before beginning work on its sister ships; this idea gained some support before the majority "Cartel" of National Liberals and Conservatives ultimately prevailed. The outlay for 1889–90—58.7 million marks, only a slight increase from the previous year's 55.8 million—meant that little work would be done on the ships in the upcoming year.[16] Nevertheless, during 1890 construction began on all four *Brandenburg*s. The imperial shipyard in Wilhelmshaven built the *Kurfürst Friedrich Wilhelm,* which in June 1891 became the first to be launched. The remaining three were laid down in private shipyards: the *Brandenburg* and *Weissenburg* by A.G. Vulcan of Stettin, and the *Wörth* by the Germaniawerft of Kiel. The *Brandenburg* and *Weissenburg* received Dillinger armor. The remaining orders went to the Krupp works, which the navy invited into the bidding in the hope that competition would bring down prices. In 1890 Friedrich Krupp did not even have a rolling mill, but after the contracts were signed he built one at the firm's complex in Essen. It was operational by the following year.[17]

Much to the dismay of the navy, Friedrich Krupp and Baron Stumm-Halberg of Dillingen concluded a corporate alliance as soon as Krupp entered the armor business. Stumm shared his license to produce compound iron-and-steel armor under the old British "Wilson system." In return, Krupp shouldered the burden of research and development for both firms. They divided contracts and fixed prices at profitable levels. While Krupp and Dillinger started to manufacture compound plates for the *Brandenburg*s, in October 1890 researchers at Krupp began experiments with all-steel plates made with nickel-steel alloys.[18] In the late 1880s the leading French armor producer, Schneider of Creusot, had begun experiments with nickel-steel armor, but with mixed results.[19] A breakthrough came in September 1890, at a United States Navy test conducted in Annapolis: imported Schneider plates, hardened by a process devised by an American, Augustus Harvey, emerged unscathed while the same fire destroyed the best British compound armor. "Harveyized" nickel-steel armor, treated with carbon and hardened in cold water, seemed indestructible. Nickel ore prices skyrocketed, and the leading naval powers scrambled to duplicate or improve upon Harvey's process.[20] Fortunately for Germany, by the late 1880s Krupp was already experimenting with nickel steel, only for gun barrels rather than armor; in 1890 these trials resulted in the decision to use nickel steel in Krupp naval artillery. In the autumn of 1890 researchers in Essen turned their attentions from guns to armor. Experiments with carbon-treated nickel-steel armor continued through 1891. In tests conducted early in 1892, in the presence of William II, the new plates proved to be 15 percent stronger than compound armor. Still in the midst of fulfilling its armor contracts of 1890, the Krupp works stopped production and re-tooled for the manufacture of nickel-steel plates, in time to deliver the new armor for the *Kurfürst Friedrich Wilhelm.*[21]

The new class of battleships did not meet with universal acclaim in Germany. Shortly after the launching of the first of the *Brandenburg*s, an anonymous critique compared their design to Britain's 14,150-ton *Royal Sovereign,* launched in February 1891 as the first of a class of eight. The British battleship was superior not only in size, but also in speed, armor, and armament. To make matters worse, many other new foreign warships were superior in various respects to the *Brandenburg* class. Critics took solace in the fact that the four battleships would give Germany clear superiority over Russia in the Baltic Sea.[22]

Monts did not live to see the completion of the *Brandenburg*s, or even the passage of the budget authorizing the onset of their construction. He died on 19 January 1889, after only six months in office. With the work of a reorganization commission still under way, William II appointed Vice Admiral Baron von der Goltz to succeed Monts as chief of the Admiralty. Goltz, at age fifty the oldest active flag officer in the service, had succeeded Monts as chief of the North Sea station just the previous summer, but his recent experience as Admiralty director under Caprivi made him no stranger to Berlin. The emperor subsequently advanced Karl Paschen and Eduard Knorr to vice admiral; Paschen replaced Goltz as chief of the North Sea station, and Knorr succeeded the retiring Vice Admiral Blanc on the Baltic station.[23]

Like Monts, Goltz had to accept the reality that his powers soon would be redefined. The uncertainty did not last long. On 20 March 1889 the new High Command (*Oberkommando*) inherited the operational leadership and the Imperial Navy Office (*Reichsmarineamt*) the administrative functions. Eight days later, William II created the Navy Cabinet (*Marinekabi-*

nett).[24] Goltz became chief of the High Command. The Admiralty director, Heusner, remained in Berlin as state secretary of the Imperial Navy Office. Captain Baron Gustav von Senden-Bibran, the emperor's naval aide-de-camp (*Flügeladjutant*) since November 1888, became chief of the Navy Cabinet. The junior member of the triumvirate, Senden (forty-two years old, twenty-sixth in seniority on the *Rangliste*), became the key figure behind the scenes. Characterized by one historian as "a bachelor of narrow interests, tactless, anglophobic, and totally dedicated to his duty," he enjoyed the trust of William II and was in a unique position to shape his naval views.[25] The reorganization gave the navy hierarchy three competing agencies, each with a leader enjoying direct access to the emperor, analogous to the army's general staff, war ministry, and military cabinet. The Reichstag questioned the wisdom of the new command structure but acquiesced in late March, after Bismarck personally endorsed it.[26]

Heusner's appointment to head the new Imperial Navy Office left him to continue in the role of chief spokesman before the parliament on budget matters. The estimates for 1890–91 were controversial from the time of their first reading in November 1889, thanks to the proposed new imperial yacht *Hohenzollern*.[27] Intended to replace the paddle steamer of the same name launched in the 1870s, the new *Hohenzollern*—marketed officially as a "dispatch boat for large formations"—displaced 4,200 tons, as much as a medium-sized cruiser. Heusner endured the attacks of Heinrich Rickert, Eugen Richter, and other Progressive politicians, with the knowledge that the "Cartel" again would carry the day for the navy. The Reichstag approved the budget just before dissolving for the campaign leading up to the elections of February 1890. The outlay for 1890–91 was an unprecedented 87.8 million marks,[28] but the opposition's targeting of a project so clearly identified with William II—the *Hohenzollern*—served notice that his close association with the navy's cause would not necessarily deter criticism or ease the passage of budgets.

A.G. Vulcan launched the new *Hohenzollern* in 1892.[29] Other unarmored warships under construction during Heusner's tenure included two vessels built by the Germaniawerft in Kiel: the 960-ton dispatch boat *Meteor* (1888–91) and the 6,100-ton cruiser *Kaiserin Augusta* (1890–92). Both were unrigged, steel-hulled vessels with armor only on their decks and conning towers. The *Kaiserin Augusta*'s engines were capable of over twenty-one knots, reflecting the dream that commerce raiding would still have its place in a future naval war.[30] The navy continued to order nominally-rigged cruisers of composite steel-and-wood construction for colonial service.

Gustav von Senden-Bibran
*Historische Sammlung der Marine-
schule Mürwik*

Four 1,600-ton vessels were laid down in the years 1888–90. The imperial
shipyard in Danzig built the *Bussard* (1888–90), *Seeadler* (1890–92), and
Cormoran (1890–93), while the imperial shipyard in Kiel completed the
Falke (1890–91).[31]

Armored projects also kept the shipyards busy; in addition to the four
*Brandenburg*s, these included the six *Siegfried*-class vessels not canceled
earlier by Monts. In future years, the budget line to continue work on the
miniature battleships would serve as an annual concession to the proponents of coastal defense in the Reichstag. The *Siegfried* was built by the
Germaniawerft of Kiel, *Beowulf* and *Frithjof* by A.G. Weser of Bremen, *Hildebrand* and *Hagen* by the imperial shipyard in Kiel, and the *Heimdall* by
the imperial shipyard in Wilhelmshaven. The *Siegfried* was commissioned
in April 1890; the last of the six, the *Hagen,* finally entered service in October 1894. That same month the *Weissenburg,* the last battleship of the
Brandenburg class, also would receive its commission. The *Siegfried*s, like
the *Brandenburg*s, were caught in the transition from compound to nickel-
steel armor; only the *Heimdall* and *Hagen* received the new product. By
then, thanks to further experimentation, Krupp was hardening the carbon-treated, nickel-steel plates in oil, a process that made them 10 percent
stronger than those hardened in water.[32]

Later critics of Tirpitz's predecessors would castigate Monts and Heusner for not presenting a grand design to the Reichstag with the first budget of William II's reign. In fact, the four battleships of the *Brandenburg* class won approval precisely because they were *not* a part of an ambitious fleet plan. If the vessels had been presented as the first step in a long-term program, dramatically expanding Germany's naval strength, the package certainly would have gone down to defeat. The alliance of parties and interests that supported the Tirpitz plan a decade later had already begun to coalesce, but public and political opinion remained unprepared for such a commitment. The wide variety of vessels under construction as of 1889 and 1890, no less than Heusner's comprehensive wish list, reflected the continuing strategic and tactical confusion wrought by the *Jeune École*. Whatever the mood of the Reichstag, the navy could experience no dramatic growth as long as its leaders had no clear idea of the best course for the future.[33]

The Politics of Naval Construction on the Eve of the Tirpitz Era (1890–1895)

A month after the stormy election campaign of February 1890, Bismarck finally left office. William II appointed Caprivi to succeed him.[34] The former chancellor's son Herbert, since 1886 state secretary of the Foreign Office, likewise resigned; Baron Adolf Marschall von Bieberstein replaced him. Following the election, the new chancellor and the naval hierarchy faced a dramatically different Reichstag. The "Cartel" parties, 55 percent of the old parliament, emerged with less than 35 percent of the seats, while the Center party, Progressives, and Social Democrats made impressive gains. As luck would have it, Heusner never faced the new Reichstag. Plagued by an ailment contracted in the tropics during his 1887–88 command of the cruiser squadron, he retired in April 1890 and died the following year. Rear Admiral Hollmann succeeded him as head of the Imperial Navy Office. Tirpitz characterized Hollmann as "a high-minded man who was, however, never quite clear as to the direction to be followed." His qualities as a courtier, rather than as an administrator, would secure his position; among other things, he shared William II's fascination with spiritualism. The emperor freely admitted Hollmann's mediocrity and is credited with giving him the derisive nickname *Hollmannikin,* yet he would stand by him for seven stormy years. Heartened by a promotion to vice admiral, in November 1890 Hollmann presented the navy's estimates for 1891–92.[35]

Things got off to a bad start when Hollmann revealed to the Reichstag

Cruiser *Kaiserin Augusta* (laid down 1890; launched January 1892)
U.S. Naval Institute Photographic Collection

Friedrich Hollmann
*Historische Sammlung der Marine-
schule Mürwik*

that the navy had underestimated the cost of the construction projects approved in the past two years. Criticism mounted after the retired Vice Admiral Henk, a conservative representative in the Reichstag, questioned the projected speed of the *Brandenburg*-class battleships. Others asked why the navy did not have a comprehensive fleet plan, a fundamental change from the mood two years earlier. After Center leader Ludwig Windthorst proposed a one-year hiatus in new construction projects, the Progressives and Social Democrats joined his party in an anti-navy coalition. Prominent figures from other parties joined them, including Rudolf von Bennigsen of the National Liberals and industrialist Wilhelm von Kardorff of the Free Conservatives. Hollmann's few defenders included the Prussian Polish leader Joseph von Koscielski, a naval enthusiast on anti-Russian grounds.[36] Chancellor Caprivi acquiesced in the Reichstag's postponement of new warship projects, except for two *Siegfried*-class coast defenders, *Hagen* and *Heimdall,* which were laid down as scheduled during 1891. Otherwise, construction starts in 1891 were limited to a pair of light vessels funded in previous budgets, both begun by private shipbuilders. The Hamburg firm of Blohm & Voss, which would eventually build the *Bismarck* of World War II fame, laid down its first warship ever, the 1,600-ton overseas cruiser *Condor,* which it completed in 1892. Meanwhile, A.G. Vulcan began work on the 990-ton dispatch boat *Comet,* eventually commissioned in 1893.[37]

The onset of these projects, along with continuing work on the four *Brandenburg*s and other ships, pushed the outlay for 1891–92 to 94.7 million marks, another record.[38] Nevertheless, the partial hiatus in new construction aroused fears among navy leaders monitoring the progress of other fleets. In May 1891 Captain Wilhelm Büchsel, a department head in the Imperial Navy Office and good friend of Tirpitz's, argued that the entire armored fleet, apart from the four *Brandenburg*s, would be obsolete by the mid-1890s. The four *Ausfallkorvetten* and the *Oldenburg* could be overhauled, but the navy needed five replacements for older battleships still on the active list. His argument for fourteen battleships was based upon the number of larger armored warships prescribed by Stosch in 1873, in the most recent fleet plan.[39] The lack of battleship contracts would have caused a crisis in the German shipbuilding industry if not for the demands of the leading steamship lines. At the urging of William II, Albert Ballin of the Hamburg-Amerika Line began to patronize domestic shipyards; the North German Lloyd soon followed suit. A.G. Vulcan, Blohm & Voss of Hamburg, and Schichau's new Danzig shipyard began building passenger ships the size of battleships. By 1895 the number of German shipyard workers topped thirty-one thousand. Without this boom in ocean liner construction, the shipyards would not have been as well prepared later to accommodate the Tirpitz plan.[40]

Over the winter of 1891–92, Hollmann took Büchsel's arguments of German naval weakness to the Reichstag. He came away with more construction money in the 1892–93 budget, but the outlay of 95.4 million marks again included nothing for new high seas battleships. Unarmored projects included the 3,700-ton cruiser *Gefion,* laid down by Schichau in Danzig; it was completed in 1894. Built of steel and wood like other vessels designed for overseas service, it also had no rigging and an armored deck and conning tower, like the *Kaiserin Augusta* and the modern smaller cruisers.[41] To placate coastal defense advocates, the Reichstag also funded two 3,550-ton modified *Siegfried*-class warships. The imperial shipyard in Kiel laid down the *Ägir* in 1892; it was commissioned in September 1896. The imperial shipyard in Danzig delayed the onset of work on the *Odin* until 1893; it finally entered service in October 1896. The two vessels received the same oil-hardened, carbon-treated nickel-steel plates as the *Heimdall* and *Hagen,* even though by the time they were finished the Krupp works had made another advance in armor technology. At the end of 1892 Krupp introduced the "gas-cementing" process, which used gas to carburize the nickel-steel surface. The plates were then hardened in running water. With no big battleship contracts in sight, the Essen works took advantage of the respite to perfect the new technique. Eventually, plates hardened by a high-pressure water spray proved to have a strength equal to compound armor twice as thick, and they also outperformed the best foreign "Harveyized" armor. The development revolutionized armor production and made the Krupp works the world leader of the industry.[42]

At a time when France and Russia were solidifying their new alliance, the effects of Russian naval expansion initiated in the 1880s were finally being felt: during 1892 Russia surpassed Germany in armored tonnage for the first time in a decade.[43] And yet, when Hollmann went to the Reichstag with his estimates for 1893–94, a badly needed replacement for the old battleship *Preussen* was the most controversial item. Concurrent furor over a new army bill—Caprivi's response to the Franco-Russian friendship—overshadowed the debate over the navy budget. Nevertheless, in March 1893 the chancellor finally spoke out on behalf of the navy, defending the need for armored warships and torpedo boats to drive off an enemy blockade, and cruisers to protect German commerce on the high seas. His speech cast these tasks in terms of a mission "to secure our existence dur-

ing a land war." Germany continued to industrialize rapidly, and its agri-
cultural sector no longer could feed a booming population without outside help. Caprivi prophetically observed that "if during a war we can no
longer count on imports, our existence can be seriously threatened." The
legislators reduced the estimates all the same, to 90.9 million marks.
Among the proposed new projects, only two small warships received funding. During 1893 A.G. Weser laid down the 2,000-ton *Hela*, a steel-hulled
dispatch vessel, and the imperial shipyard in Wilhelmshaven started work
on the *Geier*, a sixth overseas cruiser of the 1,600-ton *Bussard* class. Both
entered service in 1895.[44]

Meanwhile, in May 1893, the failure of Caprivi's army bill brought the
dissolution of the Reichstag and the scheduling of elections for mid-June.
The proposals regarding the army naturally dominated the campaign, but
naval expansion also became an issue. Debate over the army bill split the
Progressive party into factions that would remain apart for two decades.
Of the parties opposing the bill, the Social Democrats made modest gains
and the Center suffered mild losses; the latter, however, remained the largest party, with almost a quarter of the seats in the Reichstag. The conservative parties, National Liberals, Poles, and the anti-Semitic fringe all
emerged stronger than before. Their votes, along with those of the pro-
army faction of Progressives, finally passed the army bill.[45]

The composition of the new Reichstag promised to make life somewhat
easier for Hollmann as he presented his 1894–95 estimates late in 1893. Besides trying again for a replacement battleship for the *Preussen,* the state
secretary included in his budget the initial funding for the navy's first armored cruiser, a 10,700-ton project designated *Ersatz Leipzig,* ostensibly a
replacement for a 4,000-ton corvette. Hollmann met with criticism from
Eugen Richter, leader of the Progressive faction opposed to defense in-
creases, and Social Democratic leaders August Bebel and Wilhelm
Liebknecht. The navy expected political trouble after an explosion in February 1894 aboard the new *Brandenburg* killed over forty men, but the
mishap attracted little attention. In the budget vote of March, Hollmann
emerged partially victorious thanks to a change of heart by the Center. After Ernst Lieber, Windthorst's successor as party leader, spoke in favor of
the *Ersatz Preussen,* the ship secured approval by a margin of forty votes. In
a subsequent poll, the *Ersatz Leipzig* lost by twenty-two votes. Overall, the
outlay fell again, to 85.5 million marks.[46] In 1895 the imperial shipyard in
Wilhelmshaven started work on the *Ersatz Preussen,* a ship eventually
christened *Kaiser Friedrich III* in honor of William II's late father. The lay-

out of guns for the 11,100-ton design followed the pattern that had become customary for the pre-dreadnought battleships of the great powers, rather than the innovative precedent of the *Brandenburg* class. The primary armament, four 9.4-inch guns paired in turrets fore and aft, was lighter than that of the *Brandenburgs*, while the secondary battery, eighteen 6-inch guns, was much heavier. The ship was launched in July 1896.[47]

Lieber's position in the debate over the 1894–95 budget signaled the start of a drift toward a pro-navy position by the powerful Center party, improving the prospects for a long-term fleet plan. Especially among the officers of the High Command, the ineffective Hollmann, rather than the Reichstag, came to be viewed as the main obstacle to a brighter future.[48] In 1894, two years after Russia's naval expansion dropped Germany to fifth in armored tonnage among European fleets, the completion of the *Brandenburgs* enabled the navy to pass Italy and recover fourth place. In 1896 Germany finally passed Italy in total warship tonnage.[49] But Italy was an ally, and Hollmann's critics could point to the fact that the German navy failed to gain strength vis-à-vis its potential enemies.

In sharp contrast to his later support for Tirpitz and the battle fleet, until the mid-1890s William II usually aligned himself with the "cruiser school," thanks to the influence of Senden, the chief of the Navy Cabinet.[50] The emperor remained a cruiser advocate even after "devouring Captain [Alfred Thayer] Mahan's book," *The Influence of Sea Power upon History*, during 1894, and vowing "to learn it by heart."[51] The embattled Hollmann's own sentiments continued to lean toward the *Jeune École* mentality and away from battleships, as reflected in his budget proposal for 1895–96. The estimates included a variety of cruiser and torpedo boat projects, at the expense of one or more sister ships for the *Kaiser Friedrich III*. Even these were in trouble until March 1895, when the foreign secretary, Marschall, intervened to argue the navy's case in the Reichstag. Four new cruisers received funding: the armored *Ersatz Leipzig*, rejected the previous year, and three second-class cruisers of the 5,700-ton *Hertha* class. One large and eight small torpedo boats rounded out the program, which drove the estimates back up to 93.9 million marks. In the words of one historian, "these four [cruisers] saved Hollmann's neck."[52]

The 10,700-ton *Ersatz Leipzig*, eventually christened *Fürst Bismarck*, was laid down in 1895 by the imperial shipyard in Kiel. It carried the same primary armament—four 9.4-inch guns paired in turrets fore and aft—as the new battleship *Kaiser Friedrich III*, laid down earlier the same year. Its secondary armament consisted of a dozen 5.9-inch guns, and its speed of just under nineteen knots was roughly two knots faster than the newest battleship. Almost a decade would pass before Germany laid down a larger armored cruiser. Upon its launching in September 1897 the *Fürst Bismarck* would have been the navy's first armored cruiser, if not for a stopgap measure that rebuilt the old battleships *König Wilhelm, Kaiser,* and *Deutschland* as cruisers. The renovation included removal of their masts, rigging, and heavy guns. They emerged armed with lighter guns appropriate for their new duties but remained painfully slow, lacking the speed to function as cruisers. Their reconstruction proved to be a poor investment; only the *Kaiser* and *Deutschland* ever saw duty on overseas stations, and all three would be relegated to harbor duties in 1904.[53]

The 5,700-ton *Hertha* and its sister ships supposedly were in the same category as the *Kaiserin Augusta* but shared few of its characteristics. They were slower by two knots, had a higher freeboard and some side armor, and a much heavier armament: two 8.25-inch guns and eight 5.9-inch guns, compared with the four 5.9-inch of the *Kaiserin Augusta.* They were laid down before the end of 1895: the *Hertha* by A.G. Vulcan, the *Victoria Louise* by A.G. Weser, and the *Freya* by the imperial shipyard in Danzig. All three were launched in the spring of 1897.[54] For the battleship *Kaiser Friedrich III* and the four cruisers approved for 1895–96, the navy ordered the latest "gas-cemented" Krupp armor, the only variety produced after 1895.[55]

A change in the naval hierarchy followed the passage of the budget for 1895–96, ironically affecting the High Command rather than the Imperial Navy Office. While Hollmann retained his post, Goltz stepped down for health reasons. The fifty-seven-year-old admiral, the senior officer in the service, suffered from a lung ailment but would live on in retirement until 1906. William II appointed Admiral Knorr to succeed him; Rear Admiral August Thomsen replaced Knorr as chief of the Baltic station. On 13 May 1895, the date of Goltz's retirement, the emperor also promoted Alfred Tirpitz to rear admiral.[56]

The Navy, Great Power Competition, and War Plans (1890–1896)

After Bismarck left office in March 1890, his successor Caprivi led Germany on a fateful "new course" in foreign policy. The Russo-German "Reinsurance Treaty" was allowed to lapse, and Russia drifted toward an alliance with France. The Triple Alliance with Italy and Austria-Hungary assumed a more central place in German grand strategy, and good relations with Britain took on greater importance.[57] In July, Germany and Britain concluded

Cruiser *Victoria Louise* (laid down 1895; launched March 1897)
U.S. Naval Institute Photographic Collection

Armored cruiser *Fürst Bismarck* (laid down 1895; launched September 1897)
U.S. Naval Institute Photographic Collection

the Helgoland-Zanzibar Treaty, which secured the island of Helgoland for Germany in return for a British protectorate over Zanzibar and a promise of no further German colonial expansion in East Africa. The deal helped secure the route between Wilhelmshaven and the western mouth of the Kiel Canal for the future redeployment of warships between the North Sea and Baltic. At this stage the British did not consider the canal a danger to themselves; like German strategists, they looked forward to its completion for the flexibility it would give the German navy against a Franco-Russian threat at sea.

German naval activities during the last half of 1890 brought together the threads of friendship with Britain and Austria-Hungary and a new vigilance against the threat from Russia. In August 1890 William II went to Cowes aboard his yacht *Hohenzollern*, accompanied by the cruiser *Irene*, then attended the ceremonial cession of Helgoland from Britain to Germany, where his escort included the entire maneuver fleet: the four newest battleships in the I Division (*Baden, Bayern, Württemberg,* and *Oldenburg*), four older battleships in the II Division (*Kaiser, Deutschland, Friedrich der Grosse,* and *Preussen*), the *Irene,* and the torpedo flotilla.[58] The emperor also attended the autumn maneuvers, commanded by Vice Admiral Karl Deinhard and held in conjunction with the army. The eight battleships, two old corvettes, and a division of seven torpedo boats played the role of an "eastern" (i.e., Russian) fleet blockading Kiel. The torpedo flotilla, consisting of the *Blitz* and fourteen boats, operated out of Flensburg as the only active "western" (German) force, harassing the blockaders. In army exercises, troops from the IX Corps were divided into "western" defenders and "eastern" attackers, the latter moving inland as an enemy would after an amphibious landing. An Austro-Hungarian squadron visited Kiel during the maneuvers. For the winter of 1890–91 the II Division again became the "training squadron," with the ancient *Friedrich Carl* replacing the *Friedrich der Grosse.* Under the command of Rear Admiral Wilhelm Schröder, the ships cruised to the Mediterranean.[59]

Within the restructured naval hierarchy, the High Command had jurisdiction over operations and planning, but the reforms of 1888–89 also created staffs for the North Sea and Baltic stations to carry out similar work. It was as Baltic station chief of staff, from September 1890 to January 1892, that Alfred Tirpitz established his reputation as a tactician and strategist. After his years with the Torpedo Inspection, he commanded the old battleships *Preussen* and *Württemberg* in the years 1889–90 before becoming chief of staff in Kiel, where he served under Vice Admiral Knorr. As early as 1891 William II considered Tirpitz the navy's most gifted thinker.[60] It is difficult to determine precisely when Tirpitz underwent the conversion from torpedo to battleship proponent. He later contended that he had believed in the primacy of the battle fleet even during his years at the Torpedo Inspection, yet there is little evidence (other than his own word, after the fact) that this was the case. In any event, the publication of Mahan's *The Influence of Sea Power upon History* coincided with his appointment to head Knorr's staff, and the following spring found Tirpitz clearly in the battleship camp. In an April 1891 memorandum, he cited Clausewitz's maxim regarding war as an extension of politics. Tirpitz ignored the fact that many navy men still subscribed to *Jeune École* thinking, arguing that "unanimity reigns regarding the necessity to defeat the enemy sea power in open battle."[61] Tirpitz's memorandum included scenarios for a war against France or Russia, or against both powers, but he ridiculed earlier plans to attack the French channel ports or blockade the Russian Baltic ports. The navy could not implement such grand schemes because it had never addressed the practical problems of how to move a large fleet over great distances or to maintain it in enemy waters for days or weeks of operations.[62] To remedy this weakness, Tirpitz called for a practical link between tactical planning and the training of the fleet. The German navy had a remarkably bad record when it came to accidents; the *Grosser Kurfürst* sinking remained the lone catastrophic loss suffered during squadron or fleet maneuvers, but there had been other collisions at sea involving everything from battleships to torpedo boats. Tirpitz argued that the best tactics were worthless if the captains and crews of the fleet could not execute simple maneuvers. He advocated a systematic training program to ensure that officers and seamen could operate individual ships competently, as a prerequisite to maneuvering with other ships in a squadron.[63] Harking back to ancient Greece for an analogy, he cited the need to train "the individual Hoplites, before one organizes the Phalanx."[64] Tirpitz continued to stress the need for training after his appointment, in January 1892, to the post of chief of staff to Goltz in the High Command.

Meanwhile, in June 1891 William II decreed new designations for battleship formations, which would remain in effect through World War I. Henceforth a squadron would consist of eight battleships, while a division would have four.[65] More important, he made "chief of the maneuver fleet" a formal position. For the past two decades of regular maneuvers, admirals were assigned to the command almost as a sabbatical from their high posts on land; before the *Grosser Kurfürst* disaster, commanders (Henk and

Batsch) came from the Admiralty in Berlin; after 1878 the maneuver chief was usually a station chief or his second-in-command. The creation of a permanent fleet command was an important step in improving the war-readiness of a peacetime navy.[66]

Vice Admiral Deinhard, commander of the previous year's maneuvers, became first chief of the maneuver fleet. As in 1890, his forces included eight battleships: the new 3,500-ton *Siegfried* joined the *Baden, Bayern,* and *Oldenburg* in the I Division, and the four older battleships of the winter training squadron made up the II Division. Torpedo forces again included the *Blitz* and twenty-one torpedo boats. The new cruiser *Prinzess Wilhelm* and three old corvettes at various times simulated enemy warships. During the first half of September 1891, Deinhard presided over a series of four exercises. The scenarios simulated defensive warfare against a combination of Russia and either France or Denmark. Whereas in previous years the torpedo flotilla usually played the German role and the battleships that of the enemy, in three of the four simulations of 1891 at least the newer battleships of the I Division "fought" on the German side. Much to the dismay of Goltz, the enemy was judged the victor in all but one of the simulations.[67] In a November 1891 report to William II, Goltz pointed out that the side commanded by Deinhard (the enemy in the first simulation, the Germans in the others) had lost each time. He also lamented the "coastal warfare" focus of this and most previous maneuvers, because it did nothing to prepare the navy for combat on the high seas.[68] Thus the campaigns to get rid of Deinhard and to include high seas simulations—two initiatives usually credited to Tirpitz—were already under way two months before Tirpitz became Goltz's chief of staff in Berlin. In May 1892 Vice Admiral Schröder replaced Deinhard as chief of the maneuver fleet, but Goltz announced he would personally command exercises that autumn.[69] As for the maneuver program, change came slowly; there were no high seas simulations until 1895.

In 1892, for the third year in a row, eight battleships made up the core of the maneuver fleet. In the I Division, the new *Beowulf* replaced its sister ship *Siegfried,* and the *Württemberg* replaced the *Oldenburg.* Among the old battleships, the retirement of the *Preussen* and the conversion of the *Kaiser* into an armored cruiser brought the *Kronprinz* and *Friedrich der Grosse* to Rear Admiral Hans Koester's training squadron for the winter of 1891–92; both stayed on in the II Division for 1892. The torpedo flotilla again included the *Blitz* and twenty-one boats. Another two divisions, which played the role of enemy forces for much of the maneuvers, included old corvettes and lighter vessels but also the armored warships *Siegfried* and *Sachsen*. Other than vessels on overseas stations or laid up for repairs, virtually every warship in the navy played at least some role; the same would be true in subsequent years. The autumn exercises included three simulations, with situations similar to those of previous years. The first featured "a naval power of the first rank" (France) blockading both Kiel and Wilhelmshaven without attacking the German coast. The second exercise repeated the first, only with the blockaders actively attacking the coastline. The third concerned an attempt by "an eastern power" (Russia) to cross the Baltic and blockade Kiel. Again, Goltz was not pleased with the results.[70]

For the winter of 1892–93, Rear Admiral Guido Karcher commanded a training squadron that for the first time included new armored ships, the *Siegfried* and *Beowulf*, along with the old *König Wilhelm* and *Deutschland*. The ships were not available early enough to represent Germany at Italy's celebration of the four hundredth anniversary of Columbus's voyage to America. The navy sent only one warship, the cruiser *Prinzess Wilhelm*, to the ceremonies held at Genoa in September 1892.[71] The snub reflected the cooling trend in German-Italian relations under Caprivi's chancellorship. When King Umberto visited Berlin in June 1892, his foreign minister, former admiral Benedetto Brin, appealed for a Triple Alliance naval agreement. Weeks later, before German maneuvers, Tirpitz attended Italian naval exercises, and the following spring William II viewed maneuvers while visiting Venice. Both went home unimpressed, dashing Italian hopes for a naval treaty.[72]

Vice Admiral Schröder exercised personal command over the maneuver fleet of 1893. Armored warships involved included the four "sortie corvettes"; the old battleships *König Wilhelm*, *Friedrich der Grosse*, and *Deutschland*; and the *Siegfried*'s sister ships *Beowulf* and *Frithjof*, the latter making its first appearance. Five old corvettes, an armored gunboat, six lighter vessels, and dozens of torpedo boats rounded out the fleet. The first exercise, in the North Sea in late August, subjected "a superior enemy fleet" (French) to hit-and-run attacks, including night sorties, by smaller units based in Wilhelmshaven. The action ranged from Helgoland to the coast of Schleswig. A second simulation, in the Baltic Sea in mid-September, assumed a German defeat in the North Sea by "a superior western naval power" (France), which would then enter the Baltic; again, the action centered around smaller units harassing the enemy fleet. The Baltic exercise involved warships not used in the North Sea, including the *Sachsen* and several torpedo boats. The results of the 1893 maneuvers were no better than those of previous years. A harsh critique of the maneuvers, signed by Goltz, bore the mark of his chief of staff, Tirpitz. The piece criticized the officer corps for its deficient education in "tactics and strategy" and encouraged the "study of naval history," especially "the works of Captain Mahan."[73]

After the exercises, the "maneuver fleet" was redesignated "maneuver squadron," with the title of its new chief, Vice Admiral Koester, altered accordingly. The winter training squadron, under Rear Admiral Otto von Diederichs for 1893–94, became the "II Division of the maneuver squadron," a label it would wear on a year-round basis. More than just a cosmetic change, the latter reflected Tirpitz's view that the fleet should have "permanent formations . . . organized and led the same in peacetime as in wartime."[74] It marked another step on the navy's path to year-round battle-ready condition. Diederichs's division included the 10,000-ton *Brandenburg*, commissioned in November 1893, along with the *König Wilhelm*, *Deutschland,* and *Friedrich der Grosse.* The ships were not on hand for William II's visit to the Mediterranean and Adriatic in the spring of 1894; when the emperor called at Pola, the *Hohenzollern* was escorted by the old corvette *Moltke.*[75]

In 1893 Tsar Alexander III formally dedicated a naval base under construction at Libau (Liepaja) on the Latvian coast. Besides bringing the Russian Baltic fleet much closer to Germany, the new base, unlike Kronstadt, would normally be free of ice year-round.[76] The project, which would take years to complete, caused no immediate concern for German navy leaders; the main simulation of the 1894 autumn maneuvers assumed that "Libau is not yet completed as a naval base." The scenario postulated a two-front war in which the two newest divisions of battleships would remain in the North Sea to assure German "command of the sea (*Seeherrschaft*)" over the "western" (French) enemy fleet. Meanwhile, the "eastern" (Russian) enemy fleet, represented in the exercise by the four "sortie corvettes" of the I Division and Diederichs's II Division, with torpedo boats and other light vessels, steamed southward from the direction of the Gulf of Finland. The III Division (four old corvettes) simulated a division of old battleships at Kiel, while the IV Division (three *Siegfried*-class warships, including the new *Hildebrand*) was based at Danzig with torpedo boats. A total of two torpedo flotillas (the *Blitz* plus twenty-nine boats) participated in the maneuvers, which also included a scout group led by the cruiser *Prinzess Wilhelm.* For the first time since 1890, William II observed the maneuvers. The new battleship *Wörth*, sister ship of the *Brandenburg*, served as Koester's fleet flagship and home to the emperor when he and his entourage were not aboard the *Hohenzollern*. As in all previous years, the exercises posed a defensive, rather than offensive, problem for the German side. Torpedo boats again played a central role, while most of the battleships simulated the enemy. The torpedo flotilla also figured prominently in the biggest summer exercise preceding the maneuvers, a late-August nighttime attack against the battleships from the North Sea station while they were en route to the Baltic. Thus the scenario for 1894, with its reference to "command of the sea," bore the mark of Tirpitz's (Mahan's) strategic thought, while the maneuver itself reflected the defensive thinking of the *Jeune École* with its emphasis on the torpedo flotilla, ironically a strategy Tirpitz himself had promoted only too well in his years as head of the torpedo forces.[77]

On an abstract tactical level, Tirpitz spent the years 1892–94 developing the so-called *Lineartaktik*, reviving for modern battleships the traditional line-ahead battle formation common in the days of the sailing ships of the line. In his memoranda on linear tactics, Tirpitz even referred to the battleships of the fleet as "ships of the line (*Linienschiffe*)," a designation dormant since the onset of the age of armor.[78] Tirpitz's papers on operations included recommendations for the materiel of the fleet of the future. In his

Battleship *Wörth*, of the *Brandenburg* class (laid down 1890; launched August 1892)
Courtesy of Conway Maritime Press, from Steam, Steel and Shellfire: The Steam Warship, 1815–1905. © *1992 Conway Maritime Press*

famous *Dienstschrift IX* of June 1894 he called for a fleet of seventeen battleships (*Linienschiffe*), six large and twelve small cruisers, and six flotillas
of torpedo boats.[79] The German battle fleet, as an instrument for "the
strategic offensive," would be concentrated in the North Sea rather than
the Baltic.[80] Reflecting his reading of Mahan, Tirpitz argued that the "experience of history shows that the availability of a strong battle fleet is a
much more effective means to deter conflicts or to decide conflicts to our
advantage than an equally great number of cruisers [scattered] to all parts
of the earth."[81] For twenty-five years the navy had maintained a battleship
force for European waters and a cruiser force for overseas duty; Stosch,
Caprivi, and other navy leaders complained about their "dual fleet" dilemma but saw no alternative to it. Tirpitz resolved the problem by formulating an ideology based upon the premise that a battle fleet in home
waters sufficed to command respect worldwide. Cruisers were indispensable but clearly secondary in importance.

In evidence of the increasing impact of Tirpitz's ideas, after the maneuvers of 1894 the navy created a new "cruiser division," which would be
available to show the flag in the Mediterranean during the winter months,
or in more distant waters, if needed. This freed the battleships of the II Division to remain in home waters, where they could conduct winter exercises with the I Division. Thanks to the commissioning of the last two
Brandenburg-class warships during 1894—the *Kurfürst Friedrich Wilhelm*
and *Weissenburg*—Vice Admiral Koester had two homogeneous squadrons
of battleships (the *Brandenburg*s in the I Division, the "sortie corvettes" in
the II Division) for the inaugural two-week training cruise during the
winter of 1894–95. The following spring, the same eight battleships went
on another cruise, from Kiel to the Orkney and Shetland Islands; in the autumn exercises of 1895 they would practice abstract tactical maneuvers
based upon Tirpitz's *Lineartaktik*. Meanwhile, the new cruiser division,
under Rear Admiral Paul Hoffmann, immediately demonstrated its usefulness. At the end of November 1894 the cruiser *Irene* steamed to Casablanca
following the murder of a German businessman there. The *Irene* then went
on to East Asian waters, where conditions in the wake of the Sino-Japanese
War would require the cruiser division to remain for the next several
years.[82]

Although the navy's operations and maneuvers gradually came to show
Tirpitz's influence, no one had to listen to his fleet plans as long as he
served in the High Command. Under the separation of powers of 1889, the
Imperial Navy Office had jurisdiction over construction projects. Tirpitz

also encountered resistance to his ideas on materiel for other, more personal, reasons. As a brash captain in his forties ("convinced of his own excellence," according to Senden), Tirpitz had few supporters among older captains and admirals, many of whom bristled at his harsh criticism of the competence of ship commanders and training of crews. Furthermore, it was a mixed blessing that in his days in the Torpedo Inspection Tirpitz had developed his own circle of protégés, including Hunold von Ahlefeld, August von Heeringen, and Otto Braun, which he managed to reassemble after coming to the High Command. This small "corps within a corps" personally loyal to Tirpitz became a target of resentment for those outside the clique.[83]

Tirpitz always promoted the interests of whatever department he happened to be serving, but his arrogance and ambition also tended to sour relations with his immediate superiors, even those who recognized and appreciated his talents. After serving for three years under Goltz, in the spring of 1895 he welcomed the baron's retirement and hoped for better times under the new head of the High Command, Admiral Knorr. But Knorr, who had had Tirpitz as his chief of staff in Kiel from 1890 to 1892, apparently did not look forward to resuming their relationship. Upon taking office in Berlin, the fiery Knorr made known his desire to function without a chief of staff. William II did not grant his wish, but he kept peace within the High Command by giving Tirpitz a long furlough until relieving him of his post at the end of the autumn maneuvers.[84]

By the time Knorr replaced Goltz at the High Command, navy leaders were already focusing their attention on the opening ceremonies of the Kiel Canal, scheduled for 21 June 1895. The sixty-one-mile waterway, officially the *Kaiser Wilhelm-Kanal* after William I, had taken eight years to complete. William II presided at the opening, accompanied by Germany's naval, industrial, and political leaders; the latter included Prince Chlodwig zu Hohenlohe-Schillingsfürst, who had succeeded Caprivi as chancellor the previous October. Spectators witnessed the grandest international fleet review since the various Columbus commemorations of 1892. German warships present included the four battleships of the *Brandenburg* class, the four "sortie corvettes," and four of the *Siegfried* class. The *Kaiserin Augusta* led an unarmored contingent of twenty-one vessels. Britain sent the largest foreign contingent, ten warships, led by the 14,150-ton *Royal Sovereign* and three of its sister ships. Italy sent nine vessels, including the 13,900-ton *Sardegna*. Austria-Hungary and the United States each sent four warships. Reflecting the state of their relations with Germany, France and

Russia each sent only three.[85] The size of some of the foreign warships made the German navy's best appear modest in comparison. The list of visiting vessels larger than the 10,000-ton *Brandenburg*s included four British, four Italian, one French, and one Russian. Even the largest warships of 1895 could make it through the canal with room to spare; the lone mishap came when the Italian *Sardegna* accidentally ran aground.[86] No one imagined that in just over a decade, the size of battleships would increase so dramatically that the canal would have to be widened and deepened, and the size of its locks more than doubled, at a cost surpassing that of the original project.[87]

In his dedication speech, William II did not refer to the obvious strategic significance of the canal. He opened by observing that it had been "planned in peacetime and built in peacetime," and closed with the remark that Germany would operate the waterway "in the service of peace."[88] Of course, in practical terms, the Kiel Canal increased German naval power dramatically; in the future, the vessels of the Baltic and North Sea stations could be united quickly in either sea to confront an adversary. The British were not overly concerned about the new canal; they continued to consider it an enhancement of German capabilities against the French and Russians.[89] The Germans themselves viewed the waterway in the same terms. During the ceremonies at Kiel, their vigilance against spying centered on the Russians.[90]

Nevertheless, the camaraderie at Kiel belied the fact that the Anglo-German relationship was deteriorating. In recent years the British had grown increasingly wary of the rise of German industrial and commercial power, and by the summer of 1895 the two powers were at odds over a series of issues ranging from South Africa to the Near East and Far East. Things did not improve in the weeks that followed. In July, after the murder of two German merchants in Morocco, Germany demanded 250,000 marks in damages. With the new cruiser division occupied in the Far East, the navy sent a makeshift squadron of four ships—the cruiser *Kaiserin Augusta,* the coast defender *Hagen,* and the old corvettes *Marie* and *Stosch*—for a demonstration to secure the payment.[91] Critics abroad, including in Britain, called it a response out of proportion to the crime. In August, William II made his annual trip to Cowes aboard the yacht *Hohenzollern.* His diplomats advised a low-key visit; instead, he used the occasion to show off the navy's newest, largest battleships, the four *Brandenburg*s. To make matters worse, articles in the London press critical of Germany appeared upon his arrival, and William felt snubbed when the prime minister, Salisbury, missed a meeting with him just before his departure.[92]

The autumn maneuvers of 1895 emphasized high seas operations rather than coastal defense. As Koester steamed home from Britain with the I Division, Diederichs came out of Wilhelmshaven with the four "sortie corvettes" of the II Division, and the two groups simulated a North Sea battleship encounter. As the full program of exercises got under way, all four of the principal formations included homogeneous quartets of warships: the I Division (*Brandenburgs*), the II Division ("sortie corvettes"), the III Division (old fully-rigged corvettes of the *Stosch* class), and the IV Division (four *Siegfrieds*). Abstract tactical maneuvers in the Baltic, devised by Tirpitz and the High Command staff, matched the first two divisions (called the I Squadron, under Koester) against the third and fourth (the II Squadron, under Diederichs). Each side practiced steaming in line-ahead formation, turning away in a group, re-forming a line, and intercepting the opposing column at various angles. A "scout group" of cruisers attached to each squadron practiced reconnaissance strategies and signaling systems. Each squadron also had a torpedo flotilla, but the boats played a marginal role. For the battle fleet, the maneuvers marked a great step forward in Tirpitz's campaign to train the "Hoplites" and organize the "Phalanx."[93]

The busy summer and autumn brought a truce in the navy's internal battles, but Hollmann's critics soon redoubled their efforts to oust him. Knorr now led the opposition. In November 1895 the new chief of the High Command sent a memorandum to William II predicting that by 1901 the battle fleet would be vastly inferior to a Franco-Russian combination. The paper, probably authored by Tirpitz's protégé Otto Braun, proposed a fleet of twenty-five armored warships, including the eight *Siegfried*-class coast defenders. The number of larger battleships (seventeen) was the same as in Tirpitz's *Dienstschrift IX* of 1894, but this time all figures were based on the argument that the navy should have a strength 30 percent greater than either the French northern fleet or the Russian Baltic fleet. This introduced the notion that the size of the German navy should be linked to the size of one or more potential rivals. The same "principle of the fixed ratio of strength" would provide the framework for Germany's naval race against Britain before 1914.[94]

During a visit to Kiel in December 1895, William II instructed Hollmann to prepare a long-term fleet plan that would provide for twenty-five battleships, including the *Siegfrieds*. At least on this occasion, he came out strongly in favor of Tirpitz's idea of a concentration of strength in home waters.[95] Days later Senden contacted Tirpitz, then in Kiel awaiting reassignment, to ask that he send the emperor his own ideas for a fleet plan. It was an odd request, considering the prevailing philosophical differences and bitter infighting. In contrast to Tirpitz's strong preference for battleships, the chief of the Navy Cabinet favored a balanced fleet of battleships and cruisers. The two men also were not on the best of terms; indeed, Bernhard von Bülow, future chancellor, recalled years later that Senden "personally detested" Tirpitz. Nevertheless, Senden's "love for the navy" caused him to support Tirpitz, "because he thought he was the only man whose organizing ability and enthusiasm would ensure the swift and necessary expansion of the fleet."[96]

In his memorandum of late December, Tirpitz repeated the arguments William II had already heard from Knorr. Instead of twenty-five battleships he called for twenty-seven, including the eight *Siegfried*s. In the same vein as Mahan, he cited the alleged lessons of history to support the concentrated battle fleet. Tirpitz linked the battleship program and a popular expansion of the navy with foreign policy and domestic political needs, arguing that it would bolster Germany's great power status abroad and the government's internal position against the rise of the Social Democrats. Foreshadowing the "risk theory" of later years, he theorized that a strong German battle fleet would prompt "even the greatest sea state of Europe" to "be more conciliatory towards us."[97] In the atmosphere of early January 1896, William II read Tirpitz's remarks "with great interest." The emperor was fuming over the infamous Jameson Raid on the Transvaal in late December 1895, which had been launched from the British Cape Colony. On 3 January, the same day Tirpitz sent his memorandum to William II, the emperor sent a telegram to the Transvaal's President Paul Kruger, congratulating him on the capture of Jameson and the other raiders.[98]

Colonial and Overseas Interests (1888–1896)

The Anglo-German tensions over South Africa in the mid-1890s contrasted sharply with the cooperative relationship of the two powers earlier in the reign of William II, ironically even in African affairs. The collaboration leading up to the Helgoland-Zanzibar exchange of 1890 included a blockade of East Africa late in 1888 to stop the local slave trade and interdict imports of weapons. The German navy contributed the cruiser squadron under Rear Admiral Deinhard and the gunboats of the East African station, six ships in all.[99] At the same time, the navy continued to punish

Alfred Tirpitz *U.S. Naval Institute Photographic Collection*

local resistance to German rule. At the end of 1888, Deinhard's flagship *Leipzig* bombarded and destroyed most of the port city of Bagamoyo after the local Muslim leader continued to fly the flag of the sultan of Zanzibar instead of the German flag.[100] Early in 1889 a landing party from the *Sophie* intervened in Dar es Salaam. Faced with growing unrest, an exasperated Deinhard recommended the abandonment of the East African colony. Instead he received the cruiser *Schwalbe* and the dispatch vessel *Pfeil* as reinforcements; the latter was the first unrigged, steel-hulled warship ever assigned to a German African mission. By the autumn of 1890 the situation stabilized and the squadron lifted its blockade. That November the German East African Company turned the colony over to direct imperial rule.[101]

Following the Helgoland-Zanzibar Treaty, Britain and Germany cooperated to suppress East African resistance to European rule. In 1891 the death of the sultan of Zanzibar touched off unrest on the British-controlled island and the adjacent German-dominated mainland. Instability continued to plague Zanzibar and German East Africa until 1898.[102] By comparison, a relative tranquility reigned in Germany's West African possessions. Nevertheless, in 1891 and again in 1893, landing parties from station gunboats intervened in Cameroon to suppress uprisings, in some cases marching well into the interior. In 1894 a company of naval infantry was posted to Cameroon, but it saw no action before being withdrawn. For East Africa, Germany established a special *Schutztruppe* under former army and navy officers.[103]

Germany's commercial stake in Africa grew as colonial control tightened. By 1893 the Woermann Line operated four routes linking Hamburg to the West African coast, from Morocco in the north to Angola in the south. In 1898 the line finally extended service to German Southwest Africa, with a new Hamburg-Swakopmund route. In 1890 Adolph Woermann also established the German East Africa Line (Deutsche Ost-Afrika-Linie, or DOAL). Its main line ran from Hamburg to Lourenço Marques (Delagoa Bay) in Mozambique via the Suez Canal and Zanzibar. In 1892 the DOAL extended this line to Durban, South Africa, and added service from Durban to Bombay. Four years later the company added an Atlantic route, a Hamburg-Capetown-Durban-Lourenço Marques line that, ironically, bypassed all of the German West African colonies.[104]

While German merchants expanded into new African markets, their counterparts in the South Pacific continued to control the Samoan economy. Throughout the 1890s, German traders handled at least half of all Samoan imports and more than 80 percent of exports, but elsewhere in Polynesia the outlook was less encouraging. In Tonga, for example, the British became the leading players. In the early 1890s the Deutsche Handels- und Plantagen-Gesellschaft der Südsee (DHPG) sold all of its Tongan plantations, and between 1887 and 1897 the German share of Tongan exports fell from 76 to 25 percent.[105] The navy's South Pacific activity continued to center around Samoa, where British and American warships also were frequent visitors. During unrest in December 1888, the gunboats *Adler* and *Eber* sent parties ashore; an ambush left fifteen sailors dead and forty-one wounded. The mutilation of the German dead by Samoan warriors outraged Captain Ernst Fritze and the local German consul, prompting the latter to call for the immediate annexation of the island. Stronger voices echoed the appeal in Berlin. In February 1889 the DHPG threatened to liquidate its Samoan assets if Germany did not establish colonial rule.[106]

In the wake of the incident the British showed little sympathy for the Germans, the Americans even less. Indeed, the United States supported the Samoan faction that had inflicted the casualties. During the landing operation, the American sloop *Nipsic* came very close to firing on the *Adler* and

Eber. By March the corvette *Olga* had arrived in Apia Bay to reinforce the German gunboats; the United States sent the frigate *Trenton* and sloop *Vandalia* to join the *Nipsic.* The British, meanwhile, protected their interests with the corvette *Calliope.* Fortunately, nature intervened to defuse the tension, albeit with considerable loss of life: on 15 March 1889 a typhoon struck Samoa, wrecking the *Adler* and *Eber* along with the American *Trenton* and *Vandalia.* The *Olga* and *Nipsic* ran aground but were refloated later. Only the British *Calliope* emerged relatively unscathed. Suddenly driven to cooperate against the elements, Germans and Americans joined forces in rescue efforts. Ninety-three Germans died in the disaster, a heavy blow in the wake of the losses in the ambush on the island just weeks earlier. The Americans lost fifty men. The corvette *Alexandrine* soon arrived to replace the wrecked German gunboats.[107]

From April to June 1889 representatives of Germany, the United States, and Britain met in Berlin to decide the fate of Samoa. In the Berlin Final Act of 14 June 1889, Bismarck gave up the de facto protectorate that Germany had established with the naval action of August 1887, agreeing to a formal tripartite supervision of a Samoan monarchy. This system hinged not only on the cooperation of the three powers but on the goodwill of the Samoans themselves. The situation stabilized, but in 1893 another civil war broke out. The following year the light cruisers *Bussard* and *Falke* joined the British cruiser *Curaçao* in shelling the forts of Samoan rebels.[108] In 1895 Tirpitz condemned the navy's Samoan deployments for being "out of proportion to . . . the interests that are at stake."[109] The British and Americans were just as exasperated, and another Samoan civil war convinced all three powers that colonial rule was the solution. In 1899 they partitioned the islands.[110]

The onset of the Wilhelmine era found the navy active elsewhere in the Pacific. Between 1891 and 1897 gunboats conducted punitive expeditions in the Gilberts, the Marshalls, the Bismarck Archipelago, and along the coast of New Guinea.[111] For the first half of the decade the Far East station continued to be served by just two warships, and often these were very small gunboats—the 490-ton *Iltis* and *Wolf* in 1890, for example. The cruiser squadron at times reinforced the station, but in April 1893 the squadron was abolished.[112] Meanwhile, the German commercial stake in China continued to grow; in 1893 and again in 1894, the total value of Germany's Chinese trade almost reached 50 million marks, much more than the value of trade with all of its new colonies combined.[113] In the wake of Japan's decisive victory in the Sino-Japanese War of 1894–95, Germany joined France and Russia in pressuring the Japanese to return most of the territory the Chinese had ceded in the harsh Treaty of Shimonoseki (17 April 1895). Britain opposed the initiative, and Germany's involvement in it strained Anglo-German relations. Germany's pro-Chinese posture also prompted a reorientation in Japan's strategic outlook, laying the foundation for the Anglo-Japanese alliance of 1902.[114] During the war, Germany sent the new cruiser division, just established in the autumn of 1894, to back up its East Asian diplomacy. The modern cruisers *Irene* and *Prinzess Wilhelm* were joined during 1895 by the old converted battleship *Kaiser,* light cruiser *Cormoran,* corvette *Arcona,* and gunboat *Iltis.*[115]

The increasing focus on Africa, the South Pacific, and East Asia came at the expense of attention to Latin America. When civil war erupted in Chile in 1890–91, it took six months for Rear Admiral Viktor Valois to arrive from the Far East with the old cruiser squadron. In August 1891 the corvettes *Sophie, Alexandrine,* and *Leipzig* landed three hundred men in Valparaiso to protect the property of German merchants. After the situation stabilized, Valois returned to the Far East by way of Cape Horn and Capetown, South Africa. The forced circumnavigation strained the obsolete cruisers enough to prompt the decision, in April 1893, to abolish the old flying squadron.[116] Subsequent demonstrations occurred during unrest in Brazil, Venezuela, and Haiti; in 1896, Cuba's rebellion against Spain brought German corvettes to Havana.[117] Cool relations with the United States, primarily over Samoa, limited German visits to American ports. An exception came in the spring of 1893, when the cruiser *Kaiserin Augusta* and its escort *Seeadler* went to New York for the belated American celebration of the four hundredth anniversary of Columbus's first voyage.[118]

At the start of 1896, less than two years before the passage of Tirpitz's First Navy Law, fully-rigged warships still showed the German flag worldwide. Other than on the East Asian station, recently reinforced by the new cruiser division, modern cruisers were almost nowhere to be found; even in the Far East, the representation included a mixture of new and obsolete warships. The overseas stations contrasted sharply with the Baltic and North Sea, where, as early as 1894, two divisions of battleships were available for year-round duty. The debate of "cruisers-versus-battleships" still raged within the emperor's inner circle and among the admirals and politicians, but the evidence at sea showed that the battle fleet had won. Two decades before World War I, the heyday of gunboat diplomacy had already passed. In his *Dienstschrift IX* of June 1894, Tirpitz argued that "a strong battle fleet" at home would command respect worldwide, more so than a fleet of cruisers actually distributed around the globe. After the turn of the century, as the Tirpitz plan unfolded, Germany continued to concentrate its naval resources in home waters, and the other powers of Europe followed suit, making the prophecy self-fulfilling.

• • •

At the beginning of 1896, the navy still lacked a plan for the future. Nevertheless, much progress had been made since 1888. Mahan's works redefined the philosophical parameters of the naval debate, and battle fleet advocates clearly had gained the upper hand. German battleships operated on a year-round basis, and in annual maneuvers divisions of battleships simulated high seas encounters. Meanwhile, with Krupp leading the way, German industry had developed the capacity to construct battleships as good as any in the world, using domestic resources. As for the politicians, the Reichstag elected in 1893 included a majority favorable to a buildup, if navy leaders proposed a coherent program.

The badly needed catalyst emerged from the furor over William II's telegram of 3 January 1896 to President Kruger of the Transvaal, congratulating him for having withstood the Jameson Raid. Britain's silent uneasiness over the rise of German power now ended. In the words of Tirpitz, the "eruption of hatred, jealousy, and rage against Germany" in the British press, public, and government "helped more than any other factor to open the eyes of a broad sector of the German people to our actual situation and the necessity of the construction of the fleet." While only alarmists spoke of a German naval threat, British commentators no longer saw German sea power in the same positive light as they had earlier, as recently as the opening of the Kiel Canal.[119] Their outcry sparked a backlash of anglophobia in Germany, in which the anti-British sentiments of prominent navy men such as Senden and Tirpitz no longer seemed quite so mad. Senden in particular would use his position within the inner circle to encourage the more bellicose side of William II's complex sentiments toward the British. For the emperor as well as for the man on the street, anglophobia became the yeast that caused German navalism to rise.

TO THE TIRPITZ PLAN

he deterioration in Anglo-German relations following the Kruger telegram gave German navalism its clearest focusing crisis since the Danish blockades of 1848–49 and 1864. A powerful army commanded the respect of Germany's continental rivals, France and Russia, but only a strong battle fleet would do the same with Britain. At this stage, it was a matter of respect, not of preparation for a future war; indeed, Tirpitz's memorandum, which reached William II just after he had sent the Kruger telegram, spoke of a fleet that would compel Britain to "be more conciliatory" toward Germany.[1] Like Friedrich List more than half a century earlier, he cast the naval question in terms of the defense of national dignity. In the atmosphere of the moment, such arguments touched the right nerve with William II.[2] The emperor had known Tirpitz since his Torpedo Inspection years and praised his strategic outlook as early as 1891; nevertheless, it remained to be seen just how much weight the rear admiral's advice would carry in the broader scheme of things.

The Kruger telegram presented the navy with an opportunity, but it also provided fresh evidence that William II's enthusiasm, for any cause, had to be harnessed and channeled to ensure that it would do more good than harm. And although the industrial and political variables had already fallen into place, the navy still had to overcome internal obstacles before it united behind one admiral and one philosophy of expansion. The result, in 1897, would be the rebirth of *Marinepolitik,* the pursuit of a naval program for the first time since the *Grosser Kurfürst* disaster had discredited Stosch in 1878. This time, the program would serve the goals of Germany's *Weltpolitik,* the drive for world power.

The Social and Ideological Transformation
of the Officer Corps (to 1897)

By the beginning of the Wilhelmine era, the days had long passed when one had to understand Plattdeutsch to serve with Germans at sea. After 1848 the cultural divide between the coastal regions and the rest of Germany gradually broke down. The growing navy and merchant marine attracted increasing numbers of inlanders into their ranks, and the shipbuilding boom brought a migration of workers to the seaports. Nevertheless, in the navy of 1888, the vast majority of the officers and seamen still hailed from the north. The same would be true twenty years later.[3]

By the time William II came to the throne, the "militarization" or "prussianization" of the officer corps had been under way for almost two decades. More than 60 percent of the sea officers of 1888 had entered the corps since the Franco-Prussian War, and thus had never served under a chief of the Admiralty who was not a Prussian general. During the Caprivi years the navy continued to draw most of its officers from among the sons of officers and civil servants, but it also attracted more sons of noblemen than in the Stosch era. These gains were balanced off, however, by retirements of officers from the generation that had entered the corps in the 1850s, including several men holding noble titles. Thus, in the autumn of 1888, 107 sea officers held noble titles, compared with 103 in 1883. During the same five years, the corps as a whole (not including cadets) grew from 417 men to 514, causing the share of noblemen to decline from 24.7 percent to 20.8 percent.[4]

The goal of social exclusivity became even more problematic after the accession of William II, when the growth of the navy required a further expansion of the officer corps. Between 1888 and 1897 the navy's common manpower (including deck officers and NCOs) grew from just over 15,000 men to just under 20,000. During the same years, the corps of sea officers expanded from 514 to 746. Whereas the average entering "crew" under Caprivi had comprised 38 cadets, the average "crew" of 1891–97 numbered 72. Cadets holding noble titles averaged 13 per year for the years 1891–97, compared with 10 per year under Caprivi; nevertheless, the nobility simply could not match the pace of expansion. In 1895, for example, officers with noble titles accounted for 15 of the 36 sea officers and cadets who died, retired, or quit the service, but only 11 of the 71 entering cadets.[5] As the army would learn in the years preceding World War I, overall expansion of the service naturally brought an expansion in the non-noble element of the officer corps. An imperial order of March 1890 seemed to acknowledge this fact. William II cited "the increased level of education" as a factor that made "the sons of . . . honorable bourgeois homes" desirable officer candidates. In the future, "nobility of outlook (*Gesinnung*)" as well as "nobility of birth" would qualify young men for careers as officers.[6]

Tirpitz likewise emphasized the importance of the character or mentality of officer candidates. He was fond of citing George Washington's famous axiom that "only gentlemen" should be taken on as officers. Tirpitz himself was a commoner, the son of a civil servant, and did not place great value on bloodlines until after the turn of the century, when the emperor elevated him to the nobility. Before he became head of the Imperial Navy Office, he stressed ideological over social homogeneity. In his memorandum to the emperor in December 1895, he cited the need for the sea officer corps to share common views not just in "strategic thinking" but "in all questions."[7]

In Wilhelmine Germany, the most important ideological questions concerned socialism and the manner in which the empire and its institutions would cope with the rise of Social Democracy. By the mid-1890s Tirpitz considered the internal threat of socialism the greatest danger to Germany's rise to greatness; he sought to link the domestic battle against it to the drive for world power status that the navy would facilitate. In his memorandum to William II, he marketed the fleet plan as a rallying point for the German nation and a panacea "against educated and uneducated Social Democracy" at home.[8] Thus, Tirpitz wanted a corps of sea officers united not only behind the battleship program but against the socialist threat.

This would require a change in attitude, given the navy's past record on the matter. In the wake of the antisocialist law of 1878, even Tirpitz's mentor Stosch had accepted the fact that "the overwhelming majority" of his imperial shipyard workers still supported the Social Democrats. As chief of the Admiralty, Caprivi defended the navy's hiring of workers while they were on strike from jobs in private shipyards and machine shops, a practice common in Kiel during the 1880s.[9] The navy's leaders took a greater interest only when the suspected socialist sympathizers were aboard ship. After Prussian police, early in 1888, found evidence linking a boatswain on active duty to a civilian found in possession of illegal Social Democratic literature, the navy monitored the sailor's activities for a full year. Caprivi, Monts, Goltz, Hollmann, and Paschen all were involved in the inconclusive case at one time or another, but they never removed the boatswain from his post.[10]

Ironically, the navy leadership's posture vis-à-vis the Social Democrats hardened only after the antisocialist law lapsed in 1890, thanks largely to the vigilance of the Imperial Navy Office under Hollmann. Late in 1891 Hollmann forwarded information to Caprivi in the Reich Chancellery concerning a Social Democratic rally in the Kiel suburb of Friedrichsort, site of the navy's torpedo factory. In the autumn of 1894, after a joint memorandum from the interior and war ministries cited the need "to hinder as much as possible" the entry of Social Democrats into the armed forces, the navy adopted the army's policy of questioning all incoming volunteers about their political affiliations. Hollmann subsequently required each installation and command to file an annual report of its number of Social Democrats, due every April 15. The numbers registered in 1895, 1896, and 1897 were small, with most commanders reporting no men admitting being Social Democrats and none reporting any problems. Once the navy had its short list of names, Hollmann took an interest in disciplinary cases involving confessed Social Democrats, but these were rare indeed: in 1895 one man received a two-month prison term for inflicting serious bodily harm (*gefährlicher Körperverletzung*) in a fight, and in 1896 another received two months for showing disrespect (*Achtungsverletzung*) to a superior. Hollmann also cooperated with the police in investigating the records of former seamen and navy workers active in the Social Democratic movement after their discharge. These efforts likewise unearthed no evidence of past socialist proselytizing within the service.[11]

Not all officers conformed to the antisocialist spirit Hollmann sought to introduce to the corps. In the wake of the Reichstag election of 1893, a local *Landrat* in Holstein advised the navy to fire an employee of the Friedrichsort torpedo factory because he was a socialist "agitator" and had participated in a Social Democratic rally in Laboe, near Kiel. The factory's *Kapitänleutnant* Theodor Harms issued an angry response: "The torpedo factory considers it wrong to dismiss workers because of their political conduct outside of the workplace and working hours." The case went to Knorr, then chief of the Baltic station, who supported Harms's contention that the man in question, "a useful worker and chairman of the worker's committee of the torpedo factory," should not be fired for his political convictions.[12] Hollmann eventually claimed jurisdiction in the matter, which became lost amid the general infighting plaguing the naval hierarchy.[13] In the light of the strong animosities among the navy's leaders, Knorr's stand must be seen as more of a defense of the prerogatives of the office of station chief than an endorsement of a worker's freedom of conscience. In general, given the meager results of Hollmann's vigilance against the phantom socialist threat within the navy, these efforts must be characterized as a waste of time. Nevertheless, by the time Tirpitz succeeded Hollmann at the Imperial Navy Office, officers were accustomed to doing required paperwork on Social Democrats as a part of their annual routine. During his years as chief of staff in the High Command (1892–95), Tirpitz was relentless in his criticism of Hollmann's leadership and strategic outlook; it is no small irony that Hollmann was also the man most responsible for encouraging and institutionalizing the antisocialist ideology Tirpitz so strongly advocated.

As head of the Imperial Navy Office, Tirpitz feared that higher education would endanger an officer candidate's ideological reliability. He even warned that the increasing number of cadets holding the *Abitur*— young men whose social backgrounds also tended to be less prestigious— would cause "internal political" problems in the corps of sea officers. Perhaps it is not surprising that Tirpitz, a *Realschule* dropout who entered the navy just days after his sixteenth birthday, did not place much value on the *Abitur,* or even the completion of school. Others in his camp included Koester, ironically so, since his father held a Ph.D. Senden also doubted the value of a completed civilian education, but his eventual successor as head of the Navy Cabinet, Georg Alexander von Müller, would show a strong preference for candidates with the *Abitur*. In the 1890s entering cadets reflected a mix of educational backgrounds, ranging from an increasing share with the *Abitur* to a significant number who had failed to complete school before entering the navy. In 1894, 40 percent of those entering held the *Abitur;* over the next twenty years, the number increased to 90 percent. In 1885 Caprivi had to raise the navy's entrance standards to conform to those of the army; ironically, after 1900 the typical navy officer candidate was far better educated than his army counterpart, and the de facto higher standards actually became a deterrent for applicants with weaker academic backgrounds.[14]

In the debate over the constitution of an ideal sea officer, Tirpitz had strong views on the questions of class, ideology, education, and strategic outlook. Above all else, however, he valued and rewarded personal loyalty. After he became the navy's dominant personality, he would give no quarter to those he deemed undesirable but always made room for old protégés, even if they did not pass all of his other litmus tests. As Goltz's chief of staff after 1892, he had secured transfers to the High Command of many of his former subordinates from the Torpedo Inspection; he would repeat the

process again after 1897, when he took over the Imperial Navy Office. Indeed, Tirpitz's inclination to trust former torpedo men overrode considerations that would otherwise disqualify them, in his eyes, for positions of
influence. In some cases he continued to advance the careers of men who
remained advocates of cruisers and torpedo boats rather than battleships.
And Tirpitz did not know—or perhaps did not care—that Captain Theodor Harms was "soft" on socialism. The former head of the torpedo factory in Friedrichsort, who had entered the torpedo service under Tirpitz in
the late 1880s, followed his mentor to the Imperial Navy Office. His appointment to the office staff, in 1897, came just four years after his ringing
defense of a navy worker's right to be an active Social Democrat.[15]

From Hollmann to Tirpitz: The Navy and Naval Policy after the Kruger Telegram (1896–1897)

In early January 1896 the heads of all three agencies of the navy—Hollmann of the Imperial Navy Office, Knorr of the High Command, and
Senden of the Navy Cabinet—supported the decision to send the "Kruger
telegram."[16] Their endorsement came despite the fact that in the short
term, a war with the British would have been disastrous for the German
fleet. Thus, long before Tirpitz tied the future of the navy to his high-stakes
"risk theory," its leaders recognized that they had much to gain from a
deterioration of relations with Britain, and were also willing to support a
gamble that might pay off over time. They could count upon Senden, in
particular, to fan the flames of William II's anglophobia, using his unique
position within the inner circle and daily contact with the emperor. Bernhard von Bülow later recalled that Senden "liked to meddle in foreign policy . . . in an anti-English sense" and "had a deplorable influence . . . on Anglo-German relations."[17]

The expansion of German overseas interests helped create the Anglo-
German tensions in South Africa that flared up during and after the Transvaal crisis. The navy's African station cruisers, though small and unarmored, had played a role, too, in heightening British anxieties over
German support for the Boers. By the 1890s Germany's booming export
economy jeopardized British interests in several markets, but from the
British perspective the threat was greatest in South Africa. Through the
German East Africa Line, Adolph Woermann linked Hamburg not only
with German East Africa but also with the ports of British South Africa
and Portuguese Mozambique, thus greatly expanding Germany's stake in
the southern African economy. In 1889 Germany exported only 8.4 million

marks' worth of goods to South Africa; six years later the total departing through Hamburg alone reached 22.3 million. Concurrent German involvement in financing the construction of a railway between the Transvaal capital, Pretoria, and the port of Lourenço Marques led to rumors of a German annexation of Mozambique. In January 1895, fearing a preemptive British annexation of Mozambique, the Germans sent the light cruisers *Seeadler* and *Condor* to safeguard their interests. The *Condor* remained off Lourenço Marques for ceremonies celebrating the opening of the railway, and a reception for President Kruger aboard the cruiser caused a sensation in Britain.[18]

The Jameson Raid of December 1895 prompted the German community in Pretoria to appeal for German intervention. The consulate even called for a landing party from the *Seeadler,* then docked at Lourenço Marques, to come via the new railway to the Transvaal capital. Back in Berlin, the chief of the High Command, Admiral Knorr, and the foreign secretary, Marschall, both favored the move.[19] William II avoided such a direct confrontation, but his subsequent "Kruger telegram" was provocative enough. In case of a war over South Africa, Germany would have been able to give only some initial token support to the Boers; afterward, the navy's African cruisers and isolated warships on other stations would easily fall prey to British cruisers. Thus, even a brief period of hostilities—brought to an end by diplomacy within weeks, before the British battle fleet blockaded the German coast—still would be devastating for the navy. Not willing to take the risk, the emperor ordered home the *Condor* and *Seeadler* from Mozambique, and the *Kaiser* and *Arcona* from the Far East. On 21 January 1896 he proposed the recall of all overseas cruisers, ostensibly as a gambit to impress commercial and pro-colonial circles of the gravity of the situation and rally them behind a new fleet plan. He backed down after Chancellor Hohenlohe advised him that the British would interpret such moves as a sign of weakness. The cruiser division remained intact in the Far East, and one warship, the *Seeadler,* stayed at Lourenço Marques.[20]

William II's confusion and wavering in the wake of the "Kruger telegram" kept Tirpitz's memorandum of December 1895 from having the desired impact. The prospect of superior British cruiser forces sweeping the overseas stations of German cruisers even prompted the emperor to return, temporarily, to his earlier preference for cruisers over battleships. Within the government and the imperial suite, only Senden stood firmly in Tirpitz's corner. Hollmann and Hohenlohe believed the Reichstag would not support dramatic naval expansion, no matter which type of ship dominated the program. In response, Senden resolved to persuade William II to sack both of them.[21] The chief of the Navy Cabinet spread rumors of an imperial coup d'état against Hohenlohe, with the desired effect. The chancellor came out in favor of a fleet plan, thus saving his job. Hollmann likewise endured considerable anxiety; in late January 1896 he confided in Hohenlohe that an angry William II had upbraided him at a drinking party hosted by Senden.[22] Within days, the emperor summoned Tirpitz to an audience and, according to the admiral's later recollections, informed him that he would soon succeed Hollmann.[23]

Tirpitz quickly drafted wide-ranging plans to transform the Imperial Navy Office into a "super-ministry" he would inherit: an office controlling the navy, merchant marine, and colonial policy. Senden and the Navy Cabinet gave him enthusiastic support. His mentor Stosch, then lingering near death, also encouraged him. Stosch had advocated a similar conglomeration of agencies as early as the 1870s, and again before the reorganization of 1889. Unfortunately for Tirpitz, the sweeping nature of the proposal shocked William II.[24] Tirpitz's lack of seniority also posed a problem. In January 1896 he ranked thirteenth among admirals, and to make him head of the Imperial Navy Office, even without the expanded powers, would have been an unprecedented step. In any event, the emperor decided to grant Hollmann another reprieve. He sanctioned the budget proposals for 1896–97 on the condition that within a year, Hollmann would prepare a plan for naval expansion to submit to the Reichstag. With the fresh vote of confidence came a promotion to full admiral. Tirpitz, meanwhile, received command of the cruiser division on the East Asian station. His supporters considered the forced exile a blessing. Fully expecting Hollmann to fail, they were confident that Tirpitz would succeed him soon enough. Until then, the Far East command allowed Tirpitz to enhance his professional credentials (he had never commanded a formation so large) while avoiding further controversy.[25]

Tirpitz's year in East Asia was far from uneventful. In July 1896, shortly after he arrived to assume command of the cruiser division, the gunboat *Iltis* burned and sank in the China Sea. The accident claimed seventy-six lives, including Captain Otto Braun, a protégé of Tirpitz since his days at the Torpedo Inspection.[26] The recent increase in the number of German warships operating in Chinese waters brought to the forefront the issue of establishing a permanent base. In September 1896, Tirpitz recommended Kiaochow Bay. Berlin soon confirmed the choice, but the pretext for seizing the territory did not arise until after he was recalled to Germany. In early November 1897, five months after Tirpitz's departure, William II gave his successor in the Far East, Vice Admiral Diederichs, permission to take the bay. German officials cited the recent murder of two Catholic missionaries on the Shantung Peninsula as their reason. Over the next several years the fishing village of Tsingtao (Qingdao), on Kiaochow Bay, would grow into a bustling German naval base.[27]

Meanwhile, in the Reichstag debate over the 1896–97 navy budget, Hollmann benefited from the support of the Free Conservative leader Wilhelm von Kardorff, an opponent earlier in the decade. In his speeches, Kardorff pointed to the pace of naval construction in other countries. Eugen Richter again led the anti-navy camp, but those advocating at least some cuts included Alois Fritzen of the Center. Despite this troubling reminder that Ernst Lieber had not yet maneuvered the Catholic party firmly behind the navy, in March 1896 the Reichstag approved Hollmann's estimates for 1896–97. The package included funds for a division of torpedo boats, three cruisers, and a second battleship of the *Kaiser Friedrich III* class, as a replacement for the old *Friedrich der Grosse*. The imperial shipyard in Wilhelmshaven laid down the new battleship, the future *Kaiser Wilhelm II*, later in 1896. Two of the cruisers were larger, 5,900-ton versions of the *Hertha*-class design: the *Hansa*, built by A.G. Vulcan of Stettin, and *Vineta*, by the imperial shipyard in Danzig. Both were laid down in 1896 and launched in the winter of 1897–98. The navy's Danzig shipyard began the third cruiser, the 2,650-ton *Gazelle*, in 1897.[28]

The approval of all of Hollmann's proposed projects for 1896–97 raised the outlay to 99 million marks. Nevertheless, by June 1896 the state secretary again aroused the emperor's ire by doubting the prospects for naval expansion. Much to Senden's astonishment and dismay, William II then agreed with Hollmann that "the big plan" would not pass the Reichstag and should be postponed.[29] In the autumn of 1896 Hollmann proposed a budget for 1897–98 including 70 million marks for construction alone, but instead of a program he offered more of the same mixed fare of previous years: three small *Gazelle*-class cruisers, two gunboats, a division of torpedo boats, and only one battleship, the future *Kaiser Wilhelm der Grosse*, a third 11,100-ton vessel of the *Kaiser Friedrich III* class.[30] His proposal still sufficed to provoke a negative response from at least one British newspaper, the *Morning Post,* which in December 1896 warned of the day when "Germany should be strong enough to overcome the British Channel fleet and convoy an army of invasion."[31]

The cost of the proposal provoked a storm in the Reichstag, and Holl-

Battleship *Kaiser Wilhelm II*, of the *Kaiser Friedrich III* class (laid down 1896; launched September 1897) *Historische Sammlung der Marineschule Mürwik*

Gazelle-class light cruiser, at turn of century
Naval Historical Center, Basic Collection

mann mishandled it terribly. Lieber and the Center party, which had been moving toward a pro-navy posture over the past three years, joined those refusing to support the package as presented. In mid-March 1897 the budget commission reduced the estimates by 19 percent. The lone battle-ship, marketed as a replacement for the thirty-year-old *König Wilhelm*, survived the cut, as did the two gunboats, but the three cruisers and the torpedo boat division did not. Even after the reductions, the outlay for 1897–98 was an unprecedented 130.6 million marks. The Germaniawerft of Kiel received the contract for the *Kaiser Wilhelm der Grosse* and began work on the ship in 1898.[32]

Unaware of the machinations of the inner circles of the German navy, British leaders dismissed the sort of fears the *Morning Post* sought to pro-voke. Indeed, they took some solace in the fact that the German budget might have been even bigger. But alongside the unofficial initiative to sab-otage Hollmann, during the year after the "Kruger telegram" the officers of the High Command also devoted considerable time to their official duties of drafting war plans, with special attention to Britain. The sentiments of Tirpitz, reflected in their personal attacks against Hollmann, likewise shaped the High Command's thinking regarding the theoretical attacks against Britain. In February 1896, just before his departure for the Far East, Tirpitz himself had produced a sketch for a war against Britain, emphasiz-ing the element of surprise. The navy would "proceed into the Thames . . . with everything that can crawl" for a suicide mission immediately after the declaration of war, attack the British merchant marine, and lob shells into the London suburbs.[33] Plans drafted by Tirpitz's old protégés on Knorr's staff in the High Command show similar thinking. In March 1896 Captain Heeringen introduced only minor modifications to his mentor's grand de-sign, advocating mining the mouth of the Thames rather than shelling London.[34] Planning for a war against Britain gained momentum in the spring of 1897. Scenarios included army-navy cooperation and an "expedi-tionary force," which either embarked for an actual invasion or posed a threat to support German diplomacy in an Anglo-German crisis. Plans for a rendezvous of troopships in the mouth of the Schelde hinged on Dutch cooperation, to be obtained by force if necessary.[35]

Schemes for securing the coast of the Netherlands and Belgium had rel-evance not only for an invasion of Britain but also for a war against the Franco-Russian combination; in the latter scenario a German fleet de-ployed off the Low Countries would prevent the French navy from operat-ing in the North Sea.[36] Such proposals struck a responsive chord with the army. Count Alfred von Schlieffen, chief of the general staff since 1891, considered an invasion of Britain completely unfeasible, but his evolving plan for a two-front war against France and Russia considered the value of naval help against Belgium and the Netherlands.[37] For his part, Knorr could not ignore the souring of Anglo-German relations in his view of the navy's Franco-Russian scenario. In 1897 he admitted that a German fleet could not undertake an attack on the French channel coast without Britain's benevolent neutrality.[38] An active alliance of Britain, France, and Russia against Germany was considered beyond the realm of possibility and received no attention at all.

Even with Tirpitz in the Far East, the program for maneuvers still reflected his influence. For 1896 the navy employed the same lineup of warships as the previous year except for the II Division, which consisted of two "sortie corvettes" (the *Sachsen* and *Württemberg*) and the *König Wilhelm,* the latter renovated in 1895–96 by Blohm & Voss of Hamburg for future duty as an armored cruiser. The remaining "sortie corvettes" *Bayern* and *Baden* were temporarily out of service, having their obsolete "sandwich" armor replaced by new Krupp armor; after their return, the *Sachsen* and *Württemberg* were to undergo the same renovation. In August 1896 tactical exercises in the Baltic matched Vice Admiral Koester's I Squadron (the I and II Division) against the II Squadron (III and IV Division) under Rear Admiral Karl Barandon. Once again, each squadron had a group of scout cruisers and a torpedo flotilla. The abstract maneuver followed the same model of the previous year; in issuing the initial instructions, Admiral Knorr even used Tirpitz's term *Linienschiffe* to describe the battleships. In September the focus shifted to the North Sea, where a ten-day "strategic maneuver" simulated a German defense against an attack on the Elbe estuary by an enemy battle fleet. The squadrons used the Kiel Canal for the first time, steaming from Wilhelmshaven to the Baltic at the onset of the tactical maneuvers in August. En route back to the North Sea, they used the Kattegat and Skagerrak.[39]

Though the navy had always divided its largest armored warships between Wilhelmshaven and Kiel, for years the Baltic had been the focal point of the autumn maneuvers. Senden calculated the Baltic component at 80 percent in the 1894 exercises, then only 55 percent in 1895 and 45 percent in 1896. There were major Baltic maneuvers in the future, but the North Sea no longer would be slighted. Other changes in the navy's routine related even more directly to the souring of relations with Britain. Koester's spring cruise with the I and II Division, which went to the

British-owned Orkney and Shetland Islands the previous year, in 1896 included visits to ports in the Netherlands and Norway. William II did not make his usual early August trip to Cowes, freeing the navy from the burden of providing an escort.[40]

The maneuvers of 1896 were the fourth in a row commanded by Koester, but shortly after the exercises ended he exchanged jobs with the chief of the Baltic station, Vice Admiral Thomsen. Prince Henry, a rear admiral since 1895, took over II Division. The ships of the I and II Division, now formally designated the "I Squadron" on a year-round basis, remained active throughout the winter of 1896–97. For the third consecutive year, their routine included a two-week winter cruise. In February 1897 Germany agreed to participate in an international demonstration off Crete. The six great powers organized the operation after Greece proclaimed its annexation of the island, which for centuries had been an Ottoman Turkish possession. The navy kept its battleships in home waters, contributing only the cruiser *Kaiserin Augusta,* but the other Triple Alliance navies were well represented. Italy committed the largest contingent to the blockading fleet.[41] After the *Kaiserin Augusta* went on to the Far East, the casemate ship *Oldenburg,* idle for the past five years, showed the German flag off Crete.[42] A compromise solution ultimately left Crete under Turkish sovereignty but with a Greek prince as governor. The outcome pleased Germany and Austria-Hungary less than the other powers; in a sign of dissatisfaction, they would withdraw their ships early, in March 1898. The Italians, already hedging their bets amid the growing Anglo-German animosity, stayed on until the end of the demonstration, cooperating with the British, French, and Russian forces.[43]

In first weeks of the action off Crete, William II cited naval weakness as the reason for Germany's failure to play a more dominant role.[44] Nevertheless, on another occasion in 1897 he deliberately sent a weak representation. In June, Prince Henry captained the *König Wilhelm* as Germany's lone representative at the naval review commemorating Queen Victoria's sixtieth jubilee.[45] The renovated ship, now technically an armored cruiser, ironically had been built in Britain three decades earlier. As a standard-bearer for the navy, it stood in sharp contrast to the contingents that had accompanied the emperor on his visits to Cowes in 1895 and earlier. In the summer of 1897 William II again missed Cowes, but his itinerary aboard the *Hohenzollern* kept the navy busy in the weeks before autumn maneuvers. In July he called at ports in Norway and Sweden, escorted by the cruiser *Gefion.* In early August, during the week of the Cowes Regatta, he visited Tsar Nicholas II. During the emperor's stay in Russia, Thomsen anchored the I and II Division at Kronstadt, with the *Hohenzollern, Gefion,* two dispatch vessels, and the training corvette *Charlotte.*[46]

For the autumn maneuvers of 1897, the navy for the first time assembled four divisions of armored warships. The four *Brandenburg*-class battleships made up the I Division, while the makeshift II Division again included the *Sachsen, Württemberg,* and *König Wilhelm.* The remaining two divisions also included three ships rather than four, all from the *Siegfried* class. In each of the past five autumn maneuvers, fully-rigged corvettes of the *Stosch* class had formed the III Division, pretending to be battleships; such charades no longer would be necessary. Two groups of scout cruisers and two torpedo flotillas also participated in the maneuvers, which started at Danzig to accommodate the emperor's Russian travel plans. In late August and September, Thomsen and Knorr presided over a "strategic maneuver" in the Baltic, an abstract tactical exercise in the western Baltic, and a second "strategic maneuver" in the North Sea. The last exercise included four of the seldom-used armored gunboats based at Wilhelmshaven, designated the V Division.[47]

By the time the autumn maneuvers of 1897 ended, Tirpitz was back in Berlin as the head of the Imperial Navy Office. His return from the Far East, after only one year, came when William II finally lost patience with Admiral Hollmann. Early in 1897 the emperor formed a special committee to define precisely the prerogatives of the Imperial Navy Office, the High Command, and the Navy Cabinet. Hollmann objected to the committee, fearing that it would curtail his powers. On 4 March 1897, during a visit to Wilhelmshaven, William II and Hollmann quarreled openly over the matter in the officers' mess. A week later, after the Reichstag budget commission reduced the initial naval estimates for 1897–98, Hollmann submitted his resignation. The emperor characteristically wavered before accepting it. On 30 March Hollmann received an extended leave of absence, and the following day Tirpitz was appointed state secretary of the Imperial Navy Office.[48]

Denouement: The Formulation and Passage of the First Navy Law (1897–1898)

Tirpitz learned of his appointment quickly enough but took his time returning home from the Far East, traveling eastward via the United States. He reached Berlin at the beginning of June. Meanwhile, his friend Rear Admiral Büchsel served as interim head of the Imperial Navy Office. In April

1897 William II and Hohenlohe agreed that the German navy should be built up to half the size of the combined Franco-Russian strength in northern waters.[49] Knorr and his staff then laid the groundwork for the new fleet plan. Reflecting some compromise with cruiser advocates, in May 1897 the High Command produced a plan for a fleet of 25 battleships, 8 large (armored) cruisers, 46 medium and small cruisers, 5 gunboats, and 110 torpedo boats, to be completed by 1910 at a cost of 833 million marks. The battleships included existing vessels as old as the 4 "sortie corvettes" (commissioned in 1878–83), as well as the 8 small *Siegfrieds*. This first draft of a Navy Law also called for the automatic replacement of battleships after twenty-five years, and of smaller warships after shorter fixed terms of service.[50]

Tirpitz took office on 15 June 1897, the ninth anniversary of William II's accession to the throne. He was one of five state secretaries appointed that month; other newcomers included Bernhard von Bülow to the Foreign Office. Within the navy, the retirements of Hollmann and another admiral elevated Tirpitz to eleventh in seniority. Of those ahead of him, Senden (eighth on the *Rangliste*) also had direct access to the emperor; the others, including station, division, and squadron commanders, were under Knorr and the High Command. Captains August von Heeringen and Friedrich Ingenohl promptly joined Tirpitz's staff; both had been with him before, at the Torpedo Inspection and the High Command. Former torpedo men Hugo Pohl and Max Fischel were already at the Imperial Navy Office, having served under Hollmann. Tirpitz would transfer other trusted protégés to Berlin over the months and years to come.[51]

In his initial audience, Tirpitz presented William II with a memorandum describing Britain as Germany's "most dangerous enemy . . . against which we most urgently require a certain measure of naval force as a political power factor." He then presented his own proposal for the Navy Law. As in his memorandum of December 1895, he called for an armored fleet of nineteen *Linienschiffe* and the eight *Siegfried*-class coast defenders. Other ships included twelve large and thirty small cruisers, and twelve divisions of torpedo boats. Compared to the High Command's draft of May 1897, Tirpitz proposed two more battleships, four more large (armored) cruisers, sixteen fewer lighter cruisers, no new gunboats, and some two dozen fewer torpedo boats. The goals would be met by 1905, not 1910, at a cost of 58 million marks per year over the seven-year period 1898–1905. Because the Reichstag had already granted 58 million for construction for 1897–98, the estimate appeared reasonable enough.[52]

Like the draft of May 1897, Tirpitz's calculations counted battleships as old as the four "sortie corvettes." Along with the eight newer battleships (*Oldenburg*, the four *Brandenburgs*, and the three battleships of the *Kaiser Friedrich III* class already approved by the Reichstag), these left Tirpitz only seven short of his goal. In the category of large cruisers, Tirpitz counted the renovated old battleships (armored cruisers) *König Wilhelm, Kaiser,* and *Deutschland,* the unarmored *Kaiserin Augusta,* and six warships then under construction (the three vessels of the *Hertha* class, the *Hertha*'s half-sisters *Vineta* and *Hansa,* and the armored cruiser *Fürst Bismarck*), leaving just two to be built. The small cruisers included nineteen vessels already with the fleet, ranging from the *Blitz* (commissioned in 1883) to the *Hela* (1896), as well as the four *Gazelle*-class warships then under construction, leaving seven to be built. The new warship projects, which represented a 30 percent expansion in the size of the fleet, naturally attracted the most attention at the time, obscuring the key to the Tirpitz plan: the provision for the automatic replacement of battleships after twenty-five years, large cruisers after twenty years, and smaller cruisers after fifteen years.[53]

Tirpitz wasted no time rounding up support for the plan. Outside Berlin he focused his efforts on the Hanseatic cities. Hamburg, in particular, had always opposed excessive naval ambitions, fearing grand designs that might provoke a naval war and economic ruin. The leading Hanseatic families still sent their sons into the officer corps of the merchant marine rather than to the navy; as late as the onset of the Caprivi era, only one sea officer above the rank of lieutenant hailed from Hamburg, Bremen, or Lübeck. But on a crucial visit to Hamburg in September 1897, Tirpitz took a giant step toward dispelling old fears. Heeringen, functioning as his chief of propaganda, arranged a banquet at the Hamburg Rathaus with a program of pro-navy speakers including Hamburg's own Adolph Woermann; dignitaries attending included the Hamburg-Amerika Line's director, Albert Ballin. Tirpitz put on a masterful performance and received a warm welcome. Woermann subsequently hosted the admiral and his naval entourage to a reception at his home, affording a further opportunity to convert local commercial and political leaders to the cause. Afterward, Woermann and Ballin mobilized their peers in Hamburg and the commercial community as a whole behind the cause of the fleet.[54]

In the autumn of 1897 Tirpitz began to lay the foundation for the upcoming campaign in the Reichstag, focusing on the largest party, the Center, whose support for Hollmann's last two budgets had been lukewarm at best. In an October interview with Ernst Lieber he secured a promise of support, sealed with a modest contribution to cover the party leader's "expenses."[55] The following month, the murder of the Catholic missionaries in China (in the incident used to justify the seizure of Kiao-chow Bay) helped Lieber persuade his party of the need for a larger navy.[56] After the deliberations began, Tirpitz benefited from the strong support of the Free Conservative leader Kardorff, influential chairman of the Reichstag budget commission.[57]

Over the winter, Tirpitz's plan received endorsements from a host of leading figures outside the Reichstag. Albert Ballin stressed the navy's importance to the promotion and defense of overseas commerce. For a country with a 1.6 million–ton merchant marine on the high seas, the plan would be a good investment: "The expenditure . . . appears to me to be extraordinarily small in comparison to the huge losses which the German national fortune would suffer" in case of a blockade.[58] Bismarck, who would die the following July, gave his blessing in a personal letter in early December, just days before Tirpitz's first speech to the Reichstag.[59] Supporters from German academia included Ernst Haeckel, who used appropriate Darwinist language in calling the fleet "indispensable, if the German Reich shall survive in the struggle for existence with the other great powers of Europe."[60]

The state secretary's Reichstag speech of 6 December 1897, marking the formal onset of the battle for passage of the Navy Law, employed similar ominous language. In crafting his grand strategy, Tirpitz, like Mahan, was influenced in no small measure by the social Darwinism then in fashion: he characterized the construction of the fleet as a "question of survival" for Germany.[61] With the conservative parties, the National Liberals, and the leadership of the Center party in Tirpitz's corner, the passage of the bill was never seriously in doubt. The navy could fall short of the 199 votes it needed only if more than half the Center defied Lieber and voted against passage. The bill cleared its first reading on 24 March 1898 and became law on 10 April. The Reichstag finally divided 212 to 139 in favor of Tirpitz, with 46 abstentions. The margin of victory was almost too close for comfort. Some twenty members of the Center, including all of the Bavarian representatives except future chancellor Georg von Hertling, joined the Social Democrats and most Progressives in voting no.[62]

The navy wasted no time ordering the new warships authorized by the law, dispensing the contracts to a variety of shipyards. The *Kaiser Karl der Grosse* and *Kaiser Barbarossa,* the last two battleships of the 11,100-ton *Kaiser Friedrich III* class, were laid down later in 1898 by Blohm & Voss of Hamburg and Schichau of Danzig, respectively. They were followed by the five vessels of the 11,800-ton *Wittelsbach* class: the *Wittelsbach* (imperial shipyard, Wilhelmshaven, 1899), *Wettin* (Schichau of Danzig, 1899), *Zähringen* (Germaniawerft of Kiel, 1899), *Schwaben* (imperial shipyard, Wilhelmshaven, 1900), and *Mecklenburg* (A.G. Vulcan of Stettin, 1900). The imperial shipyard in Kiel laid down both of the new "large cruisers," the 8,900-ton armored cruiser *Prinz Heinrich* (1898) and the 9,100-ton *Prinz Adalbert* (1900). Most of the "small cruisers" were additions to the *Gazelle* class.[63] All sixteen of the newly authorized warships were still under construction in June 1900 when Tirpitz, capitalizing on an international climate that included the Boer War in South Africa and the Boxer Rebellion in China, secured passage of the Second Navy Law. The new legislation expanded the fleet to thirty-eight battleships, twenty large cruisers, and thirty-eight small cruisers. As in the 1898 law, the ships were to be replaced automatically after a fixed number of years.[64]

The automatic replacement provision gave the navy the ultimate insurance policy. As Volker Berghahn has pointed out, it meant that "a future more left-wing assembly was, constitutionally, no longer in a position to reduce the naval establishment by refusing to approve the naval estimates."[65] In addition to guaranteeing the size of the fleet, the Reichstag, in effect, also gave the navy carte blanche to "replace" small old ships with larger new ships, because it was taken for granted that replacement ships would have to reflect the state of the art of their future era. As luck would have it, the oldest existing battleships counted in the Tirpitz plan, the four 7,600-ton "sortie corvettes," came due for replacement just after the British *Dreadnought* revolutionized battleship design. The four 18,900-ton dreadnoughts of the *Nassau* class "replaced" them. The newer but smaller *Siegfried*-class coast defenders, 3,500-ton vessels counted as battleships by Tirpitz, ultimately were "replaced" by dreadnoughts of the 22,800-ton *Helgoland* class and 24,700-ton *Kaiser* class.[66] Initially, armored cruisers filled the quota of new and replacement cruisers in the "large" category; eventually these gave way to battle cruisers that rivaled the dreadnoughts in size. In his calculations of 1897, Tirpitz categorized as "large cruisers" ships as small as the 5,700-ton *Hertha*s. The *Ersatz Hertha*, when finally built, was the 27,000-ton battle cruiser *Hindenburg*.[67]

· · ·

The Reichstag victories of 1898 and 1900 set Tirpitz on a course to become the most successful political figure in the history of the Second Reich, after Bismarck. He would remain in office for nineteen years, finally resigning in the midst of World War I. His initial successes brought honors and acclaim, along with the opportunity to consolidate his power within the navy. After the passage of the First Navy Law, William II made Tirpitz a Prussian minister of state; among the previous leaders of the service, only Stosch had held this position along with an Imperial German naval port-folio. Two years later Tirpitz became one of five current and former navy officers elevated to the nobility, heretofore a rare honor accorded only to Henk (in 1878) and Knorr (in 1896). In 1899 the abolition of the High Command and fragmentation of its former powers eliminated the most likely source of opposition to Tirpitz and the Imperial Navy Office. After the turn of the century, as his old torpedo protégés became admirals, as-suming squadron and station commands, his grip over the service only tightened. According to one estimate, between 1902 and 1915 six of the seven chiefs of the reconstituted Admiralty Staff came from this circle of officers, as well as all of the commanders of the High Seas Fleet between 1913 and the end of World War I. Senden's retirement, in 1906, eliminated his last potential rival. Georg Alexander von Müller, who had served under Tirpitz at the Torpedo Inspection and in the High Command, succeeded Senden as chief of the Navy Cabinet.[68]

Meanwhile, the original seven-year Navy Law led the British Admiralty to revise its own future construction plans, taking into account "the stren-uous efforts of the Imperial German Government to increase the numbers of their battleships." But at this stage the sea lords feared the impact of the German buildup on the overall European naval balance much more than a direct German threat to Britain. They assumed that the Tirpitz plan would provoke increased construction in both France and Russia, the second and third naval powers of Europe. This, in turn, would compel Britain to build more battleships in order to preserve the sacrosanct "Two-Power Stand-ard," the established yardstick for gauging national security. In any event, the foundations of the future Anglo-German naval rivalry were firmly in place. Later in 1898 the Anglo-French "Fashoda Crisis" would spark hope for a rapprochement between Britain and Germany, but afterward the Boer War and Tirpitz's Second Navy Law set the two powers on their colli-sion course.[69]

EPILOGUE

he sea is the highway of the world. The sea is the parade ground of the nations." A half-century after Friedrich List's stirring words, Germany had the second-largest merchant marine on the highway, behind only the British. Thanks to the Tirpitz plan, the German battle fleet would become the second largest on the parade ground, likewise trailing only the British. List's prediction in 1841, that the corvette *Amazone* would be "the forefather of a greater progeny," eventually came true. Fittingly, one of the *Gazelle*-class light cruisers constructed under the First Navy Law was christened *Amazone*, the navy's first reuse of the name after the original vessel.[1]

Looking back from the passage of the First Navy Law, it is natural to ask whether such a breakthrough could have happened earlier. It is no coincidence that the Frankfurt Parliament of 1848–49 raised serious hopes not only for a united Germany, but also for a German navy. The economic cooperation and customs union achieved by the Prussian-led Zollverein failed to provide a sufficient foundation for a common German front at sea; before the creation of the North German Confederation in 1867 and the German Empire in 1871, political disunity and the smaller states' mistrust of Prussia effectively blocked the creation of a German navy. Stosch lifted the navy out of the doldrums following the Franco-Prussian War and implemented a construction program. Germany, at least briefly, had the third-largest armored fleet in the world, but his *Marinepolitik* fizzled out after the *Grosser Kurfürst* disaster. The next window of opportunity came after Bismarck's pro-navy pronouncement of the spring of 1886; prospects for an expansion program improved still more after the election of the friendly "Cartel" Reichstag in February 1887. But the confusion wrought by the *Jeune École* made it difficult for the navy to devise a coherent plan, and the chief of the Admiralty himself, Caprivi, posed an obstacle to expansion.

In his memoirs, Tirpitz himself characterized the years 1888 to 1897 as "the lost decade." He speculated that if the program of naval expansion had begun with the onset of William II's reign, the "political danger zone" could have been crossed before opposition to Germany coalesced in the international arena.[2] But from the new emperor's accession in June 1888 to the election of February 1890, the power struggle between Bismarck and William II coincided with the disruptive reorganization of the naval hierarchy. From February 1890 until June 1893 an unfriendly Reichstag made the passage of a navy law highly unlikely, even if one had been devised. Favorable conditions returned only in June 1893, with the election of a new Reichstag that subsequently passed Chancellor Caprivi's controversial army bill. These elections, held exactly five years after William II's accession, also came four years to the day before Tirpitz took over as state secretary in the Imperial Navy Office. Thus, at the most, the "wasted ten years" were a "wasted four years." Even during the period between 1893 and 1897, the shift to a pro-navy posture of the influential Center party, the key to the passage of the First Navy Law, occurred only gradually. In the spring of 1898 a substantial minority of the Center still refused to follow its leaders and support the navy. The opposition came from the party's Bavarian wing, reflecting the fact that some old divisions still existed between the coast and the interior. During the same "wasted four years" the navy finally stumbled toward a general consensus on Tirpitz's strategic and tactical outlook, as well as the conviction that an expanded fleet should be based around battleships concentrated in home waters. From the hindsight of 1919 Tirpitz called 1897–98 "too late" to start naval expansion, yet it is difficult to see how the convergence of factors and sentiments could have occurred much earlier.[3]

Of course, the German navy could not have made its ultimate rise without William II. Like Friedrich List—albeit in a more emotional, less intellectually sophisticated way—he saw Britain as Germany's role model, rival, and potential ally. The fate of the Tirpitz plan hinged on the emperor's willingness to sanction a program with such potentially dire consequences for Anglo-German relations. By placing the prestige of his office behind the expansion of the fleet, he enhanced the prestige of the navy and made it a focal point of German nationalism and national aspirations. But the emperor lacked the temperament and attention to detail to manage the systematic development of a stronger navy.[4] Even the most talented admiral could not have brought the plan to fruition without the backing of the emperor, but the emperor was just as stymied without the right admiral. This role would have to be filled by a senior officer with either the conciliatory skills or the blind ambition necessary to overcome divisions within the service and sell the program to the Reichstag.

After 1897, Germany's long-standing naval ambitions finally came to fruition under the guidance of Tirpitz, an individual with a well-established record of ambition and opportunism in his own career. In the 1870s and 1880s he tied his fate to the new torpedo service, which afforded considerable autonomy for a junior officer, as well as the opportunity to impress those at the top. After the *Jeune École* passed out of fashion, he became the leading German disciple of Mahan, arguing for a battleship navy. As chief of staff of the Baltic station, he fought for greater powers for the station chiefs. As chief of staff of the High Command, he sought to expand the prerogatives of that agency vis-à-vis the stations and the Imperial Navy Office. Then, as state secretary, he helped bring about the demise of the High Command and succeeded in making the Imperial Navy Office the dominant agency within the navy. Finally, in the wartime twilight of his career, as his precious battle fleet rusted at anchor in Wilhelmshaven, he became an advocate of unrestricted submarine warfare.[5]

More than any other single factor, the Tirpitz plan put Imperial Germany on the road to its demise in 1918. A common fear of German might on land brought together the strange bedfellows of Tsarist Russia and Republican France; without the German High Seas Fleet concentrated in the North Sea, it is difficult to imagine that Britain would have joined their camp. And in 1917 it was a naval threat—to be sure, from submarines rather than battleships—that brought the United States into World War I against Germany. Yet it is not entirely correct to give all of the blame to Tirpitz, although in his own memoirs, and the memoirs of his loyal protégés, he receives the lion's share of the credit for the existence of a German navy. Prussia had a navy long before Tirpitz joined it, and Germany had the world's third-largest armored battle fleet some fifteen years before the passage of the First Navy Law. The threads Tirpitz wove together—political and industrial, ideological and emotional—were already present in Germany, some only for a short time, others since before 1848, in the visions of men as diverse as Prince Adalbert and Friedrich List. In any event, the explosive growth of the German Navy League after its founding in 1898 attests to the strength of popular navalism among the public in the Second Reich.

In their appraisal of Tirpitz's motives, many historians have argued that the domestic antisocialist, antiparliamentary goals of William II's *Weltpolitik* were Tirpitz's own primary goals. This thesis fails to take into account the admiral's opportunism and attributes to him a depth of ideological conviction that simply did not exist, at least in the mid-1890s. He became a leading conservative political figure after his appointment to the Imperial Navy Office, but he remained, first and foremost, a navy man with naval interests. His primary goal was to gain more ships, more money, and a secure, central place for the navy in the overall grand strategy of his country. He linked his ambitious fleet plan to an antisocialist domestic agenda mostly as a means to an end.[6]

Nevertheless, the grand design of William II and Tirpitz, embodying domestic as well as foreign policy goals, was clearly antiparliamentary. Its promise of stability at home and greatness abroad, all wrapped in the cloak of patriotism, had an overwhelming appeal. Imperial Germany was far from being a political democracy; the electoral geometry of the Reichstag and the even more unjust systems of states such as Prussia guaranteed, above all, that the Social Democrats would be underrepresented.[7] Yet there was enough of a parliamentary system in place to defy the will of the emperor and block a program such as the Tirpitz plan, if a solid majority of the voting public had, indeed, opposed it. Some commercial leaders, academics, and liberal politicians later regretted the virtual blank check the Reichstag gave to William II and Tirpitz.[8] But they could never live down the fact that they had not been among the doubters in earlier years, when the foundations of *Weltpolitik* were first established. As Chancellor Hohenlohe observed in November 1897, at the onset of the Reichstag debate over the First Navy Law: "It is always said that the navy is a whim of the emperor. And yet it cannot be denied that it is the German people's fault—or if you like, their merit—that we possess a navy."[9]

MAPS

NORWAY

SWEDEN

Skagerrak

Kattegat

Jutland

DENMARK

Copenhagen

Sjaelland

Malmö

Föhr

Sylt ·Flensburg

Rügen

Amrum

Schlei ·Eckernförde

Putbus

x Battle of Jasmund
(1864)

Friedrichstadt

Friedrichsort

Fehmarn

Tönning·

·Laboe

Heiligenhafen

Stralsund

Greifswalder Bodden

Helgoland

Eider River

·Kiel

Neustadt

Warnemünde

Swinemünde

Büsum

Rendsburg

Eider Canal

Rostock

Greifswald

Brunsbüttel·

·Glückstadt

Lübeck

Cuxhaven·

Stettiner Haff

Wilhelmshaven·

·Bremerhaven

·Hamburg

Altona

Stettin·

·Emden

Geestemünde

Elbe River

Ems River

Weser River

·Bremen

Oder River

0   50   100
miles

Denmark and Northern Germany

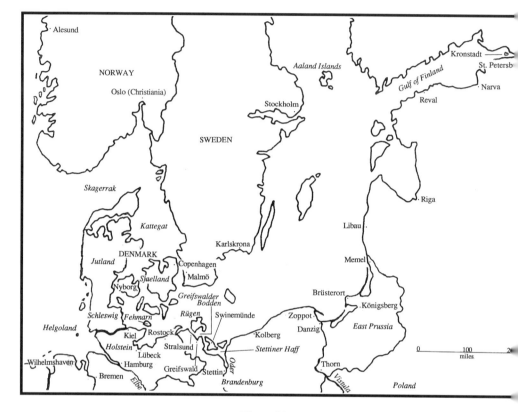

The Baltic Sea

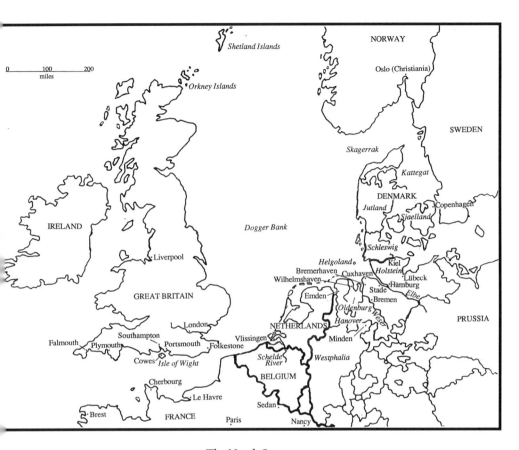

The North Sea

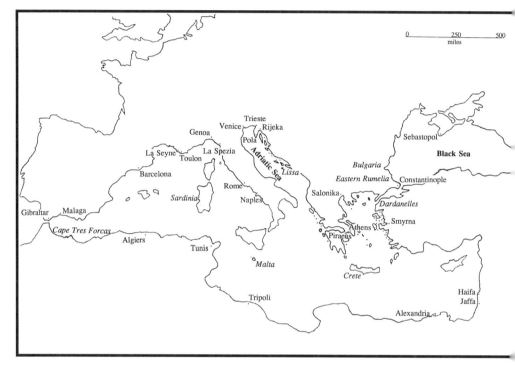

The Mediterranean Sea

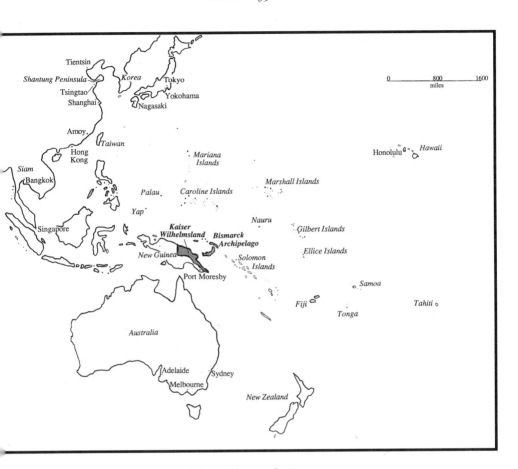

East Asia and the Pacific Ocean

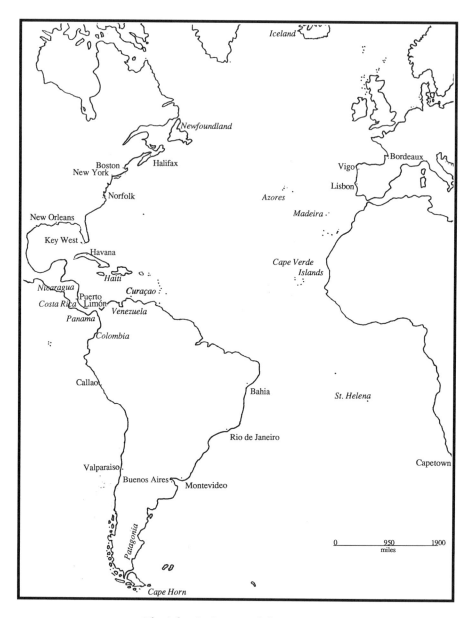

The Atlantic Ocean and the Americas

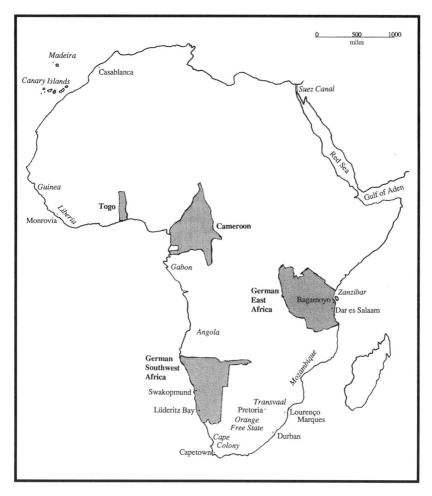

Africa

APPENDIX

Armored Warships of the German Navy (to 1898)

Name	Design[1]	Built In[2]	Laid Down	With Fleet[3]
Arminius	1,600-ton turret ship	(Britain)	1863	1865–72
Prinz Adalbert	1,400-ton ram	(France)	1863	1865–71
Kronprinz	5,800-ton battery frigate	(Britain)	1866	1867–1901
Friedrich Carl	6,000-ton battery frigate	(France)	1866	1867–95
König Wilhelm	9,800-ton battery frigate	(Britain)	1865	1869–1904[4]
Hansa	3,950-ton casemate ship	IS-Danzig	1868	1875–84 (–88)
Kaiser	7,600-ton casemate ship	(Britain)	1871	1875–1904[4]
Deutschland	7,600-ton casemate ship	(Britain)	1872	1875–1904[4]
Preussen	6,800-ton turret ship	AGV-Stettin	1871	1876–91
Friedrich der Grosse	6,800-ton turret ship	IS-Kiel	1871	1877–96
Grosser Kurfürst	6,800-ton turret ship	IS-W'haven	1869	1878
Sachsen	7,600-ton sortie corvette	AGV-Stettin	1875	1878–1902
Bayern	7,600-ton sortie corvette	IS-Kiel	1874	1881–1910
Württemberg	7,600-ton sortie corvette	AGV-Stettin	1876	1881–1906
Baden	7,600-ton sortie corvette	IS-Kiel	1876	1883–1910
Oldenburg	5,200-ton casemate ship	AGV-Stettin	1883	1886–1900
Siegfried	3,500-ton coastal battleship	GW-Kiel	1888	1890–
Beowulf	3,500-ton coastal battleship	W-Bremen	1890	1892–
Frithjof	3,500-ton coastal battleship	W-Bremen	1890	1893–
Hildebrand	3,500-ton coastal battleship	IS-Kiel	1890	1893–
Wörth	10,000-ton battleship	GW-Kiel	1890	1893–
Brandenburg	10,000-ton battleship	AGV-Stettin	1890	1893–
Kurfürst Friedrich Wilhelm	10,000-ton battleship	IS-W'haven	1890	1894–1910
Weissenburg	10,000-ton battleship	AGV-Stettin	1890	1894–1910
Heimdall	3,500-ton coastal battleship	IS-W'haven	1891	1894–
Hagen	3,500-ton coastal battleship	IS-Kiel	1891	1894–
Ägir	3,550-ton coastal battleship	IS-Kiel	1892	1896–
Odin	3,550-ton coastal battleship	IS-Danzig	1893	1896–
Kaiser Friedrich III	11,100-ton battleship	IS-W'haven	1895	1898–
Fürst Bismarck	10,700-ton armored cruiser	IS-Kiel	1895	1900–
Kaiser Wilhelm II	11,100-ton battleship	IS-W'haven	1896	1900–
Kaiser Wilhelm der Grosse	11,100-ton battleship	GW-Kiel	1898	1901–

1. Ships under 1,400 tons not included.

2. IS-Kiel—Imperial Shipyard, Kiel; IS-W'haven—Imperial Shipyard, Wilhelmshaven; IS-Danzig—Imperial Shipyard, Danzig; AGV-Stettin—A.G. Vulcan, Stettin; W-Bremen—A.G. Weser, Bremen; GW-Kiel—Germaniawerft, Kiel.

3. Ships with no deactivation date listed were still with the fleet at the beginning of World War I.

4. *König Wilhelm, Kaiser,* and *Deutschland* rebuilt as armored cruisers during the 1890s.

NOTES

Preface

1. See, e.g., Berghahn, *Der Tirpitz-Plan*, 27, and Herwig, *"Luxury" Fleet*, 9.

2. Lambi, *The Navy and German Power Politics*, 1, uses "the naval enthusiasm of 1848" as his point of departure but devotes less than one full sentence to the naval work of the Frankfurt Parliament. Herwig, *"Luxury" Fleet*, budgets eight pages for the years before 1888.

Chapter 1: Origins

1. R. Werner, *Erinnerungen und Bilder*, 4–7.

2. See, e.g., R. Werner, *Bilder aus der deutschen Seekriegsgeschichte*, 8.

3. See, e.g., Jankuhn, "Schiffahrt und Seeherrschaft der Urzeit," 21–45.

4. On the Hanseatic League see Blum, "Aus der Hansezeit," 47; Sprandel, "Gewerbe und Handel, 1350–1500," 1:348; Petter, "Deutsche Flottenrüstung," 13, 33; Bidlingmaier, *Seegeltung*, 28–38. Wollstein, *Das "Grossdeutschland" der Paulskirche*, 256, notes that in 1841 a medieval alliance of 1241 was celebrated as the six hundredth anniversary of the founding of the Hanseatic League.

5. Steltzer, *"Mit herrlichen Häfen versehen"*; Schück, *Brandenburg-Preussens Kolonial-Politik*; Auerbach, "Die brandenburgisch-preussische Marine," 697–710; Petter, "Deutsche Flottenrüstung," 24–28, 33–34.

6. Petter, "Deutsche Flottenrüstung," 30; Wislicenus, *Deutschlands Seemacht*, 51; Zorn, "Gewerbe und Handel, 1648–1800," 1:561.

7. Mantey, *Deutsche Marinegeschichte*, 37–39; Petter, "Deutsche Flottenrüstung," 30.

8. Frederick the Great, *Die Politischen Testamente*, 105.

9. Radtke, *Seehandlung*, 5–6, 41–43; Burmester, *Weltumseglung*, 18. In a second "Political Testament," written in 1768, Frederick remarked that "Prussia is a continental power. It needs a good army, but no fleet." Quoted in Born, "Die Politischen Testamente Friedrichs des Grossen," 23.

10. Bessell, *Norddeutscher Lloyd*, 8–9.

11. Petter, "Deutsche Flottenrüstung," 31, places the Prussian losses of 1806 at twelve hundred ships; Herwig, *"Luxury" Fleet,* 10, refers only to a loss of three hundred "barges and coastal vessels." See also Radtke, *Seehandlung,* 33.

12. Bundesarchiv-Militärarchiv (hereafter cited as BA-MA), RM 1/1957, 25, "Verzeichniss," [n.d., 1816?], shows the cutters *No.1, Adler, Drossel, Schwalbe,* and *Habicht,* and the merchantmen *Speculant, Indianer,* and *Adèle.* Wislicenus, *Deutschlands Seemacht,* 52, lists one merchantman rather than three. RM 1/1956, 2–6, refers to *No.1* and *Adèle,* both seized at Pillau, as later helping the Russians at Danzig. RM 1/1954 indicates that the owner of the lugger *Indianer* claimed compensation for the use of his ship at Pillau, which it guarded along with the *Habicht.*

13. For a text of Article 11 of the German Federal Act see Huber, *Dokumente zur deutschen Verfassungsgeschichte,* 1:78.

14. BA-MA, RM 1/1890, 39–43, contains a complete résumé for Longé (in French) dated Stralsund, 5 September 1815. On the six gunboats see Gröner, *Die deutschen Kriegsschiffe,* 1:155. See also Petter, "Deutsche Flottenrüstung," 41. All displacement figures should be considered approximate. As a general rule, for ships of 1,000 tons or more the displacement will be rounded off to the nearest 100 tons; for those under 1,000 tons but more than 100 tons, the displacement will be rounded off to the nearest 10 tons.

15. Frederick William III to Boyen, Berlin, 2 April 1816, BA-MA, RM 1/1644, 10; Boyen to Baron Friedrich von Schuckmann (interior minister), Berlin, 22 June 1816, RM 1/1891, 36; Count Hans von Bülow (finance minister) to Boyen, Berlin, 16 December 1816, RM 1/1953, 36; Lieutenant General Engelbrechten to War Ministry, Stralsund, 22 December 1816, ibid., 39. Governor General of Pomerania to Bülow, Stralsund, 16 May 1816, ibid., 28–31, indicates that the future *König Friedrich Wilhelm* was built by the Swedes in 1799. For specifications on the *Stralsund* see Gröner, *Die deutsche Kriegsschiffe,* 1:106; Gröner and other Prussian-German naval indexes do not count the *König Friedrich Wilhelm* as a warship.

16. Hardenberg to Boyen, Berlin, 12 June 1817, BA-MA, RM 1/1953, 51; Longé report (on initial cruise of *Stralsund*), Stralsund, 26 June 1817, RM 1/1892, 100–117. See also Gröner, *Die deutschen Kriegsschiffe,* 1:106.

17. Boyen to Hardenberg, Berlin, 17 February 1819, BA-MA, RM 1/1893, 52–54. See also Röhr, *Handbuch,* 36; Gröner, *Die deutschen Kriegsschiffe,* 1:106, 155; Petter, "Deutsche Flottenrüstung," 41–42, 45; and Mantey, *Deutsche Marinegeschichte,* 42.

18. Hardenberg to Boyen, Berlin, 26 April 1819, BA-MA, RM 1/1893, 68. Correspondence in RM 1/2060 concerns the navigation school's cruises of 1818 and 1819. See also Gröner, *Die deutschen Kriegsschiffe,* 1:106, 155.

19. Longé to Hake, Stralsund, 12 July 1820, BA-MA, RM 1/2748, 621–27.

20. Petter, "Deutsche Flottenrüstung," 43.

21. BA-MA, RM 1/2743, includes proceedings of the Rauch commission. Although the commission's plans did not come to fruition, Frederick William III accepted the notion that merchant mariners on overseas service should be exempt from conscription. In 1825 he granted the exemption for those completing certain long-distance voyages; the following year he expanded it to include everyone serving aboard Seehandlung ships, and in 1827 to all seamen involved in voyages out-

side of the Baltic. The exemption from conscription came with the qualification that in wartime, all merchant seamen over the age of twenty would be liable for naval service. See Petter, "Deutsche Flottenrüstung," 48; Donner, "Die Ereignisse zur See im Kriege 1864," 51.

22. Burmester, *Weltumseglung,* 23–24; Radtke, *Seehandlung,* 260. Burmester lists ten Seehandlung vessels, nine owned outright by the agency as well as the *Georg Foster* (a bark built in Danzig in 1848, in which the Seehandlung had a one-quarter interest), but omits the *Amerika* and *Arminius,* which were chartered in 1822.

23. See Petter, "Deutsche Flottenrüstung," 47–48; Boelcke, *So kam das Meer zu uns,* 30, 40. Three Seehandlung ships were lost at sea. Even though the crews were not subject to military law, Seehandlung captains had a successful record in maintaining discipline; for the 133 voyages, only twenty-four desertions were recorded.

24. Burmester, *Weltumseglung,* 33.

25. Bülow to Hake, Berlin, 24 May 1823, BA-MA, RM 1/2061, unnumbered, indicates that Rauch wanted to send a detachment of sappers (the 1.*Pionier-Abteilung*) from the army engineer corps to sea aboard the *Stralsund* during the summer of 1823, only to learn that the schooner already had been promised to the navigation school.

26. Bülow to War Ministry, Berlin, 5 February 1820, BA-MA, RM 1/2061, unnumbered, refers to Tobiessen's retirement. *Salmonsens Konversations Leksikon,* 3:227, provides a biography of Bille (1769–1845), who received the rank and pension of a rear admiral following his retirement to Denmark in 1838.

27. War Minister to Longé, Berlin, 5 May 1820, BA-MA, RM 1/2061, unnumbered, orders Longé to conduct the mapping project; RM 1/1644, 36–45, refers to Longé's role as a lighthouse consultant. RM 1/1959 reveals that the *König Friedrich Wilhelm* was still in Stralsund as of 1824. Longé to Kemphen, Stralsund, 22 February 1822, RM 1/1893, 119–22, refers to the construction of the new gunboat.

28. Gröner, *Die deutschen Kriegsschiffe,* 1:155–56; Petter, "Deutsche Flottenrüstung," 43. BA-MA, RM 1/2752, 237, refers to the *Garde-Mariniers* at Thorn receiving combat pay in 1831. Regarding the *Danzig's* use as a training ship for the navigation school, Gröner may have confused it with a schooner named *Danzig,* built in 1821 to serve the navigation school on short training cruises. The schooner *Danzig* is mentioned in Theodor von Schön (*Oberpräsident* of East Prussia) to Bille, Danzig, 26 February 1834, RM 1/1969, 55.

29. Biographical sketches of Longé and Murck, through January 1837, in BA-MA, RM 1/2749, 271, indicate that they were away from Stralsund from October 1822 until January 1827. Hake to Friedrich von Motz (finance minister), Berlin, 20 January 1829, RM 1/1894, 121, and Longé to Allgemeines Kriegs-Departement (hereafter A.K.D.), Stralsund, 9 December 1829, ibid., 161, refer to the demise of the *Stralsund.* RM 1/1894 and RM 1/1895 contain quarterly reports, through 1837, of payments of ninety-eight thalers to maintain the Marine Depot; "Verpflegungs-Etat für die Marine pro 1837," RM 1/2752, 20, contains the budget for 1837. See also Gröner, *Die deutschen Kriegsschiffe,* 1:106, 155; Mantey, *Deutsche Marinegeschichte,* 42–43.

30. Major Eduard von Peucker (head of artillery department of war ministry), "Bemerkungen . . . über die A.K.O. [Allerhöchste Kabinetts-Ordre] von 6. Juni 1829," Berlin, 18 February 1831, BA-MA, RM 1/2749, 90–95.

31. Ibid.; Frederick William III to Staatsministerium, Berlin, 11 February 1832, BA-MA, RM 1/2749, 114; Hake, "Votum . . . in Bezug auf die A.K.O. von 6. Juni 1829 und 11. Februar 1832," Berlin, n.d. [February 1832], ibid., 134–36.

32. Reiche to War Ministry, Berlin, 17 June 1835, 1 January 1836, BA-MA, RM 1/2749, 228, 234; Reiche to Witzleben, Berlin, 11 May 1836, ibid., 235–37; "Votum des Kriegsministeriums," Berlin, 22 July 1836, ibid., 244–50; Witzleben to Crown Prince Frederick William, Berlin, 29 January 1837, ibid., 272–78; Petter, "Deutsche Flotten-rüstung," 44; Wislicenus, "Zum hundertsten Geburtstag des Prinzen Adalbert von Preussen," 1346–47.

33. Reiche argued in vain for a definition of the relationship between the new Danzig gunboat operation and the Stralsund Marine Depot. Reiche, "Entwurf zur Organisation einer Marine-Section bei der 1. Pionier-Abtheilung," Berlin, 10 April 1841, BA-MA, RM 1/2751, 104–5; biographical sketch of Longé, n.d. [1842?], RM 1/1644, 67.

34. Rauch to Frederick William III, Berlin, 21 July 1837, BA-MA, RM 1/2749, 322–29.

35. Rauch to Reiche, Berlin, 22 May 1839, BA-MA, RM 1/2750, 13–14, refers to a royal order of 28 August 1837 supporting the hiring of an "experienced distin-guished sea officer." Reiche to War Ministry, Berlin, 8 January 1840, ibid., 55, refers to plans for the construction of the first gunboat. See also Mantey, *Deutsche Mar-inegeschichte*, 45.

36. BA-MA, RM 1/2751 and RM 1/2752, contain documentation of the con-struction of the *Kanonenjollen*. Gröner, *Die deutschen Kriegsschiffe*, 1:158, incor-rectly identifies Klawitter as the builder.

37. Frederick William IV to Count Albrecht von Alvensleben (finance min-ster), Stargard, 16 September 1840, BA-MA, RM 1/1969, 180; same to same, Sans-souci, 30 October 1841, RM 1/1970, 17; Elbertzhagen, "Memorandum of Agreement" [with shipwrights Joseph Denton, John Icely, and John Piper Icely], 16 March 1842, ibid., 50–51; Elbertzhagen report, Stettin, 22 April 1842, ibid., 48–49; Elbertzhagen to Ernst von Bodelschwingh (finance minister), Stettin, 1 June 1842, ibid., 92–93. The *Amazone*'s keel was laid on 23 May 1842. The initial correspondence refers to the ship as a brig rather than a corvette.

38. Bodelschwingh to Frederick William IV, Berlin, 4 May 1842, BA-MA, RM 1/1970, 85; Frederick William IV to Bodelschwingh, Potsdam, 31 May 1842, ibid., 96; Boyen to Bodelschwingh, Berlin, 23 June 1842, RM 1/2753, 64–65; same to same, Berlin, 22 June 1843, RM 1/1971, 19.

39. Dirckinck-Holmfeld to Finance Ministry, Stettin, 8 April 1843, BA-MA, RM 1/1971, 28; Frederick William IV to Bodelschwingh, Sanssouci, 22 September 1843, ibid., 166; Dirckinck-Holmfeld to Finance Ministry, Stettin, 10 October 1843, ibid., 172–76; Pomeranian *Regierung* to Bodelschwingh, Stettin, 3 January 1844, ibid., 262.

40. Prussian embassy to Ministry for Foreign Affairs, Constantinople, 14 June 1844, BA-MA, RM 1/1972, 221–22, notes that "around sixty ships under the Prussian

flag" had called at Constantinople over the past four months. RM 1/1973 contains dispatches from the *Amazone*'s maiden voyage. For specifications on the *Amazone* see Gröner, *Die deutschen Kriegsschiffe*, 1:107. Major General Heinrich von Scharnhorst (inspector of artillery) to Finance Ministry, Stettin, 9 November 1842, RM 1/1970, 138, and contract with Ridderstolpe, n.d. [21 October 1842], ibid., 127, document the importation of cannon from the Ridderstolpe firm of Stafsio, Sweden.

41. BA-MA, RM 1/2751, 64–74; RM 1/2752, 237; RM 1/2753, 138–50; ibid., 223–24; and RM 1/2754, 205, 211, contain documentation of the gunboat trials of 1840, 1841, 1842, 1844, and 1845.

42. Elbertzhagen to Bodelschwingh, Stettin, 3 August 1842, BA-MA, RM 1/2753, 98–99.

43. A.K.D., "Nachtrag zu dem Promemoria vom 11. März 1844," Berlin, 4 November 1844, BA-MA, RM 1/2754, 24–45; "Recapitulation des Kosten einer diesseitigen Küsten- und Fluss-Marine," Berlin, 4 November 1844, ibid., 198–202.

44. BA-MA, RM 1/1973, includes correspondence on the dispute between Elbertzhagen and Dirckinck-Holmfeld. RM 1/1974 contains dispatches from the 1845 cruise.

45. Interior and Finance Ministries to Boyen, Berlin, 12 July 1845, BA-MA, RM 1/1979, 12; Flottwell to Boyen, Berlin, 31 January 1846, ibid., 17–22.

46. Schröder, "Modifications et additions à faire aux proposition de Sa Majesté le Roi de Prusse pour entrer à Son service comme Navigations-Director," Vlissingen, 2 January 1846, BA-MA, RM 1/1979, 33.

47. "Conduiten Urtheile über den Oberst Longé," n.d. [1842], BA-MA, RM 1/1644, 69; Frederick William IV to A.K.D., Berlin, 5 March 1846, ibid., 79; A.K.D. to Generalkommando II. Armee Korps (Stettin), Berlin, 12 March 1846, ibid., 80.

48. Boyen and Flottwell to Frederick William IV, Berlin, 30 May 1846, BA-MA, RM 1/1975, 132–38; Frederick William IV to Boyen and Flottwell, Sanssouci, 19 June 1846, ibid., 163; Boyen and Flottwell to Schröder, Berlin, 7 July 1846, RM 1/1979, 48–51. See also Sondhaus, "'The Spirit of the Army' at Sea," 460.

49. Schröder, "Rapport der Reise," Danzig, 13 November 1846, BA-MA, RM 1/1975, 231–42; Moltke quoted in Maltzahn, "Jachmann," 295.

50. Schröder to Finance Ministry, Danzig, 9 December 1846, BA-MA, RM 1/1976, fol. 18–23; Peucker to Boyen, Berlin, 11 January 1847, RM 1/1979, 55–59; Frederick William IV (A.K.O.) to Boyen, Bodelschwingh (interior minister), and Duesberg, Sanssouci, 27 May 1847, RM 1/1976 (VI.1.9.1, F3214), 296. See also Sondhaus, "'The Spirit of the Army' at Sea," 461.

51. Schröder to Finance Ministry, Danzig, 20 October 1847, BA-MA, RM 1/1977, 146; Schröder, "Reise-Bericht," Danzig, 25 October 1847, ibid., 183–201.

52. On Adalbert's early life and career see Batsch, *Adalbert*, 33–136 passim; Wislicenus, *Prinzadmiral Adalbert*, 11–53 passim; Waldeyer-Hartz, "Adalbert," 267–69.

53. Frederick William III to Witzleben, Berlin, 29 December 1836, BA-MA, RM 1/2749, 254, encloses a German text (255–59) of Mingaye's plan. Batsch, *Adalbert*, 82, and most other biographers of the prince contend, incorrectly, that Adalbert was a member of the Reiche commission.

54. Batsch, *Adalbert*, 83–90. Waldeyer-Hartz, "Adalbert," 268, places Adalbert's second Russian visit in 1836 rather than 1837.

55. Batsch, *Adalbert*, 136; Wislicenus, *Prinzadmiral Adalbert*, 53; Waldeyer-Hartz, "Adalbert," 269; Major Gaede to A.K.D., Danzig, 23 May 1844, BA-MA, RM 1/2753, 207; Severin ("Ober-Baurath") to Flottwell, Berlin, 21 May 1844, RM 1/1972, 196–99. Petter, "Deutsche Flottenrüstung," 63, contends that Adalbert received a promotion to lieutenant general in 1846 and did not become General Inspector of Artillery until 1847.

56. Prince Adalbert, *Travels of His Royal Highness Prince Adalbert of Prussia, in the south of Europe and in Brazil.*

57. Ibid., 1:113–14; see also Ranke to Adalbert, Berlin, 2 February 1848, text in Batsch, *Adalbert*, 143–44.

58. List, *Schriften, Reden, Briefe*, 7:59–60.

59. Ibid., 7:60–62.

60. Ibid., 7:60–61. Contrary to List's prediction, the *Amazone* was launched without fanfare in 1843; eighteen years later it would be wrecked in a storm on the Dutch coast, leaving no remains for future generations to cherish. On the early development of the Austrian navy see Sondhaus, *The Habsburg Empire and the Sea.*

61. List also experienced considerable frustration as a railway promoter. After designing a German rail network, he helped to arrange the financing for the Saxon railway, only to be denied a role in the management of the company. See Holborn, *History of Modern Germany*, 3:22.

62. List, *Schriften, Reden, Briefe*, 7:57.

63. Petter, "Deutsche Flottenrüstung," 50.

64. In Frankfurt in 1848, Grimm represented the constituency of Mühlheim in the Ruhr. The Schleswig-Holstein question and the Danish blockade of German ports prompted him to take a strong anti-Danish position, notwithstanding his friendship with Hans Christian Andersen and other Danes. See Michaelis-Jena, *The Brothers Grimm*, 151–52. The fascinating Herwegh still lacks a biography. Among a number of dissertations concerning his life and work, Trampe, "Georg Herwegh: Sein Leben und Schaffen," is the only general biography.

65. On the overall problems of the Prussian bureaucracy on the eve of the revolution see Gillis, *The Prussian Bureaucracy in Crisis*, part one. See also Brose, *The Politics of Technological Change in Prussia.*

Chapter 2: Revolution and War

1. Lundeberg, "Sea Mines," 191, 193; Wollstein, *Das "Grossdeutschland" der Paulskirche*, 259; Röhr, *Handbuch*, 41; Giese, *Kleine Geschichte der deutschen Flotte*, 12.

2. Petter, "Deutsche Flottenrüstung," 51; idem, "Programmierter Untergang," 160.

3. Radowitz to Frankfurt Parliament, 8 June 1848, text in Wigard, *Stenographischer Bericht*, 1:252–53.

4. Friedrich Kohlparzer motion, 14 June 1848, ibid., 1:319. See also Sondhaus, "*Mitteleuropa zur See?*" 128–29. The first (and still the most comprehensive) account of the political debate over the fleet, Bär's *Die Deutsche Flotte von 1848–1852*, is based primarily on Prussian and Hanoverian archival sources, and as a result largely discounts Austria's role in the navy question.

5. Jahn, *Friedrich Ludwig Jahns Werke*, 2:1019; see also Wollstein, *Das "Grossdeutschland" der Paulskirche*, 237.

6. *Frankfurter Oberpostamts Zeitung*, 29 June 1848, no. 181; *Journal der österreichischen Lloyd*, 15 August 1848, no. 187. I thank Carey Goodman for these references.

7. Sondhaus, *"Mitteleuropa zur See?"* 129–30.

8. Güth, *Von Revolution zu Revolution*, 23; Bidlingmaier, *Seegeltung*, 70–71; Mantey, *Deutsche Marinegeschichte*, 50; Wollstein, *Das "Grossdeutschland" der Paulskirche*, 264–65.

9. According to Hildebrand, Röhr, and Steinmetz, *Die deutschen Kriegsschiffe*, 1:18, the transfer of the ships occurred on 15 October 1848.

10. Gröner, *Die deutschen Kriegsschiffe*, 1:159.

11. Heinsius, "Anfänge der Deutschen Marine," 20–21.

12. Kuby, "Politische Frauenvereine," 250–54; Häussler, *Das Ende der ersten deutschen Flotte*, 101–2.

13. See discussion in Deutsches Marine Institut, *Die deutsche Flotte im Spannungsfeld der Politik*, 43–47.

14. Prince Adalbert, *Denkschrift über die Bildung einer Deutschen Kriegsflotte*.

15. Ibid., 5–10 ("Vertheidigung der Küsten"), 23–35 ("Eine selbstständige Seemacht"), 11–23 ("Eine Kriegsmarine zur offensiven Vertheidigung und zum nothwendigsten Schutze des Handels").

16. Petter, "Deutsche Flottenrüstung," 54; Güth, *Von Revolution zu Revolution*, 23. Throughout the deliberations of 1848–49 the discussion of Baltic bases was limited to Kiel and various Prussian ports. The ports of Mecklenburg were considered too shallow even for medium-sized warships. See Bei der Wieden, "Die mecklenburgischen Häfen," 47–58.

17. Jensen, *Seestadt Kiel*, 15; Beseke, *Der Nord-Ostsee-Kanal*, 4–5. The first waterway between the Baltic and North Sea, the so-called Stecknitz Canal, opened in 1398, linking Lübeck with Lauenburg on the Elbe via the Trave, Stecknitz, and Delvenau Rivers. The modern Elbe-Lübeck Canal covers roughly the same route.

18. Schwarzenberg to Schmerling, Vienna, 22 February 1849, Österreichisches Staatarchiv, Haus- Hof- und Staatsarchiv, Politisches Archiv, II. Deutscher Bund (hereafter cited as HHSA, PA, II), Carton 86, 1849/12–13.

19. See Sondhaus, *The Habsburg Empire and the Sea*, 58–59, 62.

20. Güth, *Von Revolution zu Revolution*, 21.

21. Moltmann, *Atlantische Blockpolitik*, 150–52. The 50-gun *St. Lawrence*, one of the last sailing frigates built by the United States, was commissioned in 1847.

22. Ibid., 146, 157–58.

23. Ibid., 158–59.

24. Parker quoted in Duckwitz, *Gründung der deutschen Kriegsmarine*, 56. See also Moltmann, *Atlantische Blockpolitik*, 160–61.

25. Kudriaffsky to Schwarzenberg, Emden, 19 February 1849, HHSA, PA, II, Carton 86, 1849/140–42; Duckwitz, *Gründung der deutschen Kriegsmarine*, 18. While Duckwitz's memoir contends that he offered Kudriaffsky command of the navy, Kudriaffsky's letter characterizes the post as more of a station command. After the

248 NOTES TO PAGES 24–28

technical commission finished its work, he returned to Austria and transferred from the navy to the army, at the rank of Feldmarschalleutnant.

26. According to R. Werner, *Erinnerungen und Bilder*, 153, one of the leading Austrians in Frankfurt, Anton von Schmerling, personally wrote to Sourdeau to offer the commission and received no reply. Sourdeau, an officer of Walloon descent who had left the Austrian navy in 1843, came out of retirement in October 1848 to succeed Kudriaffsky. He retired again in March 1849, when the Danish commodore Hans Birch von Dahlerup was hired to command the Habsburg fleet. See Sondhaus, *The Habsburg Empire and the Sea*, 157–60.

27. Petter, "Admiral Brommy in der Literatur," 15–16. Brommy, *Die Marine* (1848), was reprinted in a third edition as late as 1878.

28. Anton von Martini (commander, Austrian navy) to Kriegsministerium, Trieste, 30 August 1848, Österreichisches Staatsarchiv, Kriegsarchiv (hereafter cited as KA), Marineakten, M/c 27 (1848), nr. 98-a, expresses a keen interest in Brommy, citing his authorship of the Greek navy's service regulations, but refers to the need to investigate his "personality, reputation, character, physical fitness, domestic situation, etc."

29. Petter, "Admiral Brommy in der Literatur," 15.

30. See "Liste der Offiziere, Fähnriche und Seejunker . . . nach dem Stande vom 1. Mai 1850," in Hubatsch, *Die erste deutsche Flotte*, 104–5.

31. Gröner, *Die deutschen Kriegsschiffe*, 1:66, 108–10.

32. "Liste der Offiziere, Fähnriche und Seejunker . . . nach dem Stande vom 1. Mai 1850," in Hubatsch, *Die erste deutsche Flotte*, 104–8.

33. R. Werner, *Erinnerungen und Bilder*, 169–70, 287.

34. Jahn, *Friedrich Ludwig Jahns Werke*, 2:1043.

35. Schultz, "Das Treffen vor Eckernförde," 161–67; Drees, "Vor 90 Jahren," 346–48. The most recent Danish account is Bjerg, "Affœren i Eckernförde." The manpower of the shore batteries included artillerymen from Prussia and Nassau as well as Schleswig-Holstein.

36. Bidlingmaier, *Seegeltung*, 72; Güth, *Von Revolution zu Revolution*, 23–25; R. Werner, *Erinnerungen und Bilder*, 189–96; idem, *Seekriegsgeschichte*, 410–13.

37. On the historiography of the 4 June 1849 sortie see Petter, "Admiral Brommy in der Literatur," 20–21. For a Nazi-era overview of Brommy's career see Schmitz, "Admiral Brommy," 689–97. On the British captains, Thomas King of the *Barbarossa* and Thomas Thatcher of the *Lübeck*, see R. Werner, *Erinnerungen und Bilder*, 189, and idem, *Seekriegsgeschichte*, 410. On the sortie of 14 June see idem, *Erinnerungen und Bilder*, 205–6. Werner served as an auxiliary officer aboard the *Barbarossa* during the action of June 1849.

38. Moltmann, *Atlantische Blockpolitik*, 165–75; Gröner, *Die deutschen Kriegsschiffe*, 1:67; Güth, *Von Revolution zu Revolution*, 25.

39. See text of part 2 (*Die Reichsgewalt*), article 3, section 19 of the Frankfurt constitution in Huber, *Dokumente zur deutschen Verfassungsgeschichte*, 1:377.

40. Martini to Baron Franz Cordon (war minister), Trieste, 9 December 1848, KA, Marineakten, M/c 27 (1848), no. 254 (Carton 46), reflects the Austrian naval commander's fears of subordination to a German naval command as a consequence of the proceedings at Frankfurt.

41. According to Petter, "Admiral Brommy in der Literatur," 17, Jochmus "had once served in Greece under Brommy."

42. See Huber, *Dokumente zur deutschen Verfassungsgeschichte*, 1:552. Expropriation plan discussed in Handel (Austrian minister to Württemberg) to Schwarzenberg, Stuttgart, 25 July 1849, HHSA, PA, II, Carton 86, 1849/54–56.

43. Sondhaus, "*Mitteleuropa zur See?*" 133; Brommy to Jochmus, Bremerhaven, 13 September 1849, HHSA, PA, II, Carton 86, 1849/83; Jochmus to Rechberg, Frankfurt, 12 October 1849, ibid., 1849/81–88; Archduke John to Schwarzenberg, Frankfurt, 18 October 1849, ibid., 1849/75–78; Hubatsch, "Reichsflotte und Deutscher Bund," 38.

44. "Übereinkunft zwischen Österreich und Preussen . . . ," Vienna, 30 September 1849, text in Hoor, *Erzherzog Johann von Österreich als Reichsverweser*, 97–98.

45. Sondhaus, "*Mitteleuropa zur See?*" 135. R. Werner, *Erinnerungen und Bilder*, 170–71, includes the text of Archduke John's order of 11 November 1849, promoting Brommy to rear admiral.

46. Kübeck to Schwarzenberg, Frankfurt, 10 July 1850, HHSA, PA, II, Carton 86, 1850/162; Kübeck to Schwarzenberg, Frankfurt, 8 September 1850, ibid., 1850/182–88 passim; Thun, Tagesbericht no. 38, Frankfurt, 25 November 1850, ibid., 1850/209–12. According to R. Werner, *Erinnerungen und Bilder*, 208–10, Brommy had assigned "an English captain" to the *Eckernförde*, who wanted to surrender to the Danes in September 1850; the threat of a mutiny by patriotic German officers and the crew saved the frigate.

47. On the wide variety of interpretations of the Olmütz agreement and the subsequent Dresden Conference, see Sondhaus, "Schwarzenberg, Austria, and the German Question," 7–13.

48. Jochmus memorandum, Frankfurt, 17 February 1851, HHSA, PA, II, Carton 86, 1851/119–21; Schwarzenberg to Thun, Vienna, 21 May 1851, ibid., 1851/237–41; Schwarzenberg to Thun, Vienna, 26 May 1851, ibid., 1851/243–47. Debt figure from Hildebrand, Röhr, and Steinmetz, *Die deutschen Kriegsschiffe*, 1:19.

49. Thun to Schwarzenberg, Frankfurt, 8 July 1851, HHSA, PA, II, Carton 86, 1851/318–400.

50. Bismarck, *Gedanken und Erinnerungen*, 1:96; Sondhaus, "*Mitteleuropa zur See?*" 137–38.

51. Prokesch to Schwarzenberg, Berlin, 23 July 1851, HHSA, PA, II, Carton 86, 1851/451–54. The Prussian canard was still being repeated forty years later. Koch, "Der Flottenverkauf durch Hannibal Fischer," 150, refers to disorder aboard the ships and poor leadership by officers who slept until noon. Koch also contends that sentiment within the fleet favored a Prussian takeover. See ibid., 155.

52. Häussler, *Das Ende des ersten deutschen Flotte*, 110; Prokesch to Schwarzenberg, Berlin, 8 August 1851, HHSA, PA, II, Carton 87, 1851/473–74.

53. Prokesch to Schwarzenberg, Berlin, 28 August 1851, HHSA, PA, II, Carton 87, Berichte aus Berlin/37.

54. Protocol of 7–9th Sessions of Marine Commission, Frankfurt, 23–25 October 1851, copy in HHSA, PA, II, Carton 87; Thun to Schwarzenberg, Frankfurt, 18 November 1851, ibid., 1851/767–809.

55. Bismarck to Manteuffel, Frankfurt, 19 November 1851, text in Poschinger, *Preussen im Bundestag 1851 bis 1859*, 1:44; Prokesch to Schwarzenberg, Berlin, 30 September 1851, HHSA, PA, II, Carton 87, Berichte aus Berlin/49–54; Prokesch to Schwarzenberg, Berlin, 12 January 1852, ibid., Carton 88, 1852/116–17.

56. Thun to Schwarzenberg, Frankfurt, 25 January 1852, HHSA, PA, II, Carton 88, 1852/277–82; Thun, Tagesbericht, Frankfurt, 14 February 1852, ibid., 1852/508–24.

57. Stern, *Gold and Iron*, 15–16; Thun, Tagesbericht, Frankfurt, 17 February 1852, HHSA, PA, II, Carton 88, 1852/526–49.

58. Thun to Schwarzenberg, Frankfurt, 3 March 1852, HHSA, PA, II, Carton 88, 1852/667–70; Prokesch to Schwarzenberg, Berlin, 4 March 1852, ibid., 1852/678–79; Thun, Tagesbericht, Frankfurt, 3 April 1852, ibid., 1852/811–22. On the transfer of the two ships see n. 112 below.

59. Sondhaus, "*Mitteleuropa zur See?*" 141–42; Gröner, *Die deutschen Kriegsschiffe*, 1:66–67, 108–10. After his initial review of the ships of the fleet Fischer echoed the observations of earlier visitors to Bremerhaven, praising Brommy's officers and seamen for their "order and discipline." See Häussler, *Das Ende des ersten deutschen Flotte*, 110. Otto Fischer, "Dr. Laurenz Hannibal Fischer und die Auflösung der deutschen Flotte," 250–89, especially 261–74, contends that Fischer tried to keep the German navy together despite the order to sell the ships. A son's defense of his father, the article disputes the characterization of Fischer as "gravedigger" of the first German navy, given in Bär's *Die Deutsche Flotte von 1848–1852*, which appeared in 1898.

60. Batsch, "Zur Vorgeschichte der Flotte," 778–79; on the pension issue see R. Werner, *Erinnerungen und Bilder*, 222–24, and idem, *Seekriegsgeschichte*, 421. According to Koch, "Der Flottenverkauf durch Hannibal Fischer," 152, a total of 565 officers, seamen, and supporting personnel were released on 1 May; Koch cites the figure of 367 men for 4 June 1852.

61. For a text of Brommy's farewell order of 31 March 1853 see R. Werner, *Erinnerungen und Bilder*, 224–25.

62. Stolz, *Die Schleswig-Holsteinische Marine*, 15–17, 21–22.

63. Ibid., 21; Güth, *Von Revolution zu Revolution*, 23.

64. Stolz, *Die Schleswig-Holsteinische Marine*, 22–23.

65. Ibid., 35–36.

66. Ibid., 30–32, 34, 102–5.

67. Mantey, *Deutsche Marinegeschichte*, 53; Jensen, *Seestadt Kiel*, 103; Gröner, *Die deutschen Kriegsschiffe*, 1:157.

68. Petter, "Deutsche Flottenrüstung," 52; Giese, *Kleine Geschichte der deutschen Flotte*, 17.

69. Lundeberg, "Sea Mines," 192–93. Siemens, born in Hanover in 1816, attended the artillery and engineering school in Berlin from 1835 to 1838 and became an engineering officer in the Prussian army. His three brothers also came to Kiel to serve the Schleswig-Holstein cause. See Siemens, *Lebenserinnerungen*, passim; Feldenkirchen, *Werner von Siemens*, 41.

70. Petter, "Deutsche Flottenrüstung," 52.

71. Stolz, *Die Schleswig-Holsteinische Marine*, 33.

72. Ibid., 41–45; Giese, *Kleine Geschichte der deutschen Flotte*, 17.

73. Mantey, *Deutsche Marinegeschichte*, 53.

74. Stolz, *Die Schleswig-Holsteinische Marine*, 45–46.

75. Ibid., 34, 46–47.

76. Ibid., 48. The order of April 1850 did not affect the troops aboard the frigate *Eckernförde*, who were considered to be in Prussian service.

77. Ibid., 48–50, 53; Giese, *Kleine Geschichte der deutschen Flotte*, 17.

78. Stolz, *Die Schleswig-Holsteinische Marine*, 60–61; Gröner, *Die deutschen Kriegsschiffe*, 1:158.

79. Stolz, *Die Schleswig-Holsteinische Marine*, 50–52.

80. Ibid., 49–50.

81. Ibid., 49–50, 53–55; Bidlingmaier, *Seegeltung*, 73.

82. Stolz, *Die Schleswig-Holsteinische Marine*, 55–56; Gröner, *Die deutschen Kriegsschiffe*, 1:156.

83. Jensen, *Seestadt Kiel*, 103; Bidlingmaier, *Seegeltung*, 73.

84. Stolz, *Die Schleswig-Holsteinische Marine*, 36, 64–72. According to Gröner, *Die deutschen Kriegsschiffe*, 1:109, 156–58, the Danes took possession of most of the Schleswig-Holstein vessels in March 1851.

85. Stolz, *Die Schleswig-Holsteinische Marine*, 63.

86. Reyher to Hansemann, Berlin, 8 April 1848, BA-MA, RM 1/1977, 291; Pomeranian "Rhederei" to Camphausen, 2 April 1848, Berlin, RM 1/1898, 47–48.

87. Schaper (postmaster general) to Reyher, Berlin, 12 April 1848, BA-MA, RM 1/1898, 59. The war ministry was interested in the *Preussischer Adler* upon its acquisition in May 1847; in early March 1848 Schröder traveled to Stettin to evaluate its potential as a warship. Boyen to Schaper, Berlin, 8 May 1847, ibid., 7; Schröder to Duesberg, Berlin, 6 March 1848, ibid., 45.

88. Batsch, *Adalbert*, 158.

89. Waldeyer-Hartz, "Adalbert," 269; Gröner, *Die deutschen Kriegsschiffe*, 1:158–60. Adalbert to A.K.D., Berlin, 17 May 1848, BA-MA, RM 1/1898, 110–12, indicates that the prince considered arming three Danzig merchantmen (the ships *Diamant* and *Hull* and the brig *Brillant*). None of these plans came to fruition.

90. Longé to A.K.D., Stralsund, 30 August 1848, BA-MA, RM 1/262, 3–4, reports the 10 August launching of the *Strelasund*, which was attended by Prince Adalbert. See also Gröner, *Die deutschen Kriegsschiffe*, 1:158–60; Koch, "Die deutschen Eisenindustrie," 10; and idem, "Die Sammlungen für die Deutsche Flotte," 138–39.

91. Schröder to Danzig *Regierung*, Danzig, 29 February 1848, BA-MA, RM 1/1977, 283; Schröder to Finance Ministry, Danzig, 18 April 1848, ibid., 303–5. Same to same, Danzig, 16 February 1848, RM 1/1980, 37–41, refers to Schröder's request for the transfer of Sergeant August Ferdinand Nürnberg of the 1st Artillery Brigade, who declined the offer (ibid., 45); Schröder to Ministry of Trade, Commerce, and Public Works, Danzig, 1 August 1848, RM 1/1978, 4, refers to the stoning death of sailor Johann Dircksen of the *Amazone* in a riot on 31 July.

92. War Ministry, "Denkschrift betreffend die Kriegs-Marine in Preussen," October 1849, text in Hubatsch, *Die erste deutsche Flotte*, 128; Stettin Generalkommando to War Ministry, Stettin, 22 August 1848, BA-MA, RM 1/1898, unnumbered.

As early as 15 August, a Danish ship brought 218 Prussian prisoners from Copenhagen to Swinemünde. Gröner, *Die deutschen Kriegsschiffe*, does not list the *Königin Elisabeth* as a warship.

93. War Ministry, "Denkschrift betreffend die Kriegs-Marine in Preussen," October 1849, text in Hubatsch, *Die erste deutsche Flotte*, 117–18, and Stralsund committee to Adalbert, Stralsund, 9 February 1849, BA-MA, RM 1/262, 29–41, report on the gunboat exercises of November 1848. A.K.D. to Adalbert, Berlin, 25 October 1848, ibid., 28, formally requests Schröder's services to head the gunboat exercises. Subsequent *Ranglisten* date his "commodore" title from 24 October, but in his own correspondence Schröder continued to refer to himself as navigation director until March 1849.

94. Duckwitz to Camphausen, Frankfurt, 13 December 1848, BA-MA, RM 1/1980, 62; General Karl von Stroha (war minister) to August von der Heydt (trade minister), Berlin, 14 February 1849, ibid., 66–69. Ibid., 117, is an unsigned, undated Allerhöchste Kabinetts-Ordre (A.K.O.) that would have turned over the *Amazone* and the gunboats to the German navy.

95. Hubatsch, *Der Admiralstab*, 17. See Frederick William IV to Strotha, Charlottenburg, 1 March 1849 ("Errichtung eines preussischen Marine-Oberkommandos und eines Flottenkommandos"), text in ibid., 220; A.K.D. "Promemoria," Berlin, 6 March 1849, BA-MA, RM 1/1980 (VI.1.9.2, F3215), 118–20.

96. Sondhaus, " 'The Spirit of the Army' at Sea," 462.

97. Adalbert to A.K.D., Berlin, 23 March 1849, BA-MA, RM 1/1980, 100; Adalbert to War Ministry, Berlin, 31 March 1849, RM 1/729, 2–3; Adalbert to A.K.D., Berlin, 18 April 1849, ibid., 7; A.K.D. to Okdo. der Marine, Berlin, 25 May 1849, ibid., 13. While seeking officers and NCOs abroad, Prussia rejected some foreign officer candidates. The war ministry advised Adalbert not to commission a French applicant because of "the special prejudice against the French" that "predominates . . . among the lower classes of people, from which the crews of our warships are for the most part drawn." A.K.D. to Adalbert, Berlin, 7 June 1849, ibid., 17.

98. War Ministry, "Denkschrift betreffend die Kriegs-Marine in Preussen," October 1849, text in Hubatsch, *Die erste deutsche Flotte*, 124–25. Gröner, *Die deutsche Kriegsschiffe*, does not mention the requisitioned merchantman *Danzig*.

99. Waldeyer-Hartz, "Adalbert," 269; Batsch, *Adalbert*, 168–71; Bidlingmaier, *Seegeltung*, 75; War Ministry, "Denkschrift betreffend die Kriegs-Marine in Preussen," October 1849, text in Hubatsch, *Die erste deutsche Flotte*, 125, 128.

100. Crousaz, *Kurze Geschichte*, 40, 52, 57, 62; War Ministry to Generalkommando I Armee Korps (Königsberg), Berlin, 23 December 1849, BA-MA, RM 1/200, 16–17; Schröder to Okdo. der Marine, Stettin, 19 June 1851, ibid., 43; Adalbert to A.K.D., Berlin, 17 March 1852, ibid., 58; A.K.D. to Okdo. der Marine, Berlin, 6 July 1852, ibid., 63. The truncated "Marine Corps" was renamed the *Seebataillon* in June 1852. According to Crousaz, the "Shipbuilding Corps" was created in February 1854, but contemporary correspondence uses the term *Werftcorps* as early as 1852.

101. Sondhaus, " 'The Spirit of the Army' at Sea," 462. Frederick William IV (A.K.O.) to Okdo. der Marine, Sanssouci, 20 November 1849, BA-MA, RM 31/602, fol. 16. RM 1/730 contains correspondence concerning the placement of the four cadets aboard the *St. Lawrence*.

102. Sondhaus, " 'The Spirit of the Army' at Sea," 462–63.

103. Schröder to Duesberg, Danzig, 5 January 1848, BA-MA, RM 1/1977, 260–66, complains of the *Amazone*'s size and calls for the acquisition of a frigate to replace it.

104. A.K.D. "Promemoria," Berlin, 12 October 1849, BA-MA, RM 1/2032, 1–2, indicates that the navy planned to buy or rent either the *Mercur* or the Seehandlung's *Preussischer Adler* as early as October 1849. Schröder to A.K.D., Berlin, 16 March 1850, RM 1/810, 20–22, gives the *Mercur*'s history and praises its "elegant" appearance. Donner to Mkdo. Stettin, Swinemünde, 24 July 1850, RM 1/1981, 180, refers to the *Amazone*'s collision with the brig *Norma*. Adalbert to A.K.D., Berlin, 14 September 1850, RM 1/263, 4–5, declares the *Amazone* unseaworthy. RM 1/2033 contains documentation of the *Mercur*'s repairs; RM 1/263, 75–117 passim, contains reports from the *Mercur*'s cruise.

105. Schirmacher (Okdo. adjutant) to A.K.D., Berlin, 23 June 1851, BA-MA, RM 1/2034, 226–27, and Schröder to Okdo. der Marine, Stettin, 19 June 1851, ibid., 230–32, discuss the problem of the *Mercur*'s stability, which also affected plans to arm it with more than a nominal battery. RM 1/2035 contains documentation of the *Mercur*'s Baltic cruise.

106. Lütken's *Einige Gedanken über den Gebrauch der Kanonenboote*, originally published in Copenhagen in March 1808, is an enclosure to A.K.D. (Marine-Abteilung) to Okdo. der Marine, Berlin, 4 May 1849, BA-MA, RM 1/262, 82.

107. BA-MA, RM 1/262, 154–71 passim; RM 1/810, 130–95 passim; and RM 1/806, 142–87 passim, chronicle the gunboat trials of 1849, 1850, and 1851.

108. Koch, "Die deutschen Eisenindustrie," 2; Gröner, *Die deutschen Kriegsschiffe*, 1:68, 110–11; Leckebusch, *Eisenindustrie*, 18. According to Cattaruzza, *Arbeiter und Unternehmer*, 90, Danzig was designated as site of a royal shipyard in 1844.

109. BA-MA, RM 1/2004, RM 1/2005, RM 1/2006, RM 1/2007, and RM 1/2008, contain correspondence on the construction of the *Danzig* from 1850–52. The launching was held on 13 November 1851, the queen's birthday, but the royal family was not represented. Even Prince Adalbert did not attend the modest festivities.

110. BA-MA, RM 1/61, contains material on the construction of the *Salamander* and *Nix;* RM 1/806 documents their 1851 cruises.

111. Figures from *Preussische Wehr-Zeitung*, vol. 3, no. 88 (4 May 1851). The Landtag voted the navy 1.4 million thalers for 1850, including over half a million for the *Salamander, Nix,* and the *Danzig*'s engines; another half-million went to the German navy and covered overspending from the previous year. The figure for 1851 was reduced by almost 20,000 thalers after the *Preussischer Adler* returned completely to the postal service.

112. R. Werner, *Erinnerungen und Bilder,* 221, contends that Brommy turned over the vessels on 5 April 1852. Gröner, *Die deutschen Kriegsschiffe,* 1:66, gives the date of 1 May. Other sources place the date of transfer as late as 11 May. Schmitz, "Admiral Brommy," 692–93, refers to the transfer of the seamen.

113. Frederick William IV (A.K.O.) to War Ministry, Sanssouci, 27 May 1852, BA-MA, RM 31/412, 2; Koch, "Die preussische Flottenexpedition von 1852," 435.

114. Wagner, "Die obersten Behörden der k.u.k. Kriegsmarine," 137; Petter, "Ad-

miral Brommy in der Literatur," 18. Brommy was in Austrian service from April to July 1857. On his funeral see R. Werner, *Seekriegsgeschichte,* 421.

Chapter 3: A Peaceful Interlude

1. Data on former German officers from BA-MA, RM 1/694, passim, and a comparison of rosters in *Rangliste der königlich preussischen Marine* with "Liste der Offiziere, Fähnriche und Seejunker . . . nach dem Stande vom 1. Mai 1850," in Hubatsch, *Die erste deutsche Flotte,* 104–9. See also Sondhaus, "'The Spirit of the Army' at Sea," 463.

2. BA-MA, RM 31/1827, 1–2, 43, 52.

3. Data from comparison of rosters in *Rangliste der königlich preussischen Marine; Militär-Schematismus des österreichischen Kaiserthums* (annual, title varies), and "Liste der Offiziere, Fähnriche und Seejunker . . . nach dem Stande vom 1. Mai 1850," in Hubatsch, *Die erste deutsche Flotte,* 104–9.

4. General-Direktion Seehandlung to A.K.D., Berlin, 12 October 1849, BA-MA, RM 1/2032, 16–17; Boyen to Bodelschwingh, Berlin, 23 June 1842, RM 1/2753, 64–65; Adalbert to Marineministerium, Berlin, 8 February 1862, RM 1/143, 7–12.

5. Sondhaus, " 'The Spirit of the Army' at Sea," 464.

6. Ibid., 465.

7. *Rangliste der königlich preussischen Marine,* 1852 through 1864, passim. Prince of Hessen to Adalbert, aboard HMS *Cleopatra,* 15 November 1849, BA-MA, RM 1/26, 33–34, applies for a commission in "Prussian or German naval service" upon his "return to Germany after several years."

8. See, e.g., Schröder to Okdo. der Marine, Stettin, 12 April 1851, BA-MA, RM 1/855, 1–2.

9. *Rangliste der königlich preussischen Marine,* 1853, 1862.

10. Ibid., 1854 through 1864 passim. According to legend, Frederick William IV questioned Jachmann's fitness for high rank because of his origins as a common merchant seaman and lack of formal education, but changed his mind after learning that his father had been a professor of philosophy at the University of Königsberg. See Drascher, "Zur Soziologie des deutschen Seeoffizierkorps," 556.

11. Adalbert to Marineministerium, Berlin, 8 February 1862, BA-MA, RM 1/143, 11–12. See also Heinsius, "Stellung und Besoldung der Deckoffiziere," 57–60, and Herwig, *"Luxury" Fleet,* 131–32.

12. Crousaz, *Kurze Geschichte,* 63.

13. Batsch, *Adalbert,* 179; Crousaz, *Kurze Geschichte,* 80. The twelve-year service term for seamen was codified in an order of 9 December 1858.

14. Dinter, "Albrecht Graf von Roon," 477, gives a figure of 1,022 men for 1863.

15. Adalbert to Marineministerium, Berlin, 8 February 1862, BA-MA, RM 1/143, 7–12.

16. Boelcke, *So kam das Meer zu uns,* 19.

17. Quoted in Batsch, "Zur Vorgeschichte der Flotte," 781.

18. Landerer, *Geschichte der HAPAG,* 25, 98; Prager, *Blohm + Voss,* 11. The HAPAG was founded in May 1847.

19. BA-MA, RM 1/60 and RM 1/265, document the operations of the *Nix, Sala-*

mander, and *Barbarossa* in 1852 and 1853; Burchardt to Okdo. der Marine, Swinemünde, 1 October 1852, RM 1/266, 68, refers to the mobilization of gunboat *No.31.* See also Wislicenus, *Prinzadmiral Adalbert,* 72.

20. Except where noted, the following account of the cruise of 1852–53 is based on Koch, "Die preussische Flottenexpedition von 1852," 435–43. For a text of Schröder's instructions, dated Berlin, 2 October 1852, see Boelcke, *So kam das Meer zu uns,* 47–51.

21. The *Amazone* was out of commission from September 1850 to August 1852; Adalbert to A.K.D., Berlin, 29 May 1852, BA-MA, RM 1/266, 131, orders the *Mercur*'s repairs. Both ships were repaired in the Stettin Marine Depot. Schröder, "Tagebuch," entry for 3 September 1852, RM 1/802, 5, refers to a thirteen-gun salute—appropriate for a rear admiral—that he gave to Brommy's flagship *Hansa* as the *Gefion* left Bremerhaven. At the time, the *Hansa* was one of two German navy ships not yet sold.

22. [Carl Ferdinand von Gerolt] quoted in Koch, "Die preussische Flottenexpedition von 1852," 443. According to Koch (441), Schröder and four of his officers left their ships while in Norfolk for an official visit to Washington. Schröder's diary does not mention this excursion. Koch contends that "several" sailors deserted in Buenos Aires; Schröder, "Tagebuch," entries for 6, 14 March 1853, BA-MA, RM 1/802, 75, 76, record a total of just five desertions, all in Montevideo. The squadron included almost six hundred seamen.

23. Schröder, "Tagebuch," entry for 12 August 1853, BA-MA, RM 1/802, 139.

24. Schröder, "Tagebuch," BA-MA, RM 1/802, chronicles the Mediterranean movements of the *Gefion* and *Mercur* for 1853–54, along with those of the *Danzig* for the times that the three ships cruised together.

25. On the Bomarsund and Sweaborg operations see Treue, *Der Krimkrieg,* 101–4, 110–13.

26. According to Mantey, *Deutsche Marinegeschichte,* 60–61, in 1854 seven cadets were assigned to the British navy for a three-year term; Wislicenus, *Prinzadmiral Adalbert,* 77, refers to eight cadets. Crousaz, *Kurze Geschichte,* 70, says the *Mercur* left seven cadets at Portsmouth, en route home from the Mediterranean in 1854.

27. BA-MA, RM 1/260, contains information regarding the *Nix* and *Salamander* during 1854; RM 1/805 covers the 1854 Baltic summer operations of all other warships.

28. Critics of the trade include Gröner, *Die deutschen Kriegsschiffe,* 1:110. Schröder to Okdo. der Marine, Stettin, 2 July 1852, BA-MA, RM 1/265, 10–11, notes that the *Nix* and *Salamander* are not suitably designed for use as royal yachts. Adalbert to Kdo. Baltic Station, Berlin, 31 January 1855, RM 31/643, 2, records that the exchange of ships occurred at Devonport on 12 January. RM 1/261 includes documentation of the 1855 Baltic cruises; RM 1/2043 concerns the project to purchase "a good sailing frigate" from Sweden.

29. A.K.D. to Okdo. der Marine, Berlin, 19 November 1852, BA-MA, RM 1/60, 87–88, appoints Donner chairman of the *Barbarossa* commission. Captain G. A. Indebetou, "Bericht," Deptford, 4 August 1853, RM 1/2010, 20, includes the first ref-

erence to the *Danzig*'s dry-rot problem. The unsound hull and subsequent British criticism of the Galician oak used to construct it sparked considerable bitterness on the Prussian side; in July 1852 Scott Russell's Danzig foreman, Robert Murray, had declared his "perfect satisfaction" with the Prussian execution of the British plans and called the *Danzig* "a perfect specimen of an efficient war-steamer and an honor to Prussia." Robert Murray to Captain von Wedell (superintendent, Danzig Marine Depot), Danzig, 24 July 1852, RM 1/2008, 96.

30. Sundewall to Kdo. Baltic Station, Neufahrwasser, 20, 25 April 1855, BA-MA, RM 31/643, 3, 14.

31. Batsch, *Adalbert,* 207, 211–12; Kuksz (Austrian consul), "Promemoria ueber die königlich preussische Kriegsmarine seit ihrem Entstehen im Jahre 1848 bis zum Jahre 1860," Danzig, 30 April 1861, HHSA, Administrative Registratur (hereafter cited as AR), F 44, Carton 3, Generalia 1860–70; Hubatsch, *Der Admiralstab,* 20–22. See also Frederick William IV, A.K.O. of 14 November 1853, text in ibid., 220–21.

32. See, e.g., Verchau, "Von Jachmann über Stosch und Caprivi," 54, and Herwig, *"Luxury" Fleet,* 11–12.

33. Gröner, *Die deutschen Kriegsschiffe,* 1:68–69, 111. Gröner refers to the *Arcona* and its sister ships as frigates, but contemporary sources and most subsequent literature refer to them as corvettes. The royal shipyard in Danzig built the *Hela,* while a private shipyard, Lübke of Wolgast, built the *Frauenlob.* On the funding and construction of the *Frauenlob* see Koch, "Die Sammlungen für die Deutsche Flotte," 139–42.

34. Plan of 9 April 1855 outlined in Foerster, *Politische Geschichte,* 12. The plan evolved from an earlier one of June 1853, in which Adalbert proposed nine 80-gun ships of the line (of which three would be kept in reserve), six frigates "with or without propellers," and six paddle steamers ("steam corvettes" and "steam avisos"). Adalbert's fleet plan, 15 June 1853, National Archives (hereafter cited as NA), T-1022, roll 1525. On the changes in naval technology initiated during the Crimean War see Treue, *Der Krimkrieg,* 122–34.

35. Koch, "Die Vorgeschichte von Wilhelmshaven," 475–95; Pein, "Vor 90 Jahren," 467–73; Batsch, *Adalbert,* 210; Crousaz, *Kurze Geschichte,* 71; Graser, *Norddeutschlands Seemacht,* 346–49.

36. Petter, "Deutsche Flottenrüstung," 65; Sondhaus, *The Habsburg Empire and the Sea,* 178.

37. Boelcke, *So kam das Meer zu uns,* 134–35. Woermann sent his first ship to West Africa in 1849. See Kludas, *Afrika-Linien,* 9.

38. Schramm, *Deutschland und übersee,* 253–55, 453.

39. Koch, "Die preussische Flottenexpedition von 1852," 440–41.

40. Grapow, "Gefecht S.M.S. *Danzig* bei Tres-Forkas," 772; Schröder to Admiralty, Danzig, 23 June, 12 September, 1856, BA-MA, RM 1/2036, 217, 218.

41. Batsch, *Adalbert,* 225–28; Sondhaus, *The Habsburg Empire and the Sea,* 75–76. Waldeyer-Hartz, "Adalbert," 270, gives the date of 5 December 1852 for the attack on the *Flora;* other sources place it in 1853.

42. Grabow, "Gefecht S.M.S. *Danzig* bei Tres-Forkas," 772–77; Boelcke, *So kam das Meer zu uns,* 68. Grabow cites casualties of seven killed and eighteen wounded; Boelcke, seven killed and twenty-two wounded.

43. BA-MA, RM 1/1984 and RM 1/271, chronicle the voyages of the *Thetis, Gefion,* and *Amazone* in 1857–59. On the *Grille*'s construction see Gröner, *Die deutschen Kriegsschiffe,* 1:112–13. After Schröder moved to Berlin in 1858, Sundewall served as interim Baltic station chief in 1858–59.

44. Gröner, *Die deutschen Kriegsschiffe,* 1:69, 113; Boelcke, *So kam das Meer zu uns,* 74.

45. Scott Russell to Jachmann, London, 8 March 1858, BA-MA, RM 1/2010, 207. The proposed price of the project (£31,500) also deterred the navy from accepting Russell's offer.

46. BA-MA, RM 1/1593 and RM 1/1594, contain documentation of the navy's deals with Finspong and Åker. See also Koch, "Die deutsche Eisenindustrie," 11.

47. Bessell, *Norddeutscher Lloyd,* 20, 27–29, 193–95; Neubaur, *Der norddeutsche Lloyd,* 1:19.

48. Petter, "Deutsche Flottenrüstung," 69; "Bestimmungen über die Reorganisation der Admiralität [Allgemeiner Marinebefehl Nr. 54]," Berlin, 1 May 1859, text in Hubatsch, *Der Admiralstab,* 222–23.

49. BA-MA, RM 1/272 and RM 1/273, document the mobilization of 1859; Adalbert to Kdo. Baltic Station, Danzig, 16 June 1859, RM 31/644, 135, orders even the schooners to be armed.

50. Adalbert to Marineverwaltung, Berlin, 1 March 1860, BA-MA, RM 1/275, 6–8, calls for the *Gazelle* to be activated instead of the *Danzig,* setting the tone for the subsequent exchange. Schröder to Okdo. der Marine, Berlin, 3 April 1860, ibid., 11, objects to the threatening tone of the prince's latest missive, "which I must reject categorically." William (A.K.O.) to Admiralty, Berlin, 17 May 1860, ibid., 34, did little to soothe the dispute, which fills most of this file (RM 1/275).

51. Petter, "Deutsche Flottenrüstung," 71–72; Batsch, *Adalbert,* 276–77; William I (A.K.O.) to Staatsministerium, Berlin, 16 April 1861, BA-MA, RM 1/1871, 1.

52. Moltke to Prince Regent William, Berlin, 20 January 1860, quoted in Häussler, "Küstenschutz," 319.

53. Except where noted, the following account of the German navy question of 1859–62 is based on Häussler, "Küstenschutz," 311–43.

54. On the creation of the Nationalverein see Hamerow, *Restoration, Revolution, Reaction,* 241. See also Koch, "Die Sammlungen für die Deutsche Flotte," 145–46.

55. Duckwitz served as mayor of Bremen from 1857–63 and 1866–69. He was in the Bremen Senate from 1841 until 1875; he died in 1881. See Petter, "Deutsche Flottenrüstung," 53.

56. Brenner (Austrian minister) to Rechberg, Hannover, 2 October 1861, HHSA, PA, II, Carton 89, Deutsche Flotte/1861, 114–20; Kübeck (Austrian plenipotentiary) to Rechberg, Frankfurt, 9 November 1861, ibid., 209–12.

57. Quoted in Häussler, "Küstenschutz," 336.

58. On the lingering British influence in Hamburg see Prager, *Blohm + Voss,* 12.

59. See, e.g., Rechberg to Count August von Degenfeld (Austrian war minister), Vienna, 27 February 1862, HHSA, PA, XL. Interna, Carton 114: Korrespondenz mit Militärbehörden 1862, Kriegsministerium, 55–62.

60. Gröner, *Die deutschen Kriegsschiffe*, 1:160–62. BA-MA, RM 1/276, documents the navy's activities during the summer of 1861.

61. Koch, "Die deutsche Eisenindustrie," 3; Gröner, *Die deutschen Kriegsschiffe*, 1:160–62.

62. By 1860 both Schichau and Vulcan were building ships as well as engines. In the mid-1850s Schichau became the first Prussian firm to complete a steamer with a screw propeller, while Vulcan was the first German shipyard to build iron-hulled vessels. See Neubaur, *Der norddeutsche Lloyd*, 1:19. In 1857 Vulcan received a crucial infusion of capital from the Bleichröder bank. See Cattaruzza, *Arbeiter und Unternehmer*, 28.

63. Cf. plans of 27 February 1859, in Foerster, *Politische Geschichte*, 15–16, and 2 August 1859, NA, T-1022, roll 1445; Roon to Marinekommando, Berlin, 2 March 1861, ibid.

64. Minutes of Admiralty Council, Berlin, 13 December 1861, BA-MA, RM 1/2873, 13–16.

65. Petter, "Deutsche Flottenrüstung," 61.

66. A mission to the Far East had been under discussion for the past five years. Foreign Ministry to Admiralty, Berlin, 25 September 1854, NA, T-1022, roll 1306, asks if it would be possible for the navy to send "a warship" to Japan.

67. Dell (chief of staff) to Kdo. Baltic Station, Berlin, 1 September 1859, BA-MA, RM 1/272, refers to the Prince of Hessen's request of 25 August for indefinite, unpaid leave from the navy. He never returned to active duty. Adalbert to Marineverwaltung, Berlin, 9 November 1859, NA, T-1022, roll 1445, evaluates the *Amazone* and *Mercur*. Schröder to Oberkommando, Berlin, 2 December 1859, ibid., refers to the purchase of the *Columba*, a "clipper frigate ship" of "370 Last." The sale took place on 6 December.

68. Aside from memoirs by participants, Spiess, *Die Preussische Expedition nach Ostasien*, is the most detailed account of the mission. Salewski, "Die preussische Expedition nach Japan," 39–58, is the most recent. On the negotiations with Japan see text of Sundewall report, Tokyo Bay, 25 January 1861, in Boelcke, *So kam das Meer zu uns*, 328–29. Stoecker, "Germany and China," 28, notes that Eulenburg's Chinese treaty "was a copy of the treaties Britain and France had concluded with China," giving Germans the same privileges in the "treaty ports."

69. Petter, "Deutsche Flottenrüstung," 71–72.

70. Boelcke, *So kam das Meer zu uns*, 237. Austria subsequently planned a similar expedition to the Far East, but the wars of 1864 and 1866 forced its postponement until 1868–71. See Sondhaus, *The Habsburg Empire and the Sea*, 246–47, and idem, *The Naval Policy of Austria-Hungary*, 23–24.

71. Boelcke, *So kam das Meer zu uns*, 299.

72. Ibid., 24, 130, 198, 256, and 326. R. Werner, *Die preussische Expedition*, 2:310, gives the figure of "over 100" dead. Werner captained the *Elbe* during the expedition. Petter, "Deutsche Flottenrüstung," 72, contends that "almost one-third" of the participants died during the expedition.

73. Roster of 114 men aboard the *Amazone*, signed by Donner (interim chief, Baltic station), Danzig, 8 December 1861, BA-MA, RM 1/276, 262–64. Adalbert to B.

Hebeler (Prussian consul general in London), Berlin, 4 December 1861, RM 1/26, 144, indicates that the *Amazone* was last seen on 3 November, when it passed through Danish waters en route to the North Sea. Hebeler to Adalbert, London, 11 December 1861, ibid., 145, notes that "a full cyclone" hit the North Sea on 14–15 November; thereafter, Prussian officials assumed the ship went down in that storm. RM 1/277 and RM 1/279 include documentation of an investigation of remnants of the *Amazone* that washed ashore on the Dutch coast, along with a variety of alternative explanations of its disappearance.

74. Adalbert to Marineverwaltung, Berlin, 9 November 1859, NA, T-1022, roll 1445; fleet plan of 2 August 1859, in ibid. An article from the *Kölnische Zeitung*, 4 October 1862, copy in BA-MA, RM 1/277, 166, alleges the ship was in poor condition and accuses the government of a cover-up.

75. Petter, "Deutsche Flottenrüstung," 76.

Chapter 4: The Era of German Unification

1. Pflanze, *Bismarck*, 1:164–77.

2. Foerster, *Politische Geschichte*, 21.

3. Lambi, *The Navy and German Power Politics*, 1; Dinter, "Albrecht Graf von Roon," 474–75; Batsch, *Adalbert*, 260.

4. Budget figures for 1862 and 1863 from Crousaz, *Kurze Geschichte*, 152. Minutes of Admiralty Council, Berlin, 16 December 1861, BA-MA, RM 1/2873, 26–32, refer to the selection of Jasmund on Rügen as future home of the Baltic station; rejected options included building a new base at Swinemünde and keeping the station at Danzig.

5. Gröner, *Die deutschen Kriegsschiffe*, 1:68–69, 107, 113–14, 160–62.

6. Adalbert to Marineverwaltung, Berlin, 9 November 1859, NA, T-1022, roll 1445, refers to the *Mercur* as "totally useless." Prince Regent to Admiralty, Berlin, 6 December 1860, BA-MA, RM 1/2037, 11, authorizes the sale of the *Mercur*, which occurred later that month. Captain Köhler to Marineministerium, Danzig, 15 July 1862, RM 1/284, 59–60, notes that it would have cost 8,000–10,000 thalers to refurbish the *Elbe*. Scott Russell to Bothwell (Prussian navy chief of staff), London, 8 November 1861, RM 1/26, 141–42, indicates that the initiative to purchase a British frigate (using the shipbuilder Russell as go-between) actually predated the *Amazone* disaster. See also Gröner, *Die deutschen Kriegsschiffe*, 1:66, 68, 110–12.

7. Gröner, *Die deutschen Kriegsschiffe*, 1:68–69, 113–14.

8. BA-MA, RM 1/1596, documents the negotiations with Finspong. Starting in November 1862, the Swedish firm delivered ninety-four guns to Prussia.

9. Quotes from Gerolt to Bernstorff (foreign minister), Washington, 21 February 1862, BA-MA, RM 1/750, 177–78, and unidentified newspaper clipping enclosed in Ministry for Foreign Affairs to Roon, Berlin, 14 April 1862, ibid., 205. James B. Eads, "Description of gunboat *Benton*," Washington, 6 March 1862, ibid., 184–92. W. Hunter (U.S. State Department) to Gerolt, Washington, 14 May 1862, ibid., 269, indicates that the Union navy fulfilled a request for detailed drawings of the *Monitor*.

10. Minutes of Admiralty Council, Berlin, 19 December 1862, BA-MA, RM 1/2873, 36–43.

11. Bjerg, "When the Monitors Came to Europe"; Steensen, *Vore Krydsere*, 37; idem, *Vore Panserskibe*, 137–38. The armored schooners, delivered in the summer of 1862, were the 530-ton *Absalon* and the 600-ton *Esbern Snare*.

12. Rieben to Oberkommando, Berlin, 27 February 1863, NA, T-1022, roll 1131. See also Mantey, *Deutsche Marinegeschichte*, 70–71, and Boelcke, *So kam das Meer zu uns*, 74.

13. Tegetthoff to Archduke Ferdinand Max, Piraeus, 17 October 1863, in Tegetthoff, *Aus Wilhelm von Tegetthoff's Nachlass*, 315.

14. BA-MA, RM 1/282, RM 1/284, and RM 31/413, document the 1862 cruises of the *Gazelle* and *Gefion*.

15. Roon to Okdo. der Marine, Berlin, 14 November 1863, BA-MA, RM 1/286, 101. The somewhat panicky decision was reversed just days later, but the *Niobe* and *Rover* missed the second message and returned to Danzig in late November (ibid., 104).

16. Steensen, *Vore Panserskibe*, 146, 148–49, 160–68, 178–83; Donner, "Einige Gedanken," 306. The *Peder Skram*, laid down in 1859 as a screw frigate, was launched in October 1864. There is no recent comprehensive Danish account of the navy's role in 1864. Lütken, *Søkrigsbegivenhederne i 1864*, remains the most detailed study.

17. Gröner, *Die deutschen Kriegsschiffe*, 1:68–69. Anonymous, "Die Kaiserlich Deutsche Marine," 263, indicates that thirty-eight of the forty-two wooden gunboats from 1848–49 survived to be mobilized in 1864.

18. Adalbert to Marineministerium, Berlin, 16 April 1864, BA-MA, RM 1/2011, 180. The British buyers indeed resold the ship, not to the Danes but to the Japanese. The unseaworthy steamer made it all the way to Japan and served for five years in the shogun's fleet as the *Kwaiten*. See Gröner, *Die deutschen Kriegsschiffe*, 1:68.

19. Sondhaus, *The Habsburg Empire and the Sea*, 277.

20. Sondhaus, " 'The Spirit of the Army' at Sea," 467–68.

21. Graser, *Norddeutschlands Seemacht*, 67–68, 75; Petter, "Deutsche Flottenrüstung," 79–80; Steensen, *Vore Panserskibe*, 219–20; idem, *Vore Krydsere*, 47–49.

22. Sondhaus, *The Habsburg Empire and the Sea*, 239–41.

23. Tesdorpf, "Die Tätigkeit der Flotte," 63–74; Graser, *Norddeutschlands Seemacht*, 75–77; Mantey, *Deutsche Marinegeschichte*, 76–78.

24. Donner, "Die Ereignisse zur See im Kriege 1864," 53.

25. Mantey, *Deutsche Marinegeschichte*, 79.

26. Petter, "Deutsche Flottenrüstung," 79.

27. On the Battle of Helgoland see Handel-Mazzetti, "Das Seegefecht bei Helgoland," 193–98, and Paschen, "Der blutige Tag von Helgoland," 470–76. The Danes apparently still claim Helgoland as a victory. The frigate *Jylland*, their flagship in the battle, is preserved in Copenhagen as a national historic monument. See Kjølsen, "The Old Danish Frigate," 27–33.

28. Anonymous, "Die Kaiserlich Deutsche Marine," 263; Sondhaus, *The Habsburg Empire and the Sea*, 242.

29. Donner, "Einige Gedanken," 306; Steensen, *Vore Panserskibe*, 146–48, 223.

30. Sondhaus, *The Habsburg Empire and the Sea*, 241; Pflanze, *Bismarck*, 1:250–53. On the role of the Austrian navy as an effective "fleet in being" in the

North Sea see Donner, "Einige Gedanken," 306. Naval operations during the War of 1864 cost Austria 2.1 million gulden (around 1.4 million thalers), at the time a sum equal to the price of a small armored frigate. Larisch (finance minister) to Ministerium des Äussern, Vienna, 21 April 1866, HHSA, PA, XL. Interna, Carton 123: Korrespondenz mit dem Finanzministerium 1866, nr. 1573/FM.

31. BA-MA, RM 1/288, documents winter operations in 1864–65. William I (A.K.O.) to Okdo. der Marine, Berlin, 24 March 1865, RM 1/289, 36, abolishes the squadron and names Jachmann station chief.

32. Sondhaus, " 'The Spirit of the Army' at Sea," 468–69. See also Tirpitz, *Erinnerungen*, 3; undated "Verordnung," BA-MA, RM 1/143, 105–17.

33. Sondhaus, " 'The Spirit of the Army' at Sea," 469–70. BA-MA, RM 1/143, contains several drafts of the new guidelines and curriculum; Köhler to Rieben, Danzig, 12 January 1863, ibid., 43–46.

34. See Pflanze, *Bismarck*, 1:253–58.

35. Ibid., 1:258–64. Kiel technically was a naval base of the German Confederation, from 1865 until its demise in 1866. See Salewski, "Kiel und die Marine," 277.

36. In the years 1848–65 various political authorities and engineers proposed nine different routes for a canal between the Baltic and the lower Elbe. See Beseke, *Der Nord-Ostsee-Kanal*, 5–7. William I approved the transfer of the Prussian Baltic station from Danzig to Kiel on 24 March 1865, almost two weeks before Roon's speech. See Steinmetz, *Bismarck und die deutsche Marine*, 22.

37. Jachmann to Heldt, Kiel, 5 April 1865, BA-MA, RM 1/289, 55.

38. Jensen, *Seestadt Kiel*, 47, 105.

39. Gröner, *Die deutschen Kriegsschiffe*, 1:24, 114. Gröner dates the commissioning of the *Cheops* in July 1865, but BA-MA, RM 1/2524, 37, indicates that the ram arrived in Danzig on 25 May. William I (A.K.O.) to Roon, Berlin, 29 October 1865, ibid., 113, formally renames the ram *Prinz Adalbert*.

40. BA-MA, RM 1/289, includes correspondence on the purchase and delivery of the *Arminius*. Rieben to Samuda Brothers, Berlin, 9 June 1865, RM 1/2019, unnumbered, gives the monitor high marks and opens negotiations for an armored frigate order. See also Graser, *Norddeutschlands Seemacht*, 153. Donations for the *Arminius* amounted to 458,000 thalers.

41. Gröner, *Die deutschen Kriegsschiffe*, 1:24–25, 114. Captain Andreas Schau to Okdo. der Marine, Danzig, 8 June 1865, BA-MA, RM 1/2524, 74, indicates that the *Prinz Adalbert* ran aground on 2 June; serious hull damage kept the ship out of action until July. As for the *Augusta* and *Victoria*, Graser, *Norddeutschlands Seemacht*, 85 (writing in 1870), boasts that they were as fast as the famous Confederate raider *Alabama*.

42. Gröner, *Die deutschen Kriegsschiffe*, 1:68–69, 113–14.

43. Crousaz, *Kurze Geschichte*, 152.

44. Krupp to Roon, Essen, 7 November 1862, and to Hermann Orges, Essen, 20 February 1865, in Berdrow, *Krupp*, 202, 219.

45. Ministerium des Äussern to Count Bohuslav Chotek (ambassador to Prussia), Vienna, 20 October 1864, HHSA, AR, F 44, Carton 3: Generalia 1860–70; Chotek to Mensdorff, Berlin, 2 November 1864 and 6 January 1865, ibid.

46. Foerster, *Politische Geschichte*, 23–24. Minutes of Admiralty Council, Berlin, 20 January 1865, BA-MA, RM 1/1871, 128–52, indicate that Adalbert, Roon, Jachmann, and other navy leaders devised the plan two and a half months before it was presented.

47. Lambi, *The Navy and German Power Politics*, 1.

48. Roon, speech of 5 April 1865, text in Crousaz, *Kurze Geschichte*, 135.

49. Ibid.

50. Bismarck quoted in Stern, *Gold and Iron*, 55.

51. Bismarck, speech of 1 June 1865, text in Crousaz, *Kurze Geschichte*, 142.

52. William I (A.K.O.) to Roon, Berlin, 28 November 1865, BA-MA, RM 1/2019, unnumbered; Samuda Brothers to Roon, London, 15 [?] December 1865, ibid.; "Certificat de propriété," La Seyne, 5 October 1866, RM 1/2064.

53. Koch, "Die deutsche Eisenindustrie," 12.

54. Batsch, *Adalbert*, 288–89.

55. Sondhaus, *The Habsburg Empire and the Sea*, 243. Jachmann to Okdo. der Marine, Kiel, 20 March 1866, BA-MA, RM 1/293, 41.

56. Sondhaus, *The Habsburg Empire and the Sea*, 243; Tirpitz, *Erinnerungen*, 4. Tirpitz was among the cadets aboard the *Niobe* in the spring of 1866.

57. Heldt to Bismarck, Berlin, 6 August 1865, NA, T-1022, roll 1131, confirms the departure of the *Nymphe* and *Delphin;* BA-MA, RM 31/303, documents the departure and return of the *Vineta*, which finally came home in the autumn of 1868.

58. NA, T-1022, roll 1132, contains extensive correspondence concerning the *Nymphe* and *Delphin* in 1866. Eight years before the *Delphin* ran aground in the Eider Canal, the navy was told that the yacht *Grille*, also a vessel of 350 tons, was too large to pass through the waterway. Bothwell to Admiralty, Hamburg, 11 October 1858, BA-MA, RM 1/271, unnumbered.

59. William I (A.K.O.) to Roon, Berlin, 15 May 1866, BA-MA, RM 1/292, 75.

60. Graser, *Norddeutschlands Seemacht*, 167–68, 176; Mantey, *Deutsche Marinegeschichte*, 85–86; Röhr, *Handbuch*, 51–52. In the autumn of 1866 the *Arminius*—exceptionally fast by the standards of the day—outraced the U.S. Navy's seagoing monitor *Miantonomoh* in a competition held during the latter's visit to Kiel (see Graser, 163).

61. On the Lissa campaign see Sondhaus, *The Habsburg Empire and the Sea*, 252–59. According to Tirpitz, *Erinnerungen*, 4, "in spite of the circumstances of the war (*Kriegszustand*), we celebrated Tegetthoff's naval victory at Lissa almost as if it were our own."

62. Sondhaus, " 'The Spirit of the Army' at Sea," 470; Tirpitz, *Erinnerungen*, 2.

63. Liebe to Okdo. der Marine, Kiel, 8 December 1866, BA-MA, RM 1/203, 176–86. A former army artillery officer, Liebe had directed the Schleswig-Holstein naval academy from 1849 to 1851. See Stolz, *Die Schleswig-Holsteinische Marine*, 104.

64. Crousaz, *Kurze Geschichte*, 152. In May 1865, in the wake of the Danish war, the Landtag had refused to pass a similar bill. See Stern, *Gold and Iron*, 55.

65. On the creation of the new confederation see Pflanze, *Bismarck*, 1:341–63.

66. Böhm, *Überseehandel und Flottenbau*, 27–28.

67. Text of Articles 54 and 55 in Huber, *Dokumente zur deutschen Verfassungs-*

geschichte, 2:236. According to Güth, *Von Revolution zu Revolution,* 45, the new flags were flown after 2 July 1867.

68. Dinter, "Albrecht Graf von Roon," 469–70; Verchau, "Von Jachmann über Stosch und Caprivi," 56; Pflanze, *Bismarck,* 2:137–38; Maltzahn, "Jachmann," 297.

69. Foerster, *Politische Geschichte,* 35–36.

70. [Jachmann,] "Denkschrift betreffend die Entwicklung der Kriegs-Marine des Norddeutschen Bundes . . . ," Berlin, June 1867, NA, T-1022, roll 1445, indicates that the plan initially had a timetable of eight years rather than ten. Bismarck to Roon, Berlin, 9 September 1867, ibid., refers to Jachmann as the author of the 1867 program, but Dinter, "Albrecht Graf von Roon," 476, refers to it as "Roon's third fleet plan." See also Foerster, *Politische Geschichte,* 27–28.

71. Petter, "Deutsche Flottenrüstung," 88–90.

72. The 27 officers in the Austrian navy constituted 8.8 percent of its sea officers (308) above the rank of sea cadet, while the 21 in the North German navy accounted for 14.8 percent of its sea officers (142) above the rank of sea cadet. Cf. *[Rang]liste der norddeutschen Bundesmarine,* 1868, and *Militär-Schematismus des österreichsichen Kaiserthums,* 1868.

73. *[Rang]liste der norddeutschen Bundesmarine,* 1869.

74. "Anlage zu den Protokoll vom 28 Oktober 1867," NA, T-1022, roll 1445; Federal Military Law of 9 November 1867, quoted in Güth, *Von Revolution zu Revolution,* 54–55; Graser, *Norddeutschlands Seemacht,* 503.

75. Crousaz, *Kurze Geschichte,* 153.

76. Jachmann, "Promemoria," Berlin, 28 September 1868, BA-MA, RM 1/1587, 54–58, indicates that the navy ordered Krupp guns for the *Kronprinz* and *Friedrich Carl* in May 1867, and for the *König Wilhelm* in December 1867.

77. On the *Captain* see Ballard, *The Black Battlefleet,* 100–13. The ship was built between January 1867 and January 1870.

78. Ibid., 69, 230.

79. Admiralty Council, Berlin, 28 October 1867, BA-MA, RM 1/1871, 180–88; Gröner, *Die deutschen Kriegsschiffe,* 1:28.

80. Gröner, *Die deutschen Kriegsschiffe,* 1:68–69.

81. Ibid., 1:112, 114–15, 162.

82. Paschen, *Aus der Werdezeit zweier Marinen,* 166–67.

83. Adalbert to Marineministerium, Berlin, 16 May 1867, NA, T-1022, roll 1308.

84. Henk to Oberkommando, Smyrna, 11 March 1867, ibid.; Ober-Maschinist Witzel, report of 27 March 1867, ibid.; Adalbert to Marineministerium, 15 April 1867 and 29 April 1867, ibid. The *Gazelle*'s accident, with the British steamer *Mercury,* occurred on 28 February. Histories of the navy explained the recall as a precautionary measure taken in light of the Franco-Prussian crisis over Luxembourg. See, e.g., Graser, *Norddeutschlands Seemacht,* 66, and Mantey, *Deutsche Marinegeschichte,* 92.

85. William I (A.K.O.) to Roon, Berlin, 15 February 1866, BA-MA, RM 1/292, 28; Jachmann to Okdo. der Marine, Kiel, 12 February 1867, RM 1/294, 19–20; William I (A.K.O.) to Roon, Berlin, 14 March 1867, ibid., 45–46; Jachmann to Okdo. der Marine, Kiel, 4 June 1867, ibid., 214; William I (A.K.O.) to Okdo. der Marine, Ems, 9

July 1867, ibid., 253. The corvettes *Gazelle, Hertha,* and *Arcona* would have joined the *Arminius* in the squadron of 1866.

86. Batsch to Marineministerium, Berlin, 13 August 1867, NA, T-1022, roll 1308; Rieben to Marineoberkommando, Berlin, 20 August 1867, ibid.; Jachmann telegram to Marinedepot Geestemünde, 29 April 1868, ibid.

87. Jachmann, "Promemoria," Berlin, 28 September 1868, BA-MA, RM 1/1587, 54–58; Friedrich Krupp to Marineministerium, Essen, 18 October 1868, ibid., 89. RM 1/298 contains documentation of naval operations during 1868. Budget figure from Junghänel, *Marinehaushalt,* 96.

88. BA-MA, RM 1/2533, contains information about the trials and transfer of the *König Wilhelm;* RM 1/2540 concerns the *Kronprinz.* Jachmann to Okdo. der Marine, Berlin, 3 April 1869, RM 1/144, 159–60, outlines plans to send "the armored squadron to the West Indies." RM 1/299 chronicles the delays in the Krupp deliveries and subsequent curtailment of operations in 1869.

89. Batsch, *Adalbert,* 211, 290; Wislicenus, *Prinzadmiral Adalbert,* 102; William II, *My Early Life,* 49–50.

90. Frederick III, *Tagebuch,* 3.

91. Ibid., 61–67.

92. Ibid., 94–99.

93. On Henry's adventure aboard the *Elisabeth* see Paschen, *Aus der Werdezeit zweier Marinen,* 165. William II's memoirs refer to the *Hertha* and *Elisabeth* docking at Villafranca; he recalls a visit aboard the *Hertha,* where he "stood on the decks, a boy marvelling at the wonders of this ship of war." William II, *My Early Life,* 53–54. On the visit to Toulon see ibid., 54–55. Princes William and Henry spent the entire winter of 1869–70 on the French Riviera. See Röhl, *Wilhelm II,* 172–79.

94. Cecil, *Wilhelm II,* 27; Röhl, *Wilhelm II,* p. 178.

95. Frederick III, *Tagebuch,* 99.

96. Pflanze, *Bismarck,* 1:446–74.

97. BA-MA, RM 1/302, chronicles the prewar activities of the squadron in 1870; see also Steinmetz, "Im Schatten der Armee," 213–15, and Tirpitz, *Erinnerungen,* 5. According to Graser, *Norddeutschlands Seemacht,* 176, the *Prinz Adalbert* had been assigned to the Elbe at Hamburg (Altona) in the spring of 1869, as watch ship.

98. Steinmetz, "Im Schatten der Armee," 217, 220; Mantey, *Deutsche Marinegeschichte,* 97; "Protocoll über die Sitzung des Marine-Ministeriums," Berlin, 6 August 1870, BA-MA, RM 1/1871, 189–90.

99. Gröner, *Die deutschen Kriegsschiffe,* 1:116. The *Falke* was built in Britain, initially for the Confederate States; A.G. Vulcan of Stettin built the *Pommerania* for the postal service. See also Landerer, *Geschichte der HAPAG,* 47. There is no record of the two liners actually being used during the war. The company also provided the *Teutonia,* which served as a temporary home for some French prisoners of war.

100. Dinter, "Albrecht Graf von Roon," 477, gives the prewar figure of 162 officers and 3,300 NCOs and sailors. Mantey, *Deutsche Marinegeschichte,* 96, refers to 3,655, including 680 in the *Seebataillon* and 453 in the naval artillery. Gemzell, *Organization, Conflict, and Innovation,* 36, gives the figure for 1871.

101. Ropp, *The Development of a Modern Navy,* 22–23; Kreker, "Die französische

Marine," 276–78. For a contemporary French appraisal of the strengths of the two navies going into the war see Chevalier, *La marine française*, 14–28.

102. Ropp, *The Development of a Modern Navy*, 23.

103. On the Baltic blockade see Kreker, "Die französische Marine," 278–82; on the North Sea blockade see ibid., 282–84.

104. Ropp, *The Development of a Modern Navy*, 23–24; Kreker, "Die französische Marine," 284–85.

105. William I (A.K.O.) to Roon, Berlin, 18 July 1870, BA-MA, RM 1/302, 148, relieves Adalbert of his squadron command, one day before the war began. On Adalbert at Gravelotte see Priesdorff, *Soldatisches Führertum*, 6:398. Dinter, "Albrecht Graf von Roon," 472, notes that "the supreme commander of the navy, at his own request, took part in the war against France with the army." Steinmetz, "Im Schatten der Armee," 218, is somewhat more charitable, arguing that Adalbert, who would die just three years later, already was too infirm to assume an active sea command in wartime.

106. William I to Roon, [Berlin,] 29 July 1870, text in Hubatsch, *Der Admiralstab*, 227. See also Mantey, *Deutsche Marinegeschichte*, 97–98, and Steinmetz, "Im Schatten der Armee," 218–19.

107. Kreker, "Die französische Marine," 282; Steinmetz, "Im Schatten der Armee," 217–22; Maltzahn, "Jachmann," 300. According to Tirpitz, *Erinnerungen*, 6, the two squadron sorties were the only times the *König Wilhelm* left Wilhelmshaven in 1870.

108. Kreker, "Die französische Marine," 279–80; Waldersee, "Bericht über das Gefecht der Flotillen-Division bei Hiddensee am 17. August 1870," text in Pont-Jest, *Die Campagne von 1870*, 51–53.

109. Kreker, "Die französische Marine," 280; Weickhmann, "Bericht über das Gefecht S.M.S. *Nymphe* mit dem Französischen Geschwader bei Oxhoeft," text in Pont-Jest, *Die Campagne von 1870*, 54–55.

110. William I to Bismarck and Roon, Berlin, 24 July 1870, BA-MA, RM 31/633, 3; Kuhn to Okdo. der Marine, Berlin, 24 July 1870, ibid., 2; Kuhn to North Sea Station, Berlin, 6 September 1870, ibid., 31–32. RM 31/633 reveals much confusion over pay and uniforms for the *Seewehr* and provision of coal for its ships. Any "torpedoes" used at this stage would have been spar torpedoes or mines; the navy bought its first self-propelled torpedoes in 1873.

111. Steinmetz, *Bismarck und die deutsche Marine*, 26–27.

112. Stenzel, "Flotte und Küste," 606; Mantey, *Deutsche Marinegeschichte*, 102–3. The prizes, the brig *St. Marc* and the bark *Pierre Adolphe*, each received one sea cadet and five sailors to supervise their French crews on the way to Wilhelmshaven; both vessels ended up in Norway. Weickhmann burned the iron-hulled steamer *Max*, which was too large to secure as a prize. BA-MA, RM 31/609, chronicles the fate of the *St. Marc*, which finally arrived in Kiel in late March 1871. Bismarck ultimately agreed to a French request for compensation for the *St. Marc*'s cargo, valued at 9,386 thalers. Weickhmann and his crew were still asking for their prize money in September 1872, and apparently never received it.

113. Kreker, "Die französische Marine," 286; Neubaur, *Der norddeutsche Lloyd*, 1:36; Landerer, *Geschichte der HAPAG*, 47, 98.

114. Steinmetz, "Im Schatten der Armee," 228–29.

115. Firth, "German Firms in the Pacific Islands," 4–5, 7.

116. Boelcke, *So kam das Meer zu uns,* 74, 242, 299; Graser, *Norddeutschlands Seemacht,* 66.

117. Graser, *Norddeutschlands Seemacht,* 68–69; Wislicenus, *Prinzadmiral Adalbert,* 99.

118. Boelcke, *So kam das Meer zu uns,* 30, 238, 241; Mantey, *Deutsche Marinegeschichte,* 92–93. Contract (certified Berlin, 23 October 1868) between Max von Brandt and the Pacific Mail Steamship Company, BA-MA, RM 1/819, 20–25, indicates that the Germans purchased their land in Yokohama from a British firm; the Japanese government was not a party to the arrangement.

119. Petter, "Deutsche Flottenrüstung," 86, 90–92; Köhler to Okdo. der Marine, Shanghai, 30 April 1870, BA-MA, RM 1/819, 40. On Anson Burlingame's visit to Berlin see D. Anderson, *Imperialism and Idealism,* 45.

120. Böhm, *Überseehandel und Flottenbau,* 30.

121. Landerer, *Geschichte der HAPAG,* 45; Bessell, *Norddeutscher Lloyd,* 35. In 1868 the Lloyd also opened a line to Baltimore.

122. Before the arrival of the *Augusta,* the sailing frigate *Niobe* spent the winter of 1866–67 on a training cruise to the West Indies. Heldt to Marineministerium, Berlin, 8 October 1866, NA, T-1022, roll 1308. William I (A.K.O.), Berlin, 28 August 1867, ibid., refers to a decision to send the *Augusta* to Mexico. See also Boelcke, *So kam das Meer zu uns,* 106, and Petter, "Deutsche Flottenrüstung," 95.

123. Cruise cited in Adalbert to Marineministerium, Berlin, 22 January 1870, BA-MA, RM 1/2388, 12.

124. BA-MA, RM 1/2388, includes dispatches from the 1870 cruises of the *Meteor, Niobe,* and *Arcona.*

125. Steinmetz, "Im Schatten der Armee," 228; Chevalier, *La marine française,* 97.

126. BA-MA, RM 1/2388, traces the travails of the *Arcona.* The British consul in the Azores reported that on 14 November 1870 the *Bellone* "sailed into port with colors flying, rounded close outside the *Arcona,* fired a gun and proceeded slowly out of the bay, and remained anchored outside. . . . The *Arcona* . . . remained at anchor in the bay" (ibid., 169). The ship finally reached Wilhelmshaven on 15 March 1871. See also Boelcke, *So kam das Meer zu uns,* 56; Steinmetz, "Im Schatten der Armee," 223–24; and Chevalier, *La marine française,* 97.

127. Knorr to Okdo. der Marine, Havana, 15 November 1870, BA-MA, RM 1/2388, 149–53, reports on the battle. See also Lohmann, "S.M.S. *Meteor* bei Havanna," 509–13, and R. Werner, "*Meteor* und *Bouvet* auf der Reede von Havanna," 74–77. According to the French version of the story, the captain of the *Bouvet* issued the challenge to Knorr. See Chevalier, *La marine française,* 97–98.

128. Boelcke, *So kam das Meer zu uns,* 250–51; Petter, "Deutsche Flottenrüstung," 93–94; Verchau, "Von Jachmann über Stosch und Caprivi," 58.

129. Steinmetz, "Im Schatten der Armee," 227.

130. On the effects of 1870 on Tirpitz, see Berghahn, *Der Tirpitz-Plan,* 58–59. See also *Rangliste der kaiserlich deutschen Marine,* 1871–72, 1873.

Chapter 5: Serving the New Reich

1. Cf. Huber, *Dokumente zur deutschen Verfassungsgeschichte,* 2:236, 300.

2. Lambi, *The Navy and German Power Politics,* 3.

3. William I (A.K.O.) to Bismarck and Roon, Berlin, 15 June 1871, BA-MA, RM 1/1871, 191. Pflanze, *Bismarck,* 2:138, credits Roon with reunifying the commands during 1871. On Adalbert's death see Batsch, *Adalbert,* 294. R. Werner, *Seekriegsgeschichte,* 527, cites a lung ailment as the cause. Although the prince spent 1866 and 1870 with the army, Werner notes (521) that his de facto retirement met with "the deepest regret" of the officer corps.

4. Freytag, "General von Stosch," 206.

5. Tirpitz, *Erinnerungen,* 18.

6. Paschen, *Aus der Werdezeit zweier Marinen,* 150. Paschen (171) also questions Stosch's choice of advisors.

7. Stosch, "Unsere Küsten in einem Kriege mit Frankreich."

8. See Hollyday, *Bismarck's Rival,* chapters 1–3. Manteuffel advised Stosch against accepting the new post. See Coler, "Der Sturz Albrecht von Stoschs," 704.

9. Verchau, "Von Jachmann über Stosch und Caprivi," 58, 61; Paschen, *Aus der Werdezeit zweier Marinen,* 170.

10. For Stosch's reflections on his trip to the Suez Canal see his *Denkwürdigkeiten,* 156–79.

11. Hollyday, *Bismarck's Rival,* 97, 99–100, 104, 137–38; Steinmetz, *Bismarck und die deutsche Marine,* 33. Stosch to his wife, Berlin, 7 July 1871, *Denkwürdigkeiten,* 254, refers to his possible appointment as "navy minister."

12. Pflanze, *Bismarck,* 2:138–39.

13. Ibid., 2:360, 402.

14. Coler, "Der Konflikt Bismarck-Stosch," 590.

15. Steinmetz, "Noch einmal: Bismarck-Stosch," 708. Jachmann had feuded with the chancellor's cousin, Colonel Hugo Hermann von Bismarck, during the latter's brief tenure (1864–66) as commander of the *Seebataillon,* but there is no evidence that this influenced Bismarck's later position on the appointment of Stosch, rather than Jachmann, as chief of the Admiralty. Rieben, "Promemoria," Berlin, 30 December 1865, BA-MA, RM 1/1830, 7–10, explains the origins of Jachmann's dispute with the colonel.

16. Verchau, "Von Jachmann über Stosch und Caprivi," 57. Some sources contend that Stosch never convened the Admiralty Council, but minutes in BA-MA, RM 1/1871, 241–58, indicate that it did meet in January 1879 to discuss whether the navy should dredge a second entrance to Wilhelmshaven harbor.

17. Sondhaus, " 'The Spirit of the Army' at Sea," 473. Weickhmann is characterized by future admiral Ludwig von Schröder (who served under him as a cadet aboard the *Niobe* in 1871–72) in Waldeyer-Hartz, *Ludwig von Schröder,* 34.

18. *Rangliste der kaiserlich deutschen Marine,* 1871–72, 1873. According to Tirpitz, *Erinnerungen,* 3, some of the former merchant mariners were court-martialed after 1870.

19. Hubatsch, *Kaiserliche Marine,* 467, 476.

20. Herwig, *"Luxury" Fleet*, 13; Petter, "Deutsche Flottenrüstung," 114.

21. Crousaz, *Kurze Geschichte*, 307–10; Hobson, *The German School of Naval Thought*, 16–17; Gemzell, *Organization, Conflict, and Innovation*, 41. The school had a three-year curriculum from 1875 to 1883 before reverting to the original two years.

22. Sondhaus, " 'The Spirit of the Army' at Sea," 474–75.

23. Stosch, "Zur Aufnahme in das Marine-Verordnungsblatt, Berlin, 13 May 1873, BA-MA, RM 1/145, 6–7; copy of *Verordnung über die Ergänzung des Offizierskorps der Kaiserlichen Marine nebst Allerhöchster Kabinets-Ordre vom 10. März 1874* in ibid., 202–24; Crousaz, *Kurze Geschichte*, 310; *Rangliste der kaiserlich deutschen Marine*, 1873 through 1883, passim.

24. Sondhaus, " 'The Spirit of the Army' at Sea," 475–76.

25. Paschen, *Aus der Werdezeit zweier Marinen*, 176, 178.

26. Freytag, "General von Stosch," 210.

27. Tirpitz, *Erinnerungen*, 18.

28. Petter, "Deutsche Flottenrüstung," 115.

29. Adalbert to Marineministerium, Berlin, 8 February 1862, BA-MA, RM 1/143, 7–12.

30. Petter, "Deutsche Flottenrüstung," 114. Ironically, Jachmann introduced infantry drill in 1870 for the seamen at Wilhelmshaven, to keep them busy and maintain discipline after the French blockade idled his North Sea squadron.

31. *Stenographische Berichte über die Verhandlungen des Reichstages*, 1. Legislative Period, III. Session (1872), 29. Sitzung, 559.

32. Gröner, *Die deutschen Kriegsschiffe*, 1:28–30; Wulle and Pittelkow, "Superlative aus Stettin," 34–35. According to Pistorius, "Die Vulcan-Werke A.G. Stettin," 314, the contract for the *Preussen* was not signed until 9 August 1871. William I (A.K.O.) to Roon, Berlin, 9 December 1869, BA-MA, RM 1/2607, 4, refers to the decision to equip *Grosser Kurfürst* with turrets rather than "a broadside battery," but Gröner (1:29) contends that the ship was originally designed as a casemate ship, modeled after the new *Custoza* of the Austrian navy. The same order authorizes the construction of the *Friedrich der Grosse* at Kiel. Koop, Galle, and Klein, *Von der Kaiserlichen Werft zum Marinearsenal*, 195, contend that the *Grosser Kurfürst* was laid down in 1874, but William I's 9 December 1869 letter to Roon refers to the warship as already being under construction.

33. Gröner, *Die deutschen Kriegsschiffe*, 1:28–30. According to "Protocoll über die Sitzung des Marine-Ministeriums," Berlin, 6 August 1870, BA-MA, RM 1/1871, 189–90, "preparations" for the *Friedrich der Grosse* continued during the war, while work on the *Preussen* was suspended "because the company [A.G. Vulcan] is in no position to proceed with the construction."

34. Leckebusch, *Eisenindustrie*, 16.

35. Gröner, *Die deutschen Kriegsschiffe*, 1:28–30.

36. Ibid., 1:68–69, 113–15.

37. Ibid., 1:162.

38. Foerster, *Politische Geschichte*, 30; Gerloff, *Finanz- und Zollpolitik*, 79–80. Stosch quoted in Lambi, *The Navy and German Power Politics*, 4, and Verchau, "Von Jachmann über Stosch und Caprivi," 59; Bismarck quoted in Gerloff, 79.

39. Stosch expressed these opinions shortly before taking over the Admiralty in Stosch to Freytag, Berlin, 3 December 1871, *Denkwürdigkeiten,* 272.

40. Sondhaus, *The Naval Policy of Austria-Hungary,* 47–48.

41. Lambi, *The Navy and German Power Politics,* 5; Kelly, "Tirpitz and the Origins of the German Torpedo Arm," 2. The half-dozen spar torpedo boats included three displacing 24 tons and three of 34 tons.

42. On the continued use of the Eider Canal see Jensen, *Seestadt Kiel,* 15. Lambi, *The Navy and German Power Politics,* 6, and Petter, "Deutsche Flottenrüstung," 126, allege that Stosch opposed construction of the Kiel Canal, siding with Moltke against Bismarck, but Hollyday, *Bismarck's Rival,* 107, contends that Stosch always supported the project.

43. Gerloff, *Finanz- und Zollpolitik,* 81–82; Verchau, "Von Jachmann über Stosch und Caprivi," 59; Petter, "Deutsche Flottenrüstung," 105. Hollyday, *Bismarck's Rival,* 119, notes that Stosch's friend Freytag "strongly favored" the *Kulturkampf.*

44. Anonymous, "Die Kaiserlich Deutsche Marine," 266. Figure of 95.8 million marks from Leckebusch, *Eisenindustrie,* 21n.

45. Freytag to Stosch, Leipzig, 4–5 December 1871, in Freytag, *Gustav Freytags Briefe an Albrecht von Stosch,* 82–83, indicates that the well-connected publicist Freytag helped mobilize support for the navy and advised Stosch on his relations with Reichstag members. See also Hollyday, *Bismarck's Rival,* 111–12.

46. Paschen, *Aus der Werdezeit zweier Marinen,* 174; Waldeyer-Hartz, *Ludwig von Schröder,* 55; Hollyday, *Bismarck's Rival,* 114.

47. Freytag, "General von Stosch," 206. Koch, "Die deutsche Eisenindustrie," 4–5, dismisses the "legend" that Stosch personally promoted domestic industry. He cites a Reichstag resolution of 1873, calling for the navy to patronize German firms.

48. Krupp to William I, Berlin, 16 March 1876, in Berdrow, *Krupp,* 331.

49. Güth, *Von Revolution zu Revolution,* 64.

50. R. Werner, *Seekriegsgeschichte,* 521.

51. Coler, "Der Konflikt Bismarck-Stosch," 582.

52. Steinmetz, *Bismarck und die deutsche Marine,* 39–40.

53. Coler, "Der Konflikt Bismarck-Stosch," 583.

54. Pflanze, *Bismarck,* 2:359; Hollyday, *Bismarck's Rival,* 116; Coler, "Der Konflikt Bismarck-Stosch," 584–85. Fiscal year 1876 ultimately became fiscal year 1876–77, as Germany adopted a budget calendar that did not conform to the calendar year. For 1876–77 the navy received 31.8 million marks. See Junghänel, *Marinehaushalt,* 96.

55. Hollyday, *Bismarck's Rival,* 90, 161.

56. Pflanze, *Bismarck,* 2:361; Coler, "Der Konflikt Bismarck-Stosch," 588–89.

57. Quoted in Hollyday, *Bismarck's Rival,* 166.

58. Pflanze, *Bismarck,* 2:361–63; Coler, "Der Konflikt Bismarck-Stosch," 593.

59. Arnauld de la Perière, *Prinz Heinrich,* 9. According to William II, *My Early Life,* 79, Henry officially joined the navy on his tenth birthday, in 1872.

60. Gröner, *Die deutschen Kriegsschiffe,* 1:32–33; quotes from Freytag, "General von Stosch," 208.

61. Gröner, *Die deutschen Kriegsschiffe*, 1:24–25. The *Prinz Adalbert* was scrapped in 1878; the *Arminius*, eventually used as an icebreaker and harbor tender, survived until 1901.

62. Ibid., 1:164–65.

63. Ibid., 1:70–71.

64. Ibid., 1:166.

65. Ibid., 1:116–17. Stosch to Kdo. Baltic Station, Berlin, 29 August, 10 October 1876, BA-MA, RM 31/654, 23, 25.

66. BA-MA, RM 1/1809, indicates that Stosch, in 1876–77, permitted the Russian naval attaché, Captain N. Nevakhevitch, to have drawings made of the improved installations at Kiel, Danzig, and Wilhelmshaven. Nevakhevitch contended that the plans would be used only for academic purposes at the Russian engineering academy.

67. Junghänel, *Marinehaushalt*, 96.

68. Verchau, "Von Jachmann über Stosch und Caprivi," 59.

69. Boelcke, *So kam das Meer zu uns*, 36.

70. Neubaur, *Der norddeutsche Lloyd*, 1:66; Prager, *Blohm + Voss*, 11, 17.

71. Boelcke, *So kam das Meer zu uns*, 305; Kennedy, "Bismarck's Imperialism," 264; Mantey, *Deutsche Marinegeschichte*, 136.

72. Firth, "German Firms in the Pacific Islands," 5–7.

73. Kennedy, "Bismarck's Imperialism," 264.

74. Hubatsch, *Kaiserliche Marine*, 480–89 passim. The overall number of overseas vessels does not include sailing ships used for training cruises in the North Atlantic or ships deployed in the Mediterranean.

75. Röhr, *Handbuch*, 59; Miyake, "German Cultural and Political Influence on Japan," 159–65.

76. Szippl, "Max von Brandt and German Imperialism in East Asia," 24, 32. See also Stoecker, "Germany and China," 32. Brandt's three-volume memoir, *Dreiunddreißig Jahre in Ost-Asien*, includes a volume (II) on his years in Japan and a volume (III) on his years in China.

77. Boelcke, *So kam das Meer zu uns*, 305.

78. B. Werner, *Ein deutsches Kriegsschiff in der Südsee*. Bartholomäus von Werner, not to be confused with Reinhold Werner, captained the *Ariadne*.

79. Kennedy, *The Samoan Tangle*, 16.

80. Steinmetz, *Bismarck und die deutsche Marine*, 42–43.

81. BA-MA, RM 1/2388 and RM 1/2568, chronicle the state of the Caribbean in 1871. On Imperial Germany's strong interest in Venezuela see Herwig, *Germany's Vision of Empire in Venezuela*. The navy played an important role in the life of Venezuela's small German community. In the overwhelmingly Catholic country, chaplains from visiting German warships were relied upon to perform Protestant baptisms and marriages. See ibid., 57–59.

82. Batsch to Admiralty, Cap Haytien, 14 June 1872, BA-MA, RM 1/2389, 85–87. The Haitian ships were the 7-gun *Union* and the 14-gun *Mont Organisé*, a 1,600-ton vessel almost as large as the German corvettes.

83. R. Werner, *Erinnerungen und Bilder*, 304–5, 381–82; idem, *Seekriegsge-*

NOTES TO PAGES 118–24   271

schichte, 528. The deployment of armored warships on distant stations would be rare in the late 1800s, but the overseas assignment of the *Friedrich Carl* (like the canceled 1869 Caribbean cruise plans for the entire armored squadron) reflected the Admiralty Council's earlier reasoning that the acquisition of small ironclads by Japan and some of the South American republics would require European navies to employ ironclads for their "gunboat diplomacy." Minutes of Admiralty Council, Berlin, 28 October 1867, BA-MA, RM 1/1871, 180–88.

84. BA-MA, RM 1/2389, passim. See also Güth, *Von Revolution zu Revolution,* 69.

85. Boelcke, *So kam das Meer zu uns,* 109; Paschen, *Aus der Werdezeit zweier Marinen,* 186–95. B. Werner, *Ein deutsches Kriegsschiff in der Südsee,* 46–50, has the corvette *Freya* with the *Medusa* on the Caribbean side. The *Freya* was overseas from November 1877 to September 1879. See Waldeyer-Hartz, *Ludwig von Schröder,* 97.

86. Paschen, *Aus der Werdezeit zweier Marinen,* 186, 196; Güth, *Von Revolution zu Revolution,* 64. BA-MA, RM 3/10490, 151, indicates that the *Elisabeth* visited Chile and Uruguay on its way home to Kiel.

87. Boelcke, *So kam das Meer zu uns,* 324.

88. See, e.g., Lengnick, "See-Interessen und See-Politik," 323.

89. Henk to Stosch, Berlin, 11 April 1872, BA-MA, RM 1/144, 228–31, rejecting a "flying squadron" proposal by *Kapitänleutnant* Otto Zembsch of the Admiralty. See also Pflanze, *Bismarck,* 2:360.

90. Henk to Stosch, Berlin, 11 April 1872, BA-MA, RM 1/144, 228–31.

91. Roon, speech of 5 April 1865, text in Crousaz, *Kurze Geschichte,* 135.

92. R. Werner, *Erinnerungen und Bilder,* 390–404; idem, *Seekriegsgeschichte,* 528–32; Hollyday, *Bismarck's Rival,* 146–47.

93. Hollyday, *Bismarck's Rival,* 146–47; Koop, Galle, and Klein, *Von der Kaiserlichen Werft zum Marinearsenal,* 188; Hubatsch, *Kaiserliche Marine,* 481–89. In his *Seekriegsgeschichte,* 532, R. Werner contends the ruling in his favor was "unanimous."

94. Waldeyer-Hartz, *Ludwig von Schröder,* 58–60.

95. R. Werner, *Seekriegsgeschichte,* 533.

96. BA-MA, RM 1/308, passim. See also Mantey, *Deutsche Marinegeschichte,* 125.

97. BA-MA, RM 1/310, passim; Paschen, *Aus der Werdezeit zweier Marinen,* 177.

98. Hollyday, *Bismarck's Rival,* 151–60; Boelcke, *So kam das Meer zu uns,* 59, 71; Mantey, *Deutsche Marinegeschichte,* 118–19; Röhr, *Handbuch,* 58.

99. Henk to Stosch, Berlin, 7 October 1874, BA-MA, RM 1/310, 195–216; RM 1/313, passim; Mantey, *Deutsche Marinegeschichte,* 125–26.

100. Boelcke, *So kam das Meer zu uns,* 74–75; Waldeyer-Hartz, *Ludwig von Schröder,* 64–68. Sources disagree over the identity of the three unarmored vessels.

101. BA-MA, RM 1/315, passim; RM 1/2543, passim; Waldeyer-Hartz, *Ludwig von Schröder,* 69.

102. BA-MA, RM 1/316, passim; Hubatsch, *Kaiserliche Marine,* 486–87; Boelcke, *So kam das Meer zu uns,* 75, 84; Waldeyer-Hartz, *Ludwig von Schröder,* 97; Güth, *Von Revolution zu Revolution,* 69.

103. Bernhard Ernst von Bülow (Foreign Office) to Stosch, Berlin, 2 May, and Stosch to Bülow, Berlin, 23 May 1878, BA-MA, RM 1/320, 12–14, 18.

104. Documentation in BA-MA, RM 1/2607 and RM 1/320.

Chapter 6: Disaster and Disarray

1. BA-MA, RM 1/18, contains eyewitness descriptions and testimony regarding the accident. RM 1/2304 includes several diagrams of the positions of the ships at various stages of the accident. Otto Rantzau's testimony, dated Kiel, 28 October 1878, is in RM 1/2307, 9–15.

2. Henk to William I, Berlin, 1 June 1878, BA-MA, RM 1/320, 40; Stosch to Batsch, Berlin, 3 June, and Batsch to Stosch, Wilhelmshaven, 7 June 1878, ibid., 43, 49; Philipsborn (Reich Chancellery) to Stosch, Berlin, 9 June 1878, ibid., 51.

3. Pflanze, *Bismarck,* 2:392–414, 431–41; Coler, "Palastrevolte in der Marine," 639.

4. Werner to Admiralty, Kiel, 21 July 1878, BA-MA, RM 1/18, 2–19; Werner, "Gutachten über den Zusammenstoss S.M.S. *König Wilhelm* und *Grosser Kurfürst* am 31. Mai 1878," Kiel, 21 July 1878, ibid., 20–29; Secret "Abschrift" (signed "A"), Berlin, 3 August 1878, ibid., 100–104; Batsch quoted in Batsch to Stosch, Wilhelmshaven, 28 May 1878, RM 1/320, 35–36; Stosch quoted in Coler, "Palastrevolte in der Marine," 639.

5. Güth, *Von Revolution zu Revolution,* 62, contends that Stosch required ships to be ready for service within eight days of their commissioning; Tirpitz, *Erinnerungen,* 18, says three days.

6. Stosch to Freytag, Oestrich, 2 August 1878, quoted in Coler, "Palastrevolte in der Marine," 641.

7. Ibid., 641.

8. R. Werner, *Die preussische Expedition* (1863).

9. R. Werner, *Das Buch von der deutschen Flotte* (1874), appeared initially in 1869 as *Das Buch von der norddeutschen Flotte.* It went through eight editions, the last in 1902. William II quoted in *My Early Life,* 123.

10. *Rangliste der kaiserlich deutschen Marine,* 1879, uses this language in its listing of Werner's retirement.

11. Quoted in Coler, "Palastrevolte in der Marine," 640. On the authorship of this article see Petter, "Deutsche Flottenrüstung," 122.

12. Coler, "Palastrevolte in der Marine," 641.

13. Figure for 1876 from Mantey, *Deutsche Marinegeschichte,* 121.

14. Stosch to Freytag, Oestrich, 3 October 1878, quoted in Verchau, "Von Jachmann über Stosch und Caprivi," 62n.

15. Coler, "Palastrevolte in der Marine," 642, 644–47; Hollyday, *Bismarck's Rival,* 185; Steinmetz, "Noch einmal: Bismarck-Stosch," 711. Batsch to Stosch, Wilhelmshaven, 10 December 1878, BA-MA, RM 1/19, 234, implicates Henk as an opponent of their cause. Officially, Henk, like Werner, "requested retirement." See *Rangliste der kaiserlich deutschen Marine,* 1880.

16. Testimony of Otto Rantzau, Kiel, 28 October 1878, BA-MA, RM 1/2307, 9–15; Kinderling to Stosch, Kiel, 31 October 1878, RM 1/19, 175–78; Jachmann and Klatt, "Gutachten," Kiel, 27 November 1878, ibid., 195–219. Hollen, a future vice admiral, married Stosch's only daughter, Luise, in 1874. See Priesdorff, *Soldatisches Führertum,* 8:308.

17. Batsch to Stosch, Wilhelmshaven, 10 December 1878, BA-MA, RM 1/19, 116–17; William I to Stosch, Berlin, 4 January 1879, ibid., 270–71.

18. Courts-martial, proceedings and verdict of 1 February 1879, BA-MA, RM 1/21, 1–115; proceedings and verdict of 7 June 1879, ibid., 116–82; proceedings and verdict of 25 August 1879, ibid., 183–224; Batsch to William I, Wilhelmshaven, 15 June 1879, RM 1/20, 16–25; Lieutenant General Wilhelm von Massow (fortress commandant) to Stosch, Magdeburg, 13 August 1879, ibid., 105. See also Hollyday, *Bismarck's Rival*, 182–89 passim. Although the three *Garde-Korps* courts were chaired by generals, each also included navy officers.

19. Stosch, "Qualifications-Bericht," Berlin, 11 December 1877, BA-MA, RM 1/2306, 12.

20. Coler, "Palastrevolte in der Marine," 649–52; Albedyll to Stosch, Berlin, 3 July 1879, quoted in ibid., 649.

21. William I quoted in ibid., 653.

22. Cf. *Rangliste der kaiserlich deutschen Marine*, 1879 through 1882.

23. BA-MA, RM 1/2088 through RM 1/2095, include projects up to 1903 to raise the wreck. RM 1/1715 includes correspondence from 1878–80 pondering the cost of recovering the bodies.

24. William I (A.K.O.) to Stosch, Berlin, 13 May 1879, BA-MA, RM 1/145, 198. Captain Louis von Blanc (chief of staff), "Promemoria," Berlin, 29 April 1879, ibid., 195–96, cites the need for junior officers to be able to teach their seamen to swim.

25. Hollyday, *Bismarck's Rival*, 191–94.

26. Pflanze, *Bismarck*, 3:39–40; Coler, "Palastrevolte in der Marine," 654–56; Hollyday, *Bismarck's Rival*, 180–81. According to Hollyday, 191, the plan to make Frederick Charles general inspector of the navy also involved bringing Vice Admiral Henk out of retirement to replace Stosch as chief of the Admiralty.

27. Steinmetz, *Bismarck und die deutsche Marine*, 62, and Petter, "Deutsche Flottenrüstung," 123, contend that William I supported the rear admiral's candidacy for the Danzig seat. On Rickert and the "Secession" see Pflanze, *Bismarck*, 2:537.

28. Hubatsch, *Kaiserliche Marine*, 495–508 passim.

29. Steinmetz, "Noch einmal: Bismarck-Stosch," 712.

30. Junghänel, *Marinehaushalt*, 96.

31. Figures from *Jahresbericht der k.u.k. Kriegsmarine* (1897), 118–29.

32. Gröner, *Die deutschen Kriegsschiffe*, 1:32–33.

33. Leckebusch, *Eisenindustrie*, 34–35; Koch, "Die deutschen Eisenindustrie," 6. Epkenhans, *Die wilhelminische Flottenrüstung*, 157, dates Dillingen's relationship with the navy from "1876–77."

34. Gröner, *Die deutschen Kriegsschiffe*, 1:32–33; quotes from Freytag, "General von Stosch," 208–9.

35. Gröner, *Die deutschen Kriegsschiffe*, 1:164–65, 167–68; Leckebusch, *Eisenindustrie*, 35; quotes from Freytag, "General von Stosch," 209. According to Verchau, "Von Jachmann über Stosch und Caprivi," 60, "English works . . . produced the armor plate for the first gunboats," and the first acceptable Dillinger plates were not delivered until July 1878, by which time the first five gunboats were already in serv-

ice. The change in armor suppliers caused a gap in the program; no gunboats were commissioned between February 1878 and November 1879.

36. Gröner, *Die deutschen Kriegsschiffe,* 1:117–18.

37. On the reluctance of Hamburg shipbuilders to abandon wood construction see Prager, *Blohm + Voss,* 19. Shipyard labor in the city, heavily dominated by the woodworking trades, organized its first union in reaction against the threat to its traditional livelihood. See Cattaruzza, "Organizierter Konflikt," 326–30.

38. Gröner, *Die deutschen Kriegsschiffe,* 1:166–67.

39. Ibid., 1:118–19.

40. Neubaur, *Der norddeutsche Lloyd,* 1:283.

41. Count Eulenburg (interior minister) to Stosch, Berlin, 13 January 1880, BA-MA, RM 20/9, 1, enclosing police report, "Betrifft die sozialistische Bewegung in Kiel und Umgegend," dated Kiel, 8 December 1879, ibid., 3–10; Stosch to Goltz, Berlin, 4 February 1880, ibid., 11–19; Goltz to Admiralty, Kiel, 10 February 1880, ibid., 28–33. See also Sondhaus, "The Imperial German Navy and Social Democracy," 54–55.

42. Lambi, *Free Trade and Protection in Germany,* 79.

43. Krupp to Gun Department, [Essen,] 17 February 1879, in Berdrow, *Krupp,* 355–56.

44. Krupp to Frederick William, Essen, 16 January 1880, ibid., 363.

45. Krupp to the Firm, [Essen,] undated (probably August 1881), ibid., 376.

46. Krupp to Herr Budde, [Essen,] 24 November 1882, ibid., 379. Alfred Krupp died in 1887, at the age of seventy-five.

47. Freytag, "General von Stosch," 205.

48. Ibid., 206.

49. BA-MA, RM 1/322, passim.

50. BA-MA, RM 1/324, passim.

51. Mantey, *Deutsche Marinegeschichte,* 129. Tirpitz, *Erinnerungen,* 31, recalls that he took command of the *Zieten* in May 1878, just before the *Grosser Kurfürst's* sinking. See also Kelly, "Tirpitz and the Origins of the German Torpedo Arm," 7.

52. Boelcke, *So kam das Meer zu uns,* 75.

53. BA-MA, RM 1/326, passim; William II, *My Early Life,* 230–33.

54. BA-MA, RM 1/326, passim; Paschen, *Aus der Werdezeit zweier Marinen,* 221–23; Sigel, *Germany's Army and Navy,* 108.

55. In the spring of 1882, *Obersteuermann* Meiling was arrested and imprisoned in Berlin. He allegedly received 150,000 rubles for information on German coastal defenses, signals, mines, and torpedoes. BA-MA, RM 1/1883, 28, contains a clipping on the subject from a *Berliner Tageblatt* article of 19 June 1882. Stosch to Batsch, Berlin, 21 June 1882, ibid., 29, criticizes "individuals" at the Baltic station for leaking to the press "the precise details of the investigation" of Meiling.

56. Lambi, *The Navy and German Power Politics,* 14–16.

57. BA-MA, RM 1/327, passim; Paschen, *Aus der Werdezeit zweier Marinen,* 223–25; Kelly, "Tirpitz and the Origins of the German Torpedo Arm," 9–10.

58. Lambi, *The Navy and German Power Politics,* 16.

59. Berghahn, *Der Tirpitz-Plan,* 60.

60. HHSA, AR, F 44, Carton 4, Varia ab 1871: Austausch 1874–96, indicates that throughout the 1870s and early 1880s, even after the conclusion of the Triple Alliance, the French navy exchanged much more information with the Austrians than did the Germans, on matters including artillery and torpedoes.

61. Hubatsch, *Kaiserliche Marine*, 497.

62. At the start Schwartzkopf made its torpedoes out of bronze, whereas Whitehead had used iron. See Foerster, *Politische Geschichte*, 46. Tirpitz, *Erinnerungen*, 32, indicates that Schwartzkopf started manufacturing torpedoes in the late 1870s.

63. For a text of the Triple Alliance treaty of 20 May 1882 and notes of 28 May 1882, see Bridge, *The Habsburg Monarchy*, 387–88.

64. Hubatsch, *Kaiserliche Marine*, 498; Boelcke, *So kam das Meer zu uns*, 76, 90; Waldeyer-Hartz, *Ludwig von Schröder*, 79–80.

65. Quoted in Steinberg, *Yesterday's Deterrent*, 66.

66. Hubatsch, *Kaiserliche Marine*, 492–502 passim.

67. Kennedy, "Bismarck's Imperialism," 264–66. According to B. Werner, *Ein deutsches Kriegsschiff in der Südsee*, 541–42, the *Bismarck* took over the Samoan station from the smaller corvette *Ariadne* in May 1879.

68. Firth, "German Firms in the Pacific Islands," 8; Kennedy, "Bismarck's Imperialism," 264–65. On the failure of the "Samoa bill" of 1880 see Pflanze, *Bismarck*, 2:521.

69. Boelcke, *So kam das Meer zu uns*, 301.

70. Stoecker, "Germany and China," 31–33. Brandt's aggressive promotion of German interests in China both offended and intrigued his American counterpart, John Russell Young, who conceded that his methods were effective. See D. Anderson, *Imperialism and Idealism*, 131–34.

71. Stoecker, "Germany and China," 33–36; Pistorius, "Die Vulcan-Werke A.G. Stettin," 315. Wulle and Pittelkow, "Superlative aus Stettin," 35, place the launching of the *Ting Yuen* in May 1883 and do not mention the *Chen Yuen* or the three smaller Chinese warships built later. Archival evidence indicates that the *Ting Yuen* was completed and ready for delivery by the summer of 1883; Albedyll to Caprivi, Berlin, 8 June 1883, NA, T-1022, roll 1531, discusses the possibility of "German officers and crew" being used to deliver the ship to China.

72. Siuzi Foki (Japanese ambassador) to Stosch, Berlin, 16 February 1883, NA, T-1022, roll 1531, informs the German navy of the Japanese order.

73. Böhm, *Überseehandel und Flottenbau*, 30; Boelcke, *So kam das Meer zu uns*, 324. On the voyage of the *Hansa*, Gustav Freytag quoted in Freytag, "General von Stosch," 207.

74. Güth, *Von Revolution zu Revolution*, 64; Mantey, *Deutsche Marinegeschichte*, 124, 134.

75. Boelcke, *So kam das Meer zu uns*, 136, 139; Mantey, *Deutsche Marinegeschichte*, 123. According to Mantey, the *Victoria* rather than the *Vineta* sent ashore the landing party at Nanakru in 1881.

76. Böhm, *Überseehandel und Flottenbau*, 32–35; Kludas, *Afrika-Linien*, 9.

77. Pflanze, *Bismarck*, 3:38–39.

78. Kessel, "Die Entlassung von Kameke und Stosch," 451.

79. Coler, "Der Sturz Albrecht von Stoschs," 692; Kessel, "Die Entlassung von Kameke und Stosch," 446, 451; Pflanze, *Bismarck,* 3:39.

80. Stosch to William I, Berlin, 7 March 1883, quoted in Coler, "Der Sturz Albrecht von Stoschs," 698; Stosch to Albedyll, Berlin, 7 March 1883, quoted in ibid.

81. Quoted in ibid., 699.

82. Stosch to William I, Berlin, 12 March 1883, quoted in ibid., 700.

83. *Rangliste der kaiserlich deutschen Marine,* 1884. William I to Stosch, Berlin, 15 March 1883, text in Coler, "Der Sturz Albrecht von Stoschs," 701–2, indicates that the emperor had agreed to the resignation five days earlier.

84. On the creation of the torpedo corps see Herwig, *"Luxury" Fleet,* 13.

85. Freytag, "General von Stosch," 207.

Chapter 7: Caprivi

1. Petter, "Deutsche Flottenrüstung," 129.

2. Lambi, *The Navy and German Power Politics,* 6; on Caprivi's personality see Holborn, *History of Modern Germany,* 3:303. William II, *Ereignisse und Gestalten,* 43, characterizes Caprivi as "competent, but somewhat stubborn and not completely free from vanity."

3. Paschen, *Aus der Werdezeit zweier Marinen,* 226.

4. Steinmetz, *Bismarck und die deutsche Marine,* 68–69. Petter, "Deutsche Flottenrüstung," 130, contends that there was no connection between the *Grosser Kurfürst* disaster and Batsch being passed over in favor of Caprivi.

5. Steinmetz, *Bismarck und die deutsche Marine,* 68–69. Gustav Freytag, writing in 1884, observed that "the sense of slight" caused by "the repeated appointment of an officer of the land service as head of the navy . . . found expression in the retirement of several officers of high rank." See Freytag, "General von Stosch," 207. But the *Rangliste der kaiserlich deutschen Marine,* 1883 and 1884, indicate that Batsch, Berger, and Livonius were the only admirals to retire during 1883.

6. Freytag, "General von Stosch," 208.

7. Stenzel to Monts, Wilhelmshaven, 10 September 1883, BA-MA, RM 1/1872, 1–5; Caprivi to Monts, Berlin, 10 October, and to Monts and Wickede, Berlin, 20 December 1883, ibid., 6–8, 9–10.

8. Discussing the navy's prospects in a war against France, Caprivi noted: "I have a higher faith in us, above all in our officer corps, and think less of the battle readiness of the French." Quoted in Lambi, *The Navy and German Power Politics,* 23.

9. *Rangliste der kaiserlich deutschen Marine,* 1873 through 1889 passim. For the years 1872–82, 60 of 354 entering cadets (16.9 percent) were noble, including 2 barons and 9 counts; for the years 1883–88, 60 of 229 (26.2 percent) were noble, including 7 barons and 8 counts.

10. Sondhaus, " 'The Spirit of the Army' at Sea," 478.

11. "Promemoria betreffend die Verringerung der Kosten der Carriere zum Seeoffizier," n.d., BA-MA, RM 1/2, 14–38; Monts to Caprivi, Wilhelmshaven, 26 July 1884, ibid., 69.

12. Foerster, *Politische Geschichte*, 42.

13. German emigration fell to around 90,000 in 1889 and averaged only 30,000 per year by the turn of the century. In 1889 almost 85,000 German emigrants (93.5 percent of the total) went to the United States, down from a peak of just over 210,000 in 1881. See Herwig, *Politics of Frustration*, 7.

14. Bade, "Colonial Missions and Imperialism," 314–15; Boelcke, *So kam das Meer zu uns*, 134.

15. Boelcke, *So kam das Meer zu uns*, 141, 143; Hassert, "Erwerbsgeschichte," 120. On the German experience in Southwest Africa see also Voeltz, *German Colonialism and the South West Africa Company*.

16. Boelcke, *So kam das Meer zu uns*, 141–42; Pflanze, *Bismarck*, 3:126–27.

17. Boelcke, *So kam das Meer zu uns*, 167; Hassert, "Erwerbsgeschichte," 121–22.

18. Mantey, *Deutsche Marinegeschichte*, 141–43; Boelcke, *So kam das Meer zu uns*, 146.

19. Boelcke, *So kam das Meer zu uns*, 196; Henderson, "German East Africa," 124–25.

20. Burmester, *Weltumseglung*, 33–34; Schramm, *Deutschland und Übersee*, 241; Boelcke, *So kam das Meer zu uns*, 197; Hassert, "Erwerbsgeschichte," 124.

21. Paschen, *Aus der Werdezeit zweier Marinen*, 247–53; Boelcke, *So kam das Meer zu uns*, 200.

22. Boelcke, *So kam das Meer zu uns*, 146, 201.

23. Ibid., 201; Hubatsch, *Kaiserliche Marine*, 517. BA-MA, RM 3/10528, 62–167, chronicles the *Hyäne*'s long voyage.

24. Boelcke, *So kam das Meer zu uns*, 307, 309, 361; Sigel, *Germany's Army and Navy*, 108; Schramm, *Deutschland und Übersee*, 422.

25. Paschen, *Aus der Werdezeit zweier Marinen*, 240–43; Boelcke, *So kam das Meer zu uns*, 309–10.

26. Pflanze, *Bismarck*, 3:218; Boelcke, *So kam das Meer zu uns*, 312–13; Hassert, "Erwerbsgeschichte," 129; Sigel, *Germany's Army and Navy*, 108. See also Brown, "The German Acquisition of the Caroline Islands," 137–55.

27. Boelcke, *So kam das Meer zu uns*, 314; Sigel, *Germany's Army and Navy*, 108; Firth, "German Firms in the Pacific Islands," 8, 17; Röhr, *Handbuch*, 65.

28. Firth, "German Firms in the Pacific Islands," 8; Röhr, *Handbuch*, 65.

29. See Moses, "The Extension of Colonial Rule in Kaiser Wilhelmsland," 288–312. In 1899 the company surrendered its rights to an Imperial German administration. On the punitive expedition of 1886 see Boelcke, *So kam das Meer zu uns*, 307.

30. Captain Ferdinand Krokisius (*Marie*), to Caprivi, Apia Bay, 13 November 1884, BA-MA, RM 1/2895, 12; Kennedy, "Bismarck's Imperialism," 268.

31. Kennedy, "Bismarck's Imperialism," 269, 272–73.

32. Ibid., 276; Hubatsch, *Kaiserliche Marine*, 522; Boelcke, *So kam das Meer zu uns*, 317.

33. Kennedy, "Bismarck's Imperialism," 277.

34. Bessell, *Norddeutscher Lloyd*, 50–55.

35. Firth, "German Firms in the Pacific Islands," 9.

36. Bessell, *Norddeutscher Lloyd,* 79.

37. Hubatsch, *Kaiserliche Marine,* 506–28 passim.

38. Caprivi, Denkschrift of 11 March 1884, in Güth, *Von Revolution zu Revolution,* 74.

39. Caprivi to Foreign Office, Berlin, 17 January 1885, BA-MA, RM 1/2799, 40. An opinion drafted by Hauptmann Perels of Dezernat XIII of the Admiralty, "Ausserordentliche Ausrüstung der Flotte für kolonialpolitische Zwecke," n.d., ibid., 41–47, stated that colonial protectorates were "not federal territory (*Bundesgebiet*)" and that African kingdoms did not qualify as "organized" governments, requiring a declaration of war.

40. Caprivi to Monts and Wickede, Berlin, 20 December 1883, BA-MA, RM 1/1872, 9–10, asks the Admiralty Council to consider the importance of cruiser warfare, the utility of the navy's existing unarmored ships as cruisers in wartime, and the fate of German warships on overseas stations in the event of war. RM 1/2795 indicates that the council, chaired by Monts, met ten times in January 1884 and produced *Gutachten* on each of the three questions. See also Lambi, *The Navy and German Power Politics,* 6–7, and Boelcke, *So kam das Meer zu uns,* 32.

41. Foerster, *Politische Geschichte,* 42. On the *Jeune École*'s popularity with Austrian leaders eager to contain naval spending, see Höbelt, "Von der Jeune École zur Flottenpolitik," 147–56, and Sondhaus, "Strategy, Tactics, and the Politics of Penury," 587–602.

42. Ropp, *The Development of a Modern Navy,* 155–56. See also Bueb, *Die "Junge Schule."*

43. Aube was influenced by other French critics of armored warships, most notably Captain Louis Grivel. See Ropp, *The Development of a Modern Navy,* 19, 156.

44. Ibid., 132, 159–60.

45. Marder, *The Anatomy of British Sea Power,* 86–87; Ropp, *The Development of a Modern Navy,* 160–65.

46. Ropp, *The Development of a Modern Navy,* 28–30, 157.

47. Aube quoted in ibid., 165.

48. Marder, *The Anatomy of British Sea Power,* 125.

49. Lambi, *The Navy and German Power Politics,* 7.

50. BA-MA, RM 1/335, passim. While with the squadron, Caprivi spent time aboard the battleships *Kaiser, Deutschland,* and *Kronprinz.*

51. BA-MA, RM 1/337, passim; Röhl, *Wilhelm II,* 446–47. William II quoted in *My Early Life,* 233–34.

52. BA-MA, RM 1/343, passim. There were 548 four-year volunteers aboard Stenzel's ships, accounting for almost half of his seamen. The *Niobe* was decommissioned in 1890, the sailing brigs *Rover* and *Musquito* in 1890 and 1891, respectively. See Gröner, *Die deutschen Kriegsschiffe,* 1:68, 112. RM 3/10560, 1–12, traces the armored squadron's Norwegian cruise.

53. BA-MA, RM 1/338, RM 1/343, RM 1/344, and RM 1/345.

54. Berghahn, *Der Tirpitz-Plan,* 61–62. Foerster, *Politische Geschichte,* 46, contends that Schichau started building torpedo boats in 1877. Starting in 1884, the navy designated the boats with letters and numbers, the former indicating the

shipyard of origin. For example, Schichau boats were *S-1, S-2*, etc., A.G. Vulcan boats were *V-1, V-2*, etc. See Zimmermann, "Das gesammte schwimmende Material," 73–74.

55. Lambi, *The Navy and German Power Politics,* 8; Berghahn, *Der Tirpitz-Plan,* 62–63; Herwig, *"Luxury" Fleet,* 14; Arnauld de la Perière, *Prinz Heinrich,* 29.

56. Koch, "Die deutsche Eisenindustrie," 16.

57. Lambi, *The Navy and German Power Politics,* 8.

58. Caprivi quoted in Verchau, "Von Jachmann über Stosch und Caprivi," 67.

59. Beseke, *Der Nord-Ostsee-Kanal,* 9–15. Caprivi's personal opinion of the canal project remains a subject of debate. Lambi, *The Navy and German Power Politics,* 9, contends that Bismarck intervened to overcome Caprivi's opposition to the canal, while Herwig, *"Luxury" Fleet,* 14–15, indicates that Caprivi "had a hand in" the project.

60. Lambi, *The Navy and German Power Politics,* 8–9.

61. Gröner, *Die deutschen Kriegsschiffe,* 1:34–35; Lambi, *The Navy and German Power Politics,* 9; *Krupp: A Century's History,* 192.

62. The Norddeutsche Werft went bankrupt in 1879, shortly after completing the corvettes *Bismarck* and *Blücher.* It was taken over by the Märkisch-Schlesische firm of Berlin, and in 1882 both the Kiel shipyard and the Berlin machine shop were reincorporated under the name "A.G. Germania." See Jensen, *Seestadt Kiel,* 109.

63. Figures from Cattaruzza, *Arbeiter und Unternehmer,* 19, 83.

64. Zimmermann, "Das gesammte schwimmende Material," 58–59; Gröner, *Die deutsche Kriegsschiffe,* 1:33–35; *Krupp: A Century's History,* 209, 288.

65. Boelcke, *So kam das Meer zu uns,* 32.

66. Gröner, *Die deutschen Kriegsschiffe,* 1:72, 117–18, 120–23, 166–68.

67. Zimmermann, "Das gesammte schwimmende Material," 60–65. According to Röhr, *Handbuch,* 168–69, the new classification system took effect in 1884.

68. Zimmermann, "Das gesammte schwimmende Material," 75.

69. Gröner, *Die deutschen Kriegsschiffe,* 1:114.

70. Hubatsch, *Der Admiralstab,* 42n; Gröner, *Die deutschen Kriegsschiffe,* 1:112; Röhr, *Handbuch,* 63.

71. Budget figures from Junghänel, *Marinehaushalt,* 96; international rankings from *Jahresbericht der k.u.k. Kriegsmarine* (1897): 118–29.

72. Caprivi, Denkschrift of 11 March 1884, in Güth, *Von Revolution zu Revolution,* 74.

73. Lambi, *The Navy and German Power Politics,* 17.

74. Verchau, "Von Jachmann über Stosch und Caprivi," 69. Kennedy, "German Colonial Expansion," 134–41, rejects Hans-Ulrich Wehler's argument for continuity between Bismarck's colonialism and the later German *Weltpolitik* under William II, concluding that "Bismarck's turn against England in 1884–5" was a "short-term tactical move . . . motivated by domestic considerations and by his dislike of 'liberalism' in both England and Germany" (ibid., 136).

75. Boelcke, *So kam das Meer zu uns,* 145; Pflanze, *Bismarck,* 3:131. The Congo Conference also established ground rules (the principle of "effective occupation") for future colonial annexations.

76. The largest warships of the other navies involved in the demonstration and blockade were the British *Neptune* (9,300 tons), the Russian *Dmitri Donskoi* (5,800 tons), the Italian *Ancona* (4,500 tons), and the Austro-Hungarian *Kaiser Max* (3,600 tons). See Sondhaus, *The Naval Policy of Austria-Hungary*, 105–6, 121n.

77. Herbert Bismarck to Caprivi, Berlin, 17 December 1886, NA, T-1022, roll 1531. Krupp to *Prokura* (board of managers), Essen, 23–25 February 1881, in Berdrow, *Krupp*, 371–72, ponders the fate of his Russian connections in case of a Russo-German war.

78. See Lowe, *Salisbury and the Mediterranean*, 8–25. Note from Salisbury to Károlyi (Austro-Hungarian ambassador) and Catalani (Italian ambassador), London, 12 December 1887, text in idem, *The Reluctant Imperialists*, 2:61–62.

79. On the renewal of the Triple Alliance see Bridge, *The Habsburg Monarchy*, 177–78. Lowe, *The Reluctant Imperialists*, 1:120, refers to the Mediterranean Agreements as "the nearest thing to an alliance that Britain had ever made in peacetime."

80. Mantey, *Deutsche Marinegeschichte*, 145–46. BA-MA, RM 1/345, which chronicles squadron activity during 1887, does not mention a special mobilization for the Kiel Canal dedication.

81. Arnauld de la Perière, *Prinz Heinrich*, 30–32; William II, *My Early Life*, 224–25, 236–37, 239; Röhl, *Wilhelm II*, 678–80, 682.

82. BA-MA, RM 1/345, passim; see also Hubatsch, *Kaiserliche Marine*, 519–21.

83. BA-MA, RM 1/345, 132–218 passim; Giovanni Tori (German consul) to Foreign Office, La Spezia, 18 November 1887, ibid., 190–91; Herbert Bismarck to Caprivi, Berlin, 19 November 1887, ibid., 168–69; Ropp, *The Development of a Modern Navy*, 191–92; Lowe, *Salisbury and the Mediterranean*, 35–36.

84. Caprivi to Kall, Berlin, 13 December 1887, BA-MA, RM 1/345, 218. RM 1/346, 1–37, chronicles the squadron's activities in early 1888.

85. *Jahresbericht der k.k. Kriegsmarine* (1888), 29. Austria-Hungary's contingent included five armored vessels, the most it ever sent out of the Adriatic in a single squadron. Italy sent two large battleships, the *Duilio* and *Italia*, with fifteen smaller escorts. See Sondhaus, *The Naval Policy of Austria-Hungary*, 107–8.

86. Lambi, *The Navy and German Power Politics*, 20–21.

87. Ibid., 23. On the *Moltke*'s North Atlantic cruise see Boelcke, *So kam das Meer zu uns*, 43. Captain Otto Stubenrauch (*Moltke*) to Caprivi, Buncrana, 29 July 1885, BA-MA, RM 1/1883, 98, reveals Caprivi was upset that word of the cruise was leaked to the press.

88. Lambi, *The Navy and German Power Politics*, 23, 25.

89. Ibid., 25.

90. Paschen, *Aus der Werdezeit zweier Marinen*, 263–64; Pflanze, *Bismarck*, 3:274. See also Nichols, *The Year of the Three Kaisers*.

Chapter 8: "Wasted" Years?

1. See, e.g., Boyd, "The Wasted Ten Years," 291–97.

2. Tirpitz, *Erinnerungen*, 39.

3. Lambi, *The Navy and German Power Politics*, 33.

4. Berghahn, *Der Tirpitz-Plan*, 23; Hallmann, *Schlachtflottenbau*, 53. Röhl, *Wil-*

helm II, 672, notes that in 1887, Caprivi lamented the terminal illness of Frederick III and dreaded the accession of William II.

    5. BA-MA, RM 1/2306, includes a biographical sketch of Monts up to 1878. He attended *Gymnasium* in Erfurt, leaving at age sixteen.

    6. Berghahn, *Der Tirpitz-Plan,* 23.

    7. Hubatsch, *Der Admiralstab,* 48; idem, *Kaiserliche Marine,* 524–25.

    8. BA-MA, RM 1/339, passim; William II (A.K.O.) to Monts, Kiel, 31 July 1888, ibid., 116.

    9. BA-MA, RM 1/339, passim.

    10. BA-MA, RM 1/346, passim.

    11. BA-MA, RM 1/340, passim. See also Mantey, *Deutsche Marinegeschichte,* 165–66; Boyd, "The Wasted Ten Years," 291.

    12. Boelcke, *So kam das Meer zu uns,* 76–77.

    13. Hallmann, *Schlachtflottenbau,* 56; Herwig, *"Luxury" Fleet,* 24.

    14. Gröner, *Die deutschen Kriegsschiffe,* 1:36–37. The anonymous critique "Die neuen Schlachtschiffe der kaiserlich deutschen Marine," 60, indicates that initial plans called for a heavier secondary armament of eight 6-inch guns.

    15. Hallmann, *Schlachtflottenbau,* 60. According to Hallmann, there were still nine *Siegfried*s on the drawing board at this stage.

    16. Ibid., 63–67. Figures from Junghänel, *Marinehaushalt,* 96.

    17. Gröner, *Die deutschen Kriegsschiffe,* 1:36–37; Owen, "Military-Industrial Relations," 75; *Krupp: A Century's History,* 288–89.

    18. Owen, "Military-Industrial Relations," 75; *Krupp: A Century's History,* 288; Leckebusch, *Eisenindustrie,* 36n. Weir, *Building the Kaiser's Navy,* 30, dates the Krupp-Dillinger alliance from 1893.

    19. *Krupp: A Century's History,* 289, contends that "the French plates made entirely of steel . . . split up into pieces," but Leckebusch, *Eisenindustrie,* 35, indicates that Schneider's tests were successful.

    20. On the U.S. armor tests see Cooling, *Gray Steel and Blue Water Navy,* 96–97, and Leckebusch, *Eisenindustrie,* 35.

    21. *Krupp: A Century's History,* 289–90; Leckebusch, *Eisenindustrie,* 36.

    22. "Die neuen Schlachtschiffe der kaiserlich deutschen Marine," 60–67.

    23. *Rangliste der kaiserlich deutschen Marine,* 1890. William II to Goltz, Berlin, 24 January 1889, BA-MA, RM 2/996, 22, formally appoints Goltz "commanding admiral" and interim chief of the Admiralty.

    24. Berghahn, *Der Tirpitz-Plan,* 24, 29–30.

    25. Characterization in Lambi, *The Navy and German Power Politics,* 36–37. According to Cecil, *Wilhelm II,* 294, Senden was "a virtual member of the royal household, taking all his meals with the Kaiser and his family." On Senden's character, see also Hull, *The Entourage of Kaiser Wilhelm II,* 179.

    26. Hallmann, *Schlachtflottenbau,* 68; Berghahn, *Der Tirpitz-Plan,* 28.

    27. Hallmann, *Schlachtflottenbau,* 70.

    28. Ibid., 71–72. Figures from Junghänel, *Marinehaushalt,* 96.

    29. Wislicenus, *Deutschlands Seemacht,* 127–28.

    30. Gröner, *Die deutschen Kriegsschiffe,* 1:72, 123.

31. Ibid., 1:124.

32. Ibid., 1:34–35, 37; *Krupp: A Century's History*, 290.

33. Berghahn, *Der Tirpitz-Plan*, 56.

34. On Caprivi as chancellor see Nichols, *Germany after Bismarck*.

35. Hallmann, *Schlachtflottenbau*, 68, 72; Tirpitz, *Erinnerungen*, 39; Koch, "Entwicklung der Flotte unter Wilhelm II," 84. On Hollmann as a courtier, see Bülow, *Memoirs*, 4:684; Cecil, *Wilhelm II*, 293, 302.

36. Hallmann, *Schlachtflottenbau*, 72–77.

37. Ibid., 77–78; Prager, *Blohm + Voss*, 44–49, 232; Christiansen, "99 Jahre Blohm + Voss Hamburg," 77; Gröner, *Die deutschen Kriegsschiffe*, 1:34–35, 123–24.

38. Junghänel, *Marinehaushalt*, 96.

39. Hallmann, *Schlachtflottenbau*, 82–83.

40. Landerer, *Geschichte der HAPAG*, 56, 59–60; Wulle and Pittelkow, "Superlative aus Stettin," 35; Pistorius, "Die Vulcan-Werke A.G. Stettin," 315–16; Prager, *Blohm + Voss*, 234–35; Bessell, *Norddeutscher Lloyd*, 200; Cattaruzza, *Arbeiter und Unternehmer*, 84; Henderson, *The Rise of German Industrial Power*, 199, 201–2. Ignoring the chronology of when the boom began in relation to when Tirpitz's Navy Laws were passed, Henderson argues for an opposite cause and effect: "The expansion of the German navy promoted the growth of the merchant marine. The prospect of naval orders encouraged shipbuilders to extend their dock facilities and repair workships, which benefited German shipowners" (203).

41. Gröner, *Die deutschen Kriegsschiffe*, 1:125.

42. Ibid., 1:35–36; Junghänel, *Marinehaushalt*, 96; *Krupp: A Century's History*, 290–91; Owen, "Military-Industrial Relations," 75; Leckebusch, *Eisenindustrie*, 37. Weir, *Building the Kaiser's Navy*, 31, 224n, dates the development of "420 nickel-steel armor" from July 1894; it was first used in 1895 on the battleship *Kaiser Friedrich III*.

43. Figures from *Jahresbericht der k.u.k. Kriegsmarine* (1897): 118–29.

44. Hallmann, *Schlachtflottenbau*, 87–91; Caprivi quoted, 90. See also Junghänel, *Marinehaushalt*, 96, and Gröner, *Die deutschen Kriegsschiffe*, 1:124–26.

45. Hallmann, *Schlachtflottenbau*, 90–91.

46. Ibid., 92–95; Junghänel, *Marinehaushalt*, 96. On the *Brandenburg* explosion see Jensen, *Seestadt Kiel*, 72.

47. Gröner, *Die deutschen Kriegsschiffe*, 1:37–39.

48. Lambi, *The Navy and German Power Politics*, 62.

49. Figures from *Jahresbericht der k.u.k. Kriegsmarine* (1897): 118–29.

50. Berghahn, *Der Tirpitz-Plan*, 81–82, 84, characterizes Senden and the Navy Cabinet as cruiser advocates, at least until the mid-1890s. Lambi, *The Navy and German Power Politics*, 37, calls Senden "consistent in his adherence to a battleship program," citing Steinberg, *Yesterday's Deterrent*, 101–2, concerning the summer of 1896.

51. William II quoted in Lambi, *The Navy and German Power Politics*, 34. Boyd, "The Wasted Ten Years," 293, suggests that the emperor read Mahan's work shortly after its publication, thanks to an American friend, Poultney Bigelow, who sent him a copy of it. The first German edition, *Der Einfluss der Seemacht auf die Ge-*

schichte, 1660–1763 (1895), was also the first non-English edition. According to Lambi, *The Navy and German Power Politics*, 66, the retired vice admiral Batsch translated it into German "at the request of Tirpitz and Knorr. It had a first printing of 8,000 copies, of which at least 2,000 were distributed by the Imperial Naval Office during the campaign for the first fleet law."

52. Steinberg, *Yesterday's Deterrent*, 74. See also Hallmann, *Schlachtflottenbau*, 143–47, and Junghänel, *Marinehaushalt*, 96.

53. Gröner, *Die deutschen Kriegsschiffe*, 1:26–28, 30–31, 75–76.

54. Ibid., 1:73–75.

55. *Krupp: A Century's History*, 291; Leckebusch, *Eisenindustrie*, 37–38.

56. Hallmann, *Schlachtflottenbau*, 151.

57. Kennan, *The Fateful Alliance*, 97–115, 220–22; Ropp, *The Development of a Modern Navy*, 194–95, 239, and chapter 14 passim; Lambi, *The Navy and German Power Politics*, 92.

58. BA-MA, RM 31/178, passim. See also Boelcke, *So kam das Meer zu uns*, 42–43.

59. BA-MA, RM 31/178, passim. The Austro-Hungarian squadron included the battleships *Kronprinz Rudolf* and *Kronprinzessin Stephanie* and the cruiser *Kaiser Franz Joseph I,* the three newest warships in the Habsburg navy. See Sondhaus, *The Naval Policy of Austria-Hungary*, 110.

60. Caprivi to Tirpitz, Berlin, 28 March 1891, text in Hassell, *Tirpitz*, 65, refers to the emperor's recognition of Tirpitz as a tactician and strategist. Lambi, *The Navy and German Power Politics*, 63, notes that Tirpitz did not actually take his post in Kiel until January 1891.

61. Tirpitz, "Unsere maritim-militärische Fortentwicklung," April 1891, quoted in Berghahn and Deist, *Rüstung im Zeichen der wilhelminischen Weltpolitik*, 83–84. A letter from Tirpitz to his father, dated 11 September 1871, quoted at length in Hassell, *Tirpitz*, 88–91, indicates his support for battleships, but the letter was written before Tirpitz's involvement with torpedoes (indeed, before the German navy even bought its first self-propelled torpedoes). There is no hard evidence that Tirpitz remained faithful to his battleship convictions during his torpedo years. According to Hobson, *The German School of Naval Thought*, 18–22, Tirpitz was not the first to apply Clausewitz's principles to naval strategy. Captain Alfred Stenzel, instructor at the Naval Academy (1875–81 and 1894–96), had done so long before 1894.

62. Lambi, *The Navy and German Power Politics*, 64.

63. Berghahn, *Der Tirpitz-Plan*, 72–73.

64. Tirpitz, *Erinnerungen*, 42.

65. Röhr, *Handbuch*, 66.

66. Mantey, *Deutsche Marinegeschichte*, 157.

67. Goltz, "Relation über die Herbstmanöver der Marine im Jahre 1891," Berlin, 9 November 1891, BA-MA, RM 4/62, 5–31.

68. Goltz to William II, Berlin, 10 November 1891, BA-MA, RM 4/62, 41–44.

69. Goltz to Kdo. Manöverflotte, Berlin, 23 May 1892, BA-MA, RM 4/62, 65.

70. Goltz, "Relation über die Herbstmanöver der Marine im Jahre 1892," n.d., BA-MA, RM 4/62, 75–96. Lambi, *The Navy and German Power Politics*, 74.

71. Röhr, *Handbuch*, 67.

72. Baratelli, *La marina militare italiana*, 244–45.

73. "Relation über die Herbstmanöver der Marine im Jahre 1893," BA-MA, RM 4/62, 104–84; the "Kritik" is in ibid., 160–84. See also Lambi, *The Navy and German Power Politics*, 74–75.

74. Berghahn, *Der Tirpitz-Plan*, 74.

75. *Jahresbericht der k.u.k Kriegsmarine* (1894), 49.

76. Lambi, *The Navy and German Power Politics*, 78–79; Kennan, *The Fateful Alliance*, 49. According to Hubatsch, *Kaiserliche Marine*, 96, Germany's ambassador in St. Petersburg informed Bismarck of the plans for Libau in February 1888.

77. BA-MA, RM 4/64, passim, especially "General-Idee für das Kaisermanöver 1894, n.d., ibid., 39–51.

78. Tirpitz, *Erinnerungen*, 46.

79. Tirpitz, "Taktische und Strategische Dienstschriften des Oberkommandos der Marine," Nr. IX, 16 June 1894, text in Berghahn and Deist, *Rüstung im Zeichen der wilhelminischen Weltpolitik*, 87–99.

80. Ibid., 88.

81. Tirpitz quoted in Berghahn, *Der Tirpitz-Plan*, 85.

82. BA-MA, RM 4/65, refers to the two-week "Winterreise" and the cruise to the Orkneys and Shetlands in May–June 1895. Goltz to William II, Berlin, 6 February 1895, RM 2/1584, 203, indicates that the *Irene* arrived at Hong Kong in early February.

83. Berghahn, *Der Tirpitz-Plan*, 76; Tirpitz, *Erinnerungen*, 44. Senden quoted in Steinberg, *Yesterday's Deterrent*, 69.

84. Tirpitz, *Erinnerungen*, 50; Hallmann, *Schlachtflottenbau*, 152. Tirpitz's memoirs give no hint of his personal relationship with Knorr.

85. Nees von Esenbeck, "Die Feier der Eröffnung des Kaiser-Wilhelm-Kanals," 393–417; Neubaur, *Der norddeutsche Lloyd*, 1:130. Spain, Sweden, the Netherlands, Romania, Norway, Portugal, and Turkey sent at least one warship. Denmark, its strategic significance neutralized by the new canal, sent none.

86. Bosworth, *Italy, the Least of the Great Powers*, 24.

87. The widening of the canal was authorized in 1907 and completed in 1914. See Eich, "Die Erweiterung des Kaiser Wilhelm-Kanals," 711–26, and Schultz, "Der Kaiser Wilhelm-Kanal und seine Erweiterung," 156–91.

88. "Rede Seiner Majestät des Kaisers," Kiel, 21 June 1895, text in Scheel, *Deutschlands Seegeltung*, 3–4.

89. Marder, *The Anatomy of British Sea Power*, 288.

90. Interior Ministry to Hollmann, Berlin, 12 June 1895, NA, T-1022, roll 1531, warns the navy that a Russian spy, engineering colonel Dmitri Bubnow, will be aboard one of the Russian warships at Kiel.

91. Boelcke, *So kam das Meer zu uns*, 45.

92. Steinberg, *Yesterday's Deterrent*, 76; Cecil, *Wilhelm II*, 283–84.

93. BA-MA, RM 4/65, passim.

94. Steinberg, *Yesterday's Deterrent*, 77–79. Lambi, *The Navy and German Power Politics*, 84, mentions Braun as the possible author of the memorandum of 28 No-

vember 1895. Foerster, *Politische Geschichte*, 64, provides a chart illustrating Knorr's argument. See also Hallmann, *Schlachtflottenbau*, 158.

95. Steinberg, *Yesterday's Deterrent*, 81.

96. Berghahn, *Der Tirpitz-Plan*, 90; Bülow, *Memoirs*, 1:78–79.

97. Berghahn, *Der Tirpitz-Plan*, 91–93; Tirpitz quoted in Steinberg, *Yesterday's Deterrent*, 83–84.

98. See Kennedy, *The Rise of the Anglo-German Antagonism*, 220–22; Tirpitz quoted in Berghahn, *Der Tirpitz-Plan*, 91.

99. Röhr, *Handbuch*, 65.

100. Boelcke, *So kam das Meer zu uns*, 201.

101. Ibid., 201–2; Henderson, "German East Africa," 129–30; Bidlingmaier, *Seegeltung*, 94; Foss, "Bagamoyo und Dar-es-Salam durch die Marine gehalten," 132–40. Foss, 135, contends that Deinhard requested reinforcements and gives no hint of his discouragement with the situation.

102. Boelcke, *So kam das Meer zu uns*, 203.

103. Röhr, *Handbuch*, 66–67; Boelcke, *So kam das Meer zu uns*, 149; Sigel, *Germany's Army and Navy*, 118. In the early 1890s only three navy officers transferred to the *Schutztruppe*. See *Rangliste der kaiserlich deutschen Marine*, 1892, 1894, 1895.

104. Kludas, *Afrika-Linien*, 10.

105. Firth, "German Firms in the Pacific Islands," 10.

106. Tesdorpf, *Das . . . bedeutungsvolle Jahr 1889*, 1:22–42; Kennedy, "Bismarck's Imperialism," 278; Firth, "German Firms in the Pacific Islands," 9.

107. Kennedy, "Bismarck's Imperialism," 278; Carl Tägert, "Vor 50 Jahren," 266–69; Alden, *The American Steel Navy*, 313, 318; Hassert, "Erwerbsgeschichte," 131; Tesdorpf, *Das . . . bedeutungsvolle Jahr 1889*, 1:42–63, 2:1–56.

108. Kennedy, *The Samoan Tangle*, 87–102; Boelcke, *So kam das Meer zu uns*, 308.

109. Tirpitz quoted in Boelcke, *So kam das Meer zu uns*, 319.

110. Kennedy, *The Samoan Tangle*, 105–6; 189–239.

111. Boelcke, *So kam das Meer zu uns*, 307–8, 311.

112. Hallmann, *Schlachtflottenbau*, 153.

113. Stoecker, "Germany and China," 38.

114. Steinberg, *Yesterday's Deterrent*, 75; Miyake, "German Cultural and Political Influence on Japan," 165–69.

115. Röhr, *Handbuch*, 68; Boelcke, *So kam das Meer zu uns*, 301.

116. Böhm, *Überseehandel und Flottenbau*, 38–46; Boelcke, *So kam das Meer zu uns*, 324–25; Koch, "Entwicklung der Flotte," 97.

117. Böhm, *Überseehandel und Flottenbau*, 51–55, 109–12; Boelcke, *So kam das Meer zu uns*, 112, 115, 131, 159; Gadow, *Geschichte der deutschen Marine*, 57.

118. Röhr, *Handbuch*, 67.

119. Tirpitz, *Erinnerungen*, 57. See also Marder, *The Anatomy of British Sea Power*, 288–89.

Chapter 9: To the Tirpitz Plan

1. Berghahn, *Der Tirpitz-Plan*, 91–93; Tirpitz quoted in Steinberg, *Yesterday's Deterrent*, 83–84. Foerster, *Politische Geschichte*, 72, goes to some length to disprove

a "conspiracy" theory: that Tirpitz wrote his memorandum with the knowledge that William II had sent the Kruger telegram. News of the telegram did not reach Kiel, where Tirpitz lived at the time, until 4 January, the day after he sent his report to Berlin.

2. According to Cecil, *Wilhelm II*, 298, in the wake of the crisis the emperor felt that an expanded fleet "would provide a needed corrective to Germany's status as well as his own."

3. According to Herwig, *The German Naval Officer Corps*, 41, of the 197 entering cadets in 1907, "only 25 came from south of the Mainz-Coburg line."

4. Sondhaus, " 'The Spirit of the Army' at Sea," 480.

5. Ibid., 480–81. In addition to the 746 sea officers of 1897, there were 196 sea cadets and cadets. In the remaining branches of the service there were 40 officers in the naval infantry, 73 in artillery and ordnance, 121 in the medical corps, 118 in the engineers, and 86 functioning as accountants. *Rangliste der kaiserlich deutschen Marine*, 1898.

6. Herwig, *The German Naval Officer Corps*, 39–40, and idem, "Das Offizierkorps," 144.

7. Tirpitz, *Erinnerungen*, 3; Herwig, "Das Offizierkorps," 157; Berghahn, *Der Tirpitz-Plan*, 92. Tirpitz's father, Rudolf, was a jurist and notary; his mother was the daughter of a civil servant. See Euler, "Generalität und Admiralität," 208.

8. "gegen gebildete und ungebildete Sozialdemokratie." Tirpitz memorandum, quoted in Hallmann, *Schlachtflottenbau*, 174–75. The same week, he used the same phrase in a letter to his mentor, Stosch. See Tirpitz to Stosch, Kiel, 21 December 1895, text in Berghahn and Deist, *Rüstung im Zeichen der wilhelminischen Weltpolitik*, 103.

9. Caprivi to Imperial Shipyard Kiel, Berlin, 14 February 1888, BA-MA, RM 31/654, 42.

10. BA-MA, RM 20/9, 47–57, chronicles this case of *Bootsmannsmaat* Heinze of the corvette *Stosch* and the painter Wilhelm Schweitzer of Wilhelmshaven. See also Sondhaus, "The Imperial German Navy and Social Democracy," 56.

11. BA-MA, RM 20/9, passim; RM 31/660, passim; Sondhaus, "The Imperial German Navy and Social Democracy," 58.

12. Count Rentzgau (Royal *Landrat*) to Kdo. Baltic Station, Plön, 9 August 1893, BA-MA, RM 31/660, 1; Harms to Kommandatur (Baltic station chief), Friedrichsort, 22 August 1893, ibid., 2–3; Knorr to Royal *Landrat* Plön, Kiel, 29 August 1893, ibid., 3 verso. The case concerned *Maschinenbaugehülfe* Niel Richard Martin Niess. M. Anderson, "Voter, Junker, *Landrat*, Priest," 1448–74, includes discussion of the role of the local *Landrat* in supervising the party loyalties of the people.

13. Hollmann memorandum, Berlin, 3 October 1893, BA-MA, RM 31/660, 6.

14. Sondhaus, " 'The Spirit of the Army' at Sea," 482. See also Herwig, "Das Offizierkorps," 149; Euler, "Generalität und Admiralität," 198; and Tirpitz, *Erinnerungen*, 1.

15. Sondhaus, "The Imperial German Navy and Social Democracy," 59.

16. Lambi, *The Navy and German Power Politics*, 86. According to Boelcke, *So kam das Meer zu uns*, 205, Knorr subsequently considered the telegram to have been

a mistake. For a comprehensive treatment of the ensuing crisis in Anglo-German relations see Rosenbach, *Das deutsche Reich, Grossbritannien, und der Transvaal.*

17. Bülow, *Memoirs,* 1:80, 82.

18. Boelcke, *So kam das Meer zu uns,* 204–5.

19. Ibid., 205; Lambi, *The Navy and German Power Politics,* 114.

20. Steinberg, *Yesterday's Deterrent,* 87–89. On the proposal of 21 January see Foerster, *Politische Geschichte,* 79.

21. Berghahn, *Der Tirpitz-Plan,* 91–92.

22. Steinberg, *Yesterday's Deterrent,* 89–90; Berghahn, *Der Tirpitz-Plan,* 82, 90.

23. Steinberg, *Yesterday's Deterrent,* 90.

24. Berghahn, *Der Tirpitz-Plan,* 93; Steinberg, *Yesterday's Deterrent,* 90–92.

25. Berghahn, *Der Tirpitz-Plan,* 95. *Rangliste der kaiserlich deutschen Marine,* 1897, indicates that Hollmann's promotion to full admiral took effect on 18 April 1896.

26. Gröner, *Die deutschen Kriegsschiffe,* 1:166; Steinberg, *Yesterday's Deterrent,* 103–4. The only other vessels lost during these years were the torpedo boats *S-41,* which sank in a storm off Skagen during maneuvers in August 1895, and *S-48,* which sank in the Jade in April 1896 after colliding with *S-46.* Thirteen men died in the former mishap, three in the latter. Hubatsch, *Der Admiralstab,* 42n, Röhr, *Handbuch,* 68.

27. Ganz, "The German Navy in the Far East and Pacific," 118–26. Other naval powers moved quickly to safeguard their own interests in the area. In March 1898 Russia, which had enjoyed winter anchorage rights at Kiaochow Bay, leased Port Arthur; in July 1898, Britain leased Weihaiwei.

28. Hallmann, *Schlachtflottenbau,* 167; Steinberg, *Yesterday's Deterrent,* 94–95; Gröner, *Die deutschen Kriegsschiffe,* 1:37–39, 73–75, 127.

29. Steinberg, *Yesterday's Deterrent,* 101. Budget figure from Junghänel, *Marine-haushalt,* 96.

30. Hallmann, *Schlachtflottenbau,* 214; Steinberg, *Yesterday's Deterrent,* 106.

31. Marder, *The Anatomy of British Sea Power,* 289–90. Figure from Junghänel, *Marinehaushalt,* 96.

32. Hallmann, *Schlachtflottenbau,* 225, 232–33; Junghänel, *Marinehaushalt,* 96; Gröner, *Die deutschen Kriegsschiffe,* 1:37.

33. Tirpitz quoted in Lambi, *The Navy and German Power Politics,* 119.

34. Lambi, *The Navy and German Power Politics,* 120. Kennedy, "The Development of German Naval Operations Plans against England," 173, attributes the authorship of this plan to Diederichs rather than Heeringen. Lambi, 134n, makes the case for Heeringen as the author.

35. Lambi, *The Navy and German Power Politics,* 123–24.

36. Steinberg, "A German Plan for the Invasion of Holland and Belgium," 155–56; Lambi, *The Navy and German Power Politics,* 126.

37. Lambi, *The Navy and German Power Politics,* 125, 127. The most recent work on Schlieffen, Bucholz's *Moltke, Schlieffen, and Prussian War Planning,* says nothing about the naval dimension of his plan. According to Ritter, *The Sword and the Scepter,* 2:111, Schlieffen considered the navy "an unproductive luxury."

2

38. Lambi, *The Navy and German Power Politics,* 108.

39. BA-MA, RM 4/66, passim; RM 4/83, passim. According to Kehr, "Die deutsche Flotte in den neunziger Jahren," 118, in the strategic maneuver of 1896 "the attacking ships carried the names of French battleships and cruisers and were equated with their fighting value." Kehr cites the maneuver as evidence that in 1896, naval maneuvers reflected the pre-*Weltpolitik* continental outlook of Germany. Of course the scenario calling for the defense of the Elbe estuary could just as easily apply to the British as to the French. The files documenting the maneuvers (RM 4/66 and 4/83) do not specify the French as the attacking enemy.

40. Senden memorandum, Berlin, n.d. [April 1896], BA-MA, RM 4/83, 8–9. Koester to Knorr, Kiel, 6 June 1896, RM 4/66, 116–22, describes the spring cruise of 24 April–1 June 1896. According to Marder, *The Anatomy of British Sea Power,* 266n, William II visited the British base at Malta aboard the *Hohenzollern* in April 1896, at the end of his annual Mediterranean cruise. Coming just three months after the Kruger telegram, the visit was conspicuous for its lack of fanfare.

41. Baratelli, *La marina militare italiana,* 148; Sondhaus, *The Naval Policy of Austria-Hungary,* 132.

42. Mantey, *Deutsche Marinegeschichte,* 179.

43. Seton-Watson, *Italy: From Liberalism to Fascism,* 205.

44. Lambi, *The Navy and German Power Politics,* 35.

45. *Jahresbericht der k.u.k Kriegsmarine* (1897), 83.

46. Knorr to Captain Eugen Kalau vom Hofe (naval attaché, St. Petersburg), Berlin, 27 July 1897, BA-MA, RM 4/66, 131.

47. BA-MA, RM 4/84, passim.

48. Steinberg, *Yesterday's Deterrent,* 106–16; Berghahn, *Der Tirpitz-Plan,* 106.

49. Steinberg, *Yesterday's Deterrent,* 116–17.

50. Hallmann, *Schlachtflottenbau,* 244–45; Berghahn, *Der Tirpitz-Plan,* 105–6; Foerster, *Politische Geschichte,* 101.

51. *Rangliste der kaiserlich deutschen Marine,* 1898; Kelly, "Tirpitz and the Origins of the German Torpedo Arm," 22–25.

52. Steinberg, *Yesterday's Deterrent,* 125–29. Tirpitz quoted, 126. See also Tirpitz, "Allgemeine Gesichtspunkte bei der Feststellung unserer Flotte nach Schiffsklassen und Schiffstypen," July 1897, text in Berghahn and Deist, *Rüstung im Zeichen der wilhelminischen Weltpolitik,* 122–27. During his first two months in office, Tirpitz spent much of his time trying to overcome the opposition of finance minister Johannes von Miquel; see Hallmann, *Schlachtflottenbau,* 254–87. Herwig, *Politics of Frustration,* 40, and idem, *"Luxury" Fleet,* 42, erroneously categorizes the *Siegfried* class as armored cruisers. Tirpitz, *Erinnerungen,* 100n, notes that the *Siegfried*s formed a separate category under the First Navy Law but were "rechristened, on paper, as battleships (*Linienschiffe*)" in the Second Navy Law of 1900.

53. Foerster, *Politische Geschichte,* 152–55, provides a text of the bill. Information on warships from Gröner, *Die deutschen Kriegsschiffe,* 1:32–129 passim.

54. Kehr, "Soziale und finanzielle Grundlagen der Tirpitzschen Flottenpropaganda," 133, 136–40; Böhm, *Überseehandel und Flottenbau,* 92–93; Weir, *Building the Kaiser's Navy,* 22. After the founding of the German Navy League in April 1898, Bal-

lin and Woermann were prominent members of the Hamburg chapter. See Cecil, *Albert Ballin*, 151. Two-thirds of the 155 reserve sea officers of 1897 were from the Hanseatic cities (Hamburg-Altona, 69; Bremen, 28; Lübeck, 6), reflecting a high number of *Einjährig-Freiwillige* of local origin, and the fact that merchant marine careers brought navy reserve officers born elsewhere in Germany to these cities. *Rangliste der kaiserlich deutschen Marine*, 1898.

55. According to M. Anderson, *Windthorst*, 244, "Lieber . . . departed from an interview with Admiral Alfred von Tirpitz in October 1897 . . . with 400 marks in his pocket." Tirpitz's aide, Captain Eduard Capelle, informed Lieber that the payment was "for your expenses and in the interests of the navy now and in the future."

56. Cecil, *Wilhelm II*, 317.

57. Kardorff, *Wilhelm von Kardorff*, 319.

58. Foerster, *Politische Geschichte*, 142, quoting from Ballin letter to Munich *Allgemeine Zeitung*, Hamburg, 14 December 1897. Mercantile tonnage figure from Henderson, *The Rise of German Industrial Power*, 202.

59. Bismarck to Tirpitz, Friedrichsruh, 4 December 1897, text in Foerster, *Politische Geschichte*, 130. Bismarck noted that he would have preferred more cruisers, but if he were in the Reichstag, he would not reject the bill for that reason.

60. Foerster, *Politische Geschichte*, 139, quoting from Haeckel letter to Munich *Allgemeine Zeitung*, Jena, December 1897.

61. Quoted in Herwig, *The German Naval Officer Corps*, 11.

62. See Bülow, *Imperial Germany*, 197–98, and Foerster, *Politische Geschichte*, 148–49. Cecil, *Wilhelm II*, 317, erroneously claims that the law "handily cleared the chamber 272 to 139," an impossibility, since the Reichstag had only 397 seats.

63. Gröner, *Die deutschen Kriegsschiffe*, 1:37–39, 76, 127.

64. On the Second Navy Law, see Berghahn, *Der Tirpitz-Plan*, 205–48, and Herwig, *"Luxury" Fleet*, 42–43.

65. Berghahn, "Naval Armaments and Social Crisis," 66.

66. Gröner, *Die deutschen Kriegsschiffe*, 1:46–49. The *Siegfried*s were officially reckoned as battleships in the Second Navy Law of 1900. See note 52 above.

67. Ibid., 1:83–85.

68. Kelly, "Tirpitz and the Origins of the German Torpedo Arm," 23–25.

69. Marder, *The Anatomy of British Sea Power*, 290, 296–301; quote from 297. See also Kennedy, *The Rise of the Anglo-German Antagonism*, 233, and idem, "German World Policy and the Alliance Negotiations with England," 605–25.

Epilogue

1. Gröner, *Die deutschen Kriegsschiffe*, 1:127.

2. Tirpitz, *Erinnerungen*, 39.

3. Ibid.

4. Cecil, *Wilhelm II*, 312; Boyd, "The Wasted Ten Years," 297.

5. Lambi, *The Navy and German Power Politics*, 108, notes another classic Tirpitz flip-flop: while in the Far East as commander of the cruiser squadron in 1896–97, he championed the seizure of Kiaochow Bay, but after returning to Berlin,

as state secretary of the Imperial Navy Office, he opposed the weakening of the fleet in home waters for the sake of securing the same Chinese harbor.

6. See Sondhaus, "The Imperial German Navy and Social Democracy," 60.

7. For a recent appraisal of the political culture of Imperial Germany see M. Anderson, "Voter, Junker, *Landrat*, Priest," 1448–74. For a further evaluation of the historiography of the Tirpitz plan in relation to the Social Democrats, see Sondhaus, "The Imperial German Navy and Social Democracy," 59–60.

8. See Kennedy, *The Rise of the Anglo-German Antagonism*, 408.

9. Hohenlohe to Baron Otto von Völderndorff, Berlin, 7 November 1897, in Hohenlohe, *Memoirs*, 2:487.

BIBLIOGRAPHY

Archival Sources

FREIBURG IM BREISGAU, GERMANY

Bundesarchiv
  Militärarchiv
    RM 1 [Admiralität]
    RM 2 [Marinekabinett]
    RM 3 [Reichsmarineamt]
    RM 4 [Oberkommando der Marine]
    RM 20 [Marinekommandoamt]
    RM 31 [Marinestation der Ostsee]

VIENNA, AUSTRIA

Österreichisches Staatsarchiv
  Haus- Hof- und Staatsarchiv
    Administrative Registratur, F 44 [Marinewesen]
    Politisches Archiv, II [Deutscher Bund]
  Kriegsarchiv
    Marineakten

WASHINGTON, D.C.

National Archives
  [Captured German Documents]
  T-1022 [Records of the German Navy, 1850–1945]

Published Documents, Letters, and Memoirs

Adalbert, Prince of Prussia. *Denkschrift über die Bildung einer Deutschen Kriegsflotte.* Frankfurt: Bundesdruckerei [Benjamin Krebs], 1848.

———. *Travels of His Royal Highness Prince Adalbert of Prussia, in the South of Europe and in Brazil.* Translated by Sir Robert H. Schomburgk and John Edward Taylor. 2 vols. London: David Bogue, 1849.

Berdrow, Wilhelm, ed. *Krupp: A Great Business Man Seen through His Letters.* Translated by E. W. Dickes. New York: The Dial Press, 1930.

Berghahn, Volker R., and Wilhelm Deist. *Rüstung im Zeichen der wilhelminischen Weltpolitik: Grundlegende Dokumente, 1890–1914.* Düsseldorf: Droste Verlag, 1988.

Bismarck, Otto von. *Gedanken und Erinnerungen.* 3 vols. 1898. Reprint, Stuttgart: J. G. Cotta'sche Buchhandlung Nachfolger, 1922.

Brandt, Max von. *Dreiundreißig Jahre in Ost-Asien: Erinnerungen eines deutschen Diplomaten.* 3 vols. Leipzig: G. Wigand, 1901.

Brommy, Karl Rudolf. *Die Marine.* Berlin: Verlag von Alexander Duncker, 1848.

Bülow, Bernhard von. *Imperial Germany.* Translated by Marie A. Lewenz. New York: Dodd, Mead, 1914.

———. *Memoirs of Prince von Bülow.* 4 vols. Translated by F. A. Voigt. Boston: Little, Brown, 1931–32.

Duckwitz, Arnold. *Die Gründung der deutschen Kriegsmarine.* Bremen: Verlag von C. Schünemann, 1849.

Frederick the Great. *Die Politischen Testamente.* Edited by Gustav Berthold Volz. Munich: Verlag Heinz Treu, 1941.

Frederick III, German Emperor. *Tagebuch meiner Reise nach dem Morgenlande 1869.* Edited by Hans Rothfels. 1870. Reprint, Berlin: Propyläen, 1971.

———. *The War Diary of the Emperor Frederick III, 1870–1871.* Edited and translated by A. R. Allinson. 1926. Reprint, New York: Howard Fertig, 1988.

Freytag, Gustav. *Gustav Freytags Briefe an Albrecht von Stosch.* Edited by Hans F. Helmolt. Stuttgart: Deutsche Verlags-Anstalt, 1913.

Germany. Reichstag. *Stenographische Berichte über die Verhandlungen des Reichstages, 1871–1897.* Washington, D.C.: Microcard Editions, 1966.

Hohenlohe-Schillingsfürst, Chlodwig zu. *Memoirs of Prince Chlodwig of Hohenlohe-Schillingsfuerst.* 2 vols. Edited by Friedrich Curtius. New York: Macmillan, 1906.

Hoor, Ernst, ed. *Erzherzog Johann von Österreich als Reichsverweser: Der unveröffentliche Briefwechsel mit Felix Fürst zu Schwarzenberg aus den Jahren 1848 und 1849.* Vienna: Österreichischer Bundesverlag, 1981.

Huber, Ernst Rudolf, ed. *Dokumente zur deutschen Verfassungsgeschichte.* 3 vols. Stuttgart: W. Kohlhammer Verlag, 1961–67.

Jahn, Friedrich Ludwig. *Friedrich Ludwig Jahns Werke.* Vol. 2. Edited by Carl Euler. Hof: Verlag von Rud. Lion, 1885.

List, Friedrich. *Schriften, Reden, Briefe.* Vol. 7. Edited by Erwin V. Beckerath et al. Berlin: Verlag von Reimar Hobbing, 1931.

Paschen, Karl. *Aus der Werdezeit zweier Marinen: Erinnerungen aus meiner Dienstzeit in der k.k. österreichischen und kaiserlich deutschen Marine.* Berlin: E. S. Mittler & Sohn, 1908.

Poschinger, Heinrich von, ed. *Preussen im Bundestag 1851 bis 1859.* 3 vols. 1882. Reprint, Osnabrück: Otto Zeller, 1965.

Siemens, Werner von. *Lebenserinnerungen.* Leipzig: Baustein-Verlag, 1924.

Stosch, Albrecht von. *Denkwürdigkeiten des Generals und Admirals Albrecht von Stosch.* Stuttgart: Deutsche Verlags-Anstalt, 1904.

Tegetthoff, Wilhelm von. *Aus Wilhelm von Tegetthoff's Nachlass.* Edited by Adolf Beer. Vienna: Druck und Verlag von Carl Gerold's Sohn, 1882.

Tirpitz, Alfred von. *Erinnerungen.* Leipzig: Verlag von K. F. Koehler, 1919.

Werner, Reinhold. *Erinnerungen und Bilder aus dem Seeleben.* 2nd ed. Berlin: R. Hofmann & Comp., 1881.

————. *Die preussische Expedition nach China, Japan und Siam in den Jahren 1860, 1861, und 1862.* Leipzig: F. A. Brockhaus, 1863.

Wigard, Franz, ed. *Stenographischer Bericht über die Verhandlungen der deutschen constituirenden Nationalversammlung zu Frankfurt am Main.* 9 vols. Frankfurt: Johann David Sauerländer, 1848–49.

William II, German Emperor. *Ereignisse und Gestalten aus den Jahren 1878–1918.* Leipzig: Verlag von K. F. Koehler, 1922.

————. *My Early Life.* London: Methuen, 1926.

Contemporary Periodicals, Tracts, and Reference Works

[Anonymous.] "Die Kaiserlich Deutsche Marine." *[Streffleur's] Österreichische Militärische Zeitschrift* 32, no. 4 (1891): 259–72.

[Anonymous.] "Die neuen Schlachtschiffe der kaiserlich deutschen Marine." *[Streffleur's] Österreichische Militärische Zeitschrift* 32, no. 4 (1891): 60–67.

Chevalier, Louis Edouard. *La marine française et la marine allemande pendant la guerre de 1870–1871.* Paris: H. Plon, 1873.

Freytag, Gustav. "General von Stosch and the German Navy." *Journal of the Royal United Service Institution* 28 (1884): 205–10.

Graser, Bernard. *Norddeutschlands Seemacht: Ihre Organisation, ihre Schiffe, ihre Häfen, und ihre Bemannung.* Leipzig: Friedrich Wilhelm Grunow, 1870.

Jahresbericht der k.u.k. Kriegsmarine. Annual.

Lengnick, Arthur. "See-Interessen und See-Politik." *Organ der militärwissenschaftlichen Vereine* 62 (1901): 301–37.

Lütken, Otto. *Einige Gedanken über den Gebrauch der Kanonenboote.* Berlin: Decker'schen Geheimen Ober-Hofbuchdruckerei, 1849.

Meyers Lexikon. 7th ed. Leipzig: Bibliographisches Institut, 1925.

Militär-Schematismus des österreichischen Kaiserthums. Annual, title varies.

Neues allgemeines Deutsches Adels-Lexicon. 1859–70. Reprint, Leipzig: Verlag Degener & Co., 1929.

Pont-Jest, René de. *Die Campagne von 1870 in der Nord- und Ostsee.* Bremen: Buchhandlung von J. G. Heyse, 1871.

Preussische Wehr-Zeitung.

Priesdorff, Kurt, ed. *Soldatisches Führertum.* 10 vols. Hamburg: Hanseatisches Verlagsanstalt, 1936–42.

Rangliste der kaiserlich deutschen Marine. 1871–72 through 1898. Annual, title varies.

Rangliste der königlich preussischen Marine. 1848 through 1867. Annual, title varies.

[Rang]liste der norddeutschen Bundesmarine. 1868 through 1870.

Salmonsens Konversations Leksikon. Copenhagen: J. H. Schultz Forlagsboghandel,
1915.

Stosch, Albrecht von. "Unsere Küsten in einem Kriege mit Frankreich." *Die Grenz-
boten* 26 (1867): 246–48.

Werner, Bartholomäus von. *Ein deutsches Kriegsschiff in der Südsee.* Leipzig: F. A.
Brockhaus, 1889.

Werner, Reinhold. *Das Buch von der deutschen Flotte.* Bielefeld: Belhagen & Klas-
ing, 1874.

Secondary Works

Alden, John D. *The American Steel Navy.* Rev. ed. Annapolis: Naval Institute Press,
1989.

Anderson, David L. *Imperialism and Idealism: American Diplomats in China,
1861–1898.* Bloomington: Indiana University Press, 1985.

Anderson, Margaret Lavinia. "Voter, Junker, *Landrat,* Priest: The Old Authorities
and the New Franchise in Imperial Germany." *American Historical Review* 98
(1993): 1448–74.

———. *Windthorst: A Political Biography.* Oxford: Clarendon Press, 1981.

Arnauld de la Perière, G. V. *Prinz Heinrich von Preussen: Admiral und Flieger.* Herford: Koehler, 1983.

Auerbach, Horst. "Die brandenburgisch-preussische Marine in der zweiten Hälfte
des 17. Jahrhunderts." *Militärgeschichte* 19 (1980): 697–710.

Bade, Klaus-J. "Colonial Missions and Imperialism: The Background to the Fiasco
of the Rhenish Mission in New Guinea." In *Germany in the Pacific and Far East,
1870–1914,* edited by John A. Moses and Paul M. Kennedy, 313–46. St. Lucia: University of Queensland Press, 1977.

Ballard, G. A. *The Black Battlefleet.* Edited by G. A. Osborn and N. A. M. Rodger.
Annapolis: Naval Institute Press, 1980.

Bär, Max. *Die Deutsche Flotte von 1848–1852.* Leipzig: S. Hirzel, 1898.

Baratelli, Franco Micali. *La marina militare italiana nella vita nazionale (1860–
1914).* Mursia: U. Mursia editore, 1983.

Batsch, Carl Ferdinand. *Admiral Prinz Adalbert von Preussen.* Berlin: Verlag von
Kurt Brachvogel, 1890.

———. "Zur Vorgeschichte der Flotte." *Marine Rundschau* 7 (1896): 775–86.

Bei der Wieden, Helge. "Die mecklenburgischen Häfen und die deutsche Flotte
1848/49." In *Beiträge zur mecklenburgischen Seefahrtsgeschichte,* 47–58. Cologne:
Böhlau Verlag, 1981.

Berghahn, Volker R. "Naval Armaments and Social Crisis: Germany before 1914." In
War, Economy, and the Military Mind, edited by Geoffrey Best and Andrew
Wheatcroft, 61–88. London: Croom Helm, 1976.

———. *Der Tirpitz-Plan: Genesis und Verfall einer innenpolitischen Krisenstrategie unter Wilhelm II.* Düsseldorf: Droste Verlag, 1971.

Berghahn, Volker R., and Wilhelm Deist. *Rüstung im Zeichen der wilhelminischen Weltpolitik: Grundlegende Dokumente, 1890–1914.* Düsseldorf: Droste Verlag, 1988.

Beseke, Carl. *Der Nord-Ostsee-Kanal: Seine Entstehungsgeschichte, sein Bau, und seine Bedeutung in wirthschaftlicher und militärischer Hinsicht.* 1893. Reprint, St. Peter-Ording: Verlag H. Lühr & Dircks, 1982.

Bessell, Georg. *Norddeutscher Lloyd, 1857–1957: Geschichte einer bremischen Reederei.* Bremen: Norddeutscher Lloyd, 1957.

Bidlingmaier, Gerhard. *Seegeltung in der deutschen Geschichte.* Darmstadt: Wehr und Wissen Verlagsgesellschaft, 1967.

Bjerg, Hans Christian. "Affæren i Eckernförde 5 april 1849: et 125 års minde." *Tidsskrift for Sovæsen* 145 (1974): 97–115.

———. "When the Monitors Came to Europe: The Danish Monitor *Rolf Krake*, 1863." Paper presented at the Eleventh Naval History Symposium, Annapolis, Maryland, October 1993.

Blum, Erwin. "Aus der Hansezeit." In *Grundlagen Deutscher Seegeltung,* edited by Walter Lohmann et al., 46–51. Berlin: Verlag Wehrfront Alfred Becker, 1942.

Boelcke, Willi A. *So kam das Meer zu uns: Die preussisch-deutsche Kriegsmarine in übersee, 1822 bis 1914.* Frankfurt: Ullstein, 1981.

Böhm, Ekkehard. *Überseehandel und Flottenbau: Hanseatische Kaufmannschaft und deutsche Seerüstung, 1879–1902.* Hamburg: Bertelsmann Universitätsverlag, 1972.

Born, Erich. "Die Politischen Testamente Friedrichs des Grossen." In *Seemacht und Geschichte: Festschrift zum 80. Geburtstag von Friedrich Ruge,* 13–28. Bonn: MOV-Verlag, 1975.

Bosworth, R. J. B. *Italy, the Least of the Great Powers.* Cambridge: Cambridge University Press, 1979.

Boyd, Carl L. "The Wasted Ten Years, 1888–1898: The Kaiser Finds an Admiral." *Journal of the Royal United Service Institution* 111 (1966): 291–97.

Bucholz, Arden. *Moltke, Schlieffen, and Prussian War Planning.* New York: Berg, 1991.

Bridge, F. R. *The Habsburg Monarchy among the Great Powers, 1815–1918.* New York: Berg, 1990.

Brose, Eric Dorn. *The Politics of Technological Change in Prussia: Out of the Shadow of Antiquity, 1809–1848.* Princeton, N.J.: Princeton University Press, 1993.

Brown, Richard G. "The German Acquisition of the Caroline Islands, 1898–99." In *Germany in the Pacific and Far East, 1870–1914,* edited by John A. Moses and Paul M. Kennedy, 137–55. St. Lucia: University of Queensland Press, 1977.

Bueb, Volkmar. *Die "Junge Schule" der französischen Marine: Strategie und Politik, 1875–1900.* Boppard am Rhein: Harald Boldt Verlag, 1971.

Burmester, Heinz. *Weltumseglung unter Preussens Flagge: Die Königlich Preussische Seehandlung und Ihre Schiffe.* Hamburg: Ernst Kabel Verlag, 1988.

Cattaruzza, Marina. *Arbeiter und Unternehmer auf den Werften des Kaiserreichs.* Stuttgart: Franz Steiner Verlag, 1988.

————. " 'Organizierter Konflikt' und 'Direkte Aktion': Zwei Formen des Arbeiter-
kampfes am Beispiel der Werftarbeiterstreiks in Hamburg und Triest
(1880–1914)." *Archiv für Sozialgeschichte* 20 (1980): 325–55.

Cecil, Lamar. *Albert Ballin: Business and Politics in Imperial Germany, 1888–1918.*
Princeton, N.J.: Princeton University Press, 1967.

————. *Wilhelm II: Prince and Emperor, 1859–1900.* Chapel Hill: University of
North Carolina Press, 1989.

Christiansen, Harro. "99 Jahre Blohm + Voss Hamburg: Ein kurzer Abriss der
Werftgeschichte." *Schiff und Zeit* 4 (1976): 74–80.

Coler, Christfried. "Der Konflikt Bismarck-Stosch, März/April 1877." *Wehrwissenschaftliche Rundschau* 17 (1967): 578–93.

————. "Palastrevolte in der Marine, 1878/79." *Wehrwissenschaftliche Rundschau* 17
(1967): 638–56.

————. "Der Sturz Albrecht von Stoschs, März 1883." *Wehrwissenschaftliche Rundschau* 17 (1967): 692–704.

Cooling, Benjamin Franklin. *Gray Steel and Blue Water Navy: The Formative Years
of America's Military-Industrial Complex.* Hamden, Conn.: Archon Books, 1979.

Crousaz, A. von. *Kurze Geschichte der Deutschen Kriegsmarine.* Berlin: Verlag von F.
Riemschneider, 1873.

Deutsches Marine Institut. *Die deutsche Flotte im Spannungsfeld der Politik,
1848–1945: Vorträge und Diskussionen der 25. Historisch-Taktischen Tagung der
Flotte 1985.* Herford: E. S. Mittler & Sohn, 1985.

Dinter, Elmar. "Albrecht Graf von Roon: Seine Stellung und sein Wirken als Mar-
ineminister." *Marine Rundschau* 68 (1971): 467–78.

Donner, Peter. "Die Ereignisse zur See im Kriege 1864." *Marine Rundschau* 29
(1924): 49–54.

————. "Einige Gedanken über die Erfahrungen Preussens im Seekriege von
1864." *Marine Rundschau* 39 (1934): 304–8.

Drascher, Wahrhold. "Zur Soziologie des deutschen Seeoffizierkorps." *Wehrwissenschaftliche Rundschau* 12 (1962): 555–67.

Drees. "Vor 90 Jahren: Ein Ehrentag der deutschen Artillerie (Eckernförde am 5.
April 1849)." *Marine Rundschau* 44 (1939): 346–48.

Eich. "Die Erweiterung des Kaiser Wilhelm-Kanals." *Marine Rundschau* 18 (1907):
711–26.

Epkenhans, Michael. *Die wilhelminische Flottenrüstung, 1908–1914: Weltmacht-
streben, industrieller Fortschritt, soziale Integration.* Munich: R. Oldenbourg Verlag, 1991.

Euler, Friedrich Wilhelm. "Die deutsche Generalität und Admiralität bis 1918." In
Das deutsche Offizierkorps 1860–1960, edited by Hanns Hubert Hofmann,
175–210. Boppard am Rhein: Harald Boldt Verlag, 1977.

Feldenkirchen, Wilfried. *Werner von Siemens: Inventor and International Entrepre-
neur.* Columbus: Ohio State University Press, 1994.

Firth, Stewart G. "German Firms in the Pacific Islands, 1857–1914." In *Germany in
the Pacific and Far East, 1870–1914,* edited by John A. Moses and Paul M. Kennedy, 3–25. St. Lucia: University of Queensland Press, 1977.

Fischer, Otto. "Dr. Laurenz Hannibal Fischer und die Auflösung der deutschen Flotte, 1852–53." *Historische Zeitschrift* 85 (1900): 250–89.

Foerster, Raimund. *Politische Geschichte der Preussischen und Deutschen Flotte bis zum ersten Flottengesetz von 1898.* Dresden: Druck von Wilhelm Limpert, 1928.

Foss, Max. "Bagamoyo und Dar-es-Salam durch die Marine gehalten." In *Deutschlands Seegeltung,* edited by Willy Scheel, 132–40. Halle: Verlag der Buchhandlung des Waisenhauses, 1905.

Gadow, Reinhold. *Geschichte der deutschen Marine.* Frankfurt: M. Diesterweg, 1934.

Ganz, A. Harding. "The German Navy in the Far East and Pacific: The Seizure of Kiautschou and After." In *Germany in the Pacific and Far East, 1870–1914,* edited by John A. Moses and Paul M. Kennedy, 115–36. St. Lucia: University of Queensland Press, 1977.

Gemzell, Carl-Axel. *Organization, Conflict, and Innovation: A Study of German Naval Strategic Planning, 1888–1940.* Lund: Esselte Studium, 1973.

Gerloff, Wilhelm. *Die Finanz- und Zollpolitik des Deutschen Reiches.* Jena: Verlag von Gustav Fischer, 1913.

Giese, Fritz E. *Kleine Geschichte der deutschen Flotte.* Berlin: Haude & Spener, 1966.

Gillis, John R. *The Prussian Bureaucracy in Crisis, 1840–1860: Origins of an Administrative Ethos.* Stanford, Calif.: Stanford University Press, 1971.

Grapow, F. R. "Brief eines Teilnehmers an dem Gefecht S.M.S. *Danzig* bei Tres-Forkas am 7. August 1856." *Marine Rundschau* 19 (1908): 771–77.

Gröner, Erich. *Die deutschen Kriegsschiffe, 1815–1945.* 8 vols. Coblenz: Bernard & Graefe Verlag, 1989.

Güth, Rolf. *Von Revolution zu Revolution: Entwicklungen und Führungsprobleme der Deutschen Marine, 1848–1918.* Herford: E. S. Mittler & Sohn, 1978.

Hallmann, Hans. *Der Weg zum deutschen Schlachtflottenbau.* Stuttgart: Verlag von W. Kohlhammer, 1933.

Hamerow, Theodor. *Restoration, Revolution, Reaction: Economics and Politics in Germany, 1815–1871.* Princeton, N.J.: Princeton University Press, 1958.

Handel-Mazzetti, Peter. "Das Seegefecht bei Helgoland am 9. Mai 1864." *Marine Rundschau* 39 (1934): 193–98.

Hassell, Ulrich von. *Tirpitz: Sein Leben und Wirken mit Berücksichtigung seiner Beziehungen zu Albrecht von Stosch.* Stuttgart: Chr. Belsersche Verlagsbuchhandlung, 1920.

Hassert, Kurt. "Die Erwerbsgeschichte der deutschen Schutzgebiete und die Flotte." In *Deutschlands Seegeltung,* edited by Willy Scheel, 120–32. Halle: Verlag der Buchhandlung des Waisenhauses, 1905.

Häussler, Hans-Joachim. *Das Ende der ersten deutschen Flotte: Ein Beitrag zur Geschichte der Zollvereinkrise 1852, der Reaktion und des Flottengedankens.* Berlin: Junker und Dünnhaupt Verlag, 1937.

———. "Küstenschutz und deutsche Flotte, 1859–64." *Forschungen zur brandenburgischen und preussischen Geschichte* 51 (1939): 311–43.

Heinsius, Paul. "Anfänge der Deutschen Marine." In *Die erste deutsche Flotte, 1848–1853,* edited by Walther Hubatsch, 13–27. Herford: E. S. Mittler & Sohn, 1981.

————. "Stellung und Besoldung der Deckoffiziere in der preussischen Marine." *Schiff und Zeit* 9 (1979): 57–60.

Henderson, W. O. "German East Africa, 1884–1918." In *History of East Africa,* edited by Vincent Harlow et al., 123–62. Oxford: Clarendon Press, 1965.

————. *The Rise of German Industrial Power, 1834–1914.* Berkeley: University of California Press, 1975.

Herwig, Holger H. *The German Naval Officer Corps: A Social and Political History.* Oxford: Clarendon Press, 1973.

————. *Germany's Vision of Empire in Venezuela, 1871–1914.* Princeton, N.J.: Princeton University Press, 1986.

————. *"Luxury" Fleet: The Imperial German Navy, 1888–1918.* Rev. ed. Atlantic Highlands, N.J.: Ashfield Press, 1987.

————. "Das Offizierkorps der kaiserlichen Marine vor 1918." In *Das deutsche Offizierkorps, 1860–1960,* edited by Hanns Hubert Hofmann, 139–61. Boppard am Rhein: Harald Boldt Verlag, 1977.

————. *Politics of Frustration: The United States in German Naval Planning, 1889–1941.* Boston: Little, Brown, 1976.

Hildebrand, Hans H., Albert Röhr, and Hans-Otto Steinmetz. *Die deutschen Kriegsschiffe: Biographien.* Herford: Koehler, 1979.

Höbelt, Lothar. "Von der Jeune École zur Flottenpolitik: Die Rolle der österreichisch-ungarischen Kriegsmarine im letzten Viertel des neunzehnten Jahrhunderts." *Études Danubiennes* 4 (1988): 147–56.

Hobson, Rolf. *The German School of Naval Thought and the Origins of the Tirpitz Plan, 1875–1900.* Oslo: Institutt for forsvarsstudier, 1996.

Holborn, Hajo. *A History of Modern Germany.* 3 vols. New York: Knopf, 1959–67.

Hollyday, Frederic B. M. *Bismarck's Rival: A Political Biography of General and Admiral Albrecht von Stosch.* Durham, N.C.: Duke University Press, 1960.

Hubatsch, Walther. *Der Admiralstab und die obersten Marinebehörden in Deutschland, 1848–1945.* Frankfurt: Bernard & Graefe, 1958.

————. *Kaiserliche Marine: Aufgaben und Leistungen.* Munich: J. F. Lehmanns Verlag, 1975.

————. "Reichsflotte und Deutscher Bund." In *Die erste deutsche Flotte, 1848–1853,* 29–40. Herford: E. S. Mittler & Sohn, 1981.

————, ed. *Die erste deutsche Flotte, 1848–1853.* Herford: E. S. Mittler & Sohn, 1981.

Hull, Isabel V. *The Entourage of Kaiser Wilhelm II, 1888–1918.* Cambridge: Cambridge University Press, 1982.

Jankuhn, Herbert. "Die Schiffahrt und Seeherrschaft der Urzeit bis zu den Wikingerzügen." In *Grundlagen Deutscher Seegeltung,* edited by Walter Lohmann et al., 21–45. Berlin: Verlag Wehrfront Alfred Becker, 1942.

Jensen, Jürgen. *Seestadt Kiel.* Neumünster: Karl Wachholtz Verlag, 1975.

Junghänel, Heinz. *Marinehaushalt und Marineausgabepolitik in Deutschland (1868–1930).* Lucka: Druck von Reinhold Berger, 1932.

Kardorff, Siegfried von. *Wilhelm von Kardorff: Ein Nationaler Parlamentarier im Zeitalter Bismarcks und Wilhelms II, 1828–1907.* Berlin: E. S. Mittler & Sohn, 1936.

Kehr, Eckart. "Die deutsche Flotte in den neunziger Jahren und der politisch-militärische Dualismus des Kaiserreichs." In *Der Primat der Innenpolitik*, edited by Hans-Ulrich Wehler, 111–29. Berlin: Walter de Gruyter & Co., 1965.

———. "Soziale und finanzielle Grundlagen der Tirpitzschen Flottenpropaganda." In *Der Primat der Innenpolitik*, edited by Hans-Ulrich Wehler, 130–48. Berlin: Walter de Gruyter & Co., 1965.

Kelly, Patrick J. "Tirpitz and the Origins of the German Torpedo Arm, 1877–1889." Paper presented at the Eleventh Naval Symposium, Annapolis, Maryland, October 1993.

Kennan, George F. *The Fateful Alliance: France, Russia, and the Coming of the First World War*. New York: Pantheon Books, 1984.

Kennedy, Paul M. "Bismarck's Imperialism: The Case of Samoa, 1880–1890." *Historical Journal* 15 (1972): 261–83.

———. "The Development of German Naval Operations Plans against England, 1896–1914." In *The War Plans of the Great Powers, 1880–1914*, edited by Paul M. Kennedy, 171–99. London: George Allen & Unwin, 1979.

———. "German Colonial Expansion: Has the 'Manipulated Social Imperialism' Been Ante-dated?" *Past and Present* 54 (1972): 134–41.

———. "German World Policy and the Alliance Negotiations with England, 1897–1900." *Journal of Modern History* 45 (1973): 605–25.

———. *The Rise of the Anglo-German Antagonism, 1860–1914*. London: George Allen & Unwin, 1980.

———. *The Samoan Tangle: A Study in Anglo-German-American Relations, 1878–1900*. New York: Barnes & Noble, 1974.

Kessel, Eberhard. "Die Entlassung von Kameke und Stosch im Jahre 1883." In *Forschungen zu Staat und Verfassung: Festgabe für Fritz Hartung*, edited by Richard Dietrich and Gerhard Oestreich, 441–53. Berlin: Duncker & Humblot, 1958.

Kjølsen, F. H. "The Old Danish Frigate." *The Mariner's Mirror* 51 (1965): 27–33.

Kludas, Arnold. *Die Schiffe der deutschen Afrika-Linien, 1880–1945*. Oldenburg: Stalling, 1975.

Koch, Paul. "Die deutschen Eisenindustrie und die Kriegsmarine." *Meereskunde* 7 (1913): 1–40.

———. "Entwicklung der Flotte unter Wilhelm II." In *Deutschlands Seegeltung*, edited by Willy Scheel, 83–102. Halle: Verlag der Buchhandlung des Waisenhauses, 1905.

———. "Der Flottenverkauf durch Hannibal Fischer." *Marine Rundschau* 4 (1893): 149–58.

———. "Die preussische Flottenexpedition von 1852." *Marine Rundschau* 4 (1893): 435–43.

———. "Die Sammlungen für die Deutsche Flotte." *Marine Rundschau* 7 (1896): 137–48.

———. "Die Vorgeschichte von Wilhelmshaven." *Marine Rundschau* 6 (1895): 475–95.

Koop, Gerhard, Kurt Galle, and Fritz Klein. *Von der Kaiserlichen Werft zum Marinearsenal: Wilhelmshaven als Zentrum der Marinetechnik seit 1870*. Munich: Bernard & Graefe, 1982.

Kreker, Hans-Justus. "Die französische Marine im Kriege von 1870/71." *Marine Rundschau* 70 (1973): 276–86.

Krupp: A Century's History of the Krupp Works, 1812–1912. Essen: The Krupp Works, 1912.

Kuby, Eva. "Politische Frauenvereine und ihre Aktivitäten 1848 bis 1850." In *Schimpfende Weiber und patriotische Jungfrauen: Frauen im Vormärz und in der Revolution 1848/49*, edited by Carola Lipp, 248–69. Moos and Baden-Baden: Elster Verlag, 1986.

Lambi, Ivo Nikolai. *Free Trade and Protection in Germany, 1868–1879*. Wiesbaden: Franz Steiner Verlag, 1963.

———. *The Navy and German Power Politics, 1862–1914*. Boston: Allen & Unwin, 1984.

Landerer, R. *Geschichte der Hamburg-Amerikanischen Packetfahrt-Aktien-Gesellschaft, zur Feier des fünfzigjährigen Bestehens der Gesellschaft*. Hamburg: Hamburg-Amerikanische Packetfahrt-Aktien-Gesellschaft, 1897.

Leckebusch, Günther. *Die Beziehungen der deutschen Seeschiffswerften zur Eisenindustrie an der Ruhr in der Zeit von 1850 bis 1930*. Cologne: Rheinisch-Westfälischen Wirtschaftsarchiv, 1963.

Lohmann, Walter. "S.M.S. *Meteor* bei Havanna." *Marine Rundschau* 35 (1930): 509–13.

Lowe, Cedric J. *The Reluctant Imperialists: British Foreign Policy, 1878–1902*. 2 vols. London: Routledge & Kegan Paul, 1967.

———. *Salisbury and the Mediterranean, 1886–1896*. Toronto: University of Toronto Press, 1965.

Lundeberg, Philip K. "Sea Mines in the Defense of Kiel, 1848–1849." In *Seemacht und Geschichte: Festschrift zum 80. Geburtstag von Friedrich Ruge*, 187–97. Bonn: MOV-Verlag, 1975.

Lütken, Otto George. *Søkrigsbegivenhederne i 1864*. Copenhagen: Gyldendalske Boghandels Forlag, 1896.

Maltzahn, Curt von. "Der Admiral Eduard von Jachmann." *Marine Rundschau* 38 (1933): 293–302.

Mantey, Eberhard von. *Deutsche Marinegeschichte*. Charlottenburg: Verlag "Offene Worte," 1926.

Marder, Arthur J. *The Anatomy of British Sea Power: A History of British Naval Policy in the Pre-Dreadnought Era, 1880–1905*. 1940. Reprint, New York: Octagon Books, 1976.

Michaelis-Jena, Ruth. *The Brothers Grimm*. New York: Praeger, 1970.

Miyake, Masaki. "German Cultural and Political Influence on Japan, 1870–1914." In *Germany in the Pacific and Far East, 1870–1914*, edited by John A. Moses and Paul M. Kennedy, 156–81. St. Lucia: University of Queensland Press, 1977.

Moltmann, Günter. *Atlantische Blockpolitik im 19. Jahrhundert: Die Vereinigten Staaten und der deutsche Liberalismus während der Revolution von 1848/49*. Düsseldorf: Droste Verlag, 1973.

Moses, Ingrid. "The Extension of Colonial Rule in Kaiser Wilhelmsland." In *Germany in the Pacific and Far East, 1870–1914*, edited by John A. Moses and Paul M. Kennedy, 288–312. St. Lucia: University of Queensland Press, 1977.

Nees von Esenbeck, Hans. "Die Feier der Eröffnung des Kaiser-Wilhelm-Kanals." *Marine Rundschau* 6 (1895): 393–417.

Neubaur, Paul. *Der norddeutsche Lloyd: 50 Jahre der Entwicklung, 1857–1907.* 2 vols. Leipzig: Verlag von Friedrich Wilhelm Grunow, 1907.

Nichols, J. Alden. *Germany after Bismarck: The Caprivi Era, 1890–1894.* New York: W. W. Norton, 1968.

————. *The Year of the Three Kaisers: Bismarck and the German Succession, 1887–1888.* Urbana: University of Illinois Press, 1987.

Owen, Richard. "Military-Industrial Relations: Krupp and the Imperial Navy Office." In *Society and Politics in Wilhelmine Germany,* edited by Richard J. Evans, 71–89. London: Croom Helm, 1978.

Paschen, D. "Der blutige Tag von Helgoland." *Marine Rundschau* 44 (1939): 470–76.

Pein. "Vor 90 Jahren: Preussen erwirbt das Jadegebiet." *Marine Rundschau* 48 (1943): 467–73.

Petter, Wolfgang. "Admiral Brommy in der Literatur." *Schiff und Zeit* 12 (1980): 12–22.

————. "Deutsche Flottenrüstung von Wallenstein bis Tirpitz." *Handbuch zur deutschen Militärgeschichte, 1648–1939.* Vol. 8: *Deutsche Marinegeschichte der Neuzeit.* Munich: Bernard & Graefe Verlag, 1977.

————. "Programmierter Untergang: Die Fehlrüstung der deutschen Flotte von 1848." In *Militärgeschichte: Probleme-Thesen-Wege,* edited by Manfred Messerschmidt et al., 150–70. Stuttgart: Deutsche Verlags-Anstalt, 1982.

Pflanze, Otto. *Bismarck and the Development of Germany.* 3 vols. Princeton, N.J.: Princeton University Press, 1963–90.

Pistorius, F. "Die Vulcan-Werke A.G. Stettin." *Marine Rundschau* 35 (1930): 312–22.

Prager, Hans Georg. *Blohm + Voss: Ships and Machinery for the World.* Translated by Frederick A. Bishop. London: Brassey's, 1977.

Radtke, Wolfgang. *Die preussische Seehandlung zwischen Staat und Wirtschaft in der Frühphase der Industrialisierung.* Berlin: Colloquium Verlag, 1981.

Ritter, Gerhard. *The Sword and the Scepter: The Problem of Militarism in Germany.* 4 vols. Translated by Heinz Norden. Coral Gables, Fla.: University of Miami Press, 1970.

Röhl, John C. G. *Wilhelm II: Die Jugend des Kaisers, 1859–1888.* Munich: Verlag C. H. Beck, 1993.

Röhr, Albert. *Handbuch der deutschen Marinegeschichte.* Oldenburg: Gerhard Stalling Verlag, 1963.

Ropp, Theodore. *The Development of a Modern Navy: French Naval Policy, 1871–1904.* Edited by Stephen S. Roberts. Annapolis: Naval Institute Press, 1987.

Rosenbach, Harald. *Das deutsche Reich, Grossbritannien, und der Transvaal (1896–1902): Anfänge deutsch-britischer Entfremdung.* Göttingen: Vandenhoeck & Ruprecht, 1993.

Salewski, Michael. "Kiel und die Marine." In *Geschichte der Stadt Kiel,* edited by Jürgen Jensen and Peter Wulf, 273–86. Neumünster: Karl Wachholtz Verlag, 1991.

————. "Die preussische Expedition nach Japan (1859–1861)." *Revue Internationale d'Histoire Militaire* 70 (1988): 39–58.

Scheel, Willy, ed. *Deutschlands Seegeltung.* Halle: Verlag der Buchhandlung des Waisenhauses, 1905.

Schmitz, J. "Admiral Brommy: Seine Zeit und seine Werke." *Marine Rundschau* 46 (1941): 689–97.

Schramm, Percy Ernst. *Deutschland und übersee.* Berlin: Georg Westermann Verlag, 1950.

Schück, Richard. *Brandenburg-Preussens Kolonial-Politik unter dem Grossen Kurfürsten und seinen Nachfolgern (1647–1721).* 2 vols. Leipzig: Verlag von Friedrich Wilhelm Grunow, 1889.

Schultz, Hans W. "Der Kaiser Wilhelm-Kanal und seine Erweiterung." *Jahrbuch der Schiffbautechnischer Gesellschaft* 14 (1913): 156–91.

Schultz, Karl. "Das Treffen vor Eckernförde am 5. April 1849." *Marine Rundschau* 34 (1929): 161–67.

Seton-Watson, Christopher. *Italy: From Liberalism to Fascism, 1870–1925.* London: Methuen, 1967.

Sigel, Gustav A. *Germany's Army and Navy of the Nineteenth Century.* 1900. Reprint, London: Bracken Books, 1989.

Sondhaus, Lawrence. *The Habsburg Empire and the Sea: Austrian Naval Policy, 1797–1866.* West Lafayette, Ind.: Purdue University Press, 1989.

———. "The Imperial German Navy and Social Democracy, 1878–1897." *German Studies Review* 18 (1995): 51–64.

———. "*Mitteleuropa zur See?* Austria and the German Navy Question, 1848–52." *Central European History* 20 (1987): 125–44.

———. *The Naval Policy of Austria-Hungary, 1867–1918: Navalism, Industrial Development, and the Politics of Dualism.* West Lafayette, Ind.: Purdue University Press, 1994.

———. "Schwarzenberg, Austria, and the German Question." *International History Review* 13 (1991): 1–20.

———. "'The Spirit of the Army' at Sea: The Prussian-German Naval Officer Corps, 1847–1897." *International History Review* 17 (1995): 459–84.

———. "Strategy, Tactics, and the Politics of Penury: The Austro-Hungarian Navy and the *Jeune École.*" *Journal of Military History* 56 (1992): 587–602.

Spiess, Gustav. *Die Preussische Expedition nach Ostasien während der Jahre 1860–1862.* Berlin: Verlag von Otto Spamer, 1864.

Sprandel, Rolf. "Gewerbe und Handel, 1350–1500." In *Handbuch der deutschen Wirtschafts- und Sozialgeschichte,* vol. 1, edited by Hermann Aubin and Wolfgang Zorn, 335–57. Stuttgart: Union Verlag, 1971–76.

Steensen, Robert Steen. *Vore Krydsere.* Copenhagen: Strube, 1971.

———. *Vore Panserskibe, 1863–1943.* Copenhagen: Strube, 1968.

Steinberg, Jonathan. "A German Plan for the Invasion of Holland and Belgium, 1897." In *The War Plans of the Great Powers, 1880–1914,* edited by Paul M. Kennedy, 155–70. London: George Allen & Unwin, 1979.

———. *Yesterday's Deterrent: Tirpitz and the Birth of the German Battle Fleet.* New York: Macmillan, 1965.

Steinmetz, Hans-Otto. *Bismarck und die deutsche Marine.* Herford: Koehler, 1974.

————. "Im Schatten der Armee und der grossen Politik: Eine Betrachtung zum Einsatz der preussisch-deutschen Marine im Krieg 1870/71." *Marine Rundschau* 70 (1973): 212–29.

————. "Noch einmal: Bismarck-Stosch." *Wehrwissenschaftliche Rundschau* 19 (1969): 703–13.

Steltzer, Hans Georg. *"Mit herrlichen Häfen versehen:" Brandenburgisch-preussische Seefahrt vor dreihundert Jahren.* Frankfurt: Ullstein, 1981.

Stenzel, Alfred. "Flotte und Küste." In *Krieg und Sieg 1870–71: Ein Gedenkbuch,* edited by Julius von Pflugk-Harttung, 585–611. Berlin: Schall & Grund, 1895.

Stern, Fritz. *Gold and Iron: Bismarck, Bleichröder, and the Building of the German Empire.* New York: Random House, 1977.

Stoecker, Helmuth. "Germany and China, 1861–94." In *Germany in the Pacific and Far East, 1870–1914,* edited by John A. Moses and Paul M. Kennedy, 26–39. St. Lucia: University of Queensland Press, 1977.

Stolz, Gerd. *Die Schleswig-Holsteinische Marine, 1848–1852.* Heide in Holstein: Westholsteinische Verlagsanstalt Boyens & Co., 1978.

Szippl, Richard F. "Max von Brandt and German Imperialism in East Asia in the Late Nineteenth Century." Ph.D. dissertation, University of Notre Dame, 1989.

Tägert, Carl. "Vor 50 Jahren: Der Orkan von Apia im März 1889." *Marine Rundschau* 44 (1939): 266–69.

Tesdorpf, Alfred. *Das für die Deutsche Marine unter Kaiser Wilhelm II bedeutungsvolle Jahr 1889.* 2 vols. Berlin: Verlag von R. Eisenschmidt, 1891.

————. "Die Tätigkeit der Flotte während des deutsch-dänischen Krieges 1864 (Jasmund)." In *Deutschlands Seegeltung,* edited by Willy Scheel, 63–74. Halle: Verlag der Buchhandlung des Waisenhauses, 1905.

Trampe, A. "Georg Herwegh: Sein Leben und Schaffen." Ph.D. dissertation, University of Münster, 1909.

Treue, Wilhelm. *Der Krimkrieg und seine Bedeutung für die Entstehung der modernen Flotten.* Herford: E. S. Mittler & Sohn, 1980.

Verchau, Ekkhard. "Von Jachmann über Stosch und Caprivi zu den Anfängen der Ära Tirpitz." In *Marine und Marinepolitik im kaiserlichen Deutschland, 1871–1914,* edited by Herbert Schlottelius and Wilhelm Deist, 54–72. Düsseldorf: Droste Verlag, 1972.

Voeltz, Richard Andrew. *German Colonialism and the South West Africa Company, 1884–1914.* Athens: Ohio University Center for International Studies, 1988.

Wagner, Walter. "Die obersten Behörden der k.u.k. Kriegsmarine, 1856–1918." *Mitteilungen des österreichischen Staatsarchivs.* Ergänzungsband 6 (1961).

Waldeyer-Hartz, Hugo von. *"Ein Mann": Das Leben des Admirals Ludwig von Schröder.* Braunschweig: Friedrich Vieweg & Sohn, 1934.

————. "Männer und Bilder aus der Geschichte der deutschen Seefahrt: Adalbert, Prinz von Preussen." *Marine Rundschau* 36 (1931): 267–72.

Weir, Gary E. *Building the Kaiser's Navy: The Imperial Naval Office and German Industry in the von Tirpitz Era, 1890–1919.* Annapolis: Naval Institute Press, 1992.

Werner, Reinhold. *Bilder aus der deutschen Seekriegsgeschichte: von Germanicus bis Kaiser Wilhelm II.* Munich: J. F. Lehmann's Verlag, 1899.

————. "*Meteor* und *Bouvet* auf der Reede von Havanna." In *Deutschlands Seegeltung,* edited by Willy Scheel, 74–77. Halle: Verlag der Buchhandlung des Waisenhauses, 1905.

Wislicenus, Georg. *Deutschlands Seemacht sonst und jetzt.* Leipzig: Friedrich Wilhelm Grunow, 1896.

————. *Prinzadmiral Adalbert.* Leipzig: R. Voigtländer's Verlag, 1899.

————. "Zum hundertsten Geburtstag des Prinzen Adalbert von Preussen." *Marine Rundschau* 22 (1911): 1345–55.

Wollstein, Günter. *Das "Grossdeutschland" der Paulskirche: Nationale Ziele in der bürgerlichen Revolution 1848/49.* Düsseldorf: Droste Verlag, 1977.

Wulle, Armin, and Kurt Pittelkow. "Superlative aus Stettin: Daten zur Geschichte der Stettiner Maschinenbau A.G. Vulcan." *Schiff und Zeit* 5 (1977): 34–39.

Zimmermann, Otto. "Das gesammte schwimmende Material der kaiserlich deutschen Marine." *[Streffleur's] Österreichische Militärische Zeitschrift* 30, no. 3 (1889): 57–75.

Zorn, Wolfgang. "Gewerbe und Handel, 1648–1800." In *Handbuch der deutschen Wirtschafts- und Sozialgeschichte,* vol. 1, edited by Hermann Aubin and Wolfgang Zorn, 531–73. Stuttgart: Union Verlag, 1971–76.

INDEX

Elbe River, 21, 28, 32, 36, 84, 93, 219
Elbertzhagen, Carl Alexander, ship-
builder, 8, 10, 11, 43
Elbing (Elblag). *See* Schichau of Elbing
Ellice Islands, 116
Emden, 2, 4, 84
Ems Dispatch (1870), 92
Ems River, 21, 84
Erich of Stralsund, shipbuilder, 37
Ericsson, John, shipbuilder, 73
Eulenburg, Count Friedrich zu, 67–68

Fabri, Friedrich, 154
Far East: Prussian navy cruises to, 67–69,
74, 76, 83; in German strategic consid-
erations, 86, 116, 215–16; German navy
cruises to, 97–98, 117, 144–46, 158, 198,
200, 205–6, 214–16, 220. *See also indi-
vidual countries and cities*
Fashoda Crisis (1898), 226
Federal Diet, in Frankfurt (1815–66), 4,
18, 29–32, 62–64, 74
Fehmarn, 35, 142
Ferdinand Max, Archduke, 56, 98
Fiji, 97
Finland, Gulf of, 142, 196
Finspong, Swedish armaments maker, 59,
73
Fischel, Max, Captain, 222
Fischer, Laurenz Hannibal, 32, 250 n. 59
Flags, flown by Prussian and German
ships, 3, 5, 8, 16, 20, 27, 32–33, 63, 85
Fleet plans: of Prussia, 5, 7, 8, 10–11, 55,
65–66, 69, 72, 73, 81; of Frankfurt Par-
liament, 20, 22; of North German
Confederation, 86, 90; of German
Empire, 109–10, 113–14, 116, 148, 153,
222–23
Flottwell, Eduard von, 11, 18
Föhr, 34, 35
Forges et Chantiers de la Mediterranée,
La Seyne, shipbuilder, 82, 87
France, 3, 18, 60; and Prussian-German
colonial ambitions, 68; involvement
of, in Mexico, 98; relations of, with
German Empire, 109, 114, 159, 164, 172,
176, 190, 218–19; as Pacific rival of

Germany, 117, 144; in calculations of
Triple Alliance (1882), 143; alliance of,
with Russia, 187, 190; and Sino-Japa-
nese War (1894–95), 205–6; relations
of, with Britain, 226, 229. *See also*
French navy
Francis Joseph, Emperor, 23, 77–78
Franco-Prussian War (1870–71), 92–96,
98–100
Frankfurt Parliament (German Constit-
uent National Assembly, 1848–49),
14–15, 17–20, 23, 28–29, 31–34
Frederick II (the Great), King of Prussia,
3, 241 n. 9
Frederick III, King of Prussia and Ger-
man Emperor, 63, 83, 92, 102–3, 113,
121, 141, 175
Frederick VII, King of Denmark, 19
Frederick Charles, Prince, 134
Frederick William, Crown Prince. *See*
Frederick III
Frederick William, the Great Elector, 2–3,
57
Frederick William I, King of Prussia, 3
Frederick William III, King of Prussia, 4,
7, 8, 13, 18
Frederick William IV, King of Prussia, 5,
8–9, 12–14, 18, 28, 37, 39–41, 44, 51,
53–55
Free Conservative party, 134, 186, 216,
224. *See also* Conservatives
French navy: Baltic deployment of, during Crimean War, 53; pioneers use of
armor, 55, 70; in Franco-Prussian
War, 93–96, 98–99; strength of, compared with other European navies,
135, 148, 159, 168, 200; in German war
plans and strategic considerations,
142, 169, 173–74, 193–95, 201, 218; and
Jeune École, 159–60; at Kiel Canal
opening (1895), 199–200; in demonstration off Crete (1897–98), 220
Freytag, Gustav, 102, 110–11, 129–30, 139,
149, 269 n. 45
Friedrichsort, navy torpedo factory at,
164, 211, 213
Fritze, Ernst, Captain, 204

ABOUT THE AUTHOR

Lawrence Sondhaus was born in St. Louis, Missouri, in 1958. After receiving his B.A. in 1980 from Elon College, he attended the University of Virginia, receiving his Ph.D. in 1986. In 1984–85 he studied in Vienna on a Fulbright scholarship. Currently he is an associate professor of history at the University of Indianapolis.

He is the author of numerous articles and three books—*The Habsburg Empire and the Sea: Austrian Naval Policy, 1797–1866; In the Service of the Emperor: Italians in the Austrian Armed Forces, 1814–1918;* and *The Naval Policy of Austria-Hungary, 1867–1918: Navalism, Industrial Development, and the Politics of Dualism.* His 1992 article "Strategy, Tactics, and the Politics of Penury: The Austro-Hungarian Navy and the *Jeune École,*" won the Moncado prize from the Society for Military History.

The **Naval Institute Press** is the book-publishing arm of the U.S. Naval Institute, a private, nonprofit, membership society for sea service professionals and others who share an interest in naval and maritime affairs. Established in 1873 at the U.S. Naval Academy in Annapolis, Maryland, where its offices remain today, the Naval Institute has members worldwide.

Members of the Naval Institute support the education programs of the society and receive the influential monthly magazine *Proceedings* and discounts on fine nautical prints and on ship and aircraft photos. They also have access to the transcripts of the Institute's Oral History Program and get discounted admission to any of the Institute-sponsored seminars offered around the country.

The Naval Institute also publishes *Naval History* magazine. This colorful bimonthly is filled with entertaining and thought-provoking articles, first-person reminiscences, and dramatic art and photography. Members receive a discount on *Naval History* subscriptions.

The Naval Institute's book-publishing program, begun in 1898 with basic guides to naval practices, has broadened its scope in recent years to include books of more general interest. Now the Naval Institute Press publishes about 100 titles each year, ranging from how-to books on boating and navigation to battle histories, biographies, ship and aircraft guides, and novels. Institute members receive discounts of 20 to 50 percent on the Press's nearly 600 books in print.

Full-time students are eligible for special half-price membership rates. Life memberships are also available.

For a free catalog describing Naval Institute Press books currently available, and for further information about subscribing to *Naval History* magazine or about joining the U.S. Naval Institute, please write to:

Membership Department
U.S. Naval Institute
118 Maryland Avenue
Annapolis, MD 21402-5035

Telephone: (800) 233-8764
Fax: (410) 269-7940
Web address: www.usni.org